Male Trouble

A camera obscura *book*

MALE TROUBLE
Constance Penley and Sharon Willis, editors

PRIVATE SCREENINGS
Television and the Female Consumer
Lynn Spigel and Denise Mann, editors

CLOSE ENCOUNTERS
Film, Feminism, and Science Fiction
Constance Penley, Elisabeth Lyon, Lynn Spigel,
and Janet Bergstrom, editors

Male Trouble

Constance Penley and Sharon Willis, editors

University of Minnesota Press
Minneapolis
London

Parveen Adams, "Per Os(cillation)," reprinted from James Donald (ed.), *Psychoanalysis and Cultural Theory: Thresholds* (New York: St. Martin's Press; London: Macmillan Education Ltd., 1991), pages 68–87; by permission. Material from *Camera Obscura*, volumes 17, 19, and 25–26, © The Johns Hopkins University Press, 1988, 1989, and 1991, respectively.

Published by the University of Minnesota Press
2037 University Avenue Southeast, Minneapolis, MN 55455-3092
Printed in the United States of America on acid-free paper

Library of Congress Cataloging-in-Publication Data

Male trouble / Constance Penley and Sharon Willis, editors.
    p. cm. — (A Camera obscura book)
  Includes bibliographical references and index.
  ISBN 0-8166-2171-3 (hc : acid-free)
  ISBN 0-8166-2172-1 (pb : acid-free)
  1. Men in motion pictures. 2. Sex role in motion pictures.
3. Rubens, Paul, 1953– . I. Penley, Constance, 1948– .
II. Willis, Sharon, 1955– . III. Series
PN1995.9.M46M27 1993
791.43′652041—dc20
                                              92-25407
                                              CIP

Contents

Introduction
Constance Penley and Sharon Willis

Male Trouble is a very different volume from the special issue of *Camera Obscura* on which it is based. Not only has new material been added but the context in which it appears has changed dramatically. When the issue came out in 1988 the feminist debates about masculinity were already well under way and beginning to take specific shapes. Although some critics and theorists felt the study of masculinity was as crucial as that of femininity, others expressed consternation about what it meant for feminists to be giving so much attention to the complex, heterogeneous, and conflicted construction of masculinity at a moment when it was becoming clear that renewed, concerted antagonisms toward feminism were legitimating numerous attacks on women's equality and freedom. Or, as some put it even more strongly, wasn't there a danger that a theoretically sophisticated study of masculinity, which would necessarily involve positing male subjectivity as nonmonolithic and even capable of positive or utopian moments, could entail a significant digression from a feminist project that remains underdeveloped in its attention to differences *among women*?

The *Camera Obscura* issue aimed to contribute to the increasingly animated discussions on masculinity within feminism and gay studies. These discussions and debates suggest that most found the risk of focusing on masculinity more than worth taking, and in fact crucial to understanding a world where power is divided unevenly along gendered lines.

Male Trouble thus appears in a newly redefined territory of gender relations, a territory mapped by the burgeoning of feminist work on masculinity but also by events that have marked the public consciousness and demonstrated once again the great gulf between feminists, in their claims for women's equality and self-determination, and those who believe those claims to be illegitimate. The list of those traumatic yet galvanizing events is a long one, and because the media representation has tended to put mostly women on one side of the divide and mostly men on the other, the issues tend to get trivialized as successive episodes of a spectacularized and romanticized "battle of the sexes." So too, the media's tendency to structure these events as melodrama or soap opera versions of the battle of the sexes often means that differences other than sexual ones get lost unless they also can be made into the stuff of melodrama, as was, for example, the narrative of Clarence Thomas's rise out of rural poverty into national prominence.

These events—all of which, we are claiming, demonstrate the urgency of examining male subjectivity—include, to be sure, the Clarence Thomas–Anita Hill hearings, in which for the first time in this country an issue of sexual politics claimed national attention through minute-by-minute television coverage; the media pairing of the William Kennedy Smith and Mike Tyson rape trials, which raised serious questions about the judicial system's capacity to deal adequately with the complexities of race, class, and gender as well as about the media's own capacity to treat these issues without sensationalism; the steady erosion of reproductive rights; a dramatically deteriorated economy, which always exacerbates sexual and racial scapegoating; Supreme Court decisions that follow the lead of the Reagan and Bush administrations in dismantling affirmative action; the Gulf War's construction of national identity as a virile, aggressively posturing masculinity; and the media prominence of a men's movement whose appeal is a nostalgic return to a reactionary and retrograde patriarchal masculinity as a defense against a debilitating femininity. At the same time as women are losing ground some men too are the objects of an escalated violence, as we can see in the alarming rise of gay bashing as well as systemic violence against African-American men. Because the editors of this volume are also professors, we have to include in this list the right-wing and media recruitment of Camille Paglia—in a tide of simplistic conservative attacks on "political correctness"—to trivialize or quash the nascent advances of feminists in the academy. And because we are professors of film, we have to add the storm of media protest against *Thelma and Louise* that accompanied feminist debates about its political value as well as its runaway popularity with women audiences.

Although the topic of this book is "male trouble" readers will find very little internal struggle over the now rather thoroughly discussed question of "men in feminism," or who gets to speak about masculinity. Although it is true that one recurring theme in this volume is straight masculinity (usually straight white masculinity) caught between fear of women and fear of homosexuality, the essays printed here aim to examine the structure and bases of those fears rather than hesitating over the value of turning our attention to them.

The book opens with four essays that introduce and explicate the recurring theoretical concerns of the volume. Not coincidentally, all of them examine masculinity by taking up psychoanalytic categories usually associated with femininity: hysteria, masochism, and narcissism. The idea is not simply to reverse these terms and "apply" them to masculinity. Rather, what we see here is a continuation of a move already begun by Freud and renewed by Lacan to understand these psychical positions or states as descriptive of subjectivity itself, rather than characterizing a uniquely feminine subject position. So too, the emphasis here on understanding masculinity through hysteria, masochism, and narcissism represents a move away from a sometimes narrow view of masculinity as structured primarily around voyeurism and fetishism. Such a view assigned too much masterful agency to the position of the male voyeur or fetishist—a position often theorized over the last fifteen years as *the* position of cinematic spectatorship—with a consequent pacification of the position of the female viewer or character, reduced to "to-be-looked-at-ness."

What is also apparent from the first four essays is the urgency of the wish to move toward an understanding of the ways the psychical formations and positions described by psychoanalysis are already social as well. In "Per (Os)cillation," for example, Parveen Adams shows that Freud in fact has no account of the fixing of sexual positions in relation to the femininity and masculinity that are supposed to be constituted by the Oedipus complex. Adams uses Freud's claims about masochism in "A Child Is Being Beaten" to demonstrate the arbitrariness in the way he assigns certain forms of the fantasy to men and others to women. She sees the same arbitrariness at work in Freud's attempt to show how the multiple possibilities of identification available for the subject get channeled into the relatively stable sexual positions called "masculinity" and "femininity." Where then, she asks, "do masculinities and femininities come from?" If Freud gives no theoretical proof of how these sexual positions are arrived at, he does give some idea of what masculinity means for him in three anecdotes, cited by Adams following Neil Hertz, in which it is clear that Freud's own identification is with a scientific discourse *culturally* designated as masculine.

For Kaja Silverman, too, the psychical and the social are entirely bound up with each other. In "Masochism and Male Subjectivity" she, like Adams, questions the way Freud asserts rather than proves the sexually differentiated paths taken in the masochistic fantasy of "A Child Is Being Beaten." She then goes on to describe masochism as a perversion that reflects what it undermines: "By projecting a cruel or imperious authority before whom he abases himself, the masochist only acts out in an exaggerated, anthropomorphic, and hence disruptive way the process whereby subjects are culturally spoken." She characterizes the masochist who stages this culturally charged scenario as possessing an agency of sorts, although she acknowledges that such "agency" might mean something different for feminine masochists (whether men or women)—the terms of the humiliation they dictate to themselves having already been dictated to them by the culture. Here as well the relation of the psychical to the social is apparent in Silverman's concluding argument that any libidinal deviancy—in this case male masochism, which she characterizes as a perversion of the relation to paternal law—"always represent[s] a politics 'of sorts.' " If this is a "politics 'of sorts,' " she says, feminism cannot afford to ignore it just because it is charted across the male body.

Silverman's use of notions like "agency" and "politics," although heavily qualified, might seem to suggest a voluntarist view of the unconscious, a return to an effort to evolve a "politics of the unconscious." The risk of such an effort is that it easily leads to a moralism of the psyche, in which some unconscious positions are held to be more politically correct than others, and in any case can be self-fashioned. But if anything was ever *by definition* politically incorrect and not amenable to revision, it is the unconscious. The concept of the unconscious is theoretically useless if the unconscious is held to be available to reform or recruitment. If it is not radically other and if it does not resist, it is not the unconscious. But Silverman makes no such claims for, say, the progressiveness or political correctness of male masochism in and of itself. Rather, she is concerned with how libidinal deviancy can get hooked up to a politics—is sometimes forced to become a politics—here one of challenge to patriarchy's sexual and social norms.

We are raising the issue of the problem of voluntarist interpretations of the psychoanalytic account of the unconscious because so many of the essays in this volume take psychoanalytic theory as one of their key points of reference and attempt to articulate the psychical and the social. But such a move often seems to bring with it the temptation to model progressive social prescriptions on the psyche's otherness and capacity for resistance to the imposition of symbolic law, thereby collapsing the psychical and the social, and robbing each of its own determinate specificity. One also sees an underlying wish to recruit and reform the unconscious for gay and lesbian studies, where one might find, for example, efforts to develop a positive theory and practice of lesbian self-fashioning through the psychoanalytic account of narcissism. Although theories and practices of gender bending, sexual role playing, crossdressing, and masquerade have challenged and reinvigorated feminist discussions of identity, subjectivity, and spectatorship, such approaches lose a valuable theoretical tool when they proceed from the wish that unconscious desire could be transformed into a socially desirable model for identity politics. Several of the essays in *Male*

Trouble seek to articulate the psychical and the social such that each retains the sense of its "otherness" to the other while also showing nonetheless how deeply implicated each is in the other.

Masculinity in its specific relation to national identity is the topic of Rey Chow's "Male Narcissism and National Culture: Subjectivity in Chen Kaige's *King of the Children*." Because this essay concerns non-Western culture, it offers a striking opportunity to see how the terms of subjectivity and the social — and the psychoanalytic theory used to examine and articulate them — can be very differently refracted through the lens of another culture. Chow introduces "the dialectic of social relations" into the psychoanalytic account of narcissism to describe the economy of male narcissism in Chen Kaige's film and in contemporary Chinese culture. Like Adams and Silverman, she reads Freud against himself, by first making a strategic return to his description of the category of person who is a narcissist: women, criminals, humorists — in other words, outcasts. Men, of course, are exempted from this tableau of narcissists. Chow puts them back in, especially when they too belong to the camp of outcasts. She then asks why, in the context of the repressiveness of Chinese national culture — after the catastrophe of the Cultural Revolution and the Tiananmen massacre — Chen makes his male protagonist self-absorbed, passive, and thus "feminine." She also looks at the aesthetic/sexual economy of the film as it makes of the female character a de-eroticized and nonreproductive being, a kind of clown and comrade, while idealizing the figure of the child. Chow says this configuration represents the potential of a new type of genealogical or reproductive unit, one that refuses heterosexual love, marriage, and reproduction. But, she emphasizes, it is also a configuration that, in the tradition of Chinese philosophy, skips over physicality, especially as it is embodied in the women, and dematerializes reproduction by displacing it onto the transmission of knowledge from teacher to student. In a strong concluding statement Chow argues, however, that this repression of women's physical sexuality — in both the film and the culture — is not simple misogyny but is, rather, symptomatic of a "more profound disturbance," the refusal to procreate and perpetuate a repressive culture. In a later essay in this book, Alexander Doty will also challenge the notion of a simple misogyny.

Lynne Kirby puts a strong historical spin on the idea of "male hysteria," or masculinity in disarray, in her essay on early film spectatorship, "Male Hysteria and Early Cinema." Contemporary accounts of early film spectatorship equated film viewing with the act of being run over, assaulted, and penetrated, leaving the male spectator if not feminized then at least nonmale. This same gender confusion was also a social phenomenon, with rampant outbreaks of hysteria in working-class men rather than in Victorian women, usually seen as the quintessential hysterics. The main source of hysterical symptomology, Kirby shows in fascinating detail, was the train, specifically the train seen as a dangerous instance of runaway, out-of-control technology. Many cases of hysteria were attributed to "railway brain," a traumatic neurosis brought on by fear of colliding or runaway trains.

Technology out of control, cinema out of control, masculinity out of control: Kirby shows how these three came together in films like Edison's 1910 *Asleep at the Wheel*. This undone, uncoded, hystericized spectator of early cinema got back on track only when continuity editing developed enough to forge from the chaos of modernity at least the illusion of a properly masculine and properly feminine spectator position.

Ray Barrie's "Fellowdrama," introduced by Mark Cousins, re-creates those images of male hysteria that are usually suppressed in the obstinate wish to see hysteria as feminine by definition. But, as Mark Cousins asks, in commenting on Charcot's effort to fit the image of the hysteric to the diagnostic category in his mind, "What is it that defines definition in an image?" The re-creation in "Fellowdrama" of nineteenth-century Salpetrière photographs reminds us that what several of the contributors to this book are calling "male hysteria"—men in trouble over masculinity—is not a recent phenomenon.

The next section of *Male Trouble* is devoted to four essays on *Pee-wee's Playhouse*, three from the original issue and a new one, Alexander Doty's, that specifically replies to those essays as well as to other recent commentary on Pee-wee Herman. The context for the original essays has changed, of course, in the wake of the public response to Paul Reubens's arrest. Given the general level of media discussion of sexual politics, we might take the relative lack of hysteria around the Reubens arrest as a positive sign. Although at first child experts and the media treated his arrest for indecent exposure as an infantile trauma, for once an event that brought together people's ideas about children, sexuality, sexual roles, sexual orientation, pornography, and the influence of the mass media did not result in a sustained bout of collective hysteria. Reubens went on to be eloquently defended in much of the print media, by powerful figures in the entertainment industry, and by some parents' groups.

Although none of the essays in this section unequivocally celebrates the versions of masculinity figured in the Playhouse, still one finds here some of the more utopian claims about the bewildering variety of images of contemporary masculinity thrown up by the popular media, art, and literature. In other words, these essays would not take for granted that every instance in which the standard idea of masculinity is troubled along the lines of more progressive versions of it is inevitably recuperated by a seamlessly powerful patriarchy. A polemically forceful account of that position was represented in the original "Male Trouble" issue by Tania Modleski's essay, "Three Men and Baby M," unfortunately withdrawn from the book by the author.

Constance Penley's "The Cabinet of Dr. Pee-wee: Consumerism and Sexual Terror" looks at the way the "fantasy of masculinity" is examined and subversively reconfigured right in the heart of Saturday morning children's television in its attempt to deliver the viewers to the advertisers. *Pee-wee's Playhouse* appeals to children the way all enduring folk and fairy tales do: by fictionally posing those unconscious, primal questions that children ask and that help them to order their conceptual universe: Where do I come from? What sex am I? With whom is it possible to have sexual relations? The show not only says that these are questions that continue to be posed into adulthood, it also answers them in ways that are highly untypical for children's television. *Pee-wee's Playhouse* pulls in its viewers with the deliciously scary terrors of infantile (and adult) sexual investigation, an investigation shot through with uncanny fears about castration and the uncertainty of borders, limits, boundaries. But then it puts camp to work arguing for an ethics of tolerance for all differences by making fun of the standard categories governing what counts as sexual identity—especially straight masculinity—and "normal" family relations.

Ian Balfour too looks at how Pee-wee's histrionics "unsettle culturally codified notions of masculine and feminine, indeed twist them around." "The Playhouse of the Signifier" reads *Pee-wee's Playhouse* through the last of Freud's nine theses on hysteria in "Hysterical Phantasies and Their Relation to Bisexuality": "An hysterical symptom is the expression of both a masculine and feminine unconscious sexual phantasy." Freud thus emphasizes the bisexual character of hysterical symptoms and allows for the possibility of a specifiably male hysteria. Balfour puts this characterization of hysteria together with Freud's claim that the origins of hysteria lie in the daydreams of adolescents and that "hysterics suffer principally from reminiscences" to arrive at the formula for much of the action in *Pee-wee's Playhouse*, action that revolves around the question of sexual (and cultural) difference but mainly around the question of Pee-wee's *manhood*.

To find out what children *do* with *Pee-wee's Playhouse*, Henry Jenkins threw a Pee-wee Party with his five-year-old son for a few of his son's friends. In " 'Going Bonkers!': Children, Play, and Pee-wee," we find out that children are well aware that many of their parents find *Pee-wee's Playhouse* strange and abrasive and they use that adult revulsion toward the Playhouse—but also toward all things "gross"—to carve out a play space, a cultural space "just for kids" that wards off intruding adults. Children also respond to the crazy world of the Playhouse where they are urged to "scream real loud" and make a mess, and where "grown-ups" act like children. Jenkins cites Martha Wolfenstein's study of children's humor to show why children respond with such pleasure, fascination, and anxiety to a world that makes as little sense to adults as it does to children and where the certainties of adult behavior no longer apply.

Culling information from several sources—the children's play and conversation during and after the show and drawings they made of Pee-wee and the Playhouse (several of which are reproduced in the essay)—Jenkins also claims that children use the variously sized, grotesque, often out-of-control bodies on *Pee-wee's Playhouse* to think about their own bodies, over which they are only just beginning to achieve a limited mastery. Similarly, the children use their own doubts about Pee-wee's penchant for troublemaking to develop an ethics of social behavior, even as they are attracted to a world where Pee-wee gets into all sorts of mischief without any risk of adult-imposed punishment. Finally, in his aptly titled concluding section, "The Uses of Immaturity: Television Play and Socialization," Jenkins suggests that what adults can learn from *Pee-wee's Playhouse* is the importance of, in the words of the children, "going bonkers." Adults often demand of television shows that they socialize children into maturity, but ignore shows that encourage the pleasures of fantasy rather than attempting to rationalize all experience.

Alexander Doty sets out to look at *Pee-wee's Playhouse*—and its critics—from another angle, "through a specifically queer cultural-historical context." In "The Sissy Boy, the Fat Ladies, and the Dykes: Queerness and/as Gender in Pee-wee's World," he claims that most academic and popular writing about Pee-wee Herman has discussed the ways the show deals with gender issues from a heterosexist perspective. These authors, he says, do not sufficiently recognize that the show's destabilization of gender roles, to which they give so much attention, is fueled primarily by the specific representations of gayness, lesbianism, and bisexuality that pervade it. Rather than focusing on the way the show troubles the sexual identities of straight men and straight women, it would be more pertinent to emphasize the "queer tone and context of Pee-wee and his world that allows for, and encourages, most of the gender confusion and reconceptualization." Although the authors he criticizes (including Penley and Balfour) would probably not want to give up the project of examining the radical ways *Pee-wee's Playhouse* questions and confounds straight identity—especially given the show's intervention in the world of Saturday morning children's television, which

offers the most sexually segregated and sexually stereotyped programming found on the tube—his point about the need to give additional attention to the show's queer meanings is apt.

If one does adopt a queer viewing position (which Doty argues elsewhere is ubiquitous, woven into the warp and woof of high and low
culture, and available to anyone who can handle it) then Pee-wee can
be seen not as an androgynous adolescent boy but as the feminine gay
man that he is. Although Doty agrees that, in good camp tradition, all
sexual roles and positions get satirized in the Playhouse, Pee-wee's
character can also, he insists, function for many queer viewers as an
affirmation of the look, behavior, and attitude of the feminine gay. In
so viewing the Pee-wee character one can also better understand the
complexities of the women's roles in the show, and avoid a "one-size-
fits-all" approach to male misogyny that makes no distinction between
straight and gay men's antagonism toward women. Doty claims that
gay men, here specifically feminine gay men, do not hate actual wom-
en, who are more often than not friends and political allies, but the patriarchal, stereotyped definitions of femininity that are forced upon
them in straight culture's refusal to see gay men as *men*. It may be misogyny, he says, but it is of a "distinctly queer variety, with complicated
psychological and cultural foundations of its own—perhaps more comparable to straight women's misogyny than to straight men's."

Doty goes on to discuss and defend the women's roles in the Playhouse, especially the range of lesbian roles, which has hitherto been little noted, with special emphasis on the show's butch dykes, characters
he sees as operating in the space of a lesbian reconceptualizing of masculinity rather than imitating straight men. Finally, Doty cites D. A.
Miller's account of "queer deniability"—here seen in the show's capacity to both connote and suppress queer expression—to conclude, in the
words of one of the children at the Pee-wee Party thrown by Henry
Jenkins and his son, that *Pee-wee's Playhouse* is indeed "a crazy closet."

The third and final section of *Male Trouble* is composed of four close
readings of three films and one television show—two from the fifties
and two from the past ten years, thus offering both a historical and a
contemporary perspective on figurations of masculinity in specific media texts.

Sabrina Barton's " 'Crisscross': Paranoia and Projection in *Strangers
on a Train*" makes clear, as do the other essays in the book, that the
study of masculinity is never the study of masculinity as such. Rather,
focusing on male subjectivity inevitably leads us back to issues of femininity and sexual orientation, as well as to masculinity as it is constituted in relation to race, class, and national identity. Barton paraphrases
Raymond Bellour's observation that "the not-too-obvious obviousness

of a narrative flow into heterosexual coupledom anchors mainstream cinema" to look at what happens, as in *Strangers on a Train*, when the film works to produce the obviousness and inevitability of a same-sex male couple. Although it produces Guy and Bruno as a couple, the film is even more emphatically focused on relationships between men, since it lacks what Barton calls "the blonde function"—the spectacle of Hitchcock's many blondes who together have become the quintessential "to-be-looked-at" woman.

Barton takes up the question of representations of male subjectivity in film to rethink the reductive role of female subjectivity and spectatorship in certain film theoretical models. She shows how the unstable male subjectivity in *Strangers on a Train* gets renarrativized as "a paranoid fear of the female or homosexual other." The paranoid male subject of this film differs greatly from the now conventional account of a male subject able to keep a safe voyeuristic and fetishistic distance from the image. But Barton wants to argue, with the example of the paranoid and projective masculinity evoked by this film, that women hold no monopoly on an unstable proximity to signification. "Without losing sight," she says, "of the profound asymmetries in Hollywood's representation of gender, we can explore the fissures in 'masculinity' revealed by these representations in order to help free femininity from bearing the entire burden of a split subjectivity." Barton nevertheless does not try to conclude that *Strangers on a Train* offers a critique of the privilege of the bourgeois male subject; rather she proposes that this film is of interest to feminists insofar as it takes perverse pleasure in exposing the mechanisms of the displaced violence against women and homosexuals necessary to ensure that privilege—and the man's guilty complicity in that violence.

Steven Cohan's contribution to this book offers a detailed theoretical and historical account of fifties film masculinity. In "Masquerading as the American Male in the Fifties: *Picnic*, William Holden, and the Spectacle of Masculinity in the Hollywood Film," Cohan uses as his materials for analysis not only the figure of William Holden in *Picnic* but also articles and picture spreads on Holden and other fifties leading men in fan magazines like *Photoplay*, popular magazines like *Look*, *Life*, and *Marriage and Family Living*, and news magazines like *Time* and *Newsweek*. Anyone interested in Hollywood film as both a representational system and an institutionalized regime of scopic pleasure, he says, is indebted to Laura Mulvey's influential work. Cohan, however, questions her assumption that it is always exclusively the female that is the "given stake of cinematic representation and spectatorial pleasure." Hollywood, in fact, has always been deeply invested in the spectacle of the male body, from the promotion of Douglas Fairbanks and

Rudolph Valentino to male stars of the present day. *Picnic*, he puns, is especially "revealing" (all those shots of William Holden with his shirt off) of this investment but also of the difficulties Hollywood and its publicity machines face in making sure the masculinity being staged is the right, virile, kind.

Not only is Holden's masculinity made dubious by his positioning as an erotic object, it is also undermined by the artifice associated with acting, which always puts into question the naturalness of masculinity. And, given the context of fifties anxiety about masculinity becoming feminized and a general breakdown of consensus over what constituted masculinity, it is no wonder that the studio publicity mills had to work overtime to keep this man's man a man. As Cohan argues elsewhere, even though a sense that masculinity was in jeopardy dominated much of the culture's discussion of gender and nationality, such a crisis was not unique to the fifties, to the decade, or to American culture. Every period and culture has to make sense of male subjectivity, and it is a subjectivity often perceived to be failing. Its crisis-ridden nature only serves to underscore the fragility and artifice of its construction, which takes a moment-by-moment effort to maintain.

In "Disputed Territories: Masculinity and Social Space," Sharon Willis offers another complex articulation of the psychical and the social. "To analyze cinema as a social machine," she says, "entails understanding seduction in general, not as a privatized exchange, but as part of a social libidinal channeling and mapping." In trying to describe the spatialized and depthless social imaginary that goes under the name "postmodern," Willis takes as her example the way *To Live and Die in L.A.* gives the spectator not the usual centered mastery over the scene but rather a loss of all bearings, a loss of reality, a disorienting play of simulation effects. The film first displays differences, puts them into circuits of exchange, and then ultimately confounds them: sexual, racial, and class differences, to be sure, but also differences between public and private space, real and counterfeit, high and low culture. What are the pleasure and seductive effects of such a film? Willis argues that this extremely violent film, which offers no stable point of identification but rather "a steady rhythm of reciprocal aggression," constructs us as consumers, "consumers of social conflict as well as of stylish spaces."

What Willis calls the film's male hysteria has its psychical roots in violence and repression. But the libidinized objects of that violence and repression, around which there is so much panic, exist in the social world. It is straight women, gays and lesbians, African-American men, and the poor that provide the terms of an unconscious vocabulary of seduction and aggression. It is these particular "social pressure points" that the film strives so hysterically to regulate and manage to the benefit of the one subject position that always seems to come out on top—straight white masculinity.

The intense hypermasculinity of *To Live and Die in L.A.* would seem to offer the strongest possible contrast to the kinder and gentler masculinity that Sasha Torres describes in "Melodrama, Masculinity, and the Family: *thirtysomething* as Therapy." But, according to Torres, *thirtysomething* has its own insidious ways of managing, finally, to be about straight white masculinity: "The unanswered and persistent question for the show," she says, "is masculinity, not femininity." Even though *thirtysomething* is classic family melodrama—a form associated with femininity and concerns with the family—the show attempts to renegotiate domestic melodrama's boundaries to encompass male subjectivity as well. Torres sees this renegotiation as a kind of therapeutic work on contemporary masculinity's relation to women and the domestic. But to serve as therapeutic in this way, male domestic melodrama must pull off several difficult narrative and ideological tasks: social, economic, and political issues must be recast as emotional issues; any ideological contradictions must be made part of the melodramatic plot; and, in a complicated structure of disavowal, critiques of the family must be acknowledged in ways that render them unimportant. If, Torres concludes, *thirtysomething* gives voice to, and then tries to recuperate, ideological critique of the family and gender roles, it is because, finally, a masculine interest guides this effort.

Taken together, the essays in *Male Trouble* state the need to examine masculinity from an explicitly feminist theoretical and historical perspective. They are all sharply critical of feminist arguments that implicitly assume patriarchal power to be seamless and monolithic. This assumption easily lends itself to an oversimplified gender polarization, where all women are victims and all men are unimpeded agents of patriarchy. From this position, any approach, then, that would study masculinity as a split and contradictory construction, and would cast patriarchal power as uneven and sometimes unsuccessful in its effects, represents a dangerous digression from "properly" feminist projects.

Some of the essays in *Male Trouble* do more than demonstrate the necessity of studying masculinity in the face of such criticisms. While all the essays see masculinity as fraught, divided, and therefore changeable, several of the essays crucially acknowledge the capacity of newer and shifting versions of masculinity to recuperate the power and privilege ceded to the demands of feminism and gay politics but also to the demands of capitalism itself with its increasingly voracious need for service workers, not production workers. In the essays by Sharon Willis and Sasha Torres, for example, masculinity may be in trouble but it still knows how to land on its feet. But in other essays the authors also attend to certain utopian moments of masculinity, moments when specific psychical constructions of masculinity lend themselves to "a politics of sort" (Silverman) or when masculinity makes a humorous, self-questioning spectacle of itself in unsettling ways that strike a responsive chord in both child and adult audiences (the essays on *Pee-wee's Playhouse*). The implicit argument here is that such utopian moments do occur and that feminists will do best not to dismiss them if we are to move beyond a simplistic politics of victims and victimizers—currently the view with the most popular appeal and the most press—to a more complicated and, yes, riskier politics of *possibilities*—for femininity and masculinity, for women and men.

Male Trouble

Freud (John Huston, 1962)

Per Os(cillation)
Parveen Adams

"It is in the register of the symbolic that femininity comes to acquire its meaning as only its difference from masculinity; and it is not something with a content." This is Juliet Mitchell in an interview with the editors, in m/f no. 8. It is a position that I, as one of those editors, shared at the time. More recently, reflecting on the implications of Mikkel Borch-Jacobsen's questioning of the relation between object choice and identification in Freud's texts, I began to see that a number of feminine characteristics, passivity in particular, did emerge from Freud's account of the Oedipus complex.

I do not dispute the importance of the symbolic—the "femininity" and "masculinity" that Freud is concerned with are positions taken up through different relations to the phallus. But there is another account of femininity tied up with that differentiation. The article which follows extricates this second account and shows that it doesn't work. Something appears as content and at the same time that content is not explained within the terms of Freud's psychical system.

It is important to be more precise. If something appears as content it is not as a content which is opposed to something that appears as form. To identify a content for Freud's concept of femininity is also to identify its form. This suggests that the relation to the phallus is given as a particular form/content which cannot be derived from the necessity of phallic mediation. If something is missing from Freud's account of form/content it is because something of reality has been allowed into it.

"She pictured to herself a scene of sexual gratification *per os* between the two people whose love affair occupied her mind so incessantly." So writes Freud of the unconscious fantasy underlying Dora's cough, a fantasy he describes as one of fellatio. The two people whose love affair occupied her mind so incessantly are Dora's father and his lover Frau K. Through hysterical identification Dora takes up Frau K's sexual

This essay also appears in *Psychoanalysis and Cultural Theory*, ed. James Donald (London: Macmillan, 1991).

position in the fantasy; thereby, the *os* of the fantasy is Dora's mouth. Of course, if, as Lacan suggests, the fantasy is a fantasy of cunnilingus, the *os* of the fantasy is still Dora's mouth, but this time via identification with the father. Dora's symptoms can be related to either fantasy intelligibly.

For Freud there is a certain logic of the relation between identification and object choice, for if Dora identifies with Frau K (as Freud would have it), she is thereby deemed to have her father as love object. And he would prefer her not to identify with her father for such an identification would mean that Dora's choice of love object was a woman.

It seems that it is important to specify the underlying fantasy because it concerns Dora's sexual position, that is, she takes up a masculine position if she identifies with her father, a feminine one if she identifies with Frau K. But is this the case? Once Dora identifies with the one, does she not also identify with the other? For fantasy is laid out in scenarios and the subject can take up now one position, now another in the scenario. Freud had pointed out as early as 1905 that a sadist is always also a masochist. And in 1915 the interchangeability of these positions is reiterated and extended to the positions of voyeur and exhibitionist. On the same grounds a further extension can be made, as we will see—Dora must suck and be sucked.

So Dora must take the active place *and* the passive place in the fantasy, the man's place *and* the woman's place. Given the fantasy of a scene of sexual gratification *per os*, it matters little whether we say that she is identifying with a male mouth or with a female mouth. For Dora's object choice cannot be specified through such an identification. Whether or not Dora oscillates *per* her *os*, she oscillates between a masculine and feminine position. I will argue that it is not possible to determine sexual position through identification.

Yet in Freudian theory identification is crucial at the definitive moment of sexual division, the taking up of a sexual position in the Oedipus complex. This is the moment when the multiple object choices and identifications of bisexuality are channelled into heterosexuality or homosexuality. Freud assumes that the child privileges one of its two parental love objects; that is, that the child makes a choice of love object and that this choice is followed by identification with the rival object. This double move on the child's part is crucial to the stabilization (always a somewhat precarious stability) of sexuality, the assumption of a sexed position. It is claimed that object choice locks identification into place. The trouble is that this identification, which is to produce masculinity and femininity, bears all the characteristics of oscillation already referred to.

Freud's concept of hysterical identification rests on a triangular situation which bears the Oedipal marks of object choice of one sex and rivalry and identification with the other sex. I will show that Freud's logic of object choice and identification collapses by looking at the identifications involved in the hysteric's dream of an unfulfilled wish for a supper party, the famous smoked salmon dream, the example with which the concept of hysterical identification is first introduced in 1900, and also at the identifications involved in the example of Dora's fantasy which I have already referred to. For where there is identification with the woman there is also identification with the man. Hysterical identification is characterized, it turns out, by oscillation. Of course I know that Freud recognized the bisexual identifications of the hysteric. But it is one thing to say that the hysteric identifies with both men and women and quite another to say that where there is identification with one there is also identification with the other.

What I am saying about hysterical identification has serious consequences for Freud's account of the production of femininity and masculinity at the Oedipal moment. For if it turns out that the identification which produces sexual difference within the Oedipus complex is hysterical identification, then the resolution of the Oedipus complex cannot explain the transformation of bisexuality into a fixed sexual position.

It is also possible to consider the adequacy of Freud's explanation of sexual positioning from another angle, by looking at the Freudian concepts of femininity and masculinity. Femininity appears to comprise subordination, passivity, masochism; masculinity appears to comprise superordination, activity, sadism. Notice that there are a number of pairs split up to form the masculine and feminine positions. But these pairs are those very ones which are characterized in Freud's writings as subject to oscillation. How have these interchangeable terms congealed to set up two distinct series? If it is not through the identification of the Oedipal situation which is meant to account for this coagulation, then should we seek another mechanism to account for this? Or does the problem lie in Freud's very conception of sexual positioning as the division of instinctual pairs into distinct groups? That is to say, should the problem be set up otherwise than as the fixing of that which is originally characterized as mobile and fluctuating?

An answer to this begins to emerge when the question of identification, object choice and sexual position is taken up in relation to Freud's theory of masochism as it is set out in " 'A Child Is Being Beaten'." From the structure of masochism as it is clinically understood today it is very clear that Freud's explanation of the masochistic position is untenable precisely because masochism cannot be defined and determined by fixing on one term of each of a set of pairs of oscillating terms. The subject's sexuality is simply not structured in terms of Freud's pairs. Something of reality, the masochistic scenario of the modern period, is missing from the Freudian theory of masochism. (The earliest reference I have found to this modern masochism of the bedroom is in Pico della Mirandola's *Disputationes Adversus Astrologiam Divinatricem*, 1502). But if the contemporary clinician works with that reality, nonetheless the relatively recent appearance of masochism as a sexual perversion seems of no concern to the clinician. The task of theorizing it remains.

It looks as though the way Freud determines sexual positions is mistaken. And if the characterization of the masochistic position requires an additional ingredient of another order, then so perhaps does the explanation of femininity and masculinity.

Identification in Dreams

Here is the full text of the hysteric's dream of a supper party as reported by Freud: "I wanted to give a supper-party, but I had nothing in the house but a little smoked salmon. I thought I would go out and buy something, but remembered then that it was Sunday afternoon and all the shops would be shut. Next I tried to ring up some caterers, but the telephone was out of order. So I had to abandon my wish to give a supper-party."

The hysteric's associations to this dream refer to three people: herself, her husband the butcher, and a woman friend known to them both. The woman friend liked smoked salmon though she begrudged it to herself; the hysteric herself would like a caviar sandwich every morning but had expressly asked her husband *not* to give it to her. The friend had wanted to be invited to supper. The husband, for his part, had announced that *he* was going to lose weight and to this end would accept no more invitations to supper parties. He himself liked ample women; nonetheless, he sang the praises of the woman friend who was thin.

Freud makes two successive but not contradictory analyses of this dream. Both rely on a triangular situation between the butcher, his wife, the hysteric, and their mutual female friend. That is to say that Freud gives the hysteric's jealousy of her friend as the explanation or motivation of the dream. Freud's first interpretation of the dream is that the wife is unable to give any supper parties because she wishes not to help her friend to grow any plumper since her husband admires plump women and is already singing her praises. Freud's second interpretation claims that the butcher's wife has *identified* herself with her friend, has put herself in her friend's place. This identity is expressed through the creation of a symptom, a renounced wish, both in the dream where she has to abandon her wish to have a supper party, and in real life where her friend grudges herself smoked salmon and where she herself, the butcher's wife who would love a caviar sandwich every morning, has expressly asked her husband not to give her one.

This is the moment of Freud's introduction of the concept of hysterical identification. Identification has resulted in a symptom and what the symptom signifies is "sexual relations." A hysterical woman identifies in her symptoms most readily with people with whom she has had sexual relations or with people who have had sexual relations with the same people as herself. Freud adds that for purposes of identification, mere thoughts of sexual relations would suffice. So the butcher's wife is simply following the rules of hysterical processes in expressing her jealousy of her friend through identification with her. Freud expresses the thought processes of the dream in detail: my patient put herself in her friend's place in the dream because her friend was taking my patient's place with her husband and because she (my patient) wanted to take her friend's place in her husband's high opinion. Here, in embryo, we have the Oedipal triangle and an emphasis on object choice.

Now, it is perfectly possible to construct another interpretation, standing alongside the first, the patient's identification with her friend, which is its equal in every respect. That interpretation concerns the hysteric's identification with her *husband*, the butcher. And it rests on the same triangular situation and the emphasis on object choice. So why has Freud failed to note the hysteric's identification with her husband, especially when the associations to the dream have been so replete with references to him? I will return to this question in a moment.

Freud's argument for the hysteric's identification with her friend is as follows: the dreamer's wish is that her friend's wish (for a supper party) remain unfulfilled; instead, she dreams that one of her own wishes is unfulfilled; she has thereby put herself in her friend's place. I am saying that in a perfectly parallel fashion she has also put herself in her husband's place. The identification with the husband is given in the following argument: the dreamer's wish is that her husband's wish (for plump women) remain unfulfilled; instead she dreams that one of her own wishes is unfulfilled; she has thereby put herself in her husband's place.

What elements of the analysis might uphold such an identification? In real life, the hysteric grudges herself a caviar sandwich every morning, her friend deprives herself of smoked salmon *and* the husband has announced *his* intention of depriving himself of supper parties because he is too plump! However, the element crucial to my interpretation is that the hysteric has asked her husband *not* to give her a caviar sandwich every morning even though she'd like one. This connects the husband to an unfulfilled wish and this is a wish whose fulfillment would otherwise make her plump! So she goes so far as to stop herself being plump in order that her husband's wish for plump women not be fulfilled. If she stops herself from being plump *and* the friend's wish for supper parties remains unfulfilled, then the husband's wish for plump women remains unfulfilled. It all fits together.

Nonetheless Freud does not appear to have noticed his patient's identification with the husband. We may suppose that is because, precisely, it all fits together. Which makes the identification with the husband redundant for Freud's purpose which was to explain the hysteric's dream in terms of sexual relations. The identification with the husband would add nothing to this. But for my purposes the hysteric's identification with both the man and the woman *is* important. For it shows that identification doesn't identify object choice. Perhaps it leaves open the question whether the point of identification is identification itself.

Now when Freud analyzes his own dreams, he does not use the qualifier "hysterical." Indeed, in tracking down his own identifications, Freud makes no reference to object choice or sexual explanations. And neither will I. Instead of trying to explain his dreams in terms of the analysis of the smoked salmon dream, I want to show how the smoked salmon dream works in some respects just like Freud's dream of the uncle with the yellow beard, which appeared a little later in *The Interpretation of Dreams*. Because the dream of the uncle demonstrates that identification is the whole point of the dream.

Here is the dream of the uncle with the yellow beard, itself in two parts, first a thought, then a picture. The thought: my friend R was my uncle—I had a great feeling of affection for him. The picture: I saw before me his face, somewhat changed. It was as though it had been drawn out lengthwise. A yellow beard that surrounded it stood out especially clearly.

Freud feels a resistance to interpreting the dream which he tries to say is nonsense. He gradually realizes through his associations that if his friend R was his uncle Joseph he would be saying that R was a simpleton. But the uncle was also a criminal; what comparison was he wanting to make? The preamble to the dream tells us that in 1897 Freud had been recommended for appointment as Professor Extraordinarius. But he had reasons for not having great expectations of this. Then he had been visited one evening by a friend in the same position, this friend having pressed an official at the ministry to clarify his chances and to ask whether it was not his being a Jew that was causing the delay. He was met by prevarications and excuses and of course this strengthened Freud's feeling of resignation. . . . Now, while trying to understand the dream, Freud remembered another conversation with another colleague, N, who had also been recommended for a professorship but had explained that there had been an attempt to blackmail him and that the ministry might use this against him. Freud, he said, had an unblemished character. Freud concludes that N was the criminal he was seeking. There was reason for R and N not being appointed, but these were not denominational. The facts Freud constructed were that one was a simpleton, and the other a criminal. Freud's hopes could then remain untouched.

Freud insists that he did not consider R really a simpleton, nor N a blackmailer, but the dream had indeed expressed his wish that it might be so. He then proceeds to analyze the feeling of affection in the dream as a cover, precisely, for the thoughts about his colleagues. Thus the feeling of affection serves the purpose of distortion in the dream. For the time being this is the end of the analysis of the dream which has been discussed in a chapter dealing with distortion in dreams. But fifty pages later Freud takes it up again, this time in a section on infantile material. "To our surprise," Freud says, "we find the child and the child's impulses still living on in the dream." Freud now produces another interpretation of the dream just as he has done with the smoked salmon dream, which leads once again to the moment of identification in the dream.

Let us see how Freud arrives at the identification which sets this dream in motion. Freud again takes up his worry about the contradiction in his waking and dreaming thoughts about R and N. He insists that he does not recognize in himself the pathological ambition described in his analysis of the dream. But ambition there was, and Freud traces it back to two occasions, one dating from the time of his birth, the other from his childhood. The first occasion was the prophecy of an old peasant woman at the time of this birth that he would be a great man. On the second occasion he was told by a poet that he would probably grow up to be a Cabinet Minister. This had impressed Freud greatly. Freud now sees that in mishandling his colleagues R and N because they were Jews and in treating one as a simpleton and the other as a criminal, he was behaving like the Minister, he had put himself in the Minister's place. "He had refused to appoint me Professor Extraordinarius and I had retaliated in the dream by stepping into his shoes." These are Freud's own words. The Minister's shoes are the place of the grown-up, the powerful, the superordinate. I would like to call this stepping into The Bigger Shoes, for beside them there will

always also be laid out The Smaller Shoes. After all, Freud's identification with his unfortunate colleagues suffuses the entire account of
the dream; it is the backdrop against which the identification with the
Minister is highlighted.

Certainly, the fulfillment of the dream appears to be the act of
identification itself. Retrospectively, it has become clear to Freud that
his view of his colleagues is only the means to a deeper wish, the wish
to identify with the Minister. Freud's wish to think ill of his colleagues
then becomes what I will call an intermediate wish and in a moment
we will locate what might correspond to this wish in the smoked salmon
dream.

So far, the way in which we have presented that dream has suggested
that it fits with Freud's account of hysterical identification. Freud says
that identification "expresses a resemblance and is derived from a
common element which remains in the unconscious." This common
element is often sexual in hysteria. Since the mere thought of sexual
relations suffices, the friend qualifies as the figure to be identified with.
The identification produces a symptom, in this case the renounced
wish. This wish meets the condition that hysterical identification be
marked by the similarity of symptoms, since the friend's symptom is
also a renounced wish.

On this account, the hysteric's wish that her friend's wish be unfulfilled is an expression of her jealousy in relation to her friend and
to her husband. But there is another possible explanation of the hysteric's wish. For this wish plays the same part in the analysis of the
dream as the intermediate wish did in Freud's own dream. That is to
say that thinking ill of R and N was only a means of identifying with
the Minister, and similarly, in the smoked salmon dream, the wish
that the friend's wish be unfulfilled is merely a means to the identification. So surely the hysteric no more *really* wishes her friend to
remain thin than Freud *really* wished to pass derogatory judgments
on his colleagues.

Of course, the same can be said for the intermediate wish I constructed for the hysteric in relation to her husband—her wish that his
wish for plump women remain unfulfilled. Surely she doesn't *really*
wish that—for it applies directly to her husband and herself!

I include both the friend and the husband in the summary of my
interpretation of the dream. If the butcher's wife denied herself caviar
and a supper party it was because she wished to identify herself with
her friend and with her husband. Denying herself caviar marks the
identification already present in real life. In order to maintain the
identification which has been made on the basis of the renunciation
of a wish, the hysteric has little choice but to wish that her friend's

wish for supper parties and her husband's wish for plump women be denied. It is clear that she cannot have her friend eating her favorite smoked salmon for that would lead to the collapse of her identification with her friend. And since the friend would be plump if she ate all the smoked salmon she wanted, then the hysteric's identification with the husband would also collapse. In other words, if the friend eats, the friend's wish is fulfilled and the identification collapses; if she eats she also gets plump and then the husband's wish would be satisfied and so that identification would collapse.

What follows if we accept such a reading in which identification is the aim and the relation of our hysteric to both friend and husband is secondary? Must we not reject Freud's model of hysterical identification in the dream? For that model takes the common element in hysteria to be sexual. The difficulty indeed revolves around how we understand the notion of common element because the common element does not appear to be some unconscious sexual element. In the hysteric's dream it is the renounced wish which is the basis of identification and in Freud's dream it is the derogatory judgement of R and N which is the common element. The common element appears to be something contingent which helps to set up the identification.

But it is possible to go further. If we trace back Freud's dreams to an originating moment of identification in Freud's past, we will light upon something that might be called a primal fact of identification where Freud replaces another and the common element is nowhere and nothing if it is not set up in and though the identification itself. Imagine a childhood where Freud and his nephew John, his senior by a year, are inseparable friends but often come to blows for all that. Freud constructs a fantasy about a moment that cuts across this childhood: there is a dispute over an object, each claiming to have got there before the other. Blows and might prevail over right. In this fantasy it is Freud who is the stronger and takes possession of the field. John complains to an adult and Freud defends himself, "I hit him 'cos he hit me." But Freud wins and is deeply satisfied at his victory. It is an original moment of identification with the superiority of the older boy, an identification through which he replaces John. One replaces the other and that is the point of the identification.

Identification and Object Choice in "Dora"

I would now like to turn to the case of "Dora" and ask if it serves to provide examples of hysterical identification in Freud's sense of the term. What is Dora's relation to the Oedipal triangle? I will try to give some kind of answer by considering how identification and object choice are to be separated in the account of the case, which shows precisely both bisexual object choice and bisexual identifications.

Does identification with a man, a masculine identification, imply the choice of a woman as object and identification with a woman, a feminine identification, imply the choice of a man as love object? The answer in this case at first appears to be "no." Dora's identification with her father does not imply the choice of a female object. But perhaps this is a special case because the hysteric can regress to identification while maintaining the attachment to the object. That is to say that she can identify with the love object. With this exception, which in this case is tantamount to making an exception of Dora's identification

Freud (John Huston, 1962)

with her father, it does seem that the identification with one sex implies that the object chosen is that of the opposite sex. And this holds regardless of whether the identification is with a man or a woman. But of course this bisexuality of identification so typical of the hysteric complicates the question of object choice for there are multiple object choices as there are multiple identifications. There is no basis for pre-supposing who is loved (that Herr K is still young and attractive hardly constitutes an argument that Dora loves him), but neither can it be deduced from identification whom Dora loves (when Dora identifies with a male point of view it *doesn't* follow that she loves Frau K).

My point is that the matter is even more complicated. For not only are there identifications with the man and with the woman, but an identification with one *implies* an identification with the other. Let's take as an example one of Freud's interpretations of Dora's cough, the one that takes the cough to mark an identification with Frau K through a fantasy of fellatio. Here is Freud's argument: Dora had insisted that Frau K only loved her father because he was a "man of means." Freud can demonstrate that this phrase indicates its opposite, "a man without means," a man who is impotent. Dora indeed confirms this but she knows that there is more than one way of obtaining sexual gratification, that parts of the body other than the genitals can be used for this purpose. But Dora refuses to recognize that the irritation in *her* throat and mouth could have anything to do with this.

However, Freud insists that "the conclusion was inevitable that with her spasmodic cough, which, as is usual, was referred for its exciting cause to a tickling in her throat, she pictured to herself a scene of sexual gratification *per os* between the two people whose love-affair occupied her mind so incessantly." From this Freud infers a fantasy of fellatio and hence an identification with Frau K.

This inference has not gone unchallenged. What Freud is accused of is a phallocentric option. As Neil Hertz has put it in his article on *Dora*, from Freud's sentence "she pictured to herself a scene of sexual gratification *per os*" it is not clear "who is gratifying whom, *per* whose *os* the pleasure is being procured, or with whom Dora is identifying." What precisely is left open is the possibility that the fantasy is a fantasy of cunnilingus. And indeed Hertz quotes Lacan's correction of Freud, "everyone knows that cunnilingus is the artifice most commonly adopted by 'men of means' whose powers begin to abandon them." Freud is thus accused of the phallocentric option because he has come up with the wrong fantasy.

I think this a mistaken conclusion which has ignored the fact of the interchangeability of positions within a fantasy, something established in Freud's 1915 paper *Instincts and their Vicissitudes*. Though Hertz himself refers to an interchangeability of positions, he restricts this to the possibility that the mouth, the *os* of the fantasy, might be a male *or* female mouth. The one yielding the fantasy of cunnilingus, the other yielding the fantasy of fellatio. Hertz wants a decision on this and he doesn't like Freud's decision that the fantasy is one of fellatio.

But surely the thesis of the interchangeability of positions means in this case that whichever fantasy one may opt for, Dora will take a masculine *and* a feminine position: Dora must suck and be sucked regardless. In fact, there is a close parallel between the image of Dora sucking her thumb with a profound oral gratification and the diagram Freud sets out for scopophilia and exhibitionism in his paper on the *Instincts and their Vicissitudes*. Dora is both subject and object of

sucking in just the same way as oneself looking at a sexual organ =
a sexual organ being looked at by oneself. It is this preliminary stage
of the scopophilic instinct where there is a looking at one's own sexual
organ which seems to me just like Dora sucking at an organ of her
own body and thus simultaneously being sucked. In *Instincts and their
Vicissitudes* Freud insists, using the concept of ambivalence, that the
active and passive forms of the instinct coexist and that we know this
through the mechanism of the instinct's satisfaction. Coexistence, then,
does not mean that a choice is available between the two forms but
rather that whatever the choice, the opposite form of the instinct is
also gratified.

However, Freud himself says nothing of the kind in "Dora." He
takes the persistent thumb sucking of childhood as providing the necessary somatic prerequisite for a fantasy of fellatio even in the absence
of direct knowledge of such perverse practices. After all, the thumb
was prefigured, as Dora's memories make clear, by her nurse's breast.
Freud simply substitutes "the sexual object of the moment," the penis,
for both the nipple and the thumb. And that is why his interpretation
involves a fantasy of fellatio. Even if we assume that Freud had dubious
"phallocentric" reasons for talking about fellatio, it still remains the
case that converting that fantasy into a fantasy of cunnilingus changes
nothing. Certainly the upholders of this latter interpretation are making
the same mistake as Freud in failing to take the thesis of the interchangeability of positions seriously. Perhaps this is because both sides
are caught up in the web of the relations of identifications and objects.
Certainly both sides fail to see that it is only as a consequence of the
fact that Dora must suck and be sucked regardless, that she identifies
both with the woman *and* with the man. They thereby fail to see that
object choice is not primary.

Certainly there has been much crowing over Freud's tardiness in
seeing the importance of the group of thoughts which indicate that
the object of Dora's love is Frau K. It is as though it were a question
of right and wrong conclusions: it is right to say Dora loves a woman,
Frau K; it is wrong to say Dora loves the man, Herr K. I do not think
the problem is about whom Dora loves. Dora identifies Frau K as a
woman, which is not the same thing as saying that Dora identifies
with Frau K or that she chooses her as love object.

Freud, of course, does try to establish that Frau K is Dora's object
of love. I will consider one of his arguments for this conclusion, an
argument which stems from his distinction between knowledge gained
from oral sources and knowledge gained from encyclopedic ones. On
the one hand, he assumes the woman to be the oral source of sexual
knowledge, and on the other, he assumes the encyclopedia to be a

male source of such knowledge. So the argument revolves around Dora's identification with the man's point of view (since her associations betray a knowledge of technical words that could only have been learned from an encyclopedia), an identification which allows Freud to propose an underlying fantasy of defloration from that male point of view. Frau K is then taken to be the object of this fantasy of defloration. By now you should expect that Dora will, in her turn, figure as the object of defloration in the fantasy. And indeed, Freud also speaks of Herr K in relation to the fantasy of defloration where it is Dora herself who is deflowered (an implication Freud draws from her fantasy of childbirth). Dora is both subject and object of the fantasy.

Having indicated that Freud's means of establishing the nature of Dora's relation to Frau K are insufficient to determine that relation, I want to comment on the oral/written distinction itself. First it should be clear, though Freud is not explicit on this, that if there is identification with male discourse, then there must also be identification with female discourse. Freud is saying that there are oral and written sources of sexual knowledge for Dora and that these coincide with female and male sources of knowledge. Insofar as Dora speaks of female anatomy with encyclopedic men's words she puts herself in a male place. By the same token, then, Dora's use of sexually ambiguous words that could only have been picked up from women's speech must put her in a female place.

Having said that the identification with male discourse must be matched by an identification with female discourse we should perhaps interrogate Freud's logic in the first place. That logic suggests that reading encyclopedias is a male activity and that any woman who reads encyclopedias must be identifying with a male position. Has Freud simply fabricated the oral/written distinction here? Is this sheer male, nineteenth-century prejudice? Or might it be that Dora herself is utilizing this distinction to some end, albeit unconsciously? The fabricated oral/written distinction we are dealing with fits well with a familiar mapping of, on the one hand, children, so-called primitives, the mad and women; and on the other hand, civilized society and men. That is to say that we could construct two sets of binary oppositions such that one set went with the feminine and the other with the masculine.

If Dora is making such an implicit distinction, what then does that distinction mark? I think Freud is right to pick up the distinction and infer identifications with male and female discourse. But we must note that there is something special in this identification with the place of the male and of the female, something different from the identification which has so far been characterized. The identification with the female position does not imply an identification with the male position also and neither does a reverse identification hold. This is unlike the fluidity of the positions in a fantasy where masculine implies feminine and vice versa. We appear to be dealing with something which is not quite hysterical identification.

Utilizing the "cultural" hypothesis I have just outlined leads to the suggestion that there can be a point, a resting place, a temporary arrest of the oscillation of the drive made possible by identification with one term of a culturally given distinction. That is to say that we might speak of masculine and feminine positions but that these, insofar as they imply relatively stable positions, are the product of cultural distinctions. So what exactly is the influence on what constitutes masculine and feminine positions?

We can continue to use the oral/written distinction and we can start by looking at moments in which Freud constitutes himself as feminine, moments that he retrospectively describes from a position that he takes to be fully masculine. Here I am indebted to Hertz who, in the article on Dora referred to earlier, deftly makes the links on the one hand between a knowledge gained from oral sources and Freud's femininity, and on the other between the transcending of these oral sources of knowledge and a scientific, masculine Freud. You will also see how in establishing Freud's femininity Hertz used the pairs I began with, activity/passivity, superordination/subordination.

So how does Hertz establish Freud's femininity? His argument is that Freud needs to make a separation between his knowledge and Dora's knowledge since they both derive from oral sources. And Hertz argues that pursuing this goal has consequences for the treatment of the case. But what is relevant here is that as an analogy to what is happening in the Dora case, Hertz refers to some anecdotes from the beginning of *On the History of the Psychoanalytic Movement*. There Freud tells three stories about three men, Breuer, Charcot and Chrobak, who had all communicated a piece of knowledge, the knowledge that neurosis had a sexual aetiology, without really possessing that knowledge themselves. Hertz, while arguing that Freud is almost flaunting his femininity in these anecdotes, describes Freud's role in them as what he calls the Impressionable Junior Colleague.

In the second anecdote, Freud gives an account of overhearing a conversation in French between Charcot and Brouardel. Here Hertz makes a particularly telling analysis. Charcot is saying that it is always a sexual matter; Freud is almost paralyzed by amazement but soon forgets the scene, being totally absorbed by the experimental induction of hysterical paralyses. Hertz links these two allusions to paralysis as part of his comment on this scene. I quote: "Freud's distinctly marginal relation to this scene of professional knowingness, almost out of ear-shot, listening to two men talking—in French, of course—about suggestive matters, *secrets d'alcove*, locates him close to the position of the woman in his analysis of obscene jokes, just as his being paralyzed with amazement aligns him with the (mostly female) victims of hysterical paralysis. In his innocence, in his capacity to receive impressions, he is feminized" (239).

In the third anecdote Chrobak takes Freud aside and tells him that the cause of a female patient's anxiety is her husband's impotence but that all a medical man could do was to shield the domestic misfortune with his own reputation. Hertz comments, and I continue to paraphrase, that Freud is glancing at the structure of complicity that keeps the sexual aetiology of the neuroses a well-kept smoking room secret. While he does not remain in the position of the hysteric taking in knowledge he does not know he has, he nonetheless remains outside the circle of collegiality. Freud can only put himself into the world of Oedipal rivalry by asserting his intention to be serious about this knowledge, bringing it into the light of conscious reflection and doing so by using a distinction between a casual flirtation and a legal marriage. Hertz points out that then Freud can deploy this knowledge, acquired after the manner in which the hysteric acquires *her* knowledge, as a proper *technique*.

What does this very suggestive analysis actually tell us? We start with the figure of Freud, the feminine, the junior colleague. In the end, he does succeed in overtaking his masculine seniors. That is to say that in the end he is victorious. The feminine is what is *before* taking possession of the field, before the victory. The feminine is the position of the junior colleague being beaten, the younger Freud being beaten by his older nephew, John. But Freud the hysteric, the feminized, the beaten is transformed into Freud victorious, in possession of the field.

You might well say, so there you are, the feminine can indeed be relinquished, transcended and the masculine can indeed be put in place. But I have left out the *reason* why Freud is victorious: Freud is victorious because he establishes scientific knowledge; he is victorious *qua* masculine scientist. Note that the scientist is masculine by definition, by a culturally produced definition. What stabilizes Freud's masculine position is his identification with a discourse which is culturally designated masculine. But as Hertz shows elsewhere in his article, for Freud the man, Dora's analyst, there remains a constant struggle to transcend the oral sources of knowledge which psychoanalytic practice necessarily involves, to avoid the feminine position, for there is no general sense in which he can have put himself beyond and outside it.

Masochism, Femininity and the Oedipus Complex

I now return to the question of what femininity and masculinity are for Freud. I have already indicated how Freud relates these terms to superordination/subordination and to activity/passivity. I now want to consider their relation to sadism and masochism, a relation which is largely mediated through the distinction between activity and passivity in Freud's 1919 paper " 'A Child Is Being Beaten'," which traces the vicissitudes of the instinct which lead to a masochistic position. Here we encounter a familiar problem, the problem of how the multiplicity of the positions available for identification—in a fantasy of a child being beaten, the positions of the beaten, the beater and the onlooker—can be channelled into a relatively stable sexual position that we call masochism.

Now Freud's 1919 paper is particularly interesting because it is clear that in this case the choice of object does not determine identification in any simple way. Where the beating fantasy is found in adults Freud supposes an Oedipus complex that has taken the initial form of an incestuous relation to the father for both boy and girl. But while this passive position in relation to the father leads to masochism and femininity in the case of the *boy*, the outcome for the girl is a masochistic content in a sadistic form and is *not* femininity. What then determines this difference in outcome of sexual positions? Is this a moment when Freud produces some account of fixing by explaining this difference?

Let us look at the fantasy in more detail with the help of the tabular summary which I have put together from Freud's paper.

A CHILD IS BEING BEATEN

PHASE	GIRL	BOY
I	*The father is beating the child* (the father loves me alone; I hate the other child; the father hates the other child; the father is beating the other child)	—
II	*I am being beaten by the father*	*I am being beaten by the father*
III	*A child is being beaten* boys are beaten by a male authority figure	*A child is being beaten* boys are beaten by a woman

		SEX of the BEATEN	SEX of the BEATER	PLACE of the SUBJECT	THE DRIVE
I	G	a child (masc or fem)	the father	spectator	sadistic
	B	—	—	—	—
II	G	the subject the subject	the father the father	the beaten the beaten	masochistic masochistic
III	G	children (masc)	a male authority figure	spectator	sadistic in form masochistic in content
	B	children (masc)	a woman	?	masochistic

The first point is that the conscious fantasies I have referred to so far are to be located at phase III. "A child is being beaten" is the fantasy as reported by Freud's patients and the details elaborated around that are drawn out in the course of the analysis. Freud provides verbalizations for the two preceding phases as follows: for phase I, "the father is beating the child" and for phase II, "I am being beaten by the father." The sentence for phase I and the elaborations around it are Freud's summary of the first incestuous phase of the fantasy. The sentence for phase II, "I am being beaten by the father" is an implication that Freud makes, but which is wholly unconscious in the subject.

So we can ask how the sexual positions signalled by the final conscious forms of the fantasy relate to the other earlier forms. Very briefly, phase I is the original incestuous fantasy; both the boy and the girl have a fantasy of being loved by the father. Now this Oedipal fantasy undergoes repression. But since the Oedipal wishes persist in the unconscious, a sense of guilt appears. The phase II form of the fantasy "I am being beaten by the father" is thus a punishment; but it is also a substitute for the forbidden genital relation. The original fantasy has also undergone regression to an anal-sadistic organization and in this way it still satisfies sexual love. When the unconscious fantasy of phase II is substituted for by the final conscious fantasy, we get "a child is being beaten." There has been a further repression.

I have already mentioned that the final fantasy is differently elaborated by the man and by the woman. The lower half of the tabular summary shows that four things can vary: the sex of the beaten, the sex of the beater, the place of the subject and the content of the drive. The variations can take place between phases for one sex or between sexes at any one phase. In phase II there is no such difference between the girl and the boy. However in phase III, as you know, there is significant variation. Now it is this variation that leads Freud to conclude that the man is masochistic and feminine but that the girl has given up her femininity, gets masochistic pleasure in the fantasy, but is above all a spectator.

Freud's conclusion is based on this difference in the final versions of the male and female fantasies: that in the female fantasy boys are being beaten by a male authority figure and that in the male fantasy boys are being beaten by a woman. The argument for the female fantasy is as follows: first, that the fact that it is boys who are beaten shows that the girl has given up her feminine role and wants to be a boy; second, that nonetheless the satisfaction derived from it is masochistic; and finally, that since the girl is not really herself *in* the scene, she is really a spectator *of* the scene. The argument for the male fantasy is that it retains its masochistic form because it is *boys* who continue to be beaten and it retains its genital significance and hence the feminine position for the boy because the figure doing the beating remains of the opposite sex.

Can this argument possibly be right? Is there not a certain arbitrariness in the way Freud assigns certain forms of the fantasy to men and others to women? Certainly since Freud there have been numerous accounts both of masochistic fantasies and of masochistic performances in which the masochist of either sex might occupy any of the three positions of the beating fantasy. The final form of the fantasy is not fixed, either in the sense that there is one form found in women and another in men, or in the sense that the subject occupies only one position in fantasy or in deed. Something about masochism eludes Freud.

We could also ask whether the terms "passive" and "feminine" are crucial to an account of masochism. Reading modern accounts of masochism, it seems not only that the passivity is at best secondary, but more importantly that it has nothing to do with femininity. Moreover, it seems that it is not the father who stands behind the figure of the beater; this of course undermines the derivation of the argument about the child's passivity and femininity.

So the passive, feminine position in the fantasy scenario or indeed in a real scenario is not constitutive of the masochistic position. But if masochism is not the fixing of the subject on some terrain laid out by the couples masculinity/femininity, activity/passivity, what is it? As a first step let me introduce the notion of a masochistic scenario. This is a scene of sexual excitement, an enactment of a drama whose plot is agreed and which unfolds in a contractual space: a space of precise timing, of repetition, of suspense, of signification. Partaking in this scenario is a necessary if not sufficient condition of masochism as sexual perversion. It becomes a sufficient condition when this scenario,

Freud (John Huston, 1962)

governed by a particular organization of pleasure, signifies a certain relation to the Law. It is a sufficient condition, that is, when the subject's role in the masochistic scenario signifies the abolition of the father in the symbolic and hence a subversion of the Law.

What the masochist is doing, and it is quite contrary to Freud, is to defy castration and disavow sexual difference. And this of course is a complete travesty of the Law the Oedipus complex is supposed to institute. It is important to note that the masochist's disavowal does not make him psychotic; his perversion is a stable position grounded in his refusal of the symbolic father and in his contract with the phallic mother. The masochist can subvert the Law because he too knows the paradox of conscience that Freud had recognized, the paradox that the more strictly the Law is adhered to, the greater the guilt. And he submits to the Law all the better to make a fool of it; for he takes his punishment first, in order to experience the forbidden pleasure.

Freud went wrong because rather than rely on masochists and the masochistic scenario, he thought he could develop his account on the basis of a whole set of mixed cases which had beating fantasies as the only common factor. So he develops the account on the basis of cases of hysteria, obsessional neurosis, etc. He thereby misses both the specific scenario that is of such importance to masochism and the explanation that is specific to masochism. Of course, particular fantasies are not the sole prerogative of any person or group. But it is important to see that a particular fantasy might have a particular signification in some cases; in our present context, those cases precisely that are designated masochist. And in spite of the fact that many kinds of people may have the fantasy, it is nonetheless crucial to the masochist.

So Freud did not attend to what I will call the reality of the masochistic practices which might have informed his interpretation of the fantasy. Now, contemporary psychoanalytic writings on masochistic practices give an account of the perversion which is fundamentally different from Freud's. But to say that contemporary writings show an understanding of what specifically masochism is today is not the same as saying that contemporary writings give us an explanation of the reality of masochism as a sexual position. That is to say that they don't account for the appearance of this specific perversion in our culture, for this masochism of the bedroom which is such a recent phenomenon. Contemporary analysts seem no more interested in this question than Freud. Of course analysts are not obliged to theorize reality. They are part of it; they practice at the same time and in the same place as their analysands. Nonetheless, as I have argued at length elsewhere, reality is underdetermined by the psychical and that reality remains to be theorized. We do not thereby move outside the realm of the psyche, for reality of course always exists for a subject.

Oscillation and the Oedipus Complex

I will now take up my argument that Freud has no account of the fixing of sexual positions in relation to that femininity and masculinity that are supposed to be constituted by the Oedipus complex. Here if anywhere, some mechanism to explain the fixing of sexual positions should be found. But you will be disappointed if you expect that. For what is at stake in the Oedipal situation in relation to masculinity and femininity is hysterical identification. It should be clear that given my account of hysterical identification, we will not have any satisfactory explanation of how femininity and masculinity are knotted into positions of relative fixity.

So, Freud's Oedipus complex.

In the most schematic version of the Oedipus complex the boy is supposed to end up relinquishing the mother as love object and identifying with the father, and the girl should end up identifying with the mother, though her case is much more complicated. Note that the identification of which Freud is speaking here is regressive identification. In Chapter 3 of *The Ego and the Id* Freud suggest that perhaps the sole condition under which the id can give up its objects is identification with those objects. Which is to say that object choice regresses to identification in the Oedipal situation. But this is *not* what we usually find, as Freud admits. The boy's love object was the mother but he does not identify with her; he identifies with the father. It is clear that regressive identification is not what is at stake here. Then what is? My answer is: hysterical identification.

Why do I say that hysterical identification is involved in the Oedipus complex? Well, two years earlier in *Group Psychology and the Analysis of the Ego* Freud had given an example of the complete mechanism of hysterical identification. The example was of a girl's cough, a cough identifying her with her mother, her rival in the Oedipal situation; the cough thereby signified her father as object choice. Freud was giving examples of hysterical symptom formation and this one is fully Oedipal. In this identification the ego is borrowing the features of the object so as to copy it in its relation to others. But his object is not the love object. Just such an identification appears to determine the femininity of girls and the masculinity of boys.

I have argued that hysterical identification is not a mechanism that fixes or stabilizes positions. Hysterical identification is the mechanism which allows the play of bisexuality both at the level of object choice and at the level of identification. This play of bisexuality fits in surprisingly well with Freud's account of the complete Oedipus complex in chapter three of *The Ego and the Id*. The complete complex is composed of the negative as well as the positive Oedipus complex. For example, the boy, in addition to loving the mother and being hostile to the father will show "an affectionate feminine attitude" to his father and a hostility toward the mother. Now the point is that the positive and negative forms of the Oedipus complex are not alternatives; the complete Oedipus complex is present in everyone. And this complete form of the complex which necessarily produces ambivalence towards the parents is to be attributed perhaps entirely, Freud suggests, to bisexuality and not to identification resulting from rivalry.

The Oedipus complex then, consists of four trends, affection for and hostility to the mother and affection for and hostility to the father. How do these four trends stemming from bisexuality come to result in sexual division? Freud says that the four trends produce both a mother identification and a father identification which are somehow "united with each other" to produce masculinity or femininity. Notice that for Freud the mother identification and the father identification which he attributes to bisexuality are the product of the coupling of object choice and identification. That is to say that the identification with the mother results from the taking of the father as love object and the identification with the father results from taking the mother as love object. Thus Freud has already taken an implicit step in his explanation of the fixing of sexual difference: he has separated one identification from the other. The two coexist, but one does not imply the other. He has thereby set up two sexual dispositions. But even if we accept that there are two such dispositions in each one of us, how is the choice between them made? To appeal, as Freud does, to the priority of one of the sexual dispositions is clearly no help at all as it merely contradicts the assumption of an initial bisexuality whose transformation into heterosexuality we are trying to explain.

This problem of the fixing of sexual difference was of course prefigured the moment we identified hysterical identification as the mechanism involved in the production of masculinity and femininity within the Oedipus complex, because hysterical identification as I have shown involves the oscillation, not the fixing of positions.

Of course, I am not saying that humans do not take up positions of relative fixity, live their lives as masculine, feminine, or whatever. But I *am* saying that psychoanalysis contains at least one theory of sexual difference that doesn't work, which leaves us with an insistent play of bisexuality within the complex of relations that seem to form an everpresent Oedipal situation. How that which we take to be our Oedipal resolutions comes about has to be another story.

You must be exclaiming to yourselves, "Has she really failed to see that Freud himself has told that other story about fixing, the story which features the phallus?" Indeed this feature of Freud's other story has not escaped my notice. But I do want to emphasize that there are *two* stories and that Freud conflates them. That is to say that he conflates the story concerned with the Law and the phallus with the story about the oscillation of the drive. He is right in thinking that the positions of femininity, masculinity, perversion, can be defined through the subject's relation to the phallus; he is wrong in thinking that these positions can be defined in terms of the oscillatory pairs.

Since we have identified a conflation we must separate the two things in Freud; we must separate the necessity for the subject to live its sexuality in relation to the phallus from the particular form/content of femininity/masculinity. Till now it has seemed that the latter is derived from the former. I have shown that in fact Freud tries to derive his form/content via another story which turns out, moreover, to be an unsatisfactory one. I say form/content because quite properly there is no distinction between these in Freud. The passivity, masochism, subordination of femininity is no more form than it is content (as against the argument of some feminists that there is no content in Freud's concept of femininity). But then it is not possible to relativize the Freudian notion of femininity by reference to its content alone; it is necessary to relativize the Freudian concept of femininity itself. Freud takes the form/content of masculinity/femininity to be inseparable from the necessity of the phallus. My point is a different one: Freud's form/content constitutes one particular relation to the phallus and since it cannot be derived from his argument, perhaps it is to be explained by some reference to reality. Our question must then be "Where do masculinities and femininities come from?"

WORKS CITED

Adams, Parveen. "Of Female Bondage." *Between Psychoanalysis and Feminism*. Edited by Teresa Brennan. London: Methuen, 1988.

Borch-Jacobsen, Mikkel. *Le Sujet Freudien*. Paris: Flammarion, 1982.

Deleuze, Gilles. *Masochism: An Interpretation of Coldness and Cruelty*. London: Georges Braziller, 1971.

Freud, Sigmund. *The Interpretation of Dreams (1900)*. Vols. 4 and 5 of *The Standard Edition of the Complete Psychological Works of Sigmund Freud*. Edited by James Strachey. London: Hogarth Press and the Institute of Psychoanalysis, 1962.

———. *Three Essays on the Theory of Sexuality* (1905). *Standard Edition* vol. 7.

———. "Fragment of an Analysis of a Case of Hysteria" (1905). *Standard Edition* vol. 7.

———. *Instincts and Their Vicissitudes* (1915). *Standard Edition* vol. 14.

———. " 'A Child Is Being Beaten': A Contribution to the Study of the Origin of Sexual Perversions" (1919). *Standard Edition* vol. 17.

———. *The Ego and the Id* (1923). *Standard Edition* vol. 19.

Hertz, Neil. "Dora's Secrets, Freud's Techniques." *In Dora's Case: Freud-Hysteria-Feminism*. Edited by Charles Bernheimer and Claire Kahane. New York: Columbia University Press, 1985.

m/f no. 8 (1983). Available from 24 Ellerdale Road, London NW3 6BB.

McDougall, Joyce. *A Plea for a Measure of Abnormality*. International Universities Press, 1980.

Reik, Theodor. *Masochism in Modern Man*. New York: Grove Press, 1941.

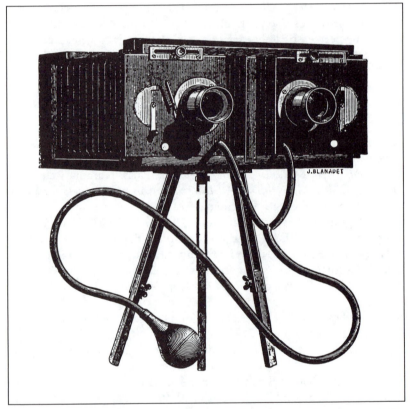

La photographie médicale (Albert Londe, preface by Charcot, 1893)

Forme fruste
Introduction to Ray Barrie's *Fellowdrama*
Mark Cousins

Above all Charcot prided himself on looking.

"He was, as he himself said, a *visuel,* a man who sees."

"He used to look again and again at the things he did not understand."

If he saw a certain chaos with his eye, gradually with his mind's eye he reduced it to nosological pictures, "and he remarked again and again on the difficulty and value of this kind of 'seeing'."

". . . or else he would recall the myth of Adam, who when God brought the creatures of Paradise before him to be distinguished and named, may have experienced to the fullest degree that intellectual enjoyment which Charcot praised so highly."

Two eyes: the eye which sees the patient, the mind's eye which sees the type.

Two images: the patient and the nosological picture.

Two patients: the type and the *forme fruste:* the type is the "extreme and complete" case; the *forme fruste* is the "long series of ill-defined cases—which branching off from one or other characteristic feature of the type, melt away into indistinctness."

The *forme fruste* refers to a blurring. In particular to the blurring of the image stamped upon a coin which is rubbed and rubbed until the image is faint and the surface is scuffed. It is older and appears less defined than what is newly minted. It has been handled and worn down.

At the same time this *fruste* does not diminish the reality of the image. Indeed it intensifies it by placing the image behind the "wear" to which it has been subjected. This "wear" functions as the opening of a space between the present "ill-defined" and the past. The *form fruste* is not some weakening of the type but the type situated in time, the splitting of the image into a past and present as if into different planes.

Freud will use the term *fruste* again in the paper "Obsessions and Phobias" and now it will also carry the signification of unreleased sexual tension. Why is there this elision, or slip, from *fruste* to *frustrée*? Why is wear and tear linked to this unrelieved sexual tension?

It is memory that fills such a gap, the lack of consummation, of a coming to be further away. For paintings, "conservation" and "restoration" try to hold back the process whereby the image keeps retreating behind itself. But this is a series of photographic images which place themselves before the division of what is well defined and what is the *form fruste*. What is it that defines definition in an image?

(All quotations are from Sigmund Freud, "Charcot" (1983), *Standard Edition* vol. 3.)

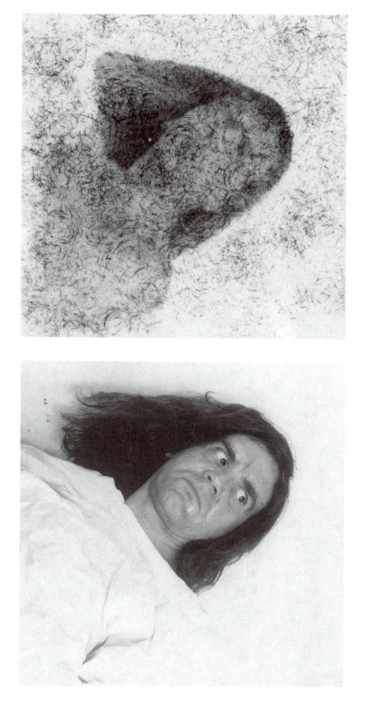

"Terreur," panels 1 and 6, 30" x 30", hand-colored positive, 1985 (Ray Barrie)

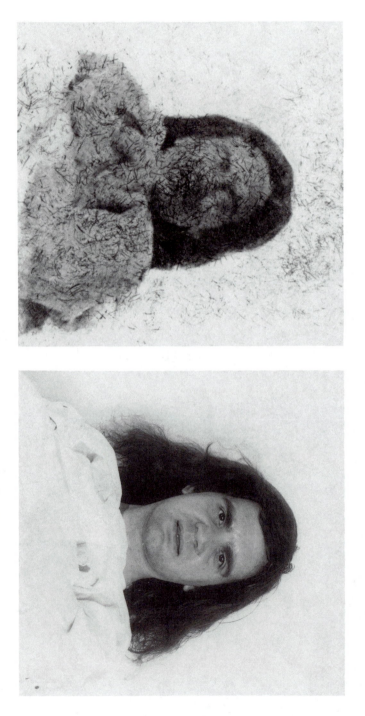

"Ironie," panels 5 and 2, 30" x 30", hand-colored positive, 1985 (Ray Barrie)

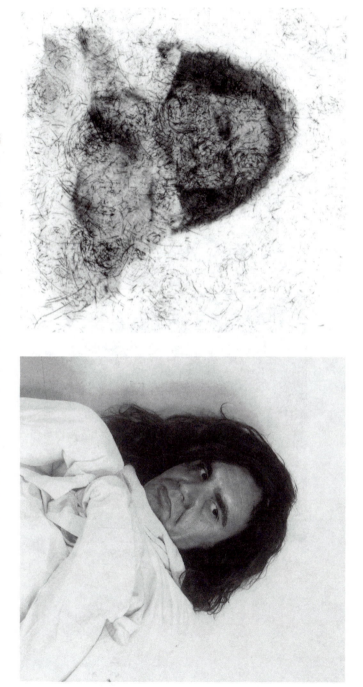

"Repugnance," panels 3 and 4, 30" x 30", hand-colored positive, 1985 (Ray Barrie)

The Martyrdom of Saint Sebastian (Mantegna)

Masochism and Male Subjectivity
Kaja Silverman

> *Perversion*: Turning aside from truth or right; diversion to an improper use. . . .
>
> (*Oxford English Dictionary*)

What is the "truth" or "right" from which perversion turns aside, and what does it improperly use? The *OED* goes some way toward answering these questions when it quotes, by way of illustration, part of a line from Francis Bacon: "Women to govern men . . . slaves freemen . . . being total violations and perversions of the laws of nature and nations." According to this grammatically "deviant" citation, perversion turns aside from both biology and the social order, and it does so through the improper deployment or negation of the binarisms upon which each regime depends — binarisms that reinforce each other in the case of gender, if not that of class. The "truth" or "right" that is thus subverted is the principle of hierarchy.

Freud's account of perversion also stresses its diversionary and decentering character. "Perversions," he writes in *Three Essays on the Theory of Sexuality*, "are sexual activities which either (a) extend, in an anatomical sense, beyond the regions of the body that are designed for sexual union, or (b) linger over the intermediate relations to the sexual object which should normally be traversed rapidly on the path towards the final sexual aim."[1] Here, in utter disregard for Western metaphysics, the "true" or "right" is heterosexual penetration. All other sexual activities belong either to the category of "foreplay," in which case they are strictly subordinated to "endpleasure," or to that of perversion.

Coitus is "ideally" a reprise in miniature of the history of infantile sexuality, a history that begins with oral gratification and culminates with genital desire for an object of the opposite gender. Here, too, the subject is exhorted to keep his or her eyes on the finish line, and to move as expeditiously as possible through the preliminary stages. But in both cases perversion intrudes as the temptation to engage in a different kind of erotic narrative, one whose organization is aleatory and paratactic rather than direct and hypotactic, preferring forepleasures to endpleasures, and browsing to discharge. Since every external and internal organ is capable of becoming an erotogenic zone, sexuality need not even be limited to the three stages Freud decreed for boys, or the four he ordained for girls. Infantile sexuality is polymorphously perverse, and even in the erotic activities of the most "normal" adult there are "rudiments which, if they had developed, would have led to the deviations described as 'perversions.' "[2]

I do not mean to suggest that polymorphous sexuality is more "natural" than genital sexuality. There is no form of human sexuality that does not marginalize need or substitute a fantasmatic object for the original and nutritive object. As Laplanche explains, "Sexuality is . . . a localized, autoerotic pleasure, a pleasure of the organ 'in place,' in opposition to a functional pleasure with all which that term implies of an opening towards the object. . . . Thus a natural, functional rhythm (that of rutting) disappears, while elsewhere there emerges a different kind of sequence, which is incomprehensible without calling into play such categories as repression, reminiscence, work of elaboration, 'deferred action.' "[3]

The notion of a deferred action has a particular relevance within the present discussion, since infantile sexuality assumes the narrative coherence of "stages" only after the fact, from the vantage point of the Oedipus complex. The concept of perversion is equally unthinkable apart from the Oedipus complex, since it derives all its meaning and force from its relation to that structuring moment and the premium it places upon genital sexuality. It is in fact something of a misnomer to characterize infantile sexuality as "polymorphously perverse," since sexuality only becomes perverse at the point where it constitutes either a retreat from Oedipal structuration or a transgressive acting out of its dictates. Perversion always contains the trace of Oedipus within it—it is always organized to some degree by what it subverts.

Those writers who have engaged theoretically with the topic of perversion tend to emphasize one of these aspects at the expense of the other. For Foucault, who stands at one extreme, perversion has no subversive edge; it merely serves to extend the surface upon which power is exercised. He insists in *The History of Sexuality* that "polymorphous conducts [are] actually extracted from people's bodies and from their pleasures" by what might be called "the society of the panopticon"— that perversion is "drawn out, revealed, isolated, intensified, incorporated, by multifarious power devices."[4] At the other extreme there is a volume like the polysexuality issue of *Semiotext(e)*, which heaps perversion upon perversion with wild abandon in the vain hope of burying Oedipus altogether.[5] Neither position is adequate to the complexities of the issues involved.

Ironically, it is a rather hateful book by Janine Chasseguet-Smirgel —a book that consistently comes down on the side of the father, "mature" sexuality, and a well-fortified ego—that seems best to intuit the challenge that perversion poses to the symbolic order. Its author cautions that "the pervert is trying to free himself from the paternal universe and the constraints of the law. He wants to create a new kind of reality and to dethrone God the Father."[6] Chasseguet-Smirgel's reading of perversion suggests that its significance extends far beyond the domain of the strictly sexual (if, indeed, such a domain ever existed)—suggests, that is, that it turns aside not only from hierarchy and genital sexuality, but from the paternal signifier, the ultimate "truth" or "right." As I will attempt to demonstrate later in this chapter with respect to masochism, at certain moments perversion may pose such a radical challenge to sexual difference as to enact precisely the scenario condemned by Bacon.

The theoretical interest of perversion extends even beyond the disruptive force it brings to bear upon gender. It strips sexuality of all functionality, whether biological or social; in an even more extreme fashion than "normal" sexuality, it puts the body and the world of objects to uses that have nothing whatever to do with any kind of "immanent" design or purpose. Perversion also subverts many of the binary oppositions upon which the social order rests: it crosses the boundary separating food from excrement (coprophilia), human from animal (bestiality), life from death (necrophilia), adult from child (pederasty), and pleasure from pain (masochism).

Of course not all perversions are equally subversive, or even equally interesting. It is unfortunate, but not surprising, that the perversion that has commandeered most of the literary and theoretical attention —sadism—is also the one that is most compatible with conventional heterosexuality. (The first thing Freud says about sadism in *Three Essays* is that "the sexuality of most male human beings contains an element of aggressiveness—a desire to subjugate." He adds that the "biological significance" of this combination "seems to lie in the need for overcoming the resistance of the sexual object by means other than the process of wooing. Thus sadism would correspond to an aggressive component of the sexual instinct which has become independent and exaggerated and, by displacement, has usurped the leading position" [157–58]. *The Ego and the Id* describes sadism's combination of cruelty and eroticism as a "serviceable instinctual fusion.")[7] The work of Sade commands enormous intellectual prestige—something inconceivable with the novels of Leopold von Sacher-Masoch, rescued from oblivion by Deleuze.[8] One thinks in this respect not only of Bataille,[9] Barthes,[10] and Gallop,[11] but also of the massive double issue of *Obliques* dedicated to Sade, which includes materials from Benoit, Klossowski, Blanchot, Robbe-Grillet, Sollers, Paulhan, Breton, Mandiargues, Masson, and Labisse, to name only a few of its contributors.[12]

The focus of this essay is the perversion that is most commonly linked with sadism, sometimes as its complement and at other times as its instinctual opposite. I refer of course to masochism,[13] variously described by Freud as an unusually dangerous libidinal infraction,[14] and as one of the "kindliest."[15]

Three Kinds of Masochism

In his last work to deal extensively with masochism, Freud distinguishes between three forms of that perversion: "erotogenic," "feminine," and "moral."[16] However, no sooner are these distinctions enumerated than they begin to erode. Erotogenic masochism, which Freud defines as "pleasure in pain," provides the corporeal basis for both feminine and moral masochism. The tripartite division thus gives way rather quickly to one of those dualisms of which Freud is so fond, with both feminine and moral masochism "bleeding" into each other at the point where each abuts onto erotogenic masochism.

The adjective "erotogenic" is one that Freud habitually links with "zone," and with which he designates a part of the body at which sexual excitation concentrates. Implicit, then, in the notion of masochism, whether feminine or moral, would seem to be the experience of corporeal pleasure, or — to be more precise — corporeal pleasure-in-pain. This stipulation poses no real conceptual difficulties with respect to the first of those categories; erotogenic masochism would seem to be literally "at the bottom" of feminine masochism, which Freud associates with fantasies of being bound and beaten, and with the desire to be "treated like . . . a naughty child."[17] It is far less clear how moral masochism could be said to have a necessary corporeal substratum, until we recall that the ego is for Freud "first and foremost a bodily ego"[18] — or, as Strachey explains in an authorized gloss, "derived from bodily sensations, chiefly from those springing from the surface of the body."[19] If, as "The Economic Problem of Masochism" suggests, the "true" masochist "always turns his cheek whenever he has a chance of receiving a blow" (165), the moral masochist's cheek is the ego. That is the erotogenic zone of choice, the site where he or she seeks to be beaten.

Curiously, after characterizing feminine masochism as "the one that is the most accessible to our observation," Freud announces that owing to the "material at [his] command," he will limit his discussion of that libidinal economy entirely to male patients.[20] The inference is obvious: feminine masochism is a specifically *male* pathology, so named because it positions its sufferer as a woman. Freud in fact says as much:

If one has an opportunity of studying cases in which the masochistic phantasies have been especially richly elaborated, one quickly discovers that they place the subject in a characteristically feminine situation; they signify, that is, being castrated, or copulated with, or giving birth to a baby. For this reason I have called this form of masochism, *a potiori*, as it were . . . the feminine form, although so many of its features point to infantile life.[21]

The reader is likely to object at this point that only five years earlier Freud had clearly identified the beating fantasy primarily with women. (Of the six patients upon whom he bases " 'A Child Is Being Beaten,' " four are female, and only two male.)[22] And from *Three Essays* until *New Introductory Lectures*, Freud was to maintain, albeit with certain crucial qualifications, the connection between femininity and masochism.[23] Yet "The Economic Problem of Masochism" is not the only major work on masochism to focus primarily upon male patients. Richard von Krafft-Ebing, who gave masochism its name and its first definition, cites thirty-three cases of male masochism, and only four of female.[24] (He also names masochism after a male masochist, Sacher-Masoch.) Theodor Reik's research had similar results, leading him to conclude that "the male sex is more masochistic than the female."[25] In his study of cruelty, Deleuze not only focuses exclusively on the novels of Sacher-Masoch, but elaborates a theoretical model of masochism in which the suffering position is almost necessarily male. What is to be made of this anomaly, whereby Freud designates as "feminine" a psychic disorder whose victims are primarily men?

While I would certainly dispute Reik's notion that men are more masochistic than women, it does seem to me that it is only in the case of men that feminine masochism can be seen to assume pathological proportions. Although that psychic phenomenon often provides a centrally structuring element of both male and female subjectivity, it is only in the latter that it can be safely acknowledged. It is an accepted—indeed, a requisite—element of "normal" female subjectivity, providing a crucial mechanism for eroticizing lack and subordination. The male subject, on the contrary, cannot avow feminine masochism without calling into question his identification with the masculine position. All of this is another way of suggesting that what is acceptable for the female subject is pathological for the male. Freud indicates as much when he tells us that whereas the beating fantasy can be effortlessly accommodated within the little girl's *positive* Oedipus complex, it can only be contained within the little boy's *negative* Oedipus complex.[26] Feminine masochism, in other words, always implies desire for the fa-

ther and identification with the mother, a state of affairs that is normative for the female subject, but "deviant" for her male counterpart.

The disruptive consequences of male masochism are also underscored by an extraordinary passage from Reik, in which he distinguishes the masochistic fantasies of women from those of men:

> Compared with the masculine masochism that of women shows a some-
> what attenuated, one could almost say anemic character. It is more of
> a trespassing of the bourgeois border, of which one nevertheless remains
> aware, than an invasion into enemy terrain. The woman's masochistic
> phantasy very seldom reaches the pitch of savage lust, of ecstasy, as does
> that of the man. Even the orgy in the phantasy does not ascend in so steep
> a curve. There is nothing in it of the wildness of the chained Prometheus,
> rather something of Ganymede's submission. One does not feel anything
> of the cyclonelike character that is so often associated with masculine
> masochism, that blind unrestricted lust of self-destruction. The maso-
> chistic phantasy of woman has the character of yielding and surrender
> rather than that of the rush ahead, of the orgiastic cumulation, of the
> self-abandonment of man. (216)

Reik suggests here that even the clinically masochistic woman does not
really exceed her subjective limits; she merely stretches them a bit. The
male masochist, on the other hand, leaves his social identity completely
behind — actually abandons his "self" — and passes over into the "enemy
terrain" of femininity. I will have more to say later about the "shattering"[27] qualities of male masochism, but suffice it to note here that the
sexual fantasies cited by Reik fully bear out these characterizations, as
do those included by Krafft-Ebing.

Not only does it turn out that feminine masochism does not have very
much to do with women, but that moral masochism does not have very
much to do with virtue. Although the moral masochist seems to be under the domination of a hyperdeveloped conscience, his or her desire for
punishment is so great as to pose a constant temptation to perform "sin-
ful" actions, which must then be "expiated." Freud warns that moral
masochism is in fact capable of swallowing up conscience altogether, of
perverting it from within.[28] This invisible sabotage occurs through the
complete reversal of the process whereby the Oedipus complex was
earlier "dissolved," i.e., of the operation whereby the paternal voice
and imago were internalized as the superego. By deriving erotic gratification from the superego's censorship and punishment, the morally
masochistic ego not only assumes an analogous position to that adopted by his or her more flamboyantly "feminine" counterpart in fantasy
or actual sexual practice, but reactivates the Oedipus complex.[29]

Significantly, what flares up with renewed intensity is that form of the Oedipus complex that is positive for the female subject, but negative for the male — the form, that is, that turns upon desire for the father and identification with the mother. Freud is quite explicit about this:

> We were able to translate the expression "unconscious sense of guilt" as meaning a need for punishment at the hands of a parental power. We know that the wish, which so frequently appears in phantasies, to be beaten by the father stands very close to the other wish, to have a passive (feminine) sexual relation to him and is only a regressive distortion of it. If we insert this explanation into the content of moral masochism, its hidden meaning becomes clear to us. (169)

Thus through moral masochism the ego is beaten/loved by the father, a situation that — once again — is "normal" for the female subject but "abnormal" for the male.

It would consequently seem that moral and feminine masochism develop out of the same "phantasmatic," to borrow a word from Laplanche and Pontalis[30] — out of the same unconsciously structuring scenario or action. However, the moral masochist remains oblivious to the passion for self-destruction that burns ferociously within; Freud observes that whereas the sadism of the superego "becomes for the most part glaringly conscious," the masochism of the ego "remains as a rule concealed from the subject and has to be inferred from his behaviour."[31] With the feminine masochist, on the other hand, the beating fantasy assumes a shape that is available to consciousness, albeit not necessarily to rational scrutiny.

Let us look rather more closely at these two categories of masochism, and at the forms they assume in both conscious and unconscious life.

Moral Masochism

With a frankness that is more alarming than engaging, Freud acknowledges in *The Ego and the Id* that under certain circumstances the superego promotes a "pure culture of the death [drive]" (53). The stronger that psychic entity — i.e., the more thoroughly the subject has been subordinated to prohibition and denial — the greater the possibility that the ego will be driven to the last extremity. In moral masochism the superego assumes titanic proportions, but even under much more auspicious conditions its authority and severity are so considerable as to call fundamentally into question the notion of a "healthy" subject, let alone one who might be said to be in a position of mastery or control. Since conventional subjectivity so closely adjoins moral masochism, I want to examine it briefly through the grid of Freud's late topography before turning once again to its pathological correlate.

We recall that the superego is the agency whereby the Oedipus complex is neutralized but its effects indefinitely prolonged. It is formed through the fantasmatization and introjection of what cannot be possessed in reality, and must consequently be renounced—the parents. This process of introjection is a complex one, more hinted at than specified in *The Ego and the Id*, but clarified somewhat in *New Introductory Lectures on Psycho-Analysis*.[32] It develops out of two sets of relationships, one of which is synonymous with the positive Oedipus complex, and the other of which is equivalent to the negative Oedipus complex, a point to which I will return in a moment. The superego would also seem to involve two different kinds of introjection, one of which I will characterize as "imaginary" and the other as "symbolic." What I mean by imaginary introjection is the psychic process whereby once-loved figures are taken into the self as subjective models or exempla, i.e., with the formation of that image or cluster of images in which the ego sees itself as it would like to be seen. Symbolic introjection, on the other hand, designates the psychic process whereby the subject is subordinated to the Law and the Name-of-the-Father. Although the category of the superego subsumes both kinds of introjection in Freud, it more specifically designates the product of symbolic introjection. Imaginary introjection, on the other hand, results in what is strictly speaking the ego ideal.

Because the subject usually goes through a negative as well as a positive Oedipus complex, he or she enters into two sets of identifications at the end of that complex: one with the imago of the mother, the other with the imago of the father.[33] One of these identifications is generally much stronger, and so tends to eclipse the other. If all goes according to cultural plan, the stronger identification conforms to the positive Oedipus complex. Nevertheless, both have a part to play in the agency that they form within the ego, an agency Freud describes as the "ego ideal or super-ego," but which is more usefully designated by the first of those appellations.

The ego ideal, I would maintain, represents one area or function of the superego but not its entirety, that "face" of each parent that is loved rather than feared. It articulates the ideal identity to which the ego aspires, and by which it constantly measures itself, but in relation to which it is always found wanting. It is the mirror in which the subject would like to see itself reflected, the repository of everything it admires.

Freud argues in *The Ego and the Id* that the introjection of these parental images desexualizes them, with the positive Oedipus complex canceling out the object-choice of the negative complex, and the negative Oedipus complex canceling out the object-choice of the positive complex. Desire for the father, in other words, gives way to identification with him, and desire for the mother to identification with her:

> The father-identification will preserve the object-relation to the mother which belonged to the positive complex and will at the same time replace the object-relation to the father which belonged to the inverted complex: and the same will be true, *mutatis mutandis,* of the mother-identification. (34)

This desexualization has grave consequences for the ego, since it results in an instinctual defusion; when object-libido changes to narcissistic libido (i.e., when love changes to identification), the aggression that was earlier commingled with that libido also loses its purchase, and turns around upon the subject's own self. No longer in the protective custody of eros, that aggression falls under the jurisdiction of the superego, which directs it against the ego (54–55).

Freud says some very inconsistent things about the gender of the superego. At some points in *The Ego and the Id* he associates it with both parents, as we have seen, but at other points he connects it exclusively with the father. In one particularly important passage, in which he places great emphasis upon the paternal identity of the superego, he refers to the "double aspect" of that psychic entity, an aspect he equates with two mutually exclusive imperatives: "You *ought to be* like this (like your father)"; and "You *may not be* like this (like your father) — that is, you may not do all that he does; some things are his prerogative" (34). The first of these commands clearly issues from the ego ideal, whose function is to promote similitude between itself and the ego, but where does the second command come from?

It comes, as Freud's reference to a "double aspect" would suggest, from another component of the superego, and one whose gender is much more delimited than that of the ego ideal. This other component is formed through the introjection of the symbolic father rather than his imaginary counterpart — through the internalization of the father as Law, gaze, voice-on-high. This element of the superego has no necessary relation to any historical figure, but its gender is irreducibly masculine, at least within the present social order. It is, quite simply, the paternal function, and the ego is always already guilty in relation to it — guilty by virtue of Oedipal desire.

Curiously, in light of the double parental complex, with the expectation it creates that both parents would have a part to play in the constitution of the superego, Freud asserts in *The Ego and the Id* that this entity is always "a substitute for a longing for the father" (37). The context in which he makes this observation indicates that he is speaking not about the ego ideal, but about what, in the strictest sense of the word, is the superego. Freud adds that the psychic entity that replaces desire for the father "contains the germ from which all religions have evolved," and produces "the self-judgment which declares that the ego falls short of its ideal." This passage from *The Ego and the Id* conse-quently has staggering implications. It suggests that what is really at is-sue in the dissolution of the male Oedipus complex — what really moti-vates Freud to insist so strenuously upon its definitive terminus — is the male subject's *homosexual attachment to the father*. The relationship of the male ego to the superego would seem to grow out of, and "ideal-ly" undo, the romance between father and son — or, to be more precise, the romance between the father in his symbolic guise and the son whose subordination is a substitute for love.[34]

The situation is even more explosive than I have so far shown it to be. There is a fundamental impossibility about the position in which the male subject is held, an impossibility that has to do with the self-canceling structure of the Oedipal imperative. The only mechanism by which the son can overcome his desire for the father is to transform ob-ject libido into narcissistic libido, and in so doing to attempt to *become* the (symbolic) father. However, this metamorphosis is precisely what the superego prohibits by decreeing: "You may not be like [your fa-ther] . . . you may not do all that he does; some things are his prerogative." The paternal law thus promotes the very thing its severity is calculated to prevent, a contradiction that must function as a con-stant inducement to reconstitute the negative Oedipus complex.

It is hardly surprising, in view of all this, that the relationship of the ego to the superego should be susceptible to sexualization; eros is in fact never far away. But what form does this "sexuality" take? Freud leaves us in no doubt on this particular point. In *Civilization and Its Discontents* he describes a situation where the ego comes to take plea-sure in the pain inflicted upon it by the superego — where fear of punish-ment gives way to the wish for it, and where cruelty and discipline come to stand for love:

> The sense of guilt, the harshness of the super-ego is . . . the same thing as the severity of the conscience. It is the perception which the ego has of being watched over in this way, the assessment of the tension between its own strivings and the demands of the super-ego. The fear of this criti-cal agency (a fear which is at the bottom of the whole relationship), the need for punishment, is an instinctual manifestation on the part of the ego, which has become masochistic under the influence of a sadistic super-ego; it is a portion . . . of the instinct towards internal destruc-tion present in the ego, employed for forming an erotic attachment to the super-ego. (136)

This description conforms precisely to what Freud was somewhat later to name "moral masochism." However, the condition it describes differs from "normalcy" only in degree and erotic intent. The prototypical male subject oscillates endlessly between the mutually exclusive commands of the (male) ego ideal and the superego, wanting both to love the father and to be the father, but prevented from doing either. The morally masochistic male subject has given up on the desire to be the father, and may in fact have turned away from the paternal ego ideal to the maternal one, and from identification with the father to identification with the mother. However, he burns with an exalted ardor for the rigors of the superego. The feminine masochist, to whom I shall return later in this chapter, literalizes the beating fantasy and brings this cruel drama back to the body.

Christian Masochism

Theodor Reik's exhaustive study of masochism warrants some attention at this point, both because it has been so extensively mined by Deleuze and others and because it manifests so extreme a sensitivity to the formal features of that pathology. Although it begins with a discussion of masochism as a sexual perversion—a discussion studded with some quite compelling fantasies, one of which we will circle back to later—its chief focus is moral (or what Reik calls "social") masochism. *Masochism in Sex and Society* characterizes that psychic economy as closed and self-referential, and associates it with exhibitionism or "demonstrativeness," revolutionary fervor, and "suspense"—a surprising catalogue at first glance. As I will attempt to demonstrate, certain parts of this definition clearly pertain to that model of moral masochism that Freud associates with the ego/superego dynamic, but other parts point toward a rather different paradigm.

Like Freud, Reik stresses that in moral or social masochism the subject functions both as the victim and as the victimizer, dispensing with the need for an external object. Even when punishment seems to derive from the external world, it is in fact the result of a skillful unconscious manipulation of "adverse incidents" (304). The psychic economy of moral masochism is therefore strikingly self-contained:

> Social masochism springs from the intermediate phase of the development of phantasy, during which the pain-inflicting and the pain-enduring person are identical, *impersonating* simultaneously object and subject. Also in the masochistic attitude toward life there is generally no object discernible that imposes the suffering and is independent of the ego. It is certainly extant in phantasy, but it does not appear in reality

and remains in the twilight where it merges into the ego. This type of masochistic character behaves almost autoerotically. (333, my emphasis)

Reik does not, however, foreground the role of the superego in moral masochism; the internal agency of punishment remains curiously unspecified in his text. He also gives fantasy a more privileged position within moral masochism than does Freud; indeed, he maintains that it plays as centrally structuring a role there as it does in what he calls "perverse" masochism. Here, again, the emphasis falls exclusively on the ego; even when other figures appear in these fantasies, they are in effect stories with a single character (314). Finally, Reik claims that the fantasies at the heart of masochism remain strictly unconscious, and that they always express the same desire—the desire to be rewarded for good behavior. Consequently, although they invariably dramatize the sufferings and defeats of the fantasizing subject, that is "only to make the final victory appear all the more glorious and triumphant" (315).

Both in its exclusive focus upon the ego, and in its apparent impulsion toward the "enhance[ment]" of that psychic entity, Reik's moral masochism would seem to differ significantly from Freud's. We will, however, discover more substantive differences between the two forms of moral masochism than those I have already noted. The latter will also evaporate upon closer scrutiny. Ultimately, the moral masochism identified by Reik occupies a theoretical position somewhere between Freud's version of that pathology and feminine masochism, manifesting aspects of both.

The second of the qualities enumerated earlier—exhibitionism or "demonstrativeness"—is one that Reik claims to be an indispensable feature, not only of moral or social masochism but of all masochism:

> In no case of masochism can the fact be overlooked that the suffering, discomfort, humiliation and disgrace are being shown and so to speak put on display. . . .
> In the practices of masochists, denudation and parading with all their psychic concomitant phenomena play such a major part that one feels induced to assume a constant connection between masochism and exhibitionism. (72)

As we will see later in this chapter, the demonstrative feature occupies a prominent place within Reik's account of feminine or "perverse" masochism. However, many of the most striking examples of exhibitionism that he cites are drawn from moral or social masochism. Once again, this places him in opposition to Freud, who claims that whereas the superego's desire to inflict injury is usually "glaringly" obvious in moral masochism, the ego's desire for punishment generally escapes the attention both of others and of the subject itself. What are we to make of this discrepancy?

A quick survey of Reik's examples suggests that his attention may be focused upon a different variety of moral masochism than that spot-lighted by Freud—that his concern may ultimately be with Christian masochism, even when he is discussing more secular instances. Not only does he devote a whole chapter to "the paradoxes of Christ," but most of the other cases of moral masochism that he cites are drawn from the lives of saints and martyrs. As in Freud's account of moral masochism, Reik's typical subject seems ardently given over to self-mortification of one kind or another (one particularly commodious sentence functions as a kind of display window, disclosing "Benedict rolling himself in thorn hedges, Macarius sitting naked on an ant-hill, [and] Anthony flagellating himself incessantly" [351]), but the psychic dynamics are otherwise quite different.[35] To begin with, an external audience is a structural necessity, although it may be either earthly or heavenly. Second, the body is centrally on display, whether it is being consumed by ants or roasting over a fire. Finally, behind all these "scenes" or "exhibits" is the master tableau or group fantasy—Christ nailed to the cross, head wreathed in thorns and blood dripping from his pierced side. What is being beaten here is not so much the body as the "flesh," and beyond that sin itself and the whole fallen world.

This last target pits the Christian masochist against the society in which he or she lives, makes of that figure a rebel or even a revolution-ary of sorts. In this particular subspecies of moral masochism there would thus seem to be a strong heterocosmic impulse—the desire to re-make the world in another image altogether, to forge a different cul-tural order. The exemplary Christian masochist also seeks to remake him- or herself according to the model of the suffering Christ, the very picture of earthly divestiture and loss. Insofar as such an identification implies the complete and utter negation of all phallic values, Christian masochism has radically emasculating implications, and is in its purest forms intrinsically incompatible with the pretensions of masculinity.[36] And since its primary exemplar is a male rather than a female subject, those implications would seem impossible to ignore. Remarkably, Christianity also redefines the paternal legacy; it is after all through the assumption of his place within the divine family that Christ comes to be installed in a suffering and castrated position.

The demonstrative feature, as I have been implicitly arguing, works very much against Reik's premise that the driving force behind moral masochism is the victory and reward of the ego. Reik suggests at one point that the moral masochist seeks to be "raised on an invisible pedestal" (315), but the passage I quoted earlier thoroughly belies this formulation. In that passage, Reik not only associates all forms of masochism with exhibitionism or self-display, but he acknowledges that what is thus rendered visible is the subject's "suffering," "discomfort," "humiliation," and "disgrace" rather than its grandeur or its triumph. The demonstrative feature also runs counter to the notion that moral masochism is an entirely self-contained system, since at least within Reik's Christian examples the gaze comes dramatically into play, either in a heavenly or an earthly guise. There are also other ways in which moral masochism opens onto the world on which it ostensibly forecloses, whether it assumes the form described by Freud or that theorized by Reik. The superego is produced through the introjection of the paternal function, and the ego through the subject's identification both with its own corporeal imago and with a whole range of other external images. The interior drama is thus the refraction of a familial structure, which itself interlocks with the whole social order. Christian masochism, as we have seen, involves a similar identificatory system.[37]

The last of the qualities associated by Reik with moral masochism—suspense—would seem to be at the center of all forms of masochism, in addition to being one of the conditions out of which conventional subjectivity develops. Reik rings some complex changes on this word, which he connects with uncertainty, dilatoriness, pleasurable and unpleasurable anticipation, apparent interminability, and—above all—excitation. Masochism exploits all these themes in one way or another because it always seeks to prolong preparatory detail and ritual at the expense of climax or consummation. Since in moral masochism this implies the endless postponement of the moment at which suffering yields to reward, and victory to defeat, suspense clearly works to elevate pain over pleasure, and so to further undermine the ego.

The larger thesis that Reik pursues over the length of his study is that the masochist is apprehensive about end pleasure because it is so fully associated with punishment and therefore seeks to delay it as long as possible ("The . . . characteristic of the masochistic tension-curve is the tendency to prolong the tension, while we meet with the opposite intention, of resolving the tension, in normal sexual life" [60]). However, Reik also maintains elsewhere in *Masochism in Sex and Society* that the masochist rushes toward the punishment he or she fears in order to get it over with as quickly as possible. Through this "flight forward" the normal sequence of pleasure and pain is reversed, and the latter is experienced before the former. This is how Reik accounts for the suffering in masochism, to which he claims the subject would never submit except as the "price" of what is always fundamentally a sexual gratification.

There is a basic contradiction here: if the masochist rushes to experience the necessary punishment *before* indulging in a pleasure so as to thereby assure an untroubled enjoyment of it, why should he or she then delay the moment of gratification for as long as possible out of fear of the consequences? This contradiction is part and parcel of Reik's refusal to admit that the masochist in fact *seeks out* punishment, of his inability to entertain the possibility that for some individuals pleasure might actually inhere in pain and in the psychic destabilization to which it leads.

Such an eventuality would represent the radical perversion of the pleasure principle, which "endeavors to keep the quantity of excitation present in [the mental apparatus] as low as possible or at least to keep it constant."[38] It would indicate, that is, that pleasure (and specifically sexual pleasure) can accompany an excruciating increase in such tension. Freud himself has, of course, prepared us for such a development. He remarks on more than one occasion that pain "trenches" into pleasure, a verb the OED glosses as "to 'cut' into, to enter into so as to affect intimately." *Three Essays* includes the observation that "nothing of considerable importance can occur in the organism without contributing some component to the excitation of the sexual instinct" (205); and "The Economic Problem of Masochism" adds that "the excitation of pain and unpleasure would be bound to have the same result too" (163). Freud's theory of pleasure is closely imbricated, however, with his account of the way in which identity is formed, i.e., with what he has to say about the secondary process and the maintenance of a quiescently cathected ego. As Leo Bersani points out in *The Freudian Body*, the introduction of large quantities of excitation into the psychic economy can only have a "shattering" effect upon this coherence, pitting the pathology of masochism (which for him means sexuality *tout court*) against identity itself:

> The pleasurable unpleasurable tension of sexual excitement occurs when the body's "normal" range of sensation is exceeded, and when the organization of the self is momentarily disturbed by sensations or affective processes somehow "beyond" those compatible with psychic organization. . . . Sexuality [i.e., masochism] would be that which is intolerable to the structured self. . . . Sexuality . . . may depend on the *décalage* or gap, in human life between the quantities of stimuli to which we are exposed and the development of ego structures capable of resisting or . . . binding those stimuli. The mystery of sexuality is that we seek not only to get rid of this shattering tension but also to repeat, even to increase it. (38–39)

What masochism really "suspends," then, is not just the pleasure principle, but the libidinal and psychic constancy that principle supports.

But what are the forms this suspense takes in moral masochism? The Christian, of course, lives his or her life in perpetual anticipation of the second coming. The figural meaning this anticipation implants in present sufferings makes it possible for them to be savored as future pleasures, with time folding over itself in such a way as to permit that retroactivity to be already experienced now, in a moment prior to its effectivity. Such is the fundamentally perverse nature of Christian suspense and the pain it sanctifies and irradiates, a suspense that works against anything approximating psychic coherence.

Freud's moral masochist also lives in suspense, but without the promise of a redemptive endpleasure. Here suspense has a double face. It signifies both the endless postponement of libidinal gratification and the perpetual state of anxiety and apprehension, which is the result of that renunciation and of the superego's relentless surveillance. Of course these forms of suspense are not limited to the moral masochist; they are also part of the cultural legacy of even the most conventionally structured of subjects. All that distinguishes the former from the latter is that his or her ego seeks to increase rather than decrease that tension, whether through the commission of misdeeds that will then elicit punishment, or—more classically—through the punctiliousness of its obedience. Freud warns us that the more perfectly the ego conforms to the superego's mandates, the more ferocious and exacting that censoring mechanism becomes.[39] It would thus seem that the ego's "goodness" can actually become a request to be beaten. The moral masochist, in short, seeks to intensify both forms of the suspense that is so (seemingly) intolerable to the "ordinary" subject. Freud is quite explicit about the challenge this poses to the stability and robustness of the ego, remarking in "The Economic Problem of Masochism" that "in order to provoke punishment from [the superego], the masochist must do what is inexpedient, must act against his own interests, must ruin the prospects which open out to him in the real world and must, perhaps, destroy his own real existence" (169–70).

Feminine Masochism

Let us now turn to feminine masochism through an examination of " 'A Child Is Being Beaten,' " which is without doubt the most crucial text for understanding that perversion. Significantly, although Freud focuses primarily upon female patients there, he manages to articulate the masochistic desire he attributes to them only through recourse to one of his male patients, who gives voice to what they cannot—the second phase of the beating fantasy.[40] Let us effect a reverse displacement and approach the male version of the beating fantasy through its female counterpart. Doing so will permit us to see how fully that fantasy subverts sexual difference.

The female fantasy consists of three phases, the first and third of which are available to analysis, but the second of which remains unconscious. Here is the complete sequence, after it has been "doctored" by Freud (the phrases within square brackets represent either his interpolations or additions made by the patient at his prompting):

Phase 1: "My father is beating the child [whom I hate]."
Phase 2: "I am being beaten by my father."
Phase 3: "Some boys are being beaten. [I am probably looking on.]"

Freud says of the first phase that it is neither sexual nor sadistic, but "the stuff from which both will later come" (187). He adds that it may not even constitute part of the fantasy proper, but may simply be a memory out of which the fantasy subsequently develops. It is savored for the erotic value it retroactively assumes, a value Freud translates with the phrase: "My father does not love this other child, *he loves only me*."

Oedipal desire and its prohibition intervene between phases 1 and 2 of the fantasy. By inserting herself into the imaginary scene in the position earlier occupied by the other child, the girl submits herself to punishment at the hands of the father, and so atones for her incestuous guilt. This new fantasy evokes intensely pleasurable feelings, however, pointing to an erotic as well as a punitive content. Phase 2 — "I am being beaten by my father"—thus functions as a mechanism for bringing about a regression to an earlier stage of sexuality; the desire that is blocked at the genitals, in other words, finds expression instead at the anus.

On account of its prohibited content, phase 2 undergoes repression. It is replaced at the level of consciousness by the third variant, which disguises the identity both of the person being beaten and of the one administering the punishment. A group of boys now replaces the little girl, and a paternal representative supplants the father. The fantasizing subject is inscribed into this scenario as an ambiguous spectator.[41] Phases 1 and 3 are ostensibly sadistic. Only phase 2 is unequivocally masochistic.

In a move equivalent in daring to Monsieur D's open concealment of the purloined letter in Poe's short story, Freud disarms his critic by acknowledging what might otherwise have been discovered about phase 2; he admits, that is, to having fabricated that sequence in the fantasy upon which he bases his entire interpretation:

> This second phase is the most important and the most momentous of all.
> But we may say of it in a certain sense that it has never had a real exis-
> tence. It is never remembered, it has never succeeded in becoming con-
> scious. It is a construction of analysis, but it is no less of a necessity on
> that account. (185)

Every time I read this passage, I find myself momentarily paralyzed
both by the audacity of the confession and by the realization that to
challenge Freud's right to speak in this way *for* his female patients
would be to place my rhetorical weight on the side of the "real" as
against the "constructed," the "authentic" against the "inauthentic."

Yet, struggle as I inevitably do against this paralysis, I can find nothing to dispute in Freud's account of phase 2, apart from the fact that
he finds what he is looking for in one of his male patient's case histories.
The change from the active to the passive form of the verb "to beat" —
from phase 1 to phase 3 — can only have been effected through the
mediation of the instinctual vicissitude indicated in phase 2. In other
words, the transition from phase 1 to phase 3 moves the subject from
heteroaggression to what appears to be sadism, and hence from the
dimension of simple self-preservation to that of sexuality. As
Laplanche has compellingly argued, that movement necessitates not
only the propping of sexuality upon aggression (i.e., upon the death
drive), but the turning around of that sexualized aggression upon the
fantasizing subject's own self (85–102). It is only in a second movement
that the now eroticized aggression can be redirected outward once
again, this time in the form of sadism. I would therefore agree with
Freud that what he identifies as phase 2 is behind phase 3, and that implicit in the later moment is a masochistic identification with the beaten
children.

At the same time, I do not think that phases 2 and 3 can be completely collapsed, or that the wish for pleasurable pain exhausts the latter's
meaning. Greater attention should be paid here to the manifest content
of the conscious fantasy, and to its substitution of boys for a girl. The
final phase attests to three transgressive desires, not one of which Freud
remarks upon, but which clamor loudly for my attention: to the desire
that it be boys rather than girls who are loved / disciplined in this way;
to the desire to be a boy while being so treated by the father; and, finally, to the desire to occupy a male subject position in some more general
sense, but one under the sign of femininity rather than that of masculinity.

These three desires clearly converge on one thing: a narcissistic investment in a subject position that it would be transgressive for a man
to occupy but that is almost unthinkable for a woman, since it implies

an identification with male homosexuality. Why should this identification fall so far outside the social pale? Because even what generally passes for "deviance" is held to a recognizable and "manageable" paradigm, i.e., to one that reinforces the binary logic of sexual difference, despite inverting its logic. Thus when a woman does not identify with a classically female position, she is expected to identify with a classically male one, and vice versa in the case of a man. The female version of the beating fantasy, then, attests to the desire for imaginary variations that fall outside the scope of the psychoanalytic paradigm.

Freud comes close on two occasions to commenting upon the last of the wishes enumerated, but both times he pulls back from what he is on the verge of discovering. At the end of Section IV he observes that

> when [girls] turn away from their incestuous love for their father, with its genital significance, they easily abandon their feminine role. They spur their "masculinity complex" . . . into activity, and from that point forward only want to be boys. For that reason the whipping-boys who represent them are boys too. (191)

Here the contradiction between having a "masculinity complex" and representing oneself as a group of "whipping-boys" goes unnoted by Freud. In a subsequent passage, however, he points out that the girl's identification with the male position does not imply an identification with activity: "[the girl] turns herself in phantasy into a man, without herself becoming active in the masculine way" (199).

In Section VI of " 'A Child Is Being Beaten,' " Freud suggests that the female subject occupies not one but *two* unconventionally masculine positions in phase 3 of the beating fantasy. In the course of describing the various shifts that occur over the history of the beating fantasy, he explicitly states that in phase 3 the girl turns herself into the group of boys (196). A few pages later, however, he indicates that in her capacity as onlooker of the beating scene, the girl occupies another position indicative of a masculinity under erasure. After observing that the girl "turns herself in phantasy into a man without herself becoming active in the masculine way," he adds that she is "no longer anything but a spectator of the event which takes the place of a sexual act" (199).

The first of these masculine positions—that of (passive) male homosexuality—is the position into which the male subject inserts himself in the masculine version of the beating fantasy, and there it has an emphatically maternal significance; Freud maintains that it is "derived from a feminine attitude toward his father" (198), i.e., from the negative Oedipus complex. The male subject thus secures access to femininity through identification with the mother. By turning herself in fantasy into the "whipping-boys," the female subject is in turn given imaginary access to this "borrowed" femininity through the image of the male body. Femininity is thus both radically denatured and posited as the privileged reference point by means of the curious relay that is set up between these two versions of the beating fantasy. But there is also an ineluctable difference at work here, since it is clearly not the same thing, socially or even psychically, for the girl to be loved/beaten by the father as it is for the boy. Through her identification with the "whipping-boys" in phase 3, the girl establishes an imaginary connection not only with a feminized masculinity but also with that difference. Is not this the beginning of a sexual relation?

It is perhaps less evident how the girl's spectatorial position in phase 3 also aligns her with an "unmanly" masculinity. Voyeurism has been heavily coded within Western culture as a male activity, and associated with aggression and sadism. Here, however, masculinity, aggression, and sadism are definitively elsewhere in the scene, concentrated in the figure of the punishing father surrogate. Like the child in the primal scene, the shadowy onlooker is more mastered than mastering.[42] The tentativeness with which Freud's female patients insert themselves into this position ("I am probably looking on") points to the irresolute character of the position itself, which is less the site of a controlling gaze than a vantage point from which to identify with the group of boys.

Before leaving the female beating fantasy, I want to note that the pronoun "I" is conspicuously missing from those parts of the fantasy that are available to consciousness, except in the adumbrative qualification about spectatorship, and in fact figures prominently only in that phrase that is "a construction of psychoanalysis"—a detail that can be attributed to heteropathic identification. Heteropathic identification is the obverse of idiopathic identification; whereas the latter conforms to an incorporative model, constituting the self at the expense of the other who is in effect "swallowed," the former subscribes to an exteriorizing logic and locates the self at the site of the other. In heteropathic identification one lives, suffers, and experiences pleasure through the other.[43] In phase 3 of the female beating fantasy, that other is, of course, the male subject.

Within the male sequence, all three phases, including the conscious one, begin with the assertion of pronominal possession. The subject position that each phase maps out, however, bends that "I" in a "feminine" direction:

> Phase 1: "I am being loved by my father."
> Phase 2: "I am being beaten by my father."
> Phase 3: "I am being beaten by my mother."

The beating fantasies confided to Freud by his male patients have also been subjected to far less censorship and distortion than those recorded by his female patients. The only significant difference between the conscious scenario (phase 3) and the unconscious scenario (phase 2) bears upon the identity of the person administering the punishment; the conscious fantasy translates into the verbal formula "I am being beaten by my mother," whereas the unconscious one reads "I am being beaten by my father" (198). Even this disguise is lightly worn, since the beating woman manifests such aggressively masculine qualities as to unmistakably resemble the paternal figure she replaces. (Phase 1, which is presumed to lie concealed behind phase 2, is not available to consciousness.)

Finally, although some effort is made to conceal the *homosexual* content of the conscious fantasy, no corresponding attempt is made to hide its *masochistic* content; the two male patients discussed by Freud, like those cited by Krafft-Ebing, Reik, and Deleuze, openly "flaunt" their desire for punishment and degradation both within their conscious fantasies and within their sexual practices. We clearly have an extreme instance here of what Reik calls the "demonstrative feature." In the conscious fantasies of the four female patients, on the other hand, masochism is concealed behind sadism, even though it is more compatible with their cultural position.

What is it precisely that the male masochist displays, and what are the consequences of this self-exposure? To begin with, he acts out in an insistent and exaggerated way the basic conditions of cultural subjectivity, conditions that are normally disavowed; he loudly proclaims that his meaning comes to him from the Other, prostrates himself before the gaze even as he solicits it, exhibits his castration for all to see, and revels in the sacrificial basis of the social contract. The male masochist magnifies the losses and divisions upon which cultural identity is based, refusing to be sutured or recompensed. In short, he radiates a negativity inimical to the social order.

All of this is spectacularly visible in one of the more highly elaborated of the male fantasies included in *Masochism in Sex and Society*. The fantasy in question was told to Reik by a thirty-seven-year-old (married) man, who depended upon it for his sexual potency:

> To an ancient barbaric idol, somewhat like the Phoenician Moloch, a number of vigorous young men are to be sacrificed at certain not too frequent intervals. They are undressed and laid on the altar one by one. The rumble of drums is joined by the songs of the approaching temple choirs. The high priest followed by his suite approaches the altar and scrutinizes each of the victims with a critical eye. They must satisfy certain requirements of beauty and athletic appearance. The high priest takes the geni-

tal of each prospective victim in his hand and carefully tests its weight
and form. If he does not approve of the genital, the young man will be
rejected as obnoxious to the god and unworthy of being sacrificed. The
high priest gives the order for the execution and the ceremony continues.
With a sharp cut the young men's genitals and the surrounding parts are
cut away. (41)

Unlike the male masochists Freud discusses in " 'A Child Is Being Beat-
en,' " the author of this fantasy is not its overt "star." He is, however,
bound to the scenario through a complex imaginary network. His immediate point of insertion occurs through the young man who will be
next to fall victim to the priest's knife, but that figure himself identifies
closely with the victim at present suffering that mutilation. Reik writes
that "the patient shares every intensive affect of this victim, feels his terror and anxiety with all the physical sensations since he imagines that
he himself will experience the same fate in a few moments" (42). This
peculiar identificatory transfer, which is once again indicative of the
heteropathic impulse implicit in feminine masochism, compounds the
specularity of the scene, making it possible for the prospective victim
(and so for the fantasizing subject himself) to see how he will be seen
when the weapon falls on his genitals. It speaks not only to the demonstrative feature of masochism—to the premium it places upon self-
display—but also to the "I saw myself seeing myself" of classic femininity,[44] and to the mirror staging that underpins all subjectivity.

What is, of course, most immediately striking about what Reik
designates the "Moloch phantasy" is the literalness with which it enacts
the "theme" of castration, the way it grounds what is normally a symbolic event at the level of the body. Once again the reader is reminded
both of the terms under which the female subject enters representation,
marked by the stigmata of a corporeal lack and of the "pound of flesh"
that is the price each of us must pay for our access to language.[45] But
even more is "at stake" in this sacrificial drama; the stipulation that
each victim must conform to a phallic ideal means that what is really
being defaced or disfigured in this fantasy is the paternal imago, and
that what is cut off and thrown away is the male subject's symbolic
legacy.

So far I have mentioned only one part of the Moloch fantasy. Later
in *Masochism in Sex and Society*, Reik describes the dramatic sequel
to the dismemberment: the castrated victims are placed on a red-hot
grate until they are thoroughly singed, and then dropped into the fire
beneath (61–63). In this fantasy nothing is salvaged, and nothing is
redeemed. It is a narrative of the darkest pain, negativity, and loss.

The Moloch fantasy also dramatizes some of the other features Reik associates with masochism. It plays with suspense, for instance, in a number of complex ways. First, there is the thrillingly terrifying anticipation built into a situation where the subject imagines himself the second person in line to suffer various atrocities, and must first watch what will later happen to himself. Then there is a narrative structure that works to defeat the apparent climax of castration by making that event only the prologue to even more profound sufferings. Suspense is literalized through the grate mechanism, which dangles the victims over the engulfing fire, and further incorporated as a dramatic device through the mandate that they be adequately singed before being dropped into the flames. The key question at this juncture—a question that pushes the suspense to an almost unbearable level of intensity—is whether the victims will be able to withstand the pain and remain on the grate until they are ceremonially ejected, or whether they will instead fling themselves onto the fire so as to achieve a quick death. A variation that is sometimes built into the middle of the fantasy further compounds the fearful tension: two of the prisoners are obliged to tend the fire that will subsequently consume them.

The "author" of the Moloch fantasy coordinates it with coitus; provided that the "synchronization" works, ejaculation occurs at the precise moment that the suspense becomes unbearable, and the victim with whom he identifies finally surrenders himself or is subjected to death. Like the other, feminine, masochists discussed by Reik, this patient seems to increase the psychic tension until there is a veritable physiological explosion. This dramatic escalation of anxiety and apprehension violates Freud's notion of the pleasure principle fully as much as does the actual implementation of sexual or religious torture, suggesting once again the shortcoming of any theoretical account of pleasure that stresses constancy over rupture and coherence over "shattering." It is no wonder that the patients whom Reik actually managed to "cure" complained to him afterward that life had lost all its color and intensity (378).

The elaborate preparations that make up the early stages of the Moloch fantasy and the seemingly interminable delay in reaching a conclusion produce an erotic narrative that conforms closely to Freud's definition of perversion; here as there, libidinal interest extends far beyond "the regions of the body which are designated for sexual union," and the "path" leading toward "the final sexual aim" is traversed far from quickly. Moreover, although ejaculation does occur, there is no representation of it within the fantasy, which always ends immediately prior to that event. (This is regularly the case with the masochistic fantasies Reik describes, as well as the masochistic practices Krafft-Ebing enumerates; there seems to be no place within either script for the ostensible goal of all forepleasure.) The male genitals do figure prominently here, but not at the grand finale; that part of the fantasy that is given over to their inspection and excision occurs around the middle, and constitutes at most a "false climax." Thus the Moloch narrative does more than linger over "the intermediate relations to the sexual object"; it actually relegates castration to the status of foreplay.

The propensity for impersonation is even more marked in feminine masochism than it is in moral (or at least Christian) masochism, which is not surprising given that it is centrally concerned with subject positioning and gender "roles." We have already looked closely at one quite flamboyant mental masquerade, a masquerade that changes its "author's" age, his historical moment, and his national identity, as well as the circumstances of his life (and death). The creator of the Moloch fantasy generates other identities for himself as well, including one where he is a Portuguese prisoner of the Aztecs who is first forced to watch a number of other men be skinned alive and is then subjected to the same fate. Krafft-Ebing recounts numerous cases of male masochists who act out the part of a slave or a page, and others where the preferred role is that of a dog, a horse, a slaughter animal, a count, a surface (such as a floor) on which women walk, and a receptacle for urine, excrement, and menstrual blood. The "hero" of Sacher-Masoch's *Venus in Furs* assumes the disguise of a servant for much of that novel, and—near the end—that of a bull.[46]

The sexual practitioners of feminine masochism generally extend the masquerade to include the person inflicting the pain or humiliation as well, and indeed the entire "scene" of the erotic adventure, in effect remaking the world. This heterocosmic impulse is particularly pronounced in the Moloch and Aztec scenarios, which relocate the fantasizing subject in another time and place altogether. It is also strikingly evident in *Venus in Furs*, where Séverin and Wanda actually leave the country in which they are living for one in which they will be better able to pass as mistress and slave. The crucial question to ask here is whether the heterocosmic impulse exhausts itself altogether in the boudoir, or whether the "play" spills over into social intercourse as well, contaminating the proprieties of gender, class, and race.[47]

Freud maintains that it is not only at the level of his sexual life, but at that of his fantasmatic and his *moi* that the male masochist occupies a female position. In " 'A Child Is Being Beaten,' " he writes that femininity assumes the status of a "subjective conviction" for the male masochist (197); he suggests, that is, that the male masochist believes himself to be a woman at the deepest level of his desire and his identity. Near the end of " 'A Child Is Being Beaten,' " he also notes that the fantasy of corporal punishment manifests itself only in "unmanly boys" and "unwomanly girls," and that it is "a trait of femininity in the boy and of masculinity in the girl which must be made responsible" for the construction of the fantasy (202). The degree to which this femininity manifests itself in the conscious existence of the male masochist depends, of course, upon the strength of the "masculine protest"[48] that he brings to bear against it — upon whether or not he fortifies himself against the "woman" within. It is, however, a significant fact that phase 3 of the male version of the beating fantasy makes no attempt to disguise the masochistic position of the fantasizing subject, although it is somewhat more reticent about the latter's homosexuality. Ironically, moreover, the transformation of the agent of punishment from the father to the mother actually functions to accentuate the male masochist's femininity, since it effects so dramatic a reversal of traditional gender roles.

Freud makes the astonishing observation in " 'A Child Is Being Beaten' " that there is no trace within the masochistic unconscious, whether male or female, of the wish to be loved by the father — of the taboo desire from which the entire condition of masochism ostensibly derives. In regressing back to the anal stage of sexuality, the masochist apparently manages to erase all record of that variant of Oedipal genitality that is generally held to be positive for the girl and negative for the boy:

> Whatever is repressed from consciousness or replaced in it by something else remains intact and potentially operative in the unconscious. The effect of *regression* to an earlier stage of the sexual organization is quite another matter. As regards this we are led to believe that the state of things changes in the unconscious as well. Thus in both sexes the masochistic phantasy of being beaten by the father, though not the passive phantasy of being loved by him, lives on in the unconscious after repression has taken place. (199–200)

If Freud is to be believed on this point, male masochism constitutes a veritable hermeneutic scandal. The passage I have just quoted suggests that the first phase of the male beating fantasy ("I am being loved by my father") is *entirely* a construction of psychoanalysis, and in a much more extreme sense than the second stage of the female sequence can be said to be. It also suggests that the unconscious significance of the fantasy is *completely* exhausted by phase 2, which as I have already noted differs from phase 3 only with respect to the gender of the person administering the punishment. Here there is no radical division of manifest from latent content. The door to the unconscious need not be picked; it is already slightly ajar and ready to yield at the slightest pressure.

There are other implications as well. If no record can be found within his unconscious of the desire to be genitally loved by the father, the male masochist cannot be domesticated by substituting the penis for the whip. His (barely) repressed desire runs directly counter to any reconciliation of father and son, attesting irrefutably to the violence of the familial and cultural contract. His sexuality, moreover, must be seen to be entirely under the sway of the death drive, devoid of any possible productivity or use value. It is no wonder that Freud pulls back from promising a psychoanalytic "cure" in the case of the feminine masochist (197).

The Mother in Male Masochism

The moment has come to do more than refer in passing to Deleuze's extremely interesting study of masochism, with which this essay has a good deal of sympathy. Deleuze argues that masochism is entirely an affair between son and mother, or to be more precise, between the male masochist and a cold, maternal, and severe woman whom he designates the "oral mother." Through the dispassionate and highly ritualized transaction that takes place between these two figures, the former is stripped of all virility and reborn as a "new, sexless man," and the latter is invested with the phallus. (Although the mother assumes a dominant position within this scenario, Deleuze stresses that she is "formed" by the son [21].) What is beaten in masochism is consequently not so much the male subject as the father, or the father in the male subject. Masochism works insistently to negate paternal power and privilege:

> A contract is established between the hero and the woman, whereby at a precise point in time and for a determinate period she is given every right over him. By this means the masochist tries to exorcise the danger of the father and to ensure that the temporal order of reality and experience will be in conformity with the symbolic order, in which the father has been abolished for all time. Through the contract . . . the masochist reaches towards the most mythical and most timeless realms, where [the mother] dwells. Finally, he ensures that he will be beaten. . . . what is beaten, humiliated and ridiculed in him is the image and likeness of the father, and the possibility of the father's aggressive return. . . . The masochist thus liberates himself in preparation for a rebirth in which the father will have no part. (58)

This argument offers a "utopian" rereading of masochism.[49] There is an obvious danger that it be taken literally, as designating the standard form of that perversion, rather than its visionary reconfiguration.

It is crucial to grasp that although Deleuze does in fact claim that masochism has nothing to do with the father, he obviously knows full well that this is not the case. His account of that libidinal infraction cannot be understood apart from the mechanism of disavowal, which he not only places at the center of *its* organization, but *himself deploys* throughout his study whenever he refuses to acknowledge the place of the father within masochism. In a key passage, Deleuze asserts that masochism "proceeds from a twofold disavowal, a positive, idealizing disavowal of the mother (who is identified with the law), and an invalidating disavowal of the father (who is expelled from the symbolic order)" (60). He thereby clearly indicates that within the masochism about which he speaks, paternal power and the law are present only negatively, through their repudiation—that the masochism he celebrates is a pact between mother and son to write the father out of his dominant position within both culture and masochism, and to install the mother in his place.

The contract between Wanda and Séverin is one dramatization of that erasing *écriture*, but *Masochism: An Interpretation of Coldness and Cruelty* is itself another. The fact that both Deleuze and his male masochist are so busy disavowing the father's phallus and the mother's lack clearly indicates that both inhabit an Oedipal universe that only the force of a radically heterocosmic imagination can unmake, and not—as one recent writer suggests—a pre-Oedipal realm from which all masochism derives.[50] Deleuze himself tells us all this in a brilliant account of disavowal and fetishism:

> Disavowal should perhaps be understood as the point of departure of an operation that consists neither in negating nor even destroying, but rather in radically contesting the validity of that which is: it suspends belief in and neutralizes the given in such a way that a new horizon opens up beyond the given and in place of it. . . . fetishism is first of all a disavowal ("No, the woman does not lack a penis"); secondly it is a defensive neutralization (since, contrary to what happens with negation, the knowledge of the situation as it is persists, but in a suspended, neutralized form); in the third place it is a protective and idealizing neutralization (for the belief in a female phallus is itself experienced as a protest of the ideal against the real; it remains suspended or neutralized in the ideal, the better to shield itself against the painful awareness of reality). (28–29)

Deleuze thus makes it possible for us to see that the mother not only stands in for the father in phase 3 of the male version of the beating fantasy, but usurps his prerogatives. In inviting the mother to beat and/or dominate him, the feminine masochist transfers power and authority from the father to her, remakes the symbolic order, and "ruins" his own paternal legacy. And that is not all. As Freud remarks of those two patients in " 'A Child Is Being Beaten,' " the conscious fantasy of being disciplined by the mother "has for its content a feminine attitude without a homosexual object-choice" (199). It thereby effects another revolution of sorts, and one whose consequences may be even more transformative than the male subject's fantasy of being beaten by the father—it constitutes a feminine yet heterosexual male subject. As with phase 3 of the female beating fantasy, phase 3 of the male beating fantasy wreaks havoc with sexual difference.

While it is true that the father is left holding the whip at the level of the unconscious fantasmatic, it is also the case that the son does not there manifest any desire to fill his boots. The mother functions as the crucial site of identification in all of the variants of the male beating fantasy. The male masochist as he is presented by Freud in " 'A Child Is Being Beaten' " thus not only prefers the masquerade of womanliness to the parade of virility, he also articulates both his conscious and his unconscious desires from a feminine position. And although he seems to subordinate himself to the law of the father, that is only because he knows how to transform punishment into pleasure and severity into bliss. This male masochist deploys the diversionary tactics of demonstration, suspense, and impersonation against the phallic "truth" or "right," substituting perversion for the *père-version* of exemplary male subjectivity.

Although I have stressed the heterocosmic tendencies of feminine masochism, I do not mean to erect it as the model for a radically reconstituted male subjectivity. As I have already remarked more than once, masochism in all of its guises is as much a product of the existing symbolic order as a reaction against it. This essay is, however, less concerned with articulating new forms of male subjectivity than with complicating our understanding of the forms it takes at present. Male subjectivity is far more heterogeneous and divided than our theoretical models would suggest; it cannot be adequately summarized by invoking either the phallus or the more flexible concept of bisexuality. Even normative masculinity is constituted through a complex interaction of the negative and positive Oedipus complexes, and the conventions sustaining "normalcy" may exercise much less force than is generally assumed. Since libidinal deviations always represent a "politics" of sorts, it seems to me that any feminism that is devoted to the interrogation of sexual difference cannot afford to ignore those that are charted across the male body or psyche.

NOTES

1. Sigmund Freud, *Three Essays on the Theory of Sexuality*, in *The Standard Edition of the Complete Psychological Works*, ed. and trans. James Strachey (London: Hogarth Press, 1953), vol. 7, 150.

2. Freud, *Three Essays on the Theory of Sexuality* 149.

3. Jean Laplanche, *Life and Death in Psychoanalysis,* trans. Jeffrey Melhman (Baltimore: The Johns Hopkins University Press, 1976) 28, 30.

4. Michel Foucault, *The History of Sexuality, Volume I: An Introduction*, trans. Robert Hurley (New York: Vintage Books, 1980) 47–48.

5. *Semiotext(e)*, vol. 4, no. 1 (1981).

6. Janine Chasseguet-Smirgel, *Creativity and Perversion* (New York: Norton, 1984) 12.

7. Sigmund Freud, *The Ego and the Id*, *Standard Edition*, vol. 19, 41.

8. Gilles Deleuze, *Masochism: An Interpretation of Coldness and Cruelty*, trans. Jean McNeil (New York: George Braziller, 1971).

9. See Georges Bataille, "The Use Value of D.A.F. de Sade," in *Visions of Excess: Selected Writings, 1927–1939*, trans. Allan Stoekl (Minneapolis: University of Minnesota Press, 1985) 91–102, and *Literature and Evil*, trans. Alastair Hamilton (New York: Urizen Books, 1973) 83–107.

10. Roland Barthes, *Sade, Fourier, Loyola,* trans. Richard Miller (New York: Hill and Wang, 1976) 15–37 and 123–71.

11. Jane Gallop, *Intersections: A Reading of Sade with Bataille, Blanchot, and Klossowski* (Lincoln: University of Nebraska Press, 1981).

12. *Obliques*, nos. 12 & 13 (1977).

13. I have returned frequently to this topic over the past eight years, but always through a literary or cinematic intermediary. See, for instance, "*Histoire d'O*: The Story of a Disciplined and Punished Body," *Enclitic*, vol. 7, no. 2 (1983): 63–81; "Changing the Fantasmatic Scene," *Framework*, no. 20 (1983): 27–36; "Male Subjectivity and the Celestial Suture: *It's a Wonderful Life*," *Framework*, no. 14 (1981): 16–21; and "Masochism and Subjectivity," *Framework*, no. 12 (1980): 2–9. This time the approach will be more insistently theoretical and speculative.

14. Sigmund Freud, "The Economic Problem of Masochism," in *Standard Edition*, vol. 19, 159.

15. See Freud, "The Economic Problem of Masochism": 166, and "Dostoevsky and Parricide," *Standard Edition*, vol. 21, 179.

16. Freud, "The Economic Problem of Masochism": 161.

17. Freud, "The Economic Problem of Masochism": 162.

18. Freud, *The Ego and the Id* 26.

19. Freud, *The Ego and the Id* 26f.

20. Freud, "The Economic Problem of Masochism": 161.

21. Freud, "The Economic Problem of Masochism": 162.

22. Sigmund Freud, " 'A Child Is Being Beaten,' " *Standard Edition*, vol. 17, 175–204.

23. The most crucial of Freud's qualifications on this point is, of course, central to the present discussion — the qualification that whereas "femininity" may indeed imply passivity, and in many cases masochism, there is no necessary connection between "woman" and "femininity." See *Civilization and Its Discontents, Standard Edition*, vol. 21, 105f., for an extremely interesting discussion of the slippage between these last two categories.

24. Richard von Krafft-Ebing, *Psychopathia Sexualis: A Medico-Forensic Study*, trans. Franklin S. Klaf (New York: Stein and Day, 1965) 86–143.

25. Theodor Reik, *Masochism in Sex and Society*, trans. Margaret H. Beigel and Gertrud M. Kurth (New York: Grove Press, 1962) 243.

26. Freud, " 'A Child Is Being Beaten' ": 194–98.

27. I borrow the concept of "shattering" from Leo Bersani, who develops it at length in his important book, *The Freudian Body: Psychoanalysis and Art* (New York: Columbia University Press, 1986).

28. Freud, "The Economic Problem of Masochism": 169.

29. Freud, "The Economic Problem of Masochism": 169.

30. In *The Language of Psycho-Analysis*, trans. Donald Nicholson-Smith (New York: Norton, 1973), Jean Laplanche and J.-B. Pontalis suggest that "the subject's life as a whole . . . is seen to be shaped and ordered by what might be called, in order to stress this structuring action, a 'phantasmatic.' This should not be conceived of merely as a thematic — not even as one characterized by distinctly specific traits for each subject — for it has its own dynamic, in that the phantasy structures seek to express themselves, to find a way out into consciousness and action, and they are constantly drawing in new material" (317). For a fuller discussion of the fantasmatic, see Chapters 4, 7, and 8 of my *Male Subjectivity at the Margins* (New York: Routledge, 1992).

31. Freud, "The Economic Problem of Masochism": 169.

32. Sigmund Freud, *New Introductory Lectures on Psycho-Analysis, Standard Edition*, vol. 22, 60–68.

33. Freud, *The Ego and the Id* 31–34.

34. For an extended discussion of the female version of the negative Oedipus

complex and its relation to feminism, see Chapters 4 and 5 of my *The Acoustic Mirror: The Female Voice in Psychoanalysis and Cinema* (Bloomington: Indiana University Press, 1988). For a further analysis of the male version, see Bersani, *The Freudian Body* 49, and Chapter 8 of *Male Subjectivity at the Margins*.

35. There are striking similarities between the degradations Reik associates with Christian masochism and those Krafft-Ebing links with the sexual perversion of masochism. See, for instance, Cases 80, 81, 82, and 83 in *Psychopathia Sexualis*.

36. Of course Christian masochism rarely exists in the form I have described here. It is more often used as the vehicle for worldly or heavenly advancement, i.e., put to extrinsic uses. Observing the expedient uses to which such suffering can be put, Reik mistakenly assumes self-advancement to be an inherent part of Christian masochism.

37. Here, too, there is an implied familial prototype, that provided by the relation of God to Christ. The Christian models himself on the latter, and directs against himself what is in effect a "divine" punishment.

38. Sigmund Freud, *Beyond the Pleasure Principle, Standard Edition*, vol. 18, 9.

39. Freud, *The Ego and the Id* 54.

40. Freud constructs phase 2 of the girl's beating fantasy by inverting phase 3 of the boy's fantasy, a discursive action that points to the asymmetrical symmetry of the two sequences.

41. For a different account of " 'A Child Is Being Beaten' " in general, and phase 3 of the girl's fantasy in particular, see D. N. Rodowick, *The Difficulty of Difference: Psychoanalysis, Sexual Difference, and Film Theory* (New York: Routledge, 1991) 1–17.

42. I discuss the primal scene and its implications for male subjectivity in *Male Subjectivity at the Margins*, Chapter 4.

43. The concepts of idiopathic and heteropathic identification derive from Max Scheler, *The Nature of Sympathy*, trans. Peter Heath (Hamden: Conn.: Archon, 1970). For a further elaboration of these two forms of identification, and their relation to sadism and masochism, see *Male Subjectivity at the Margins*, Chapter 6.

44. See Stephen Heath, "Difference," *Screen*, vol. 19, no. 3 (1978): 51–112, for an insightful discussion of this scopic regime.

45. Jacques Lacan metaphorizes that which is lost to the subject with the entry into language as a "pound of flesh."

46. Leopold von Sacher-Masoch, *Venus in Furs* 80–130, in Deleuze, *Masochism* 80–130; Deleuze, *Masochism* 96.

47. Mary Russo has some very thoughtful things to say about the social and political implications of masquerade in "Female Grotesques: Carnival and Theory," in *Feminist Studies/Critical Studies*, ed. Teresa de Lauretis (Bloomington: Indiana University Press, 1986) 213–29.

48. In " 'A Child Is Being Beaten,' " Freud writes that "it seems to be only with the girl that the masculine protest is attended with complete success. . . . With the boy the result is not entirely satisfactory; the feminine line is not given up, and the boy is certainly not 'on top' in his conscious masochistic phantasy" (203). In an essay critiquing the article from which this chapter derives, Paul Smith argues that masochism is never more than a passing moment within male subjectivity ("Action Movie Hysteria, or Eastwood Bound," *Differences*, vol. 1, no. 3 [1989]: 106). While I am clearly in disagreement with Smith's formulation, I do concur with his claim that masochism is generally narratively contained within Hollywood cinema. This, however, tells us less about the place of masochism within male subjectivity than about the normalizing operations of the dominant fiction.

49. Gayle Rubin provides another utopian reading of masochism in "The Leather Menace: Comments on Politics and S/M," in *Coming to Power*, ed. Samois (Boston: Alyson Publications, 1981) 192–335.

50. Gaylyn Studlar conflates Deleuze's oral mother with the pre-Oedipal mother of object relations psychoanalysis, and extrapolates from that conflation a highly dubious argument about the origin of masochism. According to Studlar, that perversion has its basis in the (male) child's relationship with the actual mother prior to the advent of the father, a relationship predicated upon his helpless subordination to her and the insatiability of his desire for her. Masochistic suffering consequently derives from the pain of separation from the mother and the impossible desire to fuse with her again, rather than from the categorical imperatives of the Oedipus complex and symbolic law. This is a determinedly apolitical reading of masochism, which comes close to grounding that perversion in biology. (See "Masochism and the Perverse Pleasures of the Cinema," in *Movies and Methods*, vol. 2, ed. Bill Nichols [Berkeley: University of California Press, 1985] 602–21.)

Drawing by a twelve-year-old student
(in *Erziehungsflagellantismus*, Vienna, 1932)

Railroad Raiders (J. P. McGowan, 1917)

Male Hysteria and Early Cinema
Lynne Kirby

Cinema as we know it, as an institution, as an entertainment based on the mass spectatorship of projected moving images, was born in 1895, in the Golden Age of railway travel. As the prehistory and beginnings of cinema strongly suggest, film finds an apt metaphor in the railroad. The train can be seen as providing the prototypical experience of looking at a framed, moving image, and as the mechanical double of the cinematic apparatus.[1] Both are a means of transporting a passenger to a totally different place, both are highly charged vehicles of narrative events, stories, intersections of strangers, both are based on a fundamental paradox: simultaneous motion and stillness. These are two great machines of vision that give rise to similar modes of perception, and are geared to shaping the leisure time of a mass society.

From 1895 on, the railroad occupies an important place in the vocabulary, thematic repertoire and representational strategies of film-making. It is a privileged mode of transportation in the early silent period, more than the horse, the car, the ship, the airplane. Before the train robbery, engineer, girl telegrapher, and subway pick-up films began to appear around 1902, early film-goers were treated to numberless views of trains arriving and departing, of landscapes and city streets receding rapidly before cameras mounted on the fronts of locomotives and trolleys. The very term "tracking shot" is a compelling index of the permeation of filmmaking practice by the language of the railroad. And around the world in 1895–96, the single image invoked rhetorically over and over to describe the illusionistic power of cinema, as well as film's illusion of movement, is that of a train rushing toward the camera in 3/4 view.

The marriage of the railroad and the cinema was consummated in early film exhibition practices like Hale's Tours.[2] Hale's Tours, a nickelodeon amusement first introduced at the St. Louis World's Fair in 1904, used actual train cars for a "thrill" effect. The apparatus was modeled on turn-of-the-century fairground and amusement park entertainments that seated "passengers" in railway cars while painted scenery rolled by the windows. Hale's Tours used filmed panoramic views shot from the fronts of locomotives, which placed the viewer squarely in the illusion of being on a train, while agitating the car to heighten the illusion of travel. At its most popular moment, 1906–07, Hale's Tours theaters numbered more than 500 around the U.S.

What's significant about Hale's Tours is the extent to which railway travel is invoked as a paradigm of the cinematic experience, to return to the notion of the train as a prototypical cinematic machine. The perceptual analogy of both is strongest in this particular exhibition practice, but emerges equally strongly in the kind of criticism generated by each institution. Early film critics and theorists described the film-going experience in terms remarkably similar to those used by early railroad travelers; both speak of rapid changes of scenery and point of view, of the quick appearance and disappearance of objects within a single view, of "the annihilation of space and time."

Wolfgang Schivelbusch has described how the total reorganization of time and space effected by the coming of the railroad was commonly referred to in the mid-nineteenth century as "the annihilation of space and time."[3] The speed of train travel created a temporal and spatial shrinkage, and a perceptual disorientation that tore the traveler out of the traditional space-time continuum and thrust him/her into a new world of speed, velocity and diminishing intervals between geograph-ical points. Mediated by a framed glass screen, visual perceptions multiplied to form a mobile, "panoramic" perception, such that one could only see dynamically. The landscape became evanescent. Pan-oramic perception, in contrast to traditional perception, no longer belonged to the same space as the perceived objects: the traveler saw the objects, landscape, etc. through the apparatus moving him/her through the world (41).

The importance of the frame as a condition of this vision links the train with both the photograph and the film. Schivelbusch even refers to this kind of perception as "filmic," emphasizing in addition to the frame the character of montage, of juxtaposition integral to "the new reality of annihilated in-between spaces."[4]

It is in this panoramic perception that the railroad as a perceptual paradigm for the cinema is identified by contemporary scholars.[5] There is evidence, however, that this link was not lost on early observers and makers of film. Terry Ramsaye, one of the first film historians, recounts in his *Million and One Nights* (1926) how Albert E. Smith, founder with J. Stuart Blackton of Vitagraph, solved the problem of flicker in film images while riding a train. Peering out the window while hurtling through the New Jersey landscape, Smith allegedly saw an analogy to screen flicker in the repetition of telegraph poles the train swept past.

He remarked a similar effect in the flicker produced by looking through a picket fence as the train passed through a station. "This gave him the notion," writes Ramsaye, "of dividing up the flicker of the motion picture by adding blades to the then single bladed shutter. He tried this out and found that by multiplying the flicker in fact he eliminated it in effect. The resulting betterment of projection was extraordinary." Ramsaye draws the obvious conclusion: "So the movie shutter is related to the Pennsylvania Railroad's picket fences at Manhattan Transfer."[6]

Hugo Munsterburg, whose 1916 study of the photoplay is considered one of the earliest works in film theory, absorbs the discursive paradigm of the railroad in describing the relation of film to its spectator. *The Film: A Psychological Study* makes frequent reference to the expansion of the world made possible by film's contraction of time and space. Both are effected through a montage of different views, but also through the length of individual shots, and, of course, the choice of subject. Munsterberg describes the freeing of representation — and the spectator — from the dictates of time and space in films that take the viewer around the world in a matter of minutes or even seconds. The railroad itself recurs as an example, and in one case, is cited for playing a direct role in the production and consumption of the filmic experience, when footage of the investiture of the Prince of Wales is shot in Carnarvon at 4:00 P.M., developed and edited on a train, and projected in London at 10:00 P.M. that same day.[7]

Medical discourse also took note of the train/cinema analogy. In a 1907 issue of *The Moving Picture World*, an article reports that St. Louis oculists agreed with current German research on the damage watching moving pictures can cause to the eyes, but "say there is no necessity here to declare war on the kinematograph shows, as they are doing in the German capital." A Dr. Campbell is quoted as follows: "Looking at moving pictures is like reading a book on a train. Where the focus changes all the time, it is a strain on the eye to follow the object it is looking at. Particularly is this the case if the eye is defective. Even a perfect eye cannot stand looking too long at a moving picture or watching too many telegraph poles flash by a moving train." Dr. Campbell's advice is simply "not to visit moving picture shows if your eyes are weak. They will not permanently destroy the eyesight, but they produce an irritation of the retina caused by confusion of images. All moving pictures are not equally difficult to watch. In some the quivering motion is reduced to a minimum. In others it is violent."[8]

A major feature of the perceptual overlap between the railroad and the cinema is the experience of "shock," as trauma was referred to before about 1880. In film, this is the kind of visual stimulation represented by rapid shot changes, sudden cuts to close-ups, and even attacks on vision like those represented by the train charging headlong into the camera. With the railroad, the experience of shock was emblematized by the accident, both real and anticipated, which actually gave rise to a condition known as "railway spine" and then simply "traumatic neurosis." It is around this condition that I would like to explore a fundamental sense in which the railroad can be seen as a paradigm for cinematic perception as spectatorship. Using shock as a conceptual pivot, I will suggest that the railroad accident victim becomes in relation to early train films, and early cinema more generally, the film accident victim—a traumatized, and, in one sense, hysterical spectator.

As Schivelbusch notes, early railroad travelers lived a double relation to the train journey: the pleasure of speed, the thrill of the "projectile" being shot through space, matched against the terror of collision, and its psychological effects, phobia, anxiety and, in many cases, hysteria (131). Certainly with the marked increase in railroad accidents in the U.S. after 1853, the extent to which fear of collision had become bound up with the fabric of train travel could not be doubted.[9] The medical and legal professions were in any case obliged to acknowledge and take quite seriously the connection, as lawsuits mushroomed from the mid-nineteenth century on claiming damages for victims of "railway spine."[10] "Railway spine" was a condition analyzed as a deterioration of nervous tissue, a result of physical damage to the spinal cord suffered in a railway accident. Pathological causes and effects were the only admissible evidence for claims against the railway companies, until litigants began demonstrating symptoms like anxiety, partial loss of vision, paralysis, dyspepsia, but with no corresponding physical source. Nerve disease studies taking place simultaneously in England, France, Germany and the U.S. led the medical profession to expand its view of "railway spine" to include "railway brain," a more psychologically based disease. "From the early 1880s on," writes Schivelbusch, "the purely pathological view is superseded by a new, psychopathological one, according to which the shock caused by the accident does not affect the tissue of the spinal marrow, but affects the victim psychically. Now the victim's experience of shock is the main causative factor of the ailment. By the end of the 1880s, the concept of 'railway spine' has been replaced by that of traumatic neurosis" (136).

Very soon the notion that fright alone from an accident could produce these states took hold.[11] George Drinka notes in *The Birth of Neurosis* that even though not all cases were phobias (many involved hysteria, anxiety, or nervous exhaustion), victims of train neuroses all shared the experience of being frightened while simply in the proximity

of a railroad. In short, "medical testimony and popular opinion concurred in establishing a firm connection between fright, nerves and the responsibility of the railways" (121).

If early railway travel caused its passengers considerable anxiety in anticipation of accidents, by the later nineteenth century, improvements in railway travel had led to the reduction of anxiety and the internalization of panoramic perception as second nature, such that one no longer necessarily expected a violent interruption in the train journey.[12] The term "shock" then applies all the more to the phenomenon of the accident—which, though perhaps somewhat less frequent (Schivelbush overstates the case for the U.S.), had certainly not disappeared, nor faded as a "horizon of expectation." Schivelbusch engages Freud's notion, developed in *Beyond the Pleasure Principle*, of the "stimulus shield" to describe the process of internalizing shock to form a protective shield, as it were, against further shocks (153). "Trauma" in Freud's book was the result of a particularly violent shock penetrating the protective shield of modern man's shock-habituated consciousness. Freud developed this psychic model in the context of WWI and the "war neuroses" that struck those who suffered the events of the war as a brutally violent mental, as well as physical, trauma. Schivelbusch sees "shock" as a technological and social phenomenon characteristic of modernity, of modern society since the dawn of full-scale industrialization (the railway era). Drinka is dramatic in his statement of the connection: "[T]he progressive symbols of society, such as the railways, seemed to be responsible for the breakdown of the human nervous system . . . Indeed the railway spine and brain stands [sic] forth as the classical Victorian neurosis, that is, a psychocultural illness in which the human psyche collided with the changing 19th-century environment and gave birth to an epidemic-like neurotic illness whose form and severity are rooted in the Victorian era" (122).

As part of the "changing 19th-century environment," cinema certainly had its role to play in altering the ways in which people negotiated their world. In the paradigm of "panoramic perception," and the railroad perceptual model, film might seem to be already part of the "stimulus shield," just another shock of modern life that could easily be referred to past experience. And certainly the emergence of projected moving images had its path prepared by the multitude of less dynamic screen practices assisting the birth of the new medium. The railroad accident even appears as a subject in early film. In *The Railroad Smash-up*, Edison brought together two locomotives and staged his own catastrophe. The footage was released both autonomously as *Railroad Smash-up* and as the final scene in the 1904 *Rounding Up of the*

The General (Buster Keaton and Clyde Bruckman, 1927)

Yeggmen (Edison/Porter), which follows a bank robbery from its conception at a tramp campfire, to its calamitous conclusion, the head-on crash of the locomotive the robbers had stolen for their getaway.

The immediate reference for this footage is not the train robberies so widely reported in the 1890s, and represented in stage plays, films, and popular fiction (dime novels). Rather, it is the numerous train wrecks staged at county fairs in the U.S. from 1896 through the 1920s. The first such head-on crash occurred in 1896 at Crush City, Texas, the brainchild of W. G. Crush, General Passenger Agent for the Missouri-Kansas-Texas Railroad. 30,000 people paid to see the crash, which caused the deaths of two spectators, including a little girl whose skull was attacked by a flying piece of chain. The negative press on this incident pretty much killed railroad company sponsorship of such events. But a man named "Head-On" Joe Connolly made a fortune staging these disasters as late as 1929, and charging from $.50 to $1.50 to thousands of spectators (as many as 150,000 at once).[13]

This "imagination of disaster," which clearly seems rooted in the fantasy of seeing technology go out of control (a sort of visual Luddism), had become associated with railroad travel early on.[14] As a spectacularization of technological destruction based on an equation of pleasure with terror, the "imagination of disaster" says volumes about the kinds of violent spectacle demanded by a modern public, and the transformation of "shock" into eagerly expected, digestible spectacle. Yet the rhetoric of reception of the earliest films indicates that many were not immune to the "shock of the new," to use Robert Hughes's apt phrase. Perhaps the oldest cliché of film history is the reputed reaction of the first audiences to the Lumières' *L'Arrivée d'un train* in the first public projection of films. Spectators were said to have jumped from their seats in terror at the sight of the train coming toward the camera and running beyond its purview (in 3/4 view), logically "into" the space of the spectator.[15] Descriptions of such a response, in France and elsewhere, survive in film history as rhetorical indices of film's initial novelty, and the naivete of the spectator before a two-dimensional, dynamic representation.[16]

Essentially, the idea that the train-image inspires a threatened response, and *as* a film image, returns us to the whole history of train travel as a shock paradigm for cinematic spectatorship. In one genre of early film, "shock" was the very basis of its appeal. Concerned to establish the non-narrative purpose and effects of early film camera movement, Tom Gunning focuses on several examples of films in which movement is premised on "the thrill of motion," and the "transformation of space."[17] Gunning cites an early review in the *New York Mail and Express* of a Biograph film that mounts a camera on a locomotive (one of many such films) and moves through the Haver-straw Tunnel: " 'The way in which the unseen energy swallows up space and flings itself into the distance is as mysterious and impressive almost as an allegory. . . . One holds his breathe [sic] instinctively as he is swept along in the rush of the phantom cars. His attention is held almost with the vise of fate' " (363).

In this and other examples, Gunning refers to the "enjoyable anxiety the audience felt before the illusion of motion" (363). But to refer to Freud's distinction between fright and anxiety, the spectator presum-ably banked on being frightened as well—the surprise of "unseen energy" is an indication of this. If shock was by this time a programmed unit of mass consumption, and a principle of modern perception, it could clearly turn back in on itself and frighten—or thrill—with the force of trauma. (The flicker film is a perennial tribute to this power.) Walter Benjamin recognizes this substratum of shock in his oft-quoted insight into Dada aesthetics, in which he compares the Dadaist work of art to ballistics, the effect of which—assault on the spectator—could be compared with film.[18] In the footnote to these remarks, Benjamin advances a sort of stimulus shield theory of film (predating by three years his more elaborate development of this in "On Some Motifs in Baudelaire"): "The film is the art form that is in keeping with the increased threat to his life which modern man has to face. Man's need to expose himself to shock effects is his adjustment to the dangers threatening him. The film corresponds to profound changes in the apperceptive apparatus—changes that are experienced on an individual scale by the man in the street in big-city traffic, on a historical scale by every present-day citizen" (250).

These changes were in large part brought about and imposed by the railroad. But Benjamin's remarks have a more particular thrust: big-city traffic, and modern man as urban man. Certainly a chief weapon in the bombardment of stimuli was urban traffic, notably the tram, trolley and subway trains. As Drinka points out, medical thought, especially as represented by Dr. George Miller Beard, the great Amer-ican theorist of neurasthenia, blamed modern life, progress for neu-rasthenia—the American "overwork" (stress) disease par excellence.[19] In an 1895 article, a Sir Clifford Allbutt, Professor of Medicine at Cambridge University referred nervous disability and hysteria to "the frightfulness, the melancholy, the unrest due to living at high pressure, the world of the railway, the pelting of telegrams, the strife of busi-ness. . . ." Living by the clock in a dense urban world electrified by a skein of traffic, the vulnerable urbanite succumbed to nervous disorders that, in Simmel's view at least, fueled a "higher awareness" and in-telligence in the individual.[20]

Early film registers the urban assault on the individual in its fascination with the rube in the city. In *Rube and Fender* (Edison/Porter, 1903), for example, city-conscious spectators are asked to laugh at the unwary hick who ambles down a street only to be scooped up by the fender of a trolley approaching from behind. But early film's most famous rube is Uncle Josh, who in Edison/Porter's *Uncle Josh at the Moving Picture Show* parodies the Lumière spectator responding to the train. Uncle Josh, a popular vaudeville and recording star at the turn of the century, plays himself—or rather his rube persona—in the 1902 Edison film. Seated in a loge just next to a film screen, Uncle Josh views three films, all by Edison, that elicit exaggerated responses. The first shows a dancer flinging her skirts, which titillates Josh's fancy and inspires him to leap out of the loge to test the reality of the image. The second film is *The Black Diamond Express*, which shows a train rushing at the camera at an angle that cuts much closer than in the Lumière film. Uncle Josh is terrified, and, arms flailing, panics before the image. Is this the "primitive" spectator, or the modern, train-trained subject suffering traumatic neurosis à la railway brain? In the confusion of the two in Uncle Josh, we can identify a confusion or conflation of shocks that find a common center in the early film spectator, the hysterical, traumatized subject of both the railroad and film.

Hysteria is, according to popular wisdom, the quintessential Victorian woman's condition. Read psychoanalytically (via Freud), somatic states like paralysis, speech loss, convulsions, and somnambulism were symptoms of repression—the repression of traumatic memories, specifically of a seduction scenario, and the consequent repudiation of sexuality, paradoxically considered to be a bulwark of bourgeois womanhood.[21] Read socially, hysteria was an appropriate reaction against the oppressive roles women were expected to play as wives and mothers.[22] In pre-Freudian medical thought, hysteria was nerve-related, and, as women were assumed to have more high-strung, delicate nervous systems than men, they were thought to be particularly vulnerable.[23] A basic premise of this view was that such diseases must have a pathological basis—even if traumatically induced—while a hereditary or genetic predisposition to such illness was typically assumed.[24] The "nerve literature" referred to above gradually modified its assumptions to admit a psychological dimension, but held fast to the somatic and gendered roots.

One of the major correctives to this view was the phenomenon of male hysteria, which first came to medical attention in the context of the railway accident and the corresponding "traumatic neuroses," railway spine and brain.[25] Many had remarked the appearance of neurosis in male subjects and its apparent relation to railroad accidents, as well as "shocking" accidents of a more generic industrial nature.[26] But it was Charcot who seized upon the phenomenon as a manifestation of hysteria specifically. His primary examples in *Leçons sur l'hystérie* (1888–89) are derived from cases of railroad-related trauma, including railroad accident victims.[27]

Oppenheim objected to Charcot's assimilation of "railway brain" to the hysteria model. He preferred to call it "traumatic neurosis," insisting that railway trauma gave rise to a nerve condition, with "electricity coursing through the nerves as the causative agent."[28] His railway trauma cases often showed signs of hysteria, but as often exhibited simple anxiety or nervous exhaustion. But Charcot insisted with equal conviction that hysteria was the appropriate condition— both psychically and physically. He saw all the symptoms as hysterical ones, anxiety included. "His essential proof was hypnosis," notes Michèle Ouerd in the introduction to the 1984 reprint of Charcot's *Leçons*: "since traumatic paralysis suggested all the analogies with the experimental paralysis he induced by hypnotic suggestion, the traumatic paralysis was therefore of a hysterical nature" (20). Clearly there was a problem of definition or, in semiotic terms, a crisis in signification: how many signifieds could be attached to a signifier, a symptom?

The rhetorical difficulties reemerge in Charcot's attempts to make a case for a properly male hysteria. Charcot was struck by a number of things in his studies of *male* hysterics: (1) the similarity of the symptoms to those of female hysterics—here he took pains to stretch the, his own, standard model of female hysteria to encompass male traits less typical of women patients (e.g., sustained symptoms), meaning, as Ouerd points out, he had to obliterate sexual difference: if male hysteria was to be hysteria at all, it had to resemble or *be* female hysteria, already a redundancy in the medical imagination of the period; and (2) the astonishing appearance of hysterical symptoms in very virile working-class men—the assumption having been that one might expect to find hysteria among the "effeminate" men of the idle class, the "superior," hence more neurotically disposed beings of the more delicately constituted upper classes, but among strong, vigorous proletarians, never (37–39). The way around this latter paradox was a reference to heredity—a hysterical aunt or epileptic grandfather could always be wheeled out to establish a genetic predisposition to neurosis—and an insistence on some real trauma, like the railroad accident. Still, Charcot was perplexed:

> . . . [M]ale hysteria is very common among the lower classes of society; it even seems to be more typical there than female hysteria. We're speaking

here of *la grande hystérie*, of massive hysteria as M. Marie calls it, for with mild hysteria, it's rather the reverse that one remarks. (280)

This he connected also with the appearance of male hysteria among vagabonds, tramps, society's peripatetic disenfranchised, what Ouerd refers to as "les névropathes voyageurs," those who live in their own bodies and lives the metaphor of a characteristic trait of hysteria, mobility.[29] Ouerd takes Charcot's insight into the class (or, as the case may be, non-class) position of these patients further, noting that this position reveals a pattern. If mobility of mind is one of the chief characteristics of female hysteria (the rapid ease with which the hysteric passes from tears to laughter, for example), mobility of social place is the male hysterical equivalent. Ouerd draws a parallel with the fin-de-siècle view that the working class is, in the great social body of the Republic, the migratory uterus of traditional hysteria: ". . . [I]t moves, often convulsively as in the Commune—and it is thus necessary to suppress it, to channel it into its faubourgs, care for it if possible by all the means available in hygienic, prophylactic and mental medi-cine. . . ."[30]

In a kind of mirror image of otherness, one can see that cultural displacement as massive as nineteenth-century mechanization and ur-banization—railway-assisted—made of its traumatized victims some-thing like female hysterics. In other words, it emasculated men, even if only, for some, those of a certain class. Women, proletarian men, and marginals thus bore the brunt of the shocks of modernity.

The "emasculated" male, the male hysteric, might then be seen as the boomerang of male, technological culture against itself, a vision of the railroad neurotic as a man reduced to a female, or non-male state, like the proverbial woman tied to the tracks and assaulted or traumatized by the train. The paradox: investment, or, overinvestment in the male "culture of time and space" was emasculating.

After making his own study of male hysteria in 1886, and more detailed analyses of female hysterics with Breuer in 1895, Freud would be led to posit trauma in psychic, not pathological terms. Eventually he came to see the "founding trauma" of hysteria as a fantasy of seduction, superseding his earlier view, already an advance over Char-cot, that an actual seduction early in childhood was the repressed memory that spoke, via displacement, across the body of the hysteric.[31] For the purpose of analogy, I wish to refer to Drinka's remarks on the proximity to a train as a basis for anxiety. In other words, if the mere threat of collision was enough to induce "traumatic neurosis" or hysteria in men and women, perhaps we should see "railway brain" as based on a technological seduction fantasy—imagining oneself aggressed, raped, seduced and destroyed by the train, hysteria as a fantasy of the corps morcélé, the regression to infantile scenarios of part objects and fragmented, indeed mutilated body parts, mechanically constituted as such.

Read in this context, Uncle Josh is not only hysterically funny, he's hysterical, period. His hysteria—the exaggerated fright, the bodily reaction to the train film (one easily passes from hysteria to paranoia here)—is not only a train phobia, it's a cinematic hysteria as well. As a proxy for the "naive" spectator, his reactions are to be read in relation to shock—the shock not only of the train image (the imagination of disaster, the railway brain cum railway eyes), but of the filmic image: the panic of projection. But does this then make our Uncle Josh an Auntie Josh?

In the guise of answering this question, I wish to offer an even more literal example of the kind of subject of early film I am suggesting. *The Photographer's Mishap*, a 1901 Biograph film, sets in motion the very dynamic configuration of male hysteria, train, shock and film I identify as a basis of spectatorship more generally. Read in relation to a later example of the representation of male hysteria in early film, Edison's 1910 *Asleep at the Switch*, I will suggest ways in which narrative cinema absorbs the hysterical premise for its own purposes, managing and controlling shock and its spectator.

In *The Photographer's Mishap*, a still photographer sets up a tripod on a railroad track to shoot an on-coming train. After putting his head under a hood, he is hit by the train and his camera is destroyed. The photographer springs to his feet and moves to a parallel track, only to be menaced by another approaching train, with which he narrowly escapes collision. At the end, two men arrive to escort him off the tracks, as the photographer breaks down, arms flailing, in a hysterical fit. The film is one shot, and uses stop-action photography to substitute a dummy for the actor when the train runs over him.[32]

In one sense, this film is a paradigmatic example of male hysteria induced by railway trauma: a man suffers an unbelievable accident, the result of which is not so much physical as emotional or mental trauma and shock—the joke being that he suffers no bodily harm as a result of being run down. His convulsions are echt hysterical. In psychoanalytic terms, the repetition of the train threat (the double running-over scenario) is not so much an exercise in retroactive defense and the production of protective anxiety; rather, it is the stimulus to an attack of fright, a pre-stimulus shield assault on the psyche. The hysterical symptoms point to a feminization—as emasculation—of the photographer as the victim of a metaphorical rape: run down by the train like the woman tied to the tracks (and knocked down from an erect to a prostrate position), the photographer suffers a technological seduction fantasy every bit as terrifying as the fantasies of Freud's hysterics. In a sense, within the masculinist coding of the locomotive, all obstacles run down by trains become women—or rather non-men. For what male hysteria shows us is not so much the coding of men as women, as the uncoding of men as men. Similarly, the photographer in our film exhibits many of the characteristics of the quintessential fetishist: run down once and more or less castrated, he still doesn't quite believe, and thus sets himself up for another assault. The fit at the end is a display of excess, of something that cannot be contained, as opposed to a limp, feminine subject. This photographer is in crisis.

That the butt of the visual joke is a photographer is suggestive. The other metaphor through which to read the "joke-work" of this film is that of the still vs. the moving image, photography vs. cinema. Like many an early film concerned to demonstrate within the film the superior powers of the moving image, *The Photographer's Mishap* offers graphic testimony to the ability of film to register movement, locomotion, speed (the train). The still image folds under and into the dynamism of film—both the film in question, and the train as a displaced image of cinema—and is repressed, traumatized as a result. In a sense, we have here an allegory of early film history as it emerges from photography.

The Photographer's Mishap also offers a view of spectatorship in its anticipation of *Uncle Josh at the Moving Picture Show*. The train hitting the photographer while behind his camera is an assault on vision, on a vision accustomed to static images and objects. In this case, the victim of railway brain is also a victim of cinema brain, of the aggression of the apparatus. Later it would be montage that would absorb the aggressive function of a violent interruption of a journey, a narrative—discontinuity as a shock-principle, or rather that which terrorizes vision with the shock of the unexpected. If, as is commonly asserted, the repression of discontinuity is what classical, invisible editing is all about, then perhaps we could also say that continuity editing is about the control of trauma as well.

Asleep at the Switch, for example, takes the trope of train trauma quite seriously by narrativizing it for a moral end: a lesson is to be learned about male hysteria "in the proximity of the railroad," and about the power of the moving image as a vehicle of trauma. In this film, the hystericization of the man is linked to an excessive, "train film" kind of vision. The film derives from the popular song of the same title, which enjoyed currency in the late nineteenth century.[33] In

Charles Shackford's 1897 composition, a switchman tormented by wondering if his sick child will recover, falls dead at the switch. His daughter Nell, who has come to tell him the ill son is all right, throws the switch barely in time. It turns out the railroad company president and his family were aboard the train, and Nell is handsomely rewarded for her efforts.

Though structurally similar, the film departs from the musical version in certain key aspects. In the film, the switchman falls asleep, and it is his dutiful wife who stages the last-minute rescue by resourcefully flagging the train with the dining room tablecloth. The railroad employee is given a test, which he fails, and which his wife passes. She is made to bear the burden of his failure, and to teach him a lesson in vigilance and fidelity—a function accorded to women more generally in Victorian culture, in which women were assigned the role of moral guardians, keeping watch over male laxity brought on by the stresses of the economic arena. In the film, this takes the form of an opposition between two states: that of sleep, and that of wakefulness. Ever awake, women are to keep men on the track, so to speak, and the system running.

What makes *Asleep at the Switch* interesting for the film analyst is its use of inset superimposed fantasy images designed to underscore the price of "falling down" on the job. The switchman wakes up too late, and, realizing his error, begins to hallucinate the probable outcome of his inaction. Inset in the upper left corner of the frame we see two model trains crash head-on, to the switchman's manifest horror. Later the window is filled with the rear-projected image of his would-be victims, who crowd the frame with arms outstretched. These psychic projections of guilt overpower the switchman, and he faints with remorse. Their primary function is to underline guilt, paranoia, and the moral and psychic consequences of being a negligent (if overworked and exhausted) employee, and to make the woman's sacrifice that much greater—after all, she left her child at home to save the President's Special.

To read the switchman's reactions as hysterical commands no special effort: the somnambulistic character of his hallucination, the fitful bodily response (melodramatic gesture as hysteria), the anxiety—these are familiar symptoms. And the connection with work, "overwork," to be exact, recalls the stress neurasthenia dear to American medical theory, as well as Charcot's emasculated railroad men. The film is saying something about the dangers of not only failing to perform one's job, but gender reversal as a consequence of both too much work and railroad—or cinematic—trauma. For the hallucination paralyzes and traumatizes the switchman, while his wife springs into action. It's as if he had suffered the shock of the imagined accident, or that of a traumatizing movie: a projected image like the matted-in crash.

In theoretical terms, the assaulted spectator is the hysterical spectator. The fantasies of being run over and assaulted, penetrated, produce a certain pleasure of pain—beyond the pleasure principle and in the realm of repetition compulsion—which is as much about will-to-submission, to loss-of-mastery, as it is about will-to-mastery/control. Where this becomes a threat is where the quest for thrill and shock— the roller coaster—exceeds ritualized containers of social legitimacy, to refer to Ouerd's remarks on revolution and hysteria.[34]

The *Photographer's Mishap* and *Uncle Josh* unleash male hysteria and allow it to burst forth uncontained; *Asleep at the Switch* codes it, narrativizes it, and makes the feminization explicit. The earlier films bear witness to a transitional moment in popular representation, when codes are being broken down and reformed around a dynamic, mechanical vision. Just as masculinity founders in the phenomenon of "male hysteria," which also puts into crisis definitions of femininity, so precinematic vision breaks apart in relation to film. But early cinematic perception and its aggressivity, its discontinuous excess, to use Gunning's terms, would be put back on the track, so to speak, and gender given a more strongly narrative coding, in early classical film.[35]

Does it then make sense to speak of a female subject, or a male hysteric? Is early cinematic spectatorship an emasculation, a feminization, or neither? This depends to some extent on how gender-coded society's concepts of submission, vulnerability, inability to contain and control are—and they are, of course. But before we posit some essentially "feminized" spectator—like a "feminized" railroad passenger or accident victim—we might instead consider the early film spectator as "undone," uncoded, a subject whose sexual orientation vis-à-vis spectatorship is broken down, put into crisis—hystericized. Early train films are as often involved in the undoing of sexual difference, of a set of anchors for sexual identity that floats, comically, in an age of mechanical production.[36] It's all the promise of modernity's destabilizing effects—the destruction of the old, the fixed, the taken-for-granted, the Oedipal—and all the confusion. To some extent, then, the institutionalization of classical cinema is the institutionalization of a female spectator, a properly female audience, and a regulated female point of view. If as *Asleep at the Switch* shows, feminized men, masculinized women, and excess of any sort were to be contained and narrativized, then the sex roles had to be sorted out according to the code of Woman, who began to assert a respectable influence over film from about 1909 on.

NOTES

1. See Dominique Noguez, "Fantaisie ferroviaire," *Traverses*/13 (Dec. 1978): 85–94; Mary Ann Doane, "The Moving Image," *Wide Angle* vol. 7, nos. 1–2 (1985): 42–58; Charles Musser, "The Travel Genre in 1903–1904: Moving Toward Fictional Narrative," *Iris* vol. 2, no. 1 (1984): 47–60.

2. The most comprehensive source on Hale's Tours is Raymond Fielding, "Hale's Tours: Ultrarealism in the Pre-1910 Motion Picture," in *Film Before Griffith,* ed. John Fell (Berkeley, L.A., London: University of California Press, 1983) 116–130.

3. Wolfgang Schivelbusch, *The Railway Journey,* trans. Anselm Hollo (New York: Urizen Press, 1979) 41.

4. Schivelbusch 48 (also cited by Doane 43).

5. See note 1.

6. Terry Ramsaye, *A Million and One Nights* (New York: Simon and Schuster, 1926) 351–352.

7. Hugo Munsterberg, *The Film: A Psychological Study* (New York: Dover Publications, 1970). Reprint of 1916 edition.

8. *The Moving Picture World* vol. 1, no. 16 (June 22, 1907): 249–250.

9. Robert C. Reed, *Train Wrecks* (New York: Bonanza Books, 1968) 17.

10. Schivelbusch 135ff; and George Drinka, *The Birth of Neurosis: Myth, Malady and the Victorians* (New York: Simon and Schuster, 1984) 118ff.

11. Drinka 109.

12. Schivelbusch 153.

13. Reed 59–60; Oliver Jensen, *Railroads in America* (New York: American Heritage Publishing, 1975) 186; B. A. Botkin and Alvin F. Harlow, eds., *A Treasury of Railroad Folklore* (New York: Crown Publishers, 1953) 354–356.

14. This was a horror that was well illustrated, commented upon, joked about, throughout the nineteenth century. Toward the end of the century, representation of sympathy for victims tended to fade beneath a focus on the mutilation of the machine itself, as post cards, photographs, popular illustration and film suggest. Often witnesses to accidents would have their photo made and a post card struck to send to friends or relatives. A 1909 card in the National Museum of American History, one of many

in this genre, shows a man, woman and child by a wrecked train car, as if they were posing for a studio family portrait. The card reads, "This is the car we were in when we went over. — Yours, Mr. and Mrs. J. B. Stout." Such a document of survival, and in a sense, triumph over the machine, is also clearly an orchestrated spectacle of aftermath. The Warshaw Collection and the Photo Archive of the Transportation Division of the National Museum of American History in Washington contain numerous post cards, photographs, stereographs and illustrated magazine reprints of railroad accidents from the mid-nineteenth century on. See also Reed 25ff; Schivelbusch 131–160; Anthony J. Lambert, *Nineteenth-Century Railway History Through the Illustrated London News* (London and North Pomfret, Vt.: Newton Abbot, 1984) 88ff; William C. Darrah, *The World of Stereographs* (Gettysburg, Pa.: W. C. Darrah, 1977) 185ff; and Honoré Daumier, *Les Transports en commun*, préface de Max Gallo (Paris: Editions Vilo, 1976).

15. A report on "Le Cinématographe" in the May 30, 1896 issue of the popular Paris illustrated magazine *L'Illustration* provides a typical example: "Let us repeat what has been remarked over and over about the naturalness and life-likeness of the scenes Lumière presents to us . . . The locomotive appears small at first, then immense, as if it were going to crush the audience. One has the impression of depth and relief, even though it is a single image that unfolds before our eyes" (446–447).

16. See, for example, Lewis Jacobs, *The Rise of the American Film* (New York: Teachers College, Columbia University Press, 1978) 6; and Benjamin Hampton, *A History of the Movies* (London: Noel Douglas, 1932) 13–14.

17. Tom Gunning, "An Unseen Energy Swallows Space: The Space in Early Film and Its Relation to American Avant-Garde Film," in *Film Before Griffith,* ed. John Fell (Berkeley, L.A., London: University of California Press, 1983): 362–365.

18. Walter Benjamin, "The Work of Art in the Age of Mechanical Reproduction," *Illuminations,* trans. Harry Zohn (New York: Schocken Books, 1976) 238.

19. Drinka 120ff.

20. Drinka 121. See also Schivelbusch 157; Stephen Kern, *The Culture of Time and Space* (Cambridge, Mass.: Harvard University Press, 1983) 125, on the turn-of-the-century disease known as "New Yorkitis"; and an article in the May 30, 1896 issue of *L'Illustration* on American tram conductors, who, it seems, "are exposed to a special nervous malady that appears to be caused by the excessive mental tension demanded by traffic conditions in the busy streets of the nation's big cities" (454).

21. Sigmund Freud, *The Pelican Freud Library* vol. 8, Case Histories I: "Dora" and "Little Hans" (Harmondsworth: Penguin, 1977).

22. See Toril Moi, "Representation of Patriarchy: Sexuality and Epistemology in Freud's Dora," *In Dora's Case*, eds. Charles Bernheimer and Claire Kahane (New York: Columbia University Press, 1985) 181–199.

23. Charcot, *Leçons sur l'hystérie virile,* intro. Michèle Ouerd (Paris: Le Sycamore, 1984) "Leçon 1."

24. Charcot, "Leçon 1."

25. Charcot, "Leçon 1: Apropos de six cas d'hystérie chez l'homme;" and Drinka 109–113.

26. Charcot, "Leçon 1;" and Drinka 109–113.

27. Charcot, "Leçon 1."

28. Drinka 118.

29. Charcot 214; Ouerd 26.

30. Ouerd 27. See also Neil Hertz's excellent "Medusa's Head: Male Hysteria Under Political Pressure," *Representations* no. 4 (Fall 1983): 27–54.

31. Sigmund Freud and Josef Breuer, *The Pelican Freud Library* vol. 3: "Studies on Hysteria" (Harmondsworth: Penguin, 1974); and Freud, "Dora."

32. The May 18, 1907 issue of *The Moving Picture World* relates an interesting story about the shooting of *The Photographer's Mishap* that has to do with the stop-motion technique. It seems that, although it had been explained to the train engineer that he was to run over the dummy, he refused to believe it wasn't a real man, and screeched to a halt too soon— still hitting the dummy, which upset the passengers (166).

33. See Norm Cohen, *Long Steel Rail: The Railroad in American Folksong* (Urbana/Chicago/London: University of Illinois Press, 1981) 345.

34. Cf. Hertz; and Kathy Lee Peiss, *Cheap Amusements: Working Women and Leisure in Turn-of-the-century New York* (Philadelphia: Temple University Press, 1986).

35. See Tom Gunning, "Non-continuity, Continuity, Discontinuity: A Theory of Genres in Early Film," *Iris* vol. 2, no. 1 (1984): 101–112; "The Cinema of Attraction," *Wide Angle* vol. 8, nos. 3–4 (1986): 63–70; and Miriam Hansen *Babel and Babylon: Spectatorship in American Silent Film* (forthcoming).

36. This is a notion explored at length in my dissertation, entitled "The Railroad and the Cinema, 1895–1929: Technologies, Institutions and Aesthetics," UCLA.

Male Narcissism and National Culture: Subjectivity in Chen Kaige's *King of the Children*
Rey Chow

I: The Detour

> . . . how many [teachers] (the majority) do not
> even begin to suspect the "work" the system
> (which is bigger than they are and crushes them)
> forces them to do, or worse, put all their heart
> and ingenuity into performing it with the most
> advanced awareness . . . So little do they suspect
> it that their own devotion contributes to the
> maintenance and nourishment of this ideological
> representation of the School . . .
> Louis Althusser[1]

> . . . the history of the "educated" ought to be
> materialistically presented as a function of and
> in close relation to a "history of uneducation."
> Walter Benjamin[2]

Like living things, words and phrases undergo fates inconceivable at
their moments of birth. In contemporary Chinese writings, especially
of the kind that we encounter in the media — newspaper articles, reviews
in non-academic journals, and popular political discourses — from time
to time we run across this phrase, which is used to suggest the deter-
minacy of hope: *lu shi ren zou chu lai de* (roads are made by men).
Because of the phrase's popularized nature, I have no need to cite
specific examples. Those of you who read regularly in Chinese will
recognize what I am saying immediately. The by now idiomatic nature
of this phrase shows us how an expression of hope can be standardized
through mass usage.

The phrase originated in a passage from the ending of Lu Xun's

---

This essay is a modified version of the paper I delivered at the Conference on
"Contemporary Chinese Fiction and Its Literary Antecedents," Harvard University,
May 1990. The original paper will be published in the conference volume, *From
May Fourth to June Fourth: Fiction and Film in Twentieth-Century China*, eds.
Ellen Widmer and David Wang, forthcoming.

"Guxiang" ("My Old Home," 1921). Among other things, this is a story that tells of the changed relationship between the narrator and his childhood friend, Runtu, a member of the servant class. The adult reunion of the two men who were once equals in the world of children's play is shaped by a class-consciousness that becomes painful for the narrator. Although, on first seeing Runtu again, the narrator keeps to the old familial appellation *Runtu ge* (older brother Runtu), Runtu addresses him from the place of a servant: *laoye* (old master). As in all of Lu Xun's fiction, the gap between the intellectual narrator, who belongs to the educated class, and the oppressed "others," who make up the contents of his storytelling, intensifies as the narrative progresses. In "My Old Home," this gap is "filled" at the end by a reflection on hope. Thinking of hope, the narrator becomes aware of its idolatrous nature. Doesn't his reliance on "hope" make him more similar to Runtu than he first imagined? The difference, he writes, is perhaps simply that between an accessible and an intangible idol:

> The access of hope made me suddenly afraid. When Runtu had asked for the incense-burner and candlesticks I had laughed up my sleeve at him, to think that he was still worshipping idols and would never put them out of his mind. Yet what I now called hope was no more than an idol I had created myself. The only difference was that what he desired was close at hand, while what I desired was less easily realized.[3]

After asserting the equality between himself and a member of the lower class when he is on the point of leaving the place in which Runtu is probably stuck for life, the narrator concludes his tale with the passage on hope which subsequently gave rise to the idiomatic phrase "roads are made by men." Lu Xun's text goes as follows:

> I thought: hope cannot be said to exist, nor can it be said not to exist. It is just like roads across the earth. For actually the earth had no roads to begin with, but when many men pass one way, a road is made.[4]

Why is Lu Xun's passage instructive for a discussion of the connections between early twentieth-century Chinese literature and contemporary Chinese culture? Thematically, Lu Xun's works stage the problems which continue to haunt Chinese intellectuals: the impossibility of effective social change, the unbridgeable gap between the educated class and the "people," and the fantastical nature of any form of "hope." What comes across in Lu Xun's passage is the awareness that hope is at best a form of wager. Hope is, by nature, indeterminate, but people can, if there are large numbers of them, consciously steer it in one direction. Lu Xun's text itself, however, does not do that. Instead, it remains, in a way that is ironic with respect to the positive interpretation that has been imposed upon it since, in a state that can be referred to in Chinese as *wuke naihe, wuke wubuke, wuning liangke*. The text's originary indeterminacy, in other words, is what *enables* its subsequent politicized appropriation. The interpretative production of the affirmative phrase "roads are made by men" is thus itself a historical materialization of the arbitrary process of road-making that Lu Xun describes: as more people pass one way, a road is made.

A return to the relationship between the elusiveness of an originary textual moment and its eventual honed version indicates a way of understanding the notion of the "people" and "mass" in political processes. One could say that the power of the people or mass lies in the form of an indeterminacy. Precisely because they are undecided, they can go one way or another. For something—history—to happen, it would take a forcing—an accident perhaps—in a definite direction. The new direction as such, however, always retains its originally arbitrary character.

Lu Xun's tactical understanding of the arbitrary nature of politics, though not directly stated, is implied in the way "hope" always appears as a figure of enigma in his fictional texts.[5] Because it is always *to be* decided—or arbitrated—hope cannot be known for certain in the present. We can now understand why there are so often apparently inexplicable shifts in narrative moods in his stories. Marston Anderson comments that such narrative shifts have led Lu Xun's critics to classify his work in two apparently contradictory fashions, as satirically realist, or as reminiscent and lyrical.[6] This contradiction is a politically truthful one. In the subsequent reappraisals and criticisms of the writings from the 1920s and 1930s that the Chinese communists launched, such political truthfulness was threatening because it did not cooperate or conform with the absolute clarity of direction laid down by the party. One could say that the orthodox communist criticism of textual elusiveness such as Lu Xun's implies this question: if there is hope, why aren't you writers more assertive? A more programmatic, indeed official, representation of the people and of hope therefore increasingly came to replace the kind of uncompromised incisiveness in Lu Xun's perception. However, the issues imbedded in the "making of roads" do not disappear. Although the short-story form became impermissible with the new social orthodoxy in the decades after Lu Xun's death, the problems it poses, precisely because they pertain to fundamental questions of morality, "raise their head every time there is a political thaw."[7]

As a figure of wager, hope can, I think, be redefined through "subjectivity." "Subjectivity" is one of those "politically incorrect" words that conjure up notions of "bourgeois idealism" for orthodox Marxist critics. Terry Eagleton, for instance, disapproves of it from the viewpoint of a Western European, supposedly post-Althusserian Marxist literary criticism, as a category tainted with "intransigent individualism": "it remains the case that the subject of semiotic/psychoanalytic theory is essentially the *nuclear* subject."[8] While I disagree with Eagleton, I find his statement useful in helping to clarify the Chinese situation. In Chinese communist scholarship, it is common to hear the same kind of ideological objection to the "subjective," which is mapped onto such expressions as *zhuguan, weixin zhuyi*, and so on. In a period in which cognition is intertwined with issues of politics, and in which creative energies have to be channelled toward fighting for the national cause, the literary forms that can be viewed as paradigms of explorations of subjectivity, such as biographies, autobiographies, diaries, first-person narratives, and narratives that deal explicitly with issues of sexuality, tend to live brief lives and to remain subordinated to the more conventionally "public" concerns of history and realism.

If, on the other hand, we dislodge subjectivity from the narrow "nuclear" mode in which Eagleton puts it, and instead understand it in terms of the material relationships among human beings as participants in a society—relationships that are in turn mediated by the collective cultural activities of speaking, reading, and writing—then it is an issue that is as forcefully present in modern Chinese literature and culture as it is in the West, even if it is not named as such.

I suggest that the predominant subjectivity that surfaces in the May Fourth period (mid 1910s to around 1930) is not so much a dense psychic "self," impenetrable and solipsistic, as it is a relationship between the writer, his/her object of narration, and the reader. In political terms, this is the relationship between Chinese intellectuals, the Chinese national culture, and "the people." In the writing of fiction, this relationship always presents itself as a question rather than a solution: how do we write (construct images of our culture) in order to relate to "the people"—*especially those who are socially inferior and powerless, since they are the ones who constitute the "mass" of the nation?* As such, subjectivity, even when it appears in the most "subjective" or "privatized" forms (as for instance in Yü Dafu's writings), is incomprehensible apart from its fundamental implication in the question of national culture. At the same time, it is also this tenacious relation with national culture which makes the differences between intellectuals and the masses (differences generated by the activity of literary production) a continual source of tension between Chinese intellectuals and the party state, as both hold claims to the indeterminate "mass," for whom they both want to speak.[9]

If we rethink the history of modern Chinese literature along these lines, that is, if we regard "history" as a matter of the contending claims made by the state and Chinese intellectuals on "the Chinese people"—a figure as enigmatic as hope itself—then it becomes necessary to ask how "the Chinese people" are represented. Through what kinds of aesthetic displacements and idealizations are they "constituted"?

Typically, "the Chinese people" are displaced onto figures of the powerless. Hence, I think, the large numbers of social inferiors who appear in the texts of modern Chinese literature. Literature is no longer, in the modern world, about the lives of emperors; rather, it is about the oppressed classes—the wretched of the earth. Other than the positivistic view that these are "realistic portrayals" of modern history, what else can we say about such frequent—indeed epochal—representations of the unprivileged? In other words, why does the conception and construction of a modern national culture—if writing in the post-imperialistic Third World is in part about that—take the form of an *aesthetic* preoccupation with the figures of the powerless? What does it say in terms of the things that we have been talking about—hope, the making of roads, and subjectivity?

Of all the figures of the powerless, the child is at center stage. One would need to include here not only stories about children, whether from the lower or upper classes, but also the autobiographical narratives in which Chinese writers look back to their childhood as a source for their current literary production. (The list of writers here is long: Lu Xun, Ba Jin, Bing Xin, Ding Ling, Ye Shengtao, Guo Moruo, Xiao Hong, Shen Congwen, Ling Shuhua, Luo Shu, Zhu Ziqing, Xü Dishan, and many others.) It is as if the adult thinking about China and the Chinese people always takes the route of memory in which the writing self connects with the culture at large through a specific form of "othering"—the presumably not-yet-acculturated figure of the child. In this light, the continuity among Chinese intellectuals from the May Fourth to the present period could be traced in another one of Lu Xun's enigmatic narrative endings, that of "Kuangren riji" ("The Diary of a Madman," 1918): "Jiujiu haizi . . ." ("Save the children . . ."). At Yanan in 1942, Mao Zedong would end a speech on art and literature with a couplet about children from Lu Xun, to which he supplies his own politicized interpretation:

This couplet from a poem by Lu Hsun should be our motto:
    Fierce-browed, I coolly defy a thousand pointing fingers,
    Head-bowed, like a willing ox I serve the children.
The "thousand pointing fingers" are our enemies, and we will never yield to them, no matter how ferocious. The "children" here symbolize the proletariat and the masses. All Communists, all revolutionaries, all revo-

lutionary literary and art workers should learn from the example of Lu Xun and be "oxen" for the proletariat and the masses, bending their backs to the task until their dying day.[10]

Mao's interpretation empowers the figure of the powerless child by renaming it as the proletariat and the masses. Ultimately, it was by giving this enigmatic figure, "the Chinese people," a specific politicized shape that the party state succeeded in mobilizing popular sympathies. The "powerless" is thus turned around representationally, and becomes the means to construct national culture on a "concrete" basis. The utilitarian nature of this process of empowerment is familiar to all of us. The "masses," because they are "powerless," should, ideally speaking, make use of intellectuals, who are now at their *service*.

But service here clusters around another figure—the ox/cow. Lu Xun uses this figure in a such a way as to recall not only China's agrarian origins, but also the familiar and familial process, traceable to images in classical art and poetry, of the affectionate playing between adults and children in which adults act as make-believe cows on which children ride. The image of "intellectuals becoming oxen for the masses" is thus intertwined with the realm of meanings associated with children, parents, kinship, and genealogy—a realm of meanings which Mao removed—or at least shifted away—from Lu Xun's couplet in order to consolidate his own analysis of Chinese society and its need for revolution in terms of "class" and "class struggle."[11] In ways that exceed Mao's restrictive political purpose, however, Lu Xun's image stages the philosophical struggles between the state and intellectuals over the "Chinese people" in terms of *reproduction* that continue to this day.

The components of this image—intellectuals, oxen, the masses—are what make up Chen Kaige's *Haizi wang* (*King of the Children*) (Xian Film Studio, 1987), a film based on the novel of the same title by A Cheng (1984).[12] The story of *King of the Children* takes place in the post-Cultural Revolution period in a rural area. Lao Gan, the narrator and protagonist, is posted to a school after spending years in a production unit. A Cheng's story focuses on Lao Gan's relationship with his young students and the changes he introduces into their methods of learning. Before he came, the students had "learned" by copying texts which their former teachers had copied onto the blackboard. Seeing how futile this is, Lao Gan teaches them how to read, character by character, and then proceeds to teach them composition. One student, Wang Fu, gradually emerges as the most outstanding one through his hard work. His special relationship with Lao Gan prompts the latter, when dismissed from the school at the end, to leave behind for

Wang Fu the only available Chinese dictionary, which the students revere as "the teacher of the teacher."

Both the novel and the film draw attention to children as that class of social inferiors who continue to fascinate modern Chinese intellectuals. What distinguishes the children in *King of the Children* is that they pose a specific question about national culture: the status of education. They are thus not simply members—to use the psychoanalytic categories from Lacan—of a pre-symbolic infantile state, but already participants in a major social institution, what for Althusser is the major "ideological state apparatus" of the school.[13] At the same time, the children are powerless, their future as yet undecided. This future raises the question of hope, and hope seems dismal in the aftermath of the Cultural Revolution. Although in his novel A Cheng never directly describes the Cultural Revolution as such, we feel its destructive effects unmistakably, through the impoverished state in which the Chinese education system now finds itself. What kind of a road can be made for these children? This is, I think, the primary issue in A Cheng's text; its force is a pedagogical one. As a socially powerless figure, the school-child becomes the site for cultural (re)production and its various levels of arbitration. In A Cheng, Lao Gan acts as the agent who steers these school-children away from the reproduction of the destructive culture. By training them to read and write from scratch, we are given to think, it might be possible to regenerate national culture in a positive manner. Instead of being associated with a particular political system, communism, this national culture would now be rooted in the humanistic principles of learning.[14]

For me, what makes Chen Kaige's film interesting to watch is not its faithfulness to A Cheng's novel, but the way in which it departs from the novel through its translation into the film medium. This is not a translation in the sense of producing a "filmic version" of the same story. Rather, in the translation that is *filming*, we witness a significant shift from A Cheng's *script*. What this means is that, first, the translation from writing into film removes the story from the terrain of words into a realm in which verbal language is merely one among many levels of expression. Second, and more important, the shift from script to film is also a shift *away from* the primacy of writing. Because writing occupies the central position among representational forms in the Chinese culture (in which to draw or paint, for instance, is referred to as *xiehua*, literally "to write a picture"), and also because the content of the story itself concerns the acquisition of the written word, the translation into film, in which non-verbal cultural signifiers such as visual images and sounds play a primary role, poses all the questions about literature and national culture we have raised so far—questions which are condensed in A Cheng's story into the relationship between teacher and children in the school—in entirely different ways.

In an account of the relationship between literature and film, the Russian formalist critic Boris Eikhenbaum writes:

> The cinema audience is placed in completely new conditions of perception, which are to an extent opposite to those of the reading process. Whereas the reader moved from the printed word to visualisation of the subject, the viewer goes in the opposite direction: he moves from the subject, from comparison of the moving frames to their comprehension, to naming them; in short, to the construction of internal speech. The success of film is partially connected to this new and heretofore undeveloped kind of intellectual exercise.[15]

What Eikhenbaum calls "internal speech" is interchangeable with what I have been referring to as subjectivity, namely, the relationship between the individual as participant in social activity (for instance, film-watching) and that which transcends the boundaries of his individualized physical apparatus—his own bodily vision/look. This is a relationship which is always *to be* articulated. The difference between responding to the printed word and responding to film that Eikhenbaum underscores is particularly relevant here because we are dealing with the translation of a novel into a filmic text. Where words have provided the clues to a possible relationship between Lao Gan and the world at large (he is, after all, the narrating subject in A Cheng's story), how are we to understand that relationship in the film? What is the subjectivity or internal speech that reveals itself in the *King of the Children* by Chen?

One specific *filmic* feature that departs from the novel is the way Chen uses Lao Gan's look to reopen the question of pedagogy.[16] Throughout the film, we see shots of Lao Gan staring into the distance, sometimes as if he is surprised, other times as if in a daydream. For instance, after he settles down in his lodgings at the beginning, we have a scene in which the camera, taking the shot from outside his cottage, shows him sitting by a window inside, with his hands hanging down leisurely. As he unconsciously touches himself, crossing his long graceful fingers, his eyes look into the distance. As our look follows his, we ask: what does he see? If the individual look is a response to a collective gaze, to what does his look respond? What is the larger realm which connects with this look? In the language of contemporary film criticism, this is a question about suturing—that process of subjective activation and reactivation through complex transactions between symbolic and imaginary significations, transactions that give rise to an illusory sense of unity with the field of the other and to coherence in narrative meaning. How is Lao Gan's stare sutured? In other words, with what does his look cohere?

The School

By following A Cheng's *script*, Chen shows that Lao Gan's look seeks its connection in the school-children whose education constitutes his "appointment." The protagonist's look here is the specific device through which the issue of pedagogy is addressed *filmically*. "How does one teach in the aftermath of the Cultural Revolution" becomes "how does one look into the eyes of China's future generation?" But because the question is now posed specifically in the form of vision, it leaves "subjectivity" as a matter of construction, offering us that "new and heretofore undeveloped kind of intellectual exercise" that Eikhenbaum mentions.

Lao Gan's discomfort at the question about pedagogy is evident from the time he arrives at the school. First, he discovers to his surprise that he has been assigned to a higher grade than he thought he was qualified to teach. Then, on arriving at the door of the classroom, he drops his books. As if in a confrontation, he greets with great unease the little faces that await him. This mutually responsive relationship, back and forth between teacher and school children, directs the narrative development of the story.

When Lao Gan realizes that all he can do is to copy, he is deeply frustrated. With his back to the children, he copies standardized communist texts onto the blackboard, day in and day out. The children, on their part, copy everything mechanically into their notebooks. The sounds of chalk on the blackboard and pencils on notebooks fill many scenes. As this "collective" activity intensifies, we are forced to ask: what kind of cultural production is taking place here, and with what future for these rural children? This series of copying scenes is followed by one in which Lao Gan goes home one night, holds a candle to his broken mirror, and spits at his own image. I will return to the significance of this violent act of self-degradation later.

Things change when Lao Gan begins to teach the copied texts. One of the students, Wang Fu, boldly reprimanding him for his incompetence, proclaims the principles of correct teaching. At this—what appears in every sense a public humiliation by a student, a member of the lower class in the school system—Lao Gan breaks into a laugh, as if he has finally made a connection with the school children. From then on, he proceeds to teach the students how to read and write, and slowly, each student learns to produce his or her own original thoughts in composition.

Wang Fu's persistence in copying the dictionary and his eventual "success" in producing a piece of coherent writing are the symptoms of the child who has been properly "interpellated" into the system of learning—to use Althusser's term. Wang Fu's perseverance, serious-ness, and ability to work hard are all part of the process by which the school as an apparatus of ideology solicits the voluntary cooperation of its participants.[17] The reproduction of a society, writes Althusser, is not only the reproduction of its skills but also "a reproduction of its submission to the rules of the established order, i.e., a reproduction of submission to the ruling ideology"[18] for those who are exploited.

Precisely because he is sensitive to how ideology works effectively not only through coercion (by the powerful) but more often through consent (from the powerless), Chen's film departs from the more straightforwardly humanistic direction of A Cheng's story. We see this in the way Chen handles the episode of copying. Whereas in A Cheng's novel, Lao Gan leaves the dictionary for Wang Fu as a gift, in the film he departs with these words on the table: "Wang Fu, don't copy anymore, not even the dictionary."

What Chen's film makes clear is that even though A Cheng's text is radical (since it asserts proper learning against the destructiveness of the Cultural Revolution), it leaves unasked the entire question of what it means to base culture on the act of copying. In reading A Cheng's text, one feels that it is not the act of copying that is really the problem; rather it is a matter of finding the right source from which to copy. The protest A Cheng makes, accordingly, is that the Cultural Revolution has destroyed such sources. Against such destruc-tion, A Cheng shows how one should always write *after* (one has done) something (i.e. one should copy from "life"), or else one may, as Wang Fu does, copy from the dictionary. Chen, on the other hand, does not attach to copying the value of a positive meaning as in A Cheng; rather, he sees in it a revelation of the deconstructive meanings of contem-porary Chinese culture. For Chen, the destructiveness of the Cultural Revolution is not an accident but the summation of the Chinese civ-ilization, and the act of copying, to which the students are reduced, signifies the emptiness of culture itself. This is why he says: "Culture is precisely this: it's a matter of copying."[19] Because Chen's under-standing of copying is much more drastic, he also constructs his *King of the Children* in such a way that the success of the child-as-copyist is being scrutinized and challenged through a juxtaposition with other forms of subjectivity. While A Cheng's narrative offers a more or less completed circuit of suturing between Lao Gan and the school children, especially through his special relationship with Wang Fu, this process of suturing is only one of the several crucial elements in the film.

The drastic questioning of the written word's traditional authority (and thus of the primacy of verbal language) is, I would contend, not a questioning of a moralistic kind. As I argue in a discussion of Chen's first film, *Yellow Earth* (1984),[20] the film medium allows Chen to explore the much larger issue of technological reproduction in a modern Third World culture. Although a substantial discussion of this point can only be provided on a different occasion, a brief reference to Martin Heidegger's understanding of technology helps clarify the issues somewhat.[21] In his work, Heidegger dissociates the word "technology" from its more popular associations with instrumentality. Instead, he defines the essence of technology as the bringing-forth of being—a process of revealing truth and a mode of knowing. He locates this essence of technology in the Greek word *technē*, which for him does not mean mere technique or craft, but the "bringing-forth" of that which presences into appearance. For Heidegger, modern machine technology does not depart in essence from the ancient concept of *technē*. Rather, modernity's mechanized, regulating, gigantic, and indeed dangerous apparatuses reveal *technē* as an "enframing" and a "setting-upon" of nature in ways hitherto concealed from human apprehension. Because of this, Heidegger says: "modern technology, which for chronological reckoning is the later, is, from the point of view of the essence holding sway within it, the historically earlier."[22] Having shown this about modernity, Heidegger also asks: is there a time when it is not technology (as we now know it) alone that reveals the meaning of *technē*? He finds his answer in art and especially in poetry.

In many ways, Chen's work (the three films he directed in China prior to 1989) can be seen as an exploration of the question of *technē* in the context of a devastated Third World culture which is at the same time one of the most sophisticated ancient civilizations. The intense challenge posed by Chen's *King of the Children* to the written word is a challenge to the cultured origins of Chinese history. The written script with its stable, permanent cast points to that "enframing" of being that Heidegger suggests as the essence of *technē*. Central to the power—indeed the violence—of writing is its ability to repeat itself. In China, where writing is seldom divorced from history—that is, from the notion of writing as recording and conserving—the written script is *technē* in its most basic form, the form through which the transmission and reproduction of culture is ensured. At the same time, writing is also *modern* technology in the hands of the communist state, which turns it into a pure machine for propaganda and thought-control. These two aspects of writing—first as the cumulative, unbearable burden of the past (history), and then as the technologizing imperative to construct, in the modern world, a brand new national culture (revolution)—are brought together succinctly in the mindless *copying* of the post–Cultural Revolution period.

On the night Lao Gan obtains and reads the dictionary for the first time, the scene takes on a surreal feeling as sounds of human voices reciting ancient texts are slowly echoed and magnified, creating a ghostly atmosphere that suggests the way tradition impinges upon human consciousness as so many indistinguishably repeating voices. The simple acts of reading and writing, performed here in the rural area, far away from the "centers" of urban civilization, nonetheless partake in this unmistakable sense of culture as copying, echoing, repetition. Rather than concealing it, the impoverished material circumstances help to intensify the sheer mechanism of writing as cumulative recording.

In the urban setting, of course, the unstoppable terroristic power of technology is apprehensible in more palpable forms. Chen shows this in his second film, *Da yue bing* (*The Big Parade*, 1985). In this film, the portrayal of one of the most important bases of Chinese national culture—the People's Liberation Army—is done in an admixture of a fascination with discipline (which suppresses all symptoms of the human body such as crying, fainting, vomiting, or even the physical "deformity" of bowed legs) and an ultimate sense of emotional blankness that comes with this technologized discipline. The instrumentalization of human bodies into a "collective" purpose such as the army, to the point at which material impoverishment and deprivation, including deprivation in the form of a restraint of the body's reactions to disciplinary torture, is visible on the screen through the orderliness of soldiers and other production units marching in the "big parade" in front of Tiananmen Square. It is as if the sheer regimentation of human bodies—in uniform, their faces devoid of expression, their movements absolutely identical—provides a kind of pseudo or mechanical "bridging" of the gap between the irretrievable past and the unknowable future. If this "bridging" indicates modern China's "successful" achievement of modernization, it is an achievement that, as we sense through the slow motion and funereal music in the last scenes of *The Big Parade*, requires from the individual a submission to the technologized collective goal—to technology as collective goal—in total obliteration of himself.

The rural setting of *King of the Children* does not permit the film to demonstrate the workings of technology in the graphically striking form that *The Big Parade* does. In the absence of the industrialized, militarized, and urbanized forms of technology, Chen probes the roots of *technē* in a more basic manner, through the fundamental working of verbal language itself. Here, the power of *technē*, as what brings forth the ordering of being, is demonstrated with frugal means, through a practice of traditional learning—storytelling. One day, the friends from Lao Gan's former production unit come for a visit. Out of sheer playfulness, he has them sit down like students in the classroom, whereupon he proceeds to "teach" them. As he *repeats* his words, it quickly becomes clear that this is one of those narratives which uncover the mechanism of narrating from within, so that "form" and "content" are merged and thus revealed as one:

> Once upon a time there was a mountain. In the mountain was a temple. In the temple was a Buddhist monk telling a tale. What is the tale? Once upon a time there was a mountain. In the mountain was a temple. In the temple . . .

His friends join him in what immediately becomes an uproar that reproduces the same story over and over again collectively. As they finally come to a stop, the school children, who have been eavesdropping outside the classroom, pick up where the adults have left off, and run off into the distant hills repeating exactly the same narrative with rhythm. As they disappear on the horizon, the camera returns us to Lao Gan's look. This look is one of surprise, as if he has suddenly "understood" something. What is it that he has understood? What is the content of his sudden awareness? These are questions which the film medium leaves unanswered, and which must be approached through the process of interpretation.

Such a moment of "awareness" is one of the undecidable moments of subjectivity that are crucial for the understanding of modern Chinese culture and literature. Instead of immediately supplying it with a definite meaning, such as "Lao Gan realizes how education is passed on," we should juxtapose it with other components of the film in order to grasp its range of significatory possibilities.

Nature

Side by side with the relationship between teacher and school children is another set of scenes which revolve around a character who does not exist in A Cheng's novel—a cowherd. This is, once again, a child figure, and yet unlike the school children, the cowherd belongs to "nature." Through him Chen's film creates a discourse which counters the institution of education. What is this counter-discourse like? In other words, what is the function of the nature child in this film?

"Nature" supplies an alternative form of suturing for Lao Gan's look. Oftentimes, as he stares, what he "sees" is the expansiveness of the rural landscape. While some might argue that "nature" as such is the un-suturing of the look and therefore, arguably, a non-Western type of cinematic intervention, I am reluctant to divide "West" and "East" in this facile manner by putting "nature" and "East" in the space of an "outside." There are two reasons for not taking this interpretative step. First, I see the elusiveness and fantasy that are part of nature-as-filmic-signifier as a major *political* means of resisting the overwhelmingly articulate, verbal, indeed verbose, machinery of official Chinese communist discourse with its technologies of mass control. By presenting a counter-discourse in the form of a natural muteness, therefore, directors like Chen are not exactly nostalgic about a metaphysical beyond; rather this is a politically engaged way of searching for an alternative cultural semiotics—*a detour.* Second, "nature" functions as the unconscious side of a male circuit of production. As such, it plays an indispensable role in reinforcing certain patterns of censorship, especially the censorship of the physical body and the biological reproduction through woman. This point will become clear in the second part of this essay.

The cowherd first appears in the scenes of Lao Gan's journey to the school. He is dressed in white; a large straw hat covers his face so that we cannot see his features; he is leading a herd of cows on the mountain road. He is mute throughout the film, and his "communication" with Lao Gan takes the opposite form to that of the school children—the non-verbal.[23] Two scenes demonstrate the significatory power of this non-verbalness.

One day, as Lao Gan is teaching, he sees that the cowherd is doing something on the blackboard in the classroom next door. As he goes and looks, he finds the cowherd has splattered dung on the board; meanwhile he has disappeared into the distance. A second scene shows Lao Gan meeting the cowherd face to face in the fields. He asks: "Where are you from, child? Do you go to school? Why not? I know how to read and write. I can teach you." The cowherd remains mute and goes away.

Why does Chen insert the figure of this mute child in this story about teaching? From the beginning, we feel that the cowherd's existence is a mystery, which belongs to the plane of fantasy rather than to the institutional reality to which Lao Gan is officially appointed. And yet this fantasy intrudes into his path of vision in spite—perhaps because—of its mysterious nature. Here, the use of cinematic image and sound together effects a forceful interplay between the pedagogical and the natural frames of reference. The film begins, after all, with *two* series of sounds—first, cowbells, then the sounds of writing with chalk on the blackboard. As Lao Gan travels with his friend Lao Hei to the school, the two men come across things that seem to startle them. Among these things is the cowherd. Typically, we are shown the slightly surprised look of the two male characters, especially Lao Gan; then the camera would "suture" the look by showing a scene from the mountains, a view of rocks falling from a cliff, of trees, etc. What kind of "suturing" is this? This type of scene, in which Lao Gan's human, individualized look is seen to be actively *looking*, only to be "connected" with something "natural"—that is, something mute, stationary, and uneventful—parallels his actual encounters with the cowherd, who becomes *a personified form of the non-verbal presence of a natural world* that exists side by side with (rather than meta-physically beyond) the human institution of learning. Precisely because the cowherd is non-verbal, he belongs more appropriately to the me-dium which does not rely on verbal language alone to generate its significations. The cowherd's *bodily presence* signifies the challenge of non-presence, non-participation—a form of life and a history outside formal education—which runs parallel with but remains indifferent to the history of education.

If the pedagogical subjectivity in this film is the circuit of looks that runs between Lao Gan and the school children (which is the dominant narrative in A Cheng's novel), then this mute presence of the cowherd alters this subjectivity significantly. Side by side with the pedagogical suturing, especially between Lao Gan and Wang Fu, the inheritor of book culture, is now another suture effect, which is non-verbal *on the child's side*. The non-verbal nature of the cowherd's "response" to Lao Gan forces us to think: what is the use of education? How does it reproduce itself, and for whose benefit?

The status of nature in *King of the Children* carries with it the implications of a counter-discourse which is not situated in human agency but in fantasy. On the night Lao Gan browses through the dictionary, as I have mentioned, the film supplies a chorus of muffled voices from the past reciting texts to accompany Lao Gan's reading. At the same time, this "rejoining" with the ancestral voices of education is interrupted by a noise from the outside. It is a cow, standing mys-teriously in the dark and walking away as Lao Gan opens the door and discovers it.

I hope by now I have established the terms of this part of my argument clearly. If we are to think of subjectivity in terms of the suturing of a perceiving individual and an undecidable external reality, then Lao Gan's subjectivity that emerges in the film is a bifurcated one. On the one hand, it retains the "good" Chinese tradition of a compassion for children as the socially powerless. This subjectivity directs its own "completion" in the other through the acquisition of the written word. This particular suturing process stands for the compliance with a *proper* sense of national culture, as that which has to be built from the most basic technology—writing. This subjectivity takes us in the direction of a determinate and determinable form of hope. If the children are the "masses," then education through literacy represents the hope of a definite and definitive road.

On the other hand, Chen explores Lao Gan's subjectivity through another realm in which the teacher's impulse to reach out to the socially powerless child cannot materialize into an act of pedagogy. Instead, it is met with a defiance that one must describe as at once natural, silent, mysterious, and uncooperative. This other story of subjectivity punctuates Chen's film in the form of scenes that are placed halfway between reality and fantasy—the point is that the audience cannot tell the difference and that it does not matter. What matters is that the figure of the cowherd reappears persistently, as if in a dream or a detour that swerves away from the conscious and straightforward relationship between teacher and school children.

Along this detour is a non-existent Chinese character. One day, as Lao Gan is copying texts on the board, he writes down a character which he subsequently erases:

Toward the end of the film, he recalls this episode of mis-writing in his parting words to the students. Cows are stubborn animals, he says, you can scold them and hit them, and they just blink at you. But there are times when cows go wild—that is, when you piss. This is because cows love salt. (In A Cheng's novel, Lao Gan also tells us that once you have pissed for a cow, you can make it do anything you want, for they will respect you as if you were their parents.) It was this association of "cow" and "piss," Lao Gan explains, that made him write the imaginary character "cow-water" the other day.

The significatory density of this non-existent character is, structurally speaking, what counteracts the ferocity of Wang Fu's dedication to verbal language. The "cow-water" fantasy exposes literate culture in a scandalously different manner—as excrement. This exposure takes place at various levels at once. First, the fantasy returns us to the origin of the Chinese civilization—peasant knowledge. As such, in a text which is critical of the destructiveness of the Cultural Revolution, tribute is paid to one of Chinese communism's most compelling pedagogical imperatives: intellectuals must learn from peasants. The way cows behave toward urine is an ecological fact that one acquires by being "exiled" in the countryside, not by being in the classroom.

Second, this fantasy is a story about the dialectic of submission and domination. The cows, in spite of their patient and uncomplaining nature, go wild at the rare physical pleasure of salt. Whoever provides this pleasure, in other words, also has the power to dominate them. From the human perspective, this understanding of pleasure and submission is profoundly disturbing because in it we recognize the acts of degradation and humiliation, indeed violence. An act of physical discharge, which eliminates that which stinks—how could this, from the perspective of the properly educated, possibly be a source of pleasure and an inducement to submission? To what can we compare this at the symbolic level? Is this story about animal nature also one about human culture? If so, what kind of blow has been dealt to the dignity of the latter?

The radicalness of "cow-water" lies in the way it reveals the fundamental violence of culture as a process of production. The success of "culture" is the success of subjugating those who are in need of resources (as for instance, salt in the case of cows) for productive purposes. The paradox is that, not only would the act of subjugation not make them rebel, but, because its violence is at the same time what sustains and nurtures, the dominated respond to it submissively—animalistically. To come back to making of roads: pissing is, in this light, the act that establishes a path, which is met with pleasure and followed henceforth with loyalty.

If submission as such, transposed onto the human cultural frame, is essential for the formation of "identity," then this fantasy illuminates the unutterable inequality involved in that process. The silent, fantastical text of this *other* story about Chinese national culture reads: are not the hardworking, uncomplaining masses of Chinese people like the cows—and is not "tradition," as represented and endorsed by official political orthodoxy, the pissing master? (In the modern economy, "work" is what generates "salary," which etymologically means "payment for one's work in the form of salt.") No matter how abusive this master becomes, the masses succumb to him as the source of their survival. The masses submit even as tradition and national culture crush them. Against this *equivalence* between cows and people, the direct political empowerment of the "masses" that appears in Mao's reading of Lu Xun—a reading that distinguishes between cows and people by making the former a symbol of those who should serve the latter—is at once a hope, a lie, and the making of a road by force, with blood and tears.

The conception of culture as violence and excrement also returns us to the question of copying and writing-as-reproduction. Unlike A Cheng's story, in which one feels that the point of learning is to identify the correct source from which to copy, Chen's film deconstructs cultural production itself as copying. With the insertion of the cowherd, words, texts, dictionaries, and verbal language—summations of the human learning tradition—exist on a par with piss, as the (waste) product of a violently subjugating act to which Chinese individuals, like the intelligent student Wang Fu, have no choice but submit. The nature of this submission is that of copying and reproducing precisely the source of their subjugation—in other words, cultural violence through institutionalized education itself. It is only when this "originary" act of violence is completed through the act of submission and voluntary reproduction (since it includes the possibility of pleasure and physical survival) that it becomes fully effective as cultivation and culture. (In A Cheng, the hardworking cows are compared to philosophers.) This is why, on first discovering that he cannot teach the students anything except copying—i.e., on discovering that he is not, properly speaking, helping to perpetuate culture, Lao Gan expresses physical violence toward *himself*, by spitting at his own image in the broken mirror. Meanwhile, as Wang Fu strikes back in words, he is happy: the circuit of teaching that he initiated has been properly completed by this young child's active response and can now regenerate itself.

But if human culture is violent, nature is more so. If the cows in Chen's film are not, as Mao's image suggests, the "intellectual servants" to be used by the proletariat, they are not icons of humanistic benevolence either. The cowherd's (and by implication, nature's) muteness is a form of subjugating presence to which Lao Gan, even though a teacher, submits. In the last scenes of the film, as he departs from the village, we are once again given what look like dream scenes of nature. Chief among these is a field of black stumps, which stand mysteriously and collectively. As these stumps meet our eyes, we hear cowbells and someone pissing. It is the cowherd, who faces the camera and pisses at us directly, his genitals exposed. The camera then shows us his eye under the broken straw hat—is he looking at Lao Gan or at us? With the amplification of cowbells in the wind, the cowherd disappears; we see the black stumps and his hat on one of them. The stumps are magnified and the sounds of the cowbells increase. A moment of quiet. Then the face of the cowherd without the hat: a scruffy country child, turning around, looking at us.

The fantasy of the cowherd returns nature to the cosmic indifference described by the *Dao De Jing: tiandi bu ren, yi wanwu wei chugou*

(The cosmos is without/outside human benevolence; it treats everything as mere straw dogs). It is the mute, natural world, forever untamable, which ultimately pisses at us without shame or guilt. Vis-à-vis this nature, human violence itself is, the film says, a mere copy and re-production.

II: The Road Not Yet Taken

> We have found, especially in persons whose li-bidinal development has suffered some distur-bance, as in perverts and homosexuals, that in the choice of their love-object they have taken as their model not the mother but their own selves. They are plainly seeking themselves as a love-object and their type of object-choice may be termed *narcissistic*. . . .
>
> [The child] is really to be the center and heart of creation, "His Majesty the Baby," as once we fancied ourselves to be. He is to fulfill those dreams and wishes of his parents which they never carried out. . . . At the weakest point of all in the narcissistic position, the immortality of the ego, which is so relentlessly assailed by re-ality, security is achieved by fleeing to the child.
>
> Sigmund Freud[24]

> Ultimately, a thorough-going feminist revolution would liberate more than women.
>
> Gayle Rubin[25]

It is now possible for me to turn to the issue of "male narcissism" in the title of my essay. While I am sympathetic to the deconstructive reading of culture that Chen Kaige offers through what I have been calling the detour of nature and fantasy, I think such a reading leaves certain forms of human agency which are accountable for such violence unidentified and thus unquestioned. The detour, while it may funda-mentally critique the violence of culture as pedagogical suturing, also becomes complicitous with such violence because the alternative it offers, through nature, is *silence*. It is at this point that a social criticism, however partial, of recognizable types of human agency that lurk behind cultural violence is necessary as a way out, even if such criticism does not yet lead to a new road.

By offering a feminist reading as a supplement to my analysis of the bifurcated subjectivity above, my point is not to belittle the political subversiveness at work under Chen's direction. It is rather to attempt a mode of reading which, in a way that is not autonomous from but involved with that subversiveness, locates certain excesses which fall outside Chen's detour. These excesses—what to me are possible signs of a new mass and new hope that exist in incomplete forms in the film—are to be found with "woman." By focussing on the question of woman, we will see that the structural interplay between the subjectivities in *King of the Children*—stranded between the pedagogical and the fantastic—is a closed circuit.

This supplementary reading based on woman leads to a major question. Is this closed circuit, which I term male narcissism, at bottom a way to resist the reproduction of national culture altogether? If so, why? Why do the male subjectivities in Chen's film seek to connect with the child either through the school or through nature, while bypassing woman? What is the root of this "disturbance" which manifests itself as aesthetic symptom? In other words, does the *passive* role in which Chen casts his male protagonist reflect a response to a larger force of destruction at work, so that the exclusion of woman must be seen, not simply as misogyny, but as an effort to cope with what in Lacanian terms we would call castration?

To deal with these questions, let us now "do a re-take" of interpreting *King of the Children.*

If subjectivity is possible only as the result of a certain completion of an individual viewer's look—even if that process of completion is an illusory one—the two types of subjectivity evident in Chen's film, which are held in a contentious relationship with each other, are also held *together* by the absence of women as productive agents. (The girl students are, strictly speaking, recipients, not producers.)

From the beginning, Chen gives us a world of male play. From Lao Gan's former production unit, to the school, to his special relationship with Wang Fu, to the mute cowherd, this is a world of men and men as children at play. In addition, we find several scenes in which Lao Gan is alone against the background of nature, moving around aimlessly and enjoying himself. Between the continuity of human culture through verbal pedagogy and its discontinuity through the fantasy of nature, therefore, what disappears is woman. Moreover, this disappearance of woman occurs as a chiasmus: the woman disappears as the child appears.

We turn, at this point, to Laidi, the woman cook and singer in Lao Gan's production unit. Laidi's entrance is always a disruptive one. Take, for instance, the scene near the beginning in which Lao Gan and his friends gather for a meal before he departs for his new position. Chen shows us—with what nuanced attention!—the men's comradeship in cooking: first the collective contributions to the menu, then the washing, cutting, chopping of meat and vegetables, then setting the rice to be cooked inside a section of bamboo, and finally the sharing of the cooked meal. The power of males in such a group is, as Gayle Rubin would describe it, "not founded on their roles as fathers or patriarchs, but on their collective adult maleness, embodied in secret cults, men's houses, warfare, exchange networks, ritual knowledge, and various initiation procedures."[26] By contrast, although Laidi is a cook, she is never shown cooking; instead she strikes one as always bursting onto the scene of male play, bringing with her some kind of disorder. When Laidi enters this first scene of a shared meal, she is announced by her loud voice, her plump body, her broad manners, and a very unfeminine question: "Why don't you ask me for a drink?" Although she is a singer, we never hear her sing; the voice that comes from her is rather always given in a clownish fashion, as shouting and as disharmonious *noise*.

By stripping Laidi of what are conventional feminine (erotic) qual-ities—submissiveness, shyness, slenderness, and reticence, all of which belong to Lao Gan instead—Chen leaves open the question as to his attitude toward women's role in the production of national culture. To what extent does Laidi's exclusion from the conventional feminine realm of significations constitute an exclusion of woman in the cultural symbolic? And to what extent does her *clowning* become a new type of signification, a feminine power which is in fact stronger than the male because of its libidinally uninhibited nature? Two episodes allow us to negotiate these questions.

Laidi's ambition is to become a teacher of music at the same school where Lao Gan teaches. She wants the men to see that she is more than a cook. But this wish is met with patronizing criticisms from the men, who tease her for not understanding that she has none of the professional qualifications it takes to be a teacher. What she considers to be the most important qualification—her ability to sing and compose in voice—is thus immediately dismissed as irrelevant. Lao Gan, for his part, is honest enough to recognize that he is not properly qualified to teach either. But this understanding of Laidi's *equality* with him does not prompt him to help her.

Meanwhile, Laidi is the one who, among all the people Lao Gan knows, provides him with the Chinese dictionary he needs for teaching. When she comes to his school for a visit, Lao Gan introduces her to Wang Fu as the real owner of the dictionary, whereupon Wang Fu calls her "teacher." In A Cheng's novel, Lao Gan writes down Laidi's name as well as his own as donors when he leaves behind the dictionary as a gift. What is interesting about the relationships among Laidi, Lao Gan, and Wang Fu, I think, is that they indicate the potential of a new type of genealogy or reproductive unit. The woman, the man, and the school boy form a kind of collective away from the familial reproduction restricted to "blood" and heterosexuality. But as woman is liberated from her erotic and biologically reproductive role, what does she become? What we see in the film is that she has been turned into a comic spectacle whose palpable physical dimensions exceed the closed circuit of male pedagogy and fantasy.

In what sense is this closed circuit narcissistic? I turn now to Freud's argument about narcissism for some definitions. Narcissism, as we understand it in popular usage, is the "love of the self." Freud states that narcissism is not so much a perversion in the pejorative sense as it is a means of self-preservation. Freud distinguishes between two types of libidinal development in human beings—the anaclitic, typified by the search for an object of love external to the subject, which he identifies as active and masculine; the narcissistic, typified by the subject's seeking himself as the love object, which he identifies as passive and feminine. Freud's famous tableau of narcissists goes as follows:

> [Narcissistic] *women* love only themselves with an intensity comparable to that of the man's love for them. . . . Such women have the greatest fascination for men, not only for aesthetic reasons, . . . but also because of certain interesting psychological constellations. It seems very evident that one person's narcissism has a great attraction for those others who have renounced part of their own narcissism and are seeking after object-love; the charm of a *child* lies to a great extent in his narcissism, his self-sufficiency and inaccessibility, just as does the charm of certain *animals* which seem not to concern themselves about us, such as *cats* and the *large beasts of prey*. In literature, indeed, even the great *criminal* and the *humorist* compel our interest by the narcissistic self-importance with which they manage to keep at arm's length everything which would diminish the importance of their ego. It is as if we envied them their power of retaining a blissful state of mind—an unassailable libido-position which we ourselves have since abandoned.[27]

This passage from Freud clearly reveals his bias, that is, his exclusion of "man" from his tableau of narcissists. But if we disregard this sexual bias, a far more important feature of his argument that is relevant to our present discussion surfaces. We notice that those that he identifies as narcissistic share a common status, which is the status of the outsider—marginalized, mute, or powerless—beheld from a distance. Because of this, I would de-emphasize Freud's rigid sexual division between the male and female as anaclitic and narcissistic, and instead use his argument about narcissism for a *social* analysis that would include men as well as women as narcissists. Narcissism, seen in terms of the "outcast" categories in which Freud locates it, can now be redefined as the effect of a cultural marginalization or even degradation. The narcissist's look of "independence"—a self-absorption to the point of making others feel excluded—to which Freud attributes an aesthetic significance must therefore receive a new interpretation in the form of a question: is it the sign of a lack or a plenitude? Is it the sign of insecurity or self-sufficiency? Once we introduce the dialectic of social relations here and understand the "exclusionary look" as a possible result of (or reaction to) being excluded, it becomes necessary to think of certain forms of narcissism not in terms of independence, but as the outward symptoms of a process of cultural devastation, which leaves the self recoiling inward, seeking its connection from itself rather than with external reality.

Freud's argument makes it clear that narcissism is not an intrinsic quality (even though we inevitably attribute it to persons), but a relation produced through the process of observation. In other words, the understanding of narcissism involves a viewing position from which others look narcissistic and exclusionary to us. Narcissism is thus a description of our psychological state in the other—as we feel excluded, the other becomes "narcissistic." In contemporary Chinese cinema, what does the creation of narcissistic male characters tell us about the making of film—in other words, why is narcissism *conferred upon them?* Why does Chen make his male protagonist self-absorbed, passive, and thus "feminine"? How is this related to the question of national culture?

These questions bring us back to the one I raised at the beginning, namely, why does the writing of national culture in modern China typically take the form of an aesthetic preoccupation with the powerless? If the construction of national culture is a form of empowerment, then the powerless provides a means of aesthetic transaction through which a certain emotional stability arises from *observing* the powerless as a spectacle. In this spectacle, the viewer can invest a great amount of emotional energy in the form of sympathy; at the same time, this sympathy becomes the concrete basis of an affirmative national culture precisely because it *secures the distance from the powerless* per se. The projection of narcissism—an exclusionary self-absorption—onto the other becomes thus a way (as we notice in Freud) of stabilizing, or empowering, the viewing subject's position with an inexplicable aesthetic and emotional pleasure. Such pleasure gives rise, through the illusion of a "solidarity" with the powerless, to the formation of a "unified" community. What distinguishes Chen's film from, say, classical Hollywood narrative films, is that it is male, rather than female, figures who make up the spectacle(s) of the powerless. Moreover, it is "maleness" that sutures each point of the aesthetic transaction within the director's control, from (character as) spectacle to (character as) viewer, from feelings of devastation to feelings of solidarity.

According to Freud, a person may love, in the narcissistic manner, the following:

(a) What he is himself (actually himself).
(b) What he once was.
(c) What he would like to be.
(d) Someone who was once part of himself.

These descriptions define the world of male play which provides much pleasure for the men in Chen's film. Laidi, on the other hand, makes it impossible for them to play merely as sexless children; her difference reminds them that there is a world of brute biological re- production in which they, as the inheritors of Chinese culture, are supposed to participate. Hence, for instance, an attempt at swearing at the beginning of the film was preceded by the question: "Is there any woman around?" If this question is one pertaining to social de- corum, then social decorum is an indicator of the functioning of the unconscious. The question points to a shared understanding on the part of the men that swearing, which as a rule alludes to sex or sexual organs, brings out a reality which is on a par with that of woman. As long as women are not present, however, that reality is not materialized and can remain at the level of empty male talk.

On Lao Gan's return visit to the production unit, Laidi touches him. As he refuses such touching, she retorts: "Even if you were to teach for one hundred years, I'd still know what's between your legs!" This reminder of "nature" is as defiant as the trees, the cows, and the cowherd, and yet because it is spoken by a woman—because, shall we say, it comes from a human voice other than that of the male—it cannot be relegated to the realm of fantasy and has the potential of erupting as an alternative symbolic order. Unlike the mute nature child who allows the male "look" to wander in a happy mood of self- exploration and self-projection, the woman's harsh voice keeps calling him back to the world of human culture and the burdens that await him there. For Chen, it is as if these burdens cannot be shaken off unless one becomes perverse—by taking off for the world of fantasy.

Instead of following the road opened up by the female voice, then, Chen's work follows a detour which is, seen in a feminist analysis, a well-trodden philosophical one. This detour heads for the child, voiced or voiceless, a stand-in for culture or nature, who becomes the recipient of what in psychoanalytic language is the process of idealization.

If Lu Xun's call to "save the children" provides the continuity through modern Chinese literature and culture, we need to ask whether the emotional insistence behind such a call is not at the same time an insistence on forgetting and excluding women. While the child occupies a position in modern Chinese literature and culture similar to other figures of social oppression, because of his association with infancy he also offers the illusion that he is "freer" and more originary than the others. By contrast, woman, as the recipient of every type of social structuration, is a heavily "corrupted" space—a densely written script—which offers no such illusion of freedom. Because of this, it is much easier to project onto the child the wishes that cannot be fulfilled precisely because of the oppression of culture, through the illusion that the child occupies a kind of beyond-culture status which is superior because it is outside. The extreme form of this projection, as we see in Chen's film, uses the child to personify nature's original, amoral violence. The mute, pissing cowherd is, in this light, Chen's supreme invention of a *doubled* narcissistic relation. He is the silent beast confronting the feminine man, the ultimate narcissist—nature—beheld by the human narcissist.

The idealization of the child contains a self-directed violence. This violence disguises itself as love of the self, as "narcissism." As Freud says, "At the weakest point of all in the narcissistic position, the immortality of the ego, . . . security is achieved by *fleeing to the child*" (my emphasis). Fleeing to the child—what this means is that what appears to be a love of the self, which generates the look of complete self-absorption, is actually a desperate flight to another figure, who is powerless, inferior, but therefore safest for the realization of otherwise unenactable fantasies. In the Chinese context especially, this process of flight is a complex one. The child onto whom cultural hope is projected is not simply a figure of Chinese sentimentalism. Rather, it is the formation of an ideal, and, as Freud says, "the formation of an ideal would be the condition of repression."[28]

What is repressed, and why does it need to be? The answer to this question must be sought historically and collectively rather than within the space of one essay. For now, I can only point to the visible avoidance of the physical sexuality as embodied by woman, an avoidance that aesthetically intersects with the acceptance and idealization of the child. This is, as I have already mentioned, not misogyny *tout court*, but is symptomatic of a more profound disturbance.

In the sexual economy, "woman" represents that place in which man is to find his mating other in order to procreate and perpetuate the culture of which he is the current inheritor. "Woman" therefore serves as a reminder of the duty of genealogical transmission—of *chuanzong jiedai*. The question implied in Chen's film is: do Chinese men in the post–Cultural Revolution period want to perform this duty?

In the idiomatic Chinese expression for the "mating other," *duixiang*, we find a means of understanding the sexual economy in psychoanalytic terms. *Duixiang*, in contemporary psychoanalytic language, is that mirror image which would correspond to one's self, so that when we are looking for a mate, we literally say *zhao duixiang*—"to look for the corresponding image."

In the narcissistic subjectivity, this *duixiang* is internally directed. The "natural" *duixiang* for Lao Gan would have been Laidi, who loves him and wants to be with him—her aspiration to be a music teacher is, one could say, an expression of her wish to "correspond" to him. And yet in Chen's film, the strong woman's love is presented as now farcical, now threatening. The possibilities it offers—heterosexual love, marriage, reproduction—are refused by the film. Instead, male subjectivity takes another route, and joins children as figures of idealization. It is the children, then, who have come to take the place of the corresponding image, in a way that bypasses the woman (even though she is shown in an affectionate light, as a mother or sister who tends). In bypassing the woman as the figure of reproduction, what does the film project? It projects, as I said, two types of subjectivity, each of which can now be understood in terms of a narcissistic male circuit of reproduction. Reproduction is either strictly through education, or through a submission to the awesome muteness of nature. In each we find a "suturing" between the male protagonist with a male child. The "sublimated" message of the film is: the world is generated in this interplay between pedagogy and fantasy, between "culture" and "nature"—that is, without woman and without the physical body!

In Freud's text, narcissistic gratification, involving repression, can be secured through the ego-ideal, which, besides the individual side, also has a social side, in the form of "the common ideal of a family, a class, or a nation":

> The dissatisfaction due to the non-fulfillment of this ideal liberates homosexual libido, which is transformed into sense of guilt (dread of the community). Originally this was a fear of punishment by the parents, or, more correctly, the dread of losing their love; later the parents are replaced by an indefinite number of fellow men.[29]

Would it be far-fetched to say that the narrative of modern Chinese history, culminating in the catastrophe of the Cultural Revolution and more recently in the Tiananmen Massacre, represents precisely this "dissatisfaction" of the ego-ideal in the form of the nation? The guilt felt by the educated Chinese toward their fellow men generates the massive "censorial institution of conscience"—a feeling of being watched by other men—which makes it difficult, if not impossible, to engage in the conventional procedure of searching for the "corre-sponding image." Instead, *zhao duixiang* becomes a process, not of finding the one who loves one, but of self-observation, self-watching, and self-censorship. The displacement of narcissistic emotion onto "corresponding images" that are not women—difficult partners in biological reproduction—but idealized figures of children is sympto-matic of 1) a dissatisfaction with the failure of culture at large, and 2) an attempt nonetheless to continue to bear its burden conscien-tiously, by *disembodying* the reality of culture's reproduction and displacing that reality onto the purely institutional or fantastic level. Contrary to Freud's way of dividing the sexes, a film like *King of the Children* shows us that it is in male subjectivity that the need to secure emotional stability through narcissism is most evident. We can only speculate that this is in direct proportion to the burden of cultural reproduction that publicly/symbolically falls on men. Ironically, in spite of their subordinated status, women seem exempt from this desperate route since they are considered superfluous from the outset. In this "ironically" lies what I would call "the road not yet taken."

I understand that, by equating Laidi with the physical body, I seem to be going against one of the major lessons we have learned from feminism, namely, that "woman" is not about biological reproduction alone. However, my point in emphasizing the reproductive function of woman in this context is rather to show how a criticism of the cultural violence in Chinese culture cannot be undertaken without a vigilance about how the physical aspects of life are as a rule suppressed. Because women are traditionally associated with such physical aspects, their exclusion from the symbolic realm becomes a particularly poi-gnant way of exposing this general suppression. My insistence on the biological, therefore, is not an attempt to reify it as such, but is rather a means of interrupting the tendency toward what I would, for lack of a better term, call mentalism in Chinese culture, a mentalism that we witness even in a subversive film such as *King of the Children*. Because the Chinese national culture reproduces itself biologically by means of the machinery that is women's bodies even while continuing to dismiss them on account of their femaleness, and because the Chinese communist state controls the population by controlling women's bod-ies, upon which forced abortions at advanced stages of pregnancy can be performed as "policy"—I think we must belabor women's repro-ductive role somewhat, even at the risk of "biologism."

In Laidi, we find the suggestion of a healthy narcissism which com-prises an assertiveness, spontaneity, and fearlessness to seek what she wants while at the same time letting the other be. Because of this latter ability to let the other be, Laidi's love for Lao Gan is not expressed in the exclusive form of sexual desire and conquest, but rather in the form of a general affection in which one feels the presence of the caring sister, mother, and fellow worker as well. This alternative form of narcissism does not evade the other's difference (through specularization) in order to achieve its own stability. In it we find a different form of hope, toward which the film, caught in the closed circuit of male narcissism, nonetheless gestures, even though it never materializes into a significant new direction.

King of the Children continues, in the formalist manner of Lu Xun, the exploration of the cluster of issues involving Chinese national culture that has haunted Chinese intellectuals since the beginning of the twentieth century. To the literary incisiveness of Lu Xun's conception of hope—not as a road but as a crossroads—Chen's work brings the complexity of the filmic medium, in which the suggestively specular process of *zhao duixiang*—of finding that which gives us "self-regard" and "self-esteem"—takes on collective cultural significance. If Chinese intellectuals in the twentieth century have consistently attempted to construct a responsible national culture through an investment in figures of the powerless, Chen's film indicates how such an investment, because it is inscribed in the formation of an ego-ideal in the terms I describe, excludes woman and the physical reality she represents. Chen's film offers a fantastic kind of hope—the hope to rewrite culture without woman and all the limitations she embodies, limitations that are inherent to the processes of cultural, as well as biological, reproduction. The subjectivity that emerges in Chen's film alternates between notions of culture and nature that are both based on a lineage free of woman's interference. As such, even at its most subversive/deconstructive moments (its staging of the unconscious that is nature's brute violence), it partakes of a narcissistic avoidance of the politics of sexuality and of gendered sociality that we would, in spite of the passive "feminine" form it takes, call masculine. This masculinity is the sign of a vast transindividual oppression whose undoing must become the collective undertaking for all of us who have a claim to modern Chinese culture.

NOTES

1. Louis Althusser, "Ideology and Ideological State Apparatuses: Notes towards an Investigation," *Lenin and Philosophy and Other Essays* (New York: Monthly Review Press, 1971) 157.

2. Walter Benjamin, *Moscow Diary*, ed. Gary Smith, trans. Richard Sieburth (Cambridge: Harvard University Press, 1986) 29.

3. *The Complete Stories of Lu Xun*, trans. Yang Xianyi and Gladys Yang (Beijing: Foreign Languages Press; Bloomington: Indiana University Press, 1981) 65.

4. *The Complete Stories of Lu Xun* 65.

5. In an essay called "Xiwang," Lu Xun follows the Hungarian poet and revolutionary Petöfi Sándor to say that the unfoundedness of hopelessness is similar to that of hope itself. In a poem called "Hope," Sándor compares hope to a prostitute, implying by that traditional "metaphor" its faithlessness and mystery to men. See "Xiwang," *Yecao, Lu Xun chuanji*, vol. 2 (Beijing: Renmin wenxue chubanshe, 1981).

6. Marston Anderson, "The Morality of Form: Lu Xun and the Modern Chinese Short Story," *Lu Xun and His Legacy*, ed. and intro. Leo Ou-fan Lee (Berkeley: University of California Press, 1985) 32–53. Anderson's arguments are further elaborated in his *The Limits of Realism: Chinese Fiction in the Revolutionary Period* (Berkeley: University of California Press, 1990).

7. Anderson, "The Morality of Form," 52.

8. Terry Eagleton, "Ideology, Fiction, Narrative," *Social Text*, no. 2, 71; emphasis in the original.

9. A good example of this tension in the pre-1949 period is found in Mao Dun's essay, "From Guling to Tokyo" (1928), in which he scrutinizes the question of what constitutes "proletarian literature." See "From Guling to Tokyo," *Bulletin of Concerned Asian Scholars*, trans. Yu-shih Chen, Jan.-Mar. (1976): 38–44.

10. "Talks at the Yenan Forum on Literature and Art," *Mao Tse-tung on Literature and Art* (Beijing: Foreign Languages Press, 1960, 1977) 39–40. The couplet is from Lu Xun's "Zizhao" ("Self-mockery"), *Ji wai ji, Lu Xun chuanji*, vol. 7 (Beijing: Renmin wenxue chubanshe, 1981).

11. For a helpful discussion of how to interpret this image, I am grateful to the students who took my course, "Introduction to Literary Theory for Students of Modern Chinese Literature," winter 1990, at the University of Minnesota.

12. See *A Cheng xiaoshuo: qi wang, shu wang, haizi wang* (Taipei: Haifeng chubanshe, 1988) 163–213.

13. Althusser, "Ideology and Ideology State Apparatuses."

14. Since I have already analyzed A Cheng's story at length elsewhere, my discussion of it here is brief. See "Pedagogy, Trust, Chinese Intellectuals in the 1990s—Fragments of a Post-Catastrophic Discourse," forthcoming in *Dialectical Anthropology* (Special Issue on Post-Mao China).

15. Boris Eikhenbaum, "Literature and Cinema (1926)," *Russian Formalism: A Collection of Articles and Texts in Translation*, eds. Stephen Bann and

John E. Bowlt (New York: Harper and Row Publishers, Inc., 1973) 123. For an extended version of Eikhenbaum's views on cinema, see his "Problems of Cinema Stylistics," *Russian Formalist Film Theory*, ed. Herbert Eagle (University of Michigan Slavic Publication, 1981) 55–80.

16. In a recent article, Kaja Silverman distinguishes the look, which is individualized and has a human bearer, and the gaze, which is external and collective. She argues that in Hollywood cinema, the male look is always exchangeable with the gaze because it is disburdened of lack. See "Fassbinder and Lacan: A Reconsideration of Gaze, Look, and Image," *Camera Obscura* no. 19: 54–84. While making use of these terms, I want to emphasize that the distribution of "male" and "female" characteristics in *King of the Children* reverses the Hollywood paradigm. The male look in Chen's film is the bearer of a lack; it is the male who occupies the passive (classically "feminine") position. The question is: why? As I will argue in the second half of my essay, this is a question of symbolic castration, or cultural violence, which is particularly germane to the understanding of the contemporary Chinese situation.

17. See my account of the humanistic and patriarchal meanings of Wang Fu's "success" in "Pedagogy, Trust, Chinese Intellectuals in the 1990s."

18. Althusser, "Ideology and Ideology State Apparatuses," 132.

19. Chen, interview with *Playboy*, Chinese edition, No. 22 (May 1988): 48.

20. "Silent is the Ancient Plain: Music, Film-Making, and the Conception of Reform in China's New Cinema," *Discourse* 12.2 (Spring-Summer 1990): 82–109.

21. See Martin Heidegger, "The Origin of the Work of Art," *Poetry, Language, Thought*, trans. Albert Hofstadter (New York: Harper Colophon Books, 1971) 15–87; "The Question Concerning Technology," *The Question Concerning Technology and Other Essays*, trans. and intro. William Lovitt (New York: Harper Colophon Books, 1977) 3–35.

22. Lovitt 22.

23. Chen's fascination with the inarticulate or verbally clumsy child is evident in his other films as well—for instance, Han Han in *Yellow Earth* and the young soldier Hou, who stutters, in *The Big Parade*.

24. Freud, "On Narcissism: An Introduction" (1914), *A General Selection from the Works of Sigmund Freud*, ed. John Rickman, M.D., Appendix Charles Brenner, M.D. (New York: Doubleday, 1957) 112 (emphasis in the original); 115.

25. Rubin, "The Traffic in Women: Notes on the 'Political Economy' of Sex," *Toward an Anthropology of Women*, ed. Rayna Reiter (Monthly Review Press, 1975) 200.

26. Rubin 168.

27. Freud 113; my emphases.

28. Freud 116. A perfect example of the massive destructiveness that results from the idealization of children, who are used to enact otherwise unrealizable fantasies, was Mao's mobilization of the Red Guards during the Cultural Revolution.

29. Freud 123.

p. 6   Chen Kaige   陳凱歌

p. 6   *lu shi ren zou chu lai de*   路是人走出來的

p. 7   *wuke naihe*   無可奈何

     wuke wubuke   無可無不可

     wuning liangke   毋寧兩可

p. 8   *zhuguan*   主觀

     weixin zhuyi   唯心主義

p. 9   (couplet from Lu Xun's poem)   橫眉冷對千夫指
俯首甘為孺子牛

p. 9   *Haizi wang*   孩子王

p. 10   *xiehua*   寫畫

p. 14   *Da yue bing*   大閱兵

p. 14   (quoted passage)

從前，有座山，山裏有座廟，廟裏有個和尚，
講故事。講的什麼呢？從前有座山，
山裏有座廟，廟裏有個和尚講 ——

p. 18   *Dao De Jing*   道德經

     tiandi bu ren, yi wanwu wei chugou   天地不仁，以萬物為芻狗

p. 24   *chuanzong jiedai*   傳宗接代

duixiang   對象

zhao duixiang   找對象

The Cabinet of Dr. Pee-wee: Consumerism and Sexual Terror
Constance Penley

> Every evening at lighting up o'clock sharp and until further notice in Feenichts Playhouse. . . . By arraignment, childream's hours, expercatered . . . .With nightly redistribution of parts and players by the puppetry producer. . . .
>
> James Joyce, Finnegans Wake

What goes on in *Pee-wee's Playhouse*? What goes on outside *Pee-wee's Playhouse*? On the inside we have the hi-tech, low-taste spectacle of sexually ambiguous adults, not exactly pretending to be kids, yet inhabiting this child's fantasy-land with hyperactive glee. Outside and around the Playhouse we have the world of Saturday morning television and its efforts to deliver the children to the advertisers. What then does the outside of the Playhouse have to do with the inside?

What goes on *in* the Playhouse is that Pee-wee and his guests are "playing house." This is literally so in one episode that takes place on a rainy day when everyone has to stay inside. "Let's play war!" is one suggestion. "Let's play headhunter!" is another. But it is Miss Yvonne who prevails, insisting that they "play house," even over Pee-wee's objection that "that's girl stuff." Pee-wee dutifully, if grudgingly, takes up his assignment to play Daddy to Miss Yvonne's Mommy, but balks at her demand that Daddy give Mommy a kiss. He relents, under pressure, and gives her a kiss whose passion is just this side of Ward Cleaver's. Another episode makes more explicit what playing house involves when Pee-wee, in otherwise innocent circumstances, says, "I'll show you mine if you'll show me yours." (In the second season of the show they finally get around to playing "doctor.") Indeed, the dialogue and visuals of *Pee-wee's Playhouse* abound with wienie jokes, for the most part of the size variety. "Think you got a big enough pencil there?" Reba the mail-lady asks Pee-wee as he hauls out a giant pencil to write a letter to his seafaring friend Captain Carl. But before Pee-wee can get the letter in the mail, Captain Carl shows up with an equally oversize extendable telescope as a present for *him*. On another day in the Playhouse, Mrs. Steve, the local snoop and mean-lady, is looking for Randy, the eponymous bad-boy puppet who has stolen apples from her orchard. "I have a bone to pick with you," she shrieks at Randy. "Where are you hiding the little thing," she asks Pee-wee accusingly. Tracking Randy down to his hiding place under the bunk beds, she snarls, "Come out here, you little dickens."

But what girls have, or do not have, is also the subject of investigation at the Playhouse when Pee-wee, rendered permanently invisible by a magic trick that backfires, takes the opportunity to look up Miss Yvonne's dress and begins the childhood chant, "I've seen London, I've seen France . . .," until Miss Yvonne makes her escape. ("Oh, Pee-wee!" is one of Miss Yvonne's most frequently uttered lines, always in a tone of feigned outrage.) The putative difference between little boys and little girls is once again the topic, this time of a Penny cartoon, in which the narrator rapidly and cannily speculates on a whole range of differences, wrapped up in the final observation that "girls grow to maturity faster than boys."

Frequently then in the Playhouse, "playing house" involves a fever-pitch investigation of sexual identity, most succinctly stated in Pee-wee's now notorious line, another recycled childhood taunt, "I know you are, but what am I?" Also posed throughout the show is the kindred question of the relation between the sexes. In one episode Pee-wee throws a party "to celebrate friendship." All the Playhouse regulars show up, dressed to the nines. They play Pin-the-tail-on-the-donkey and eat fifties hors d'oeuvres like pigs-in-a-blanket. Then everyone starts dancing. Among the couples is Miss Yvonne and Tito, the muscular lifeguard, usually seen only in skimpy bathing trunks, and a libidinal object for any number of the Playhouse regulars. Pee-wee taps him on the shoulder, asking "May I cut in?" Tito steps back, Pee-wee steps in, but only to turn and begin dancing with Tito, not Miss Yvonne. After a few seconds, Pee-wee gives a wicked laugh and turns back around to Miss Yvonne ("Oh, Pee-wee!). All tension is dissolved in the next scene, however, when everyone begins to dance the Hokey-Pokey, the elementary school game designed to help children make distinctions not between the sexes, but between their right foot and their left foot.

The question of sexual relations is posed once again when Miss Yvonne asks Cowboy Curtis for a date. Cowboy Curtis exclaims, "Well, if that don't beat all, a *woman* asking a *man* out on a date!" What is implied, of course, is that he has never been out with a woman before and, in fact, considers it a pretty wild idea. Worried that he "won't know how to act," he is rescued from his pre-date jitters by the Cowntess, the aristocratic bovine who claims that her specialty is "dating dilemmas." To demonstrate to Cowboy Curtis what to do on a date, the Cowntess sets up a role-playing game and asks Pee-wee to be Miss Yvonne. He objects at first, but then takes to his role with gusto. The game comes crashing to a halt, however, when Cowboy Curtis, carried away with *his* role, tries to give Miss Yvonne/Pee-wee a goodnight kiss. Things go pretty far before Pee-wee pulls back to exclaim, "No! None of that stuff! Game's over!"

It is not until the second season, however, that the inevitable question of where babies come from is raised. The King of Cartoons springs a surprise by bringing along, for the first time, the Queen of Cartoons and their new son, the Prince of Cartoons. Pee-wee plays kitchy-koo with the Prince, and then asks, "Where'd you find him, King, did a stork bring him?" "Not *exactly*," the King replies. Cowboy Curtis guesses that the Prince appeared on the castle doorstep in a basket. "No, no," the King says, "don't you know where babies come from?" Chairy offers still another hypothesis: "Silly, you buy babies in the Baby Department at the hospital." Pee-wee nods in agreement. Since Cowboy Curtis and Pee-wee have just been experimenting with sprouting a grapefruit seed, Cowboy Curtis opines that perhaps babies grow "kinda like seeds." The King agrees, "Yes, kinda like that," and then asks the ever-helpful Magic Screen "to show us some information on the subject." Magic Screen complies by showing them and us what looks like an early sixties educational film on reproduction, which is about as helpful as the preceding hypotheses on where babies come from: we are told about the "miracle of reproduction" while watching a baby chick hatch. When it is over, Pee-wee looks at the camera and says, "Gee, you learn something new every day!" But all that has been learned here is that traditional pedagogical ideas about how to give sexual information to children result in stories that are as fantasmatic as the children's own attempts to make sense of reproduction.

It is highly appropriate that it is the figure of the Sphinx that adorns the exterior of the Playhouse, inasmuch as Freud declared the Sphinx's riddle to be the very model of the sexual questions invariably posed by children.[1] The Sphinx therefore becomes the icon or emblem of infantile sexual investigation, a repetitious line of questioning that wants to know "Where did I come from?" "What sex am I?," and "With whom is possible to have sexual relations?" In its deliberate playing to two audiences, one child and the other adult, *Pee-wee's Playhouse* suggests that these are questions that never cease to insist, even in fully Oedipalized adulthood. How does the Playhouse play to two audiences? Take the following example, in which the question of "With whom is it possible to have sexual relations?," which necessarily includes the question of *how* one has sexual relations, is given, for adult viewers at least, a modern and tragic twist. In this episode, the first of the second season, after the production of the show had moved from New York to Los Angeles, Pee-wee is remodeling the Playhouse. Miss Yvonne arrives, as usual looking as if she is gliding down the Miss Universe runway. Since the Playhouse is such a mess, Pee-wee is worried that Miss Yvonne is going to get dirty. But Miss Yvonne says, "Don't worry about that, you know my motto." "No, what's that?," Pee-wee asks. "Be Prepared!," she exclaims, as she whips out a clear plastic raincoat to cover her pale chiffon dress and billowing crinolines. Pee-wee helps her put it on, along with a transparent plastic cap to protect her large, dome-shaped bouffant hairdo. They walk over to the hipster leader of the Playhouse band, a dog-puppet that speaks in syncopated rhyme. "Dig that crazy plastic dress," he exclaims. "That's in case I make a mess," Miss Yvonne coyly replies. Adults are sure to get the safe sex allusion here, but it is an allusion that is probably not immediately available to the child viewers of this show, ages 2–11. In the same way, the program's references to homosexuality, as in the episodes where Pee-wee rejects Miss Yvonne to dance with Tito or where Cowboy Curtis tries to give Pee-wee a kiss when he's playing Miss Yvonne, are probably taken by children as no more than a perfectly adequate representation of their own dismissal of the opposite sex and all that "icky stuff."

But what does the Playhouse's network, CBS, think of all that "icky stuff," heterosexual or otherwise? CBS no longer has an internal censorship board, but informal self-censorship is still very much at work. Why then did no one object, for example, to Pee-wee's giant underpants

skit, in which he places a pair of truly humongous Fruit of the Looms over his head to show how this simple, everyday garment can be turned into a nun's habit or Rapunzel's flowing hair? Once one has noticed the very adult sexual antics mixed in with the child's play on this show, one inevitably wonders how this is allowed to go on, especially on CBS, traditionally the staidest of the three major networks, indeed the "quality" or "family" network. Could it be that the CBS executives have *scotomized* the show's sexuality, and specifically its homosexuality? That is, that like children who are not yet developmentally or psychically prepared to receive certain sexual information, they *see* it but do not *register* it? I shall return to this question of CBS's sexual knowledge, or lack of it, later on.

Infantile sexual investigation is, of course, no more innocent than playing house, and it has its own terrors. Pee-wee's Playhouse is, in fact, a haunted house. There is something uncanny about it, as we shall see. CBS's decision to produce *Pee-wee's Playhouse* for the 1986 season broke a cardinal rule of Saturday morning kidvid programming: the familiarity principle. As ABC's vice-president of children's programming (awkwardly) put it: "Each of our shows has newness about it, yet with familiarity built in."[2] "Familiarity" arises from the product tie-in, the show derived from a toy, *Lady Lovely Locks and Pixietails*, for example, or the show spun off from a popular TV series or movie, like *The Flintstone Kids* or *Real Ghostbusters*. *Pee-wee's Playhouse* has none of these advantages; it lacks product recognition or an audience already *familiar* with its images. Is there then something *unfamiliar* about *Pee-wee's Playhouse*, what Freud, in his essay on "The 'Uncanny' "[3] called *unheimlich*, literally, "unhomely"? Let us look at a story that Freud confesses had an uncanny effect on him. He reports that:

> In the middle of the isolation of war-time a number of the English *Strand Magazine* fell into my hands. . . . I read a story about a young married couple who move into a furnished house in which there is a curiously shaped table with carvings of crocodiles on it. Towards evening an intolerable and very specific smell begins to pervade the house; they stumble over something in the dark; they seem to see a vague form gliding over the stairs—in short, we are given to understand that the presence of the tables causes ghostly crocodiles to haunt the place, or that the wooden monsters come to life in the dark, or something of the sort. (244–245)

"It was a naive enough story," Freud says, "but the uncanny feeling it produced was quite remarkable." This can only make us wonder what Freud would have thought of the goings-on in Pee-wee's fridge — ice cubes, popsicles, vegetables and leftovers performing trapeze acts, staging an opera, dancing the Can-Can—because it is not only crocodiles that come to life in the Playhouse. Radically anthropomorphized, everything is animated: Conky the robot, Chairy the chair, Globey the globe, Magic Screen, Mr. Kite, Mr. Window, and in the second season, Clocky the clock and Floory the floor, just to name a few. And it is precisely this animation of the inanimate that characterizes the uncanny: sentient furniture, dolls coming to life, dismembered limbs, a severed head, a hand cut off at the wrist, feet that dance by themselves. Pee-wee's Playhouse teems with such partial objects. Pee-wee himself seems like a bright-cheeked puppet that has come to life, and it is doubtless for this reason that he was chosen to play Pinocchio in Shelley Duval's *Fairy Tale Theater*. The mutant toys, Jambi's head in the genie box and the hands he receives in the mail in the original *Pee-wee Herman Show*, Pee-wee's headless torso when Jambi has been only partially successful in bringing him back from invisibility, all of these recall the *jouissance* of dismemberment and other bodily mayhem in the silly and sadistic cartoons of the thirties that set the tone for much of what goes on in the Playhouse.

For Freud, however, the uncanny does not arise simply from intellectual uncertainty (Is it alive or not?). "Something has to be added to the novel and unfamiliar in order to make it uncanny" (221). The first dictionary definition of *heimlich*, Freud shows, links it to the "homely," the "familiar," and thus its opposite, *unheimlich*, becomes that which is frightening, or arouses dread and horror, precisely because it is unfamiliar. But the second definition of *heimlich* is quite different from the first, and means "concealed," "kept from sight." Thus the second definition of *heimlich* bizarrely turns into its opposite, *unheimlich*, that which is eerie, weird. The dictionary example Freud offers takes us right back to Pee-wee: "These pale youths are *unheimlich* and are brewing heaven knows what mischief" (224). Freud uses the ambivalence in the definition of *heimlich* to demonstrate that what is unfamiliar is actually the familiar. Repetition, the instinctual compulsion to repeat, is powerful enough, he says "to overrule the pleasure principle" (238), and is a source of the uncanny. For Freud, what is repeated is that which has been previously repressed: an earlier way of psychically negotiating the world. Once again notoriously collapsing phylogeny and ontogeny, Freud argues that both primitive humans and each of us in our own earlier development had an animistic conception of the universe, manifested in the belief that the world is peopled by the spirits of human beings. This idea arises from the subject's narcissistic overvaluation of his own mental processes, the belief in the omnipotence of his own thoughts and wishes. Jambi, you will recall, allows Pee-wee one wish a day, which is (almost) always perfectly fulfilled.

For Freud, of course, this kind of uncanniness depends mainly on its proximity to the castration complex. This is perhaps why one cannot go through the saw-toothed door of Pee-wee's Playhouse without passing a giant pair of scissors hanging on the wall (although they disappear in the second season). And as for the name Pee-wee itself, beyond its myriad connotations of smallness, lurks the threat of castration. For Freud says in his essay on "The Dissolution of the Oedipus Complex," that castration threats come so often not as warnings about masturbation, but bedwetting.

But is the Playhouse, in fact, *unheimlich*, unhomely, uncanny? Freud admits that fairy tales, no matter how much they adopt animism and omniscience of thought, do not have an uncanny effect. As long as the events or objects are enclosed in a fictional world, we do not feel them as uncanny. We are not asked to decide on their reality or not; we take them as fiction. However, the situation is altered, he says, as soon as the writer begins to move in the world of common reality. I want to suggest that *Pee-wee's Playhouse* does have an uncanny effect, precisely because it moves in the world of common reality, as Freud called it, or consumer reality, as we might now call it. *Pee-wee's Playhouse* differs significantly from the fairy tale in that it does not try to pass itself off as a seamless fiction, separate from the "real world." Instead, it fully acknowledges its continuity with what is outside and around the Playhouse, namely the world of children's Saturday morning television.

We do not find a moralistic "No Trespassing" sign posted on the edge of Pee-wee's premises. First of all, there is the Chinese box or mise-en-abîme effect of the ubiquitous Broadcast Arts aesthetic (the "look" provided by the producers of the first season of the *Playhouse*). This is seen throughout the Playhouse, then in the "stay tuned" bumpers that Broadcast Arts designed for CBS to distinguish the Saturday morning programs from the commercials, and, finally, in the commercials themselves, some of them created by Broadcast Arts for the sponsors, the manufacturers of Fruit-Flavored Trix, for example. All of these bear the distinctive Broadcast Arts look, which combines live action filmmaking with a variety of special effects techniques, including clay animation, stop-motion animation, cel animation, motion graphics, motion control photography, and the use of models, miniatures, mattes and computer graphics.[5] Frequently, then, there is remarkably little visual difference between the inside and outside of *Pee-wee's Playhouse*. Broadcast Arts and Pee-wee Pictures, in both their production methods and their characteristic looks, exuberantly play up the continuity between art and commercialism.

But, one might ask, what about the figure of the Salesman, the giant puppet somewhat resembling Richard Nixon who comes to the door in each episode, only to have it slammed in his face as Pee-wee once again refuses his high-volume "incredible offer," screaming "Salesmen!" (or "Sandman!," as I heard it the first six or seven times I saw the show!)? Is not this refusal to be seen as *this* show's rejection of the blatantly manipulative commercialism that pervades children's television programming? Yes and No. While it is true that the Salesman's attempted hard-sell is exactly repeated and rejected each week during the first season, an exception is made in one episode. Pee-wee is having a party to which all the regulars have been invited. Everyone was to have brought a present for someone else, but somehow Pee-wee has been left out. When we hear the pounding on the door, we know that it is the Salesman. Pee-wee opens the door and, this time, responds to the sales pitch because his feelings are hurt at not having been given a present. Instead of slamming the door, he hesitates and asks, "What's the offer?" The Salesman makes him an offer he can't refuse, free foil for his ever-expanding foil ball. Pee-wee grabs the foil, invites the Salesman in, and even directs him to the refreshment table. Everyone has a price. Repeatedly in the Playhouse, a moral stance is established — here, an objection to the kind of corporate decision-making that turns every kids show into a half-hour commercial — and then blithely undermined.

When Stephen Oakes, executive producer of the first season of the *Playhouse*, was asked why his company had not tried to market any of the mutant toys seen by millions of kids every week on Pee-wee's toy shelf, he replied, somewhat tongue-in-cheek, "Bad management."[6] He wryly admitted, however, that it might not be such a commercially successful idea since any child can easily create his or her own mutant toy through even the most half-hearted efforts at dismemberment and recombination. Paul Reubens, who plays Pee-wee Herman both on and off screen (reporters are warned that they will be interviewing *Pee-wee*, not Paul Reubens), constantly threatens to market toys based on the show. But when he begins to discuss the Pee-wee products he would like to merchandise and license, it is clear that his ideas are only an extension of Pee-wee's typical attitude toward the Salesman. In *Interview* magazine Pee-wee revealed that "Ralston-Purina is developing a cereal with me called 'Pee-wee Chow,' and it'll be in the shape of little dog-food stars. . . . I want the television commercial for it to show a mother pouring it into a bowl and putting it on the floor, and the kids crawling over and eating it like dog food." Another of his marketing schemes involves permanent Pee-wee tattoos: "I always thought it would be fun to have permanent tattoos and not say they were permanent. Kids would put them on their arms and stuff and their parents would be scrubbing them and scrubbing them and they wouldn't come off. It would be good advertising for the show in the future. A whole generation of kids with these big Pee-wee tattoos."[7] However, a Pee-wee Herman talking doll was successfully introduced in the 1987 Christmas season and is already a collector's item.

In another way too *Pee-wee's Playhouse* is both continuous and discontinuous with the world of commercialized children's television programming. When it first appeared in 1986, the *Playhouse* was most notably different in being the only Saturday morning show to have live characters on it (even if the look and gestures of the Playhouse gang seem governed by an animated cartoon aesthetic). But it is significant that Pee-wee *leaves* the Playhouse at the end of each episode, saying goodbye to his guests and riding/flying his scooter off into an imaginary geography of America, as well as into the credits sequence, which segues into an announcement to stay tuned for *Teen Wolf* and *Galaxy High*, the CBS programs to follow. If in these numerous ways the Playhouse is not sealed off from common reality, or here, consumer reality, then, according to the Freudian notion, the viewer would be confronted with an intellectual uncertainty about the boundaries between the real and the unreal, the animate and the inanimate (or, here, the commercial and the noncommercial) that in part characterizes the uncanny. In all the senses of the uncanny *Pee-wee's Playhouse* can therefore be said to fit the bill: its investigation of sexual identity, with the threat of castration always in the wings; its animation of the inanimate, so linked to childhood narcissism and the fantasy of omnipotent thought, and the conceptual uncertainty it raises about borders, limits and boundaries.

No television show or program can be understood outside of its environment, the ads that are embedded in it and the other programs around it. *Pee-wee's Playhouse* is clearly not separate from these considerations of commercialism and scheduling, and the confusion over where the show begins and ends even contributes to its uncanny effect, as we have seen. But there is one way that *Pee-wee's Playhouse is* distinct from its surroundings. All the other Saturday morning shows, as well as most of the commercials, are marked by an extreme sexual differentiation. The network programs aim for what is called "girl appeal," especially in the 1986–1987 season with so many new girl products appearing on the market. Girls are thought to respond to "cute and cuddly" and apparently watch, in vast numbers, *Kissyfur, The Wuzzles, The Care Bears, Pound Puppies,* and *Muppet Babies.* The cheap syndicated shows, on the other hand, have captured the boy-product market with shows like *He-Man and the Masters of the Universe,* and *Inhumanoids. Pee-wee's Playhouse,* however, attempts to be a cross-over show, not only appealing to viewers of different ages but to children of opposite sexes. The fast-forward speed of *Pee-wee's Playhouse* is intended to capture the fidgety attention of little boys, and its endearing characters the sentimental devotion of little girls. But there is much more here than a grab-bag attempt to appeal to both boys and girls. *Pee-wee's Playhouse* offers something that elicits the fascinated attention of all small children. We could call it terror, the terror of sexuality, of sexual difference, and we are back again to infantile sexual investigation and even the uncanny. *Pee-wee's Playhouse* forgoes the easy channeling of children's sexual identification into either mastery for the boys (*He-Man and Masters of the Universe*) or permanent regression for the girls (*Kissyfur, The Wuzzles*). Instead the program suggests that the question of sexual difference is highly problematic and possibly never entirely settled. CBS's vice-president of children's programming has said that the network is trying to attract people to its Saturday morning line-up "who have succeeded in bringing *fantasy* to children in books, movies, or whatever."[8] Although the CBS executive does not expand upon what she or the network means by "fantasy," psychoanalytic theory tells us that unconscious fantasy typically and generically involves a strong component of the scary, and what is scary for children is more often than not the questions posed by sexuality, and the children's own highly fraught relation to sexual knowledge. That CBS is indeed aiming toward programs that are edgier and more frightening than *Kissyfur*, yet which do not emphasize triumphant mastery like *Inhumanoids*, can be seen in their choice of Chris Columbus, who wrote the very nasty and quite terrifying *Gremlins* for Steven Spielberg, to script *Galaxy High*. CBS has also announced that Maurice Sendak, the author of *Where the Wild Things Are*, may develop a show soon.[9] It should be said, though, that CBS's interest in conceiving more innovative programming for children is probably due, more than anything else, to the fact that the ratings for the syndicated cartoon shows based on toys have plunged precipitously, by about 60%, indicating that there may be a market for newer kinds of shows.[10] But in any case, CBS was willing to take a chance on its "great weird hope,"[11] Pee-wee Herman.

What do I mean by saying that CBS took a chance on Pee-wee Herman (and now I am back to the question of what CBS *knows*)? It was not only that the show would have the only live actors on Saturday morning television, or that each episode was clearly going to cost more to produce than an animated show (the first season's episodes averaged $325,000 each and employed 150 artists and technicians).[12] The risk for CBS was the challenge of transforming a sexually risqué work of performance art into a children's television program. *The Pee-wee Herman Show*, a very adult take-off on children's shows, was successfully staged in two Los Angeles theaters before being made into an HBO special. It was fully scatological (the secret word was "latrine"), and entirely sadistic and voyeuristic. There were jokes about wienies, doggy doo, underwear, open flies, vaginal smells, anal intercourse, masturbation, and sexually transmitted diseases, among others. And Jambi was already the raging queen in a box that we still see on the Playhouse. CBS wanted Broadcast Arts to do a show for them, but needed a character on which to base it. They chose Pee-wee Herman, and according to the head of Broadcast Arts, asked the innovative production company to come up with a children's show, making only two stipulations. Pee-wee Herman should not be shown coming out of the bathroom trailing a piece of toilet paper stuck to his shoe, nor should he stick pencils in potatoes. Both were done in the first season. Stephen Oakes believes that CBS is fully aware of the gay references in the Saturday morning show, but says that the network has never mentioned them to Reubens or the producers. As the show went along, CBS had, in fact, only two objections, based on objections they thought were sure to come from parents groups. First, they were concerned about the "secret word," because not only are children watching the show supposed to "scream real loud" when they hear it on the show, they are told to do so all day long, whenever they hear the word. Since the secret words are frequently-uttered ones like "this," "there," "okay," "time," or "day," the network executives feared that the effects of the show would spill over into the entire day, causing parental stress. Second, they objected to the attempt to rejuvenate the fifties game "Winky Dink" in the Connect-the-Dots sequence of the show. The idea was to sell clear, flexible plastic sheets at a franchise like McDonald's that children would attach to the TV screen and then play Connect-the-Dots with special crayons that would also be supplied. Parents groups did not like the idea because they foresaw some kids playing Connect-the-Dots without the plastic sheet. They were also worried about the children being exposed to radiation from the television set since the game required them to be right next to it. The secret word stayed but the new "Winky Dink" was cancelled.

What is surprising in all these negotiations is that CBS never questioned or censored the show's presentation of sexuality, including its clear allusions to homosexuality. I earlier suggested that the CBS executives, like the prepubescent children who make up the majority of the target audience, simply do not take in the sexual references. Admittedly, this is unlikely, since those executives are sure to be sophisticated adults, tuned in to what "the public wants," which means that there must be other reasons for the network's sudden binge of tolerance. Surely CBS *knows*, but somehow feels that things are controllable, that the sexual meanings circulated by the show will somehow be contained.

Perhaps too much has been made of the homosexual subtext in *Pee-wee's Playhouse*. I say this even though most critics have scrupulously avoided any mention of Pee-wee's sexual orientation (variously describing Pee-wee as adolescent, androgynous, polymorphously perverse, or just "weird"), or bring it up only in order to put it aside. As an article in *Film Comment* said, "if Pee-wee has to have an inordinate number of handsome young men on the show, that's his business."[13] Although the allusions to gay culture are there, it is not enough merely to point them out. Bryan Bruce does a very good job of it, however, in his *CineAction* article, "Pee-wee Herman: the Homosexual Subtext."[14] Bruce gives a list of the many "disguised allusions to a gay sensibility in both the show and the film [*Pee-wee's Big Adventure*]" (4). He says that it is not just that there are a lot of handsome men on the show, "it's rather that each represents a specific gay male icon, prominent fantasy figures in homosexual pornography (although in the context of the Playhouse made human and friendly), including the sailor (Captain Carl), the black cowboy (Cowboy Curtis), and the muscular, scantily-clad lifeguard (Tito), not to mention the escaped con (Mickey) in *Pee-wee's Big Adventure*" (5). In the film we see explicit references to gay fantasy in two instances of drag, once when Pee-wee disguises himself as Mickey's girlfriend to get them through a police roadblock (he forgets to change back into his boy clothes after they are out of danger) and again when Pee-wee makes a brief appearance as a nun near the end of the film. Bruce says the nun, in particular, is a dead giveaway in its appeal to the irreverent gay camp aesthetic (5).

It is precisely this last point about the "irreverent gay camp aesthetic" that needs to be brought more into focus. Perhaps with *Pee-wee's Playhouse* it is not a case of "disguised allusions," or latent meanings put there in the text to be discerned by a knowing gay following, but rather of an overall aesthetic, *a camp sensibility*, one in which everything is entirely on the surface. And if this camp sensibility has become so pervasive in our culture that it is no longer automatically equated with homosexuality, but has become available to a much wider set of artistic and social meanings, then this could help to explain the network's acquiescence to the Playhouse's sexual antics. It is only "troglodytes who . . . confuse camp with homosexual," claims Mark Booth in *Camp*, his definitive study of the subject, which challenges the received idea, first aired by Christopher Isherwood and then popularized by Susan Sontag, that camp originated in homosexual cliques of the thirties. Booth instead traces the origins of the camp sensibility back to the nineteenth century, to the dandyism of Beau Brummell and Oscar Wilde, then even further back, to the artifices of Restoration comedy, and finally to the seventeenth century, to the elaborate dressing up and showing off of Louis XIV's Versailles, seen by later camp figures as a sort of camp Eden. Camp behavior, costume, language and attitudes were taken up and extended in British pop, American Warholian pop, hippie exotica, punk, and most recently, in the postmodern predilection for quotation and pastiche. To say that camp cannot be equated with homosexuality is not, however, to deny that gays have been the marginal group to make the greatest *use* of a camp sensibility now widely available to every producer and consumer of popular culture.

What are the characteristics of the modern "uses of camp"? [16] For Booth, camp is distinguished by artificiality, stylization, theatricality, naivete, sexual ambiguity, tackiness, poor taste, and stylishness. The *sources* of camp are city life, pluralism, style, and learning (that is, possessing enough knowledge to be self-conscious). The *targets* of camp are conventional morality, good taste, marriage and family, suburbia, sports, and business. (And yes, the Playhouse regulars go "camping" in one episode, building a fire right in the middle of the Playhouse.) Booth sums up his description of camp and the camp persona thus, "All his life, the camp person remains a naughty child checking his elders" (57). Pee-wee Herman is, indeed, a naughty child checking his elders; but more to the point is the way the show *puts camp to work* as part of an overall strategy to playfully subvert the conventions of both sexuality and consumerism.

Camp, as an "operation of taste" [17] is everywhere apparent in the Playhouse. Booth claims that the most common manifestation of camp erudition over the past two centuries has been the habit of collecting. Beau Brummell, Robert de Montesquiou, and Boni de Castellane all had a passion for collecting. The epitome of the camp collector, however, was William Beckford, who built for himself an immense hideaway mixing Gothic, Oriental and Spanish styles. Inside this folly he amassed a huge collection of furniture, books and paintings, a place William Hazlitt described as "a cathedral turned into a toy shop" (51). Pee-wee's Playhouse too is a mad collector's dream: mixing periods (the forties, fifties and sixties); styles ("modern," "German Expressionist," "Tex-Mex," "early Easter Island," "neo-Aztec,"); and trashy retro objects, both kitsch and camp. The periods, styles and objects are, of course, not at all arbitrarily chosen: they have been selected for parodic recycling because they have their origins in what must have been the childhood and adolescence of the "real" Pee-wee Herman, the thirty-five year old Paul Reubens. Camp as cultural memory, resurrected for subversive ends, not to mention fun. Both the subversiveness and the fun lie in the way camp finds beauty in the seeming bizarre or outrageous, in the way it discovers the worthiness of something that is supposedly without value, here the debris of mass consumer culture.

But camp also has subversive fun with recycling and celebrating the kitschiest of sexual roles. We have seen how the show lovingly presents the icons of gay male pornography. And the Playhouse's ideas about femininity are equally pop: Miss Yvonne is the Burlesque Queen of camp theater, her femininity exaggerated into a parody of itself; the obese Mrs. Steve is the Divine stand-in, played by Shirley Stoler of Leonard Kastle's *The Honeymoon Killers*; and in the second season, Mrs. René is a sixties swinger decked out in mini-skirt and go-go boots. In camp, though, every sexual role can be satirized and celebrated, including the popular image of the homosexual.[18] Pee-wee's mincing step, affected gestures, exaggerated speech, obvious makeup and extreme fastidiousness are constant reminders of this popular image. It is an image most sharply brought into focus when Pee-wee plays interior decorator in the first show of the second season as he renovates the Playhouse. Ricardo, the Spanish-speaking soccer player, and Cowboy Curtis can only look on and roll their eyes as Pee-wee takes "ages" to decide where to place a chair.

It is, of course, inevitable that marriage, that haven in a heterosexual world, should come in for ridicule here. Pee-wee's stock response to the question of whether he likes something is, "Yes, but I wouldn't want to marry it!" But in the second season, during a mixed-sex slumber party at the Playhouse, Pee-wee does marry something he likes. Too excited to fall asleep, the pajama-clad guests decide to make a snack. Someone asks Pee-wee if he likes the snack and he gives his usual snappy comeback. This time, however, he has second thoughts.

"But why not?," he asks slyly. With a quick cut we find ourselves in the middle of a wedding ceremony in which Pee-wee takes as his beautiful bride . . . a bowl of fruit salad!

In advocating the dissolution of hard and inflexible sexual identities and moral rules, camp also pleads for an attitude of tolerance, for an acceptance of difference, a plea whose pathos often tips over into sentimentality. (Those who prefer the first season of *Pee-wee's Play-*

house to the second typically cite the latter's increased moralism and sentimentality.) John Waters has advanced this plea for acceptance by reconceiving one of camp's most dubious characters, the extremely fat woman. In *Hairspray*, even though Divine still *verges* on repulsiveness, both she and, especially, her daughter, played by Ricky Lake, are presented in an entirely sympathetic light and are, in fact, the lovable heroines of the film for their part in the struggle for a racially integrated Baltimore. (*Pee-wee's Playhouse*, fattist to the core, still has a ways to go here: Mrs. Steve is nasty and stupid, Mrs. René is a ditz.) In this plea for tolerance and acceptance, however, the camp figure typically exhibits a bitter wit, a form of "gay angst," the sadness of those who have internalized straight society's opinion of them.[19] But the Pee-wee persona appears to offer a new version of camp subjectivity in that one finds here no inner pathos, no inner struggle, no problem of feeling abnormal or wanting to hide it. Pee-wee's comic mode has most often been compared to that of Jerry Lewis in the way the two so spectacularly hystericize the male body. The difference, though, is that when Pee-wee turns into a woman, or oscillates between male and female, this transformation is not accompanied by any anxiety, as it always is with Lewis.[20] Perhaps this oscillation without anxiety represents a new, postmodernist stage of camp subjectivity, one distinguished by a capacity for zipping through sexual roles that is as fast and unremarkable as zapping through the channels.

Even before *Hairspray*, though, *Pee-wee's Playhouse* was already using camp to plead for the acceptance of racial difference as well as sexual difference (sexual difference, that is, in the sense of the variety of "nonstandard" or minority sexualities). One of the first and most immediate impressions of the show is the easygoing way it mixes races and ethnicities. For example, when Miss Yvonne asks Cowboy Curtis for a date, it is never mentioned (or in typical TV fashion made into an "issue" or "problem" to be addressed or resolved) that she is white and he is black. So too, in the second season much is made of Pee-wee's efforts to learn Spanish from Ricardo. Often Ricardo's lines are not translated, thus acknowledging the Hispanic children in the audience who will get them anyway. One important way the show deals with racial difference is to make it one among many differences (ethnic, sexual, cross-cultural), all of which are to be mixed together and appreciated rather than condemned: Cowboy Curtis, for example, is black, male, a cowboy and a gay pornographic icon. And in the Playhouse gang, one of the "real" little kids is Cher, an Asian girl dressed as Pocohantas. Although multiplying and celebrating "differences" can risk leveling or vitiating crucial political categories of difference, I would argue that here, in the context of Saturday morning television, the Playhouse's dizzying presentation of difference, accompanied by a constant plea for tolerance, shows a sharp understanding of how one might go about reordering (attitudes toward) difference, even under the gaze of the masters of the television universe.

The culmination of all of this campy play with difference occurs in one episode in which all questions of racial and sexual difference are projected onto a more spectacular difference, that between humans

and aliens. The camp passion for the horror/sf genre is well-known. In "Camp and the Gay Sensibility," Jack Babuscio argues that the horror genre, in particular, is susceptible to a gay interpretation.[21] Tourneur's *Cat People*, for example, could be seen as a film about the inner drives that threaten a person's equilibrium and way of life; Mamoulian's *Dr. Jekyll and Mr. Hyde*, about coping with pressures to conform and adapt; Siegal's *Invasion of the Body Snatchers*, about the masking of "abnormality" behind a facade of "normality," and so on. Thus it seems only appropriate that the Playhouse should one day be invaded by a monster from outer space, green of course, who is basically one big eye on a stalk that hops around. But after feeding the monster a submarine sandwich and getting to know it (Jambi grants Pee-wee's wish to translate monster-language into English), Pee-wee and the Playhouse gang make friends with "Roger," as he asks to be called, who soon becomes a Playhouse favorite. The moral of the story, of course, is not to be afraid of difference, whether it be sexual, racial or interplanetary.

But Roger also demonstrates the coexistence of the two perspectives on difference that I have argued are at the core of the show. As a giant eyeball, Roger is the metaphorical and metonymical equivalent of what is threatened in the fantasy of castration (an unconscious fear of difference), yet he is also "our new friend Roger" from another planet (a social and conscious wish for the acceptance of difference). Roger's pivotal role in mediating the show's two perspectives on difference is especially marked in the second season. Although he does not return to the Playhouse, except for a brief appearance at the slumber party, his huge bloodshot eyeball is embedded in Pee-wee's new helmet, which he dons at the end of each episode before waving goodbye to his friends and riding off on his scooter. Here, in the figure of Roger, we can see how the Playhouse manages to bring together all the possible conscious and unconscious valences that can be given to the familiar and the unfamiliar, the homey and the unhomey, the like-me and the not-like-me.

Although I have also argued that *Pee-wee's Playhouse* plays to both children and adults, it is obvious that those two levels of address are not and cannot be seen as entirely separate. Rather, the interest of this show lies in the way it re-presents masculinity right at the edge of the territory of the child, that morally quarantined and protected area. It is almost as if the show "recognizes" that as long as infantile sexuality remains conceptually off limits, it will not be possible to rethink sexual roles and sexed identities, masculine or otherwise. This is because the adult fantasy of childhood simplicity and happiness is a founding fantasy, one that offers the possibility of innocence to those who need to retain the idea of innocence itself. As long as this fantasy remains unexamined, so too will the fantasy of masculinity.

NOTES

1. Sigmund Freud, *Three Essays on Sexuality, The Standard Edition of the Complete Psychological Works of Sigmund Freud* (hereafter referred to

as *S.E.*), ed. James Strachey (London: Hogarth Press and the Institute of Psychoanalysis, 1962), vol. 6: 195.

2. Squire D. Rushnell, quoted by Matt Roush, "Pee-wee pops up on fall's lineup," USA Today (Sept. 9, 1986): 1D–2D.

3. Sigmund Freud, "The 'Uncanny'," *S.E.* vol. 17: 219–252.

4. Sigmund Freud, "The Dissolution of the Oedipus Complex," *S.E.* vol. 19: 175.

5. On Broadcast Arts, see *Millimeter* (September 1986), section on "Special F/X": 107–110; *Advertising Age* (May 13, 1985): 4; *On Location* (June 1982): 1.

6. I am very grateful to Stephen Oakes for answering my many questions about *Pee-Wee's Playhouse*. I particularly appreciate the response he gave to this paper when it was presented as a talk at a conference on television at Johns Hopkins University, organized by the Graduate Student Representative Organization on Mar. 7, 1987.

7. Margy Rochlin, "Pee-wee Herman" (interview), *Interview* (July 1987): 49.

8. Judy Price quoted by Roush, "Pee-wee pops up on fall's lineup" 2D.

9. Judy Price quoted by Roush, "Pee-wee pops up on fall's lineup" 2D.

10. David Diamond, "Is the Toy Business Taking Over Kids' TV?," *TV Guide* (June 13, 1987): 8. Also pushing CBS to look for newer kinds of children's programming is the growing strength of the movement to reregulate children's television in response to the consequences of the Reagan administration's radical deregulation policies.

11. Roush 2D.

12. Figures reported by Diana Loevy, "Morning Becomes Eccentric," *Channels* (Oct. 1986): 71.

13. Jack Barth, "Pee-wee TV," *Film Comment* vol. 22, no. 6 (Nov.–Dec. 1986): 79.

14. Bryan Bruce, "Pee Wee Herman: The Homosexual Subtext," *CineAction* no. 9 (Summer 1987): 3–6.

15. Mark Booth, *Camp* (London: Quartet Books, 1983).

16. Andrew Ross, "Uses of Camp," in *No Respect: American Intellectuals and Popular Culture,* forthcoming from Routledge, Chapman and Hall.

17. Ross, "Uses of Camp."

18. Booth 20: "In camp culture, the popular image of the homosexual, like the popular image of the feminine woman, is mimicked as a type of the marginal."

19. Jack Basbucio, "Camp and the Gay Sensibility," *Gays and Film,* ed. Richard Dyer (New York: New York Zoetrope, 1984) 47–48.

20. A comparison made by Joe McElhaney in his paper "I Know I Am But What Is He?: Looking at Pee-wee Herman," presented on the Lesbian/ Gay Male Reception panel at the 1986 meeting of the Society for Cinema Studies.

21. Basbucio 43.

The Playhouse of the Signifier:
Reading Pee-wee Herman
Ian Balfour

I. The Mail-Lady

I want to begin with a phrase from *Pee-wee's Playhouse*, the epithet for the character named Reba, who is called the "mail-lady," because her job is to deliver the mail. At first, the "mail-lady" seems to take her place as one among others in the system of socially-enlightened and enlightening figures in the playhouse: Cowboy Curtis (the black cowboy), Dixie (the woman taxidriver), and so on. In this simple but not too simple way, *Pee-wee's Playhouse* is one of the most progressive shows on network television. A stereotypical mailman is usually just that: a man. And to underscore the relation between the mail and the man, one Pee-wee episode features clips from a forties documentary on the United States Postal Service. The ostensible purpose of the documentary is to explain to the boys and girls at home where the "mail" comes from. And so we are treated to a panegyric on "the good old mailman" and footage of dozens of men sorting and delivering the mail, accompanied by a current voice-over chiming in "Boy! oh boy!" In the end, the enlightened Pee-wee can conclude: "Now I know everything about the mail." One of the many messages the mail-lady delivers, then, has to do with the very position from which she speaks and acts, established by the stark contrast between her and all those other mailmen. But Reba also delivers another kind of message. For Pee-wee's mail man is a "mail lady," a phrase that—given the over-determinations encoded by the sexual hijinks on the show—takes on an added resonance: the *male*-lady. And, indeed, the phrase the "mail-lady" can be switched into its converse, the lady-male, faster than one can change channels by remote.

It doesn't take very long to recognize the gay subtext, intertext, or just plain text of the Pee-wee episodes, most clearly legible in the figure of Jambi, the drag queen genie adorned with a turban, flaming red lipstick, and a single earring. Jambi—a literalization of television's ubiquitous "talking head"—is one of the few male characters on television to wear lipstick, and Pee-wee may be the only other one. In the daydream world of the playhouse, Jambi is the embodiment and purveyor of wish-fulfillment: Pee-wee's wish is Jambi's command. Upon each wish, all the boys and girls in the playhouse and television audience are directed to join in on the nonsensical ritual chant "Meck-a-lecka-high, meck-a-hiny-ho, meck-a-lecka-hi, mecka-chiny-ho," and its enunciation never fails to make the wish come true. If Jambi can grant everyone's wishes, then presumably he can grant his own as well, and Jambi obviously has chosen not to take up the mantle of the stereotypical, masculinist male.[1] (And it is no accident that the most macho character in the playhouse is also the most morally reprehensible, namely, Randy, the puppet bully who comes with all sorts of nasty ideological strings attached. It is Randy who is most often the target of object lessons like "Don't smoke," "Don't steal other people's apples" or "Don't make crank phone calls.") Pee-wee's sexuality is only somewhat more ambiguous than Jambi's, ambiguous enough to let network executives look the other way when reviewing ratings but also ambiguous enough to have caused them some consternation in the early months of the show. Perhaps the scandal of Pee-wee's sexuality is muted by his seemingly arrested development at an early age, but to judge from certain journalistic accounts Pee-wee is unnerving to many parents. Perhaps what is most unsettling about Pee-wee is the way he straddles the line between sexual knowledge and ignorance, as if he were somehow pre- and post-pubescent at the same time. In one episode of the second season, we glimpse Pee-wee reading the tail end of a story to some of the children in the playhouse. Pee-wee trails off with a sigh, saying "and so ends the story of the part-time dog." He then perks up to advise the boys and girls that next time he will tell the story of the "part-time boy." The part-time boy is, of course, Pee-wee: and this phrase too has to be understood in more than one sense. Part-time *boy*, because Pee-wee is part-time boy and part-time girl, if only in his most hysterical and histrionic moments. But also *part-time* boy because the other part of the time Pee-wee is something like a man.

The sexual asymmetry in *Pee-wee's Playhouse* is also visible in the distribution of looks—not gazes—among the male and female characters: the women are for the most part departures from TV's projected image of the attractive women, in the mode of, say, Vanna White. Of Miss Yvonne, Mrs. Steve, Dixie, Reba, and Mrs. René, only the body of Miss Yvonne—the woman known primarily for her "big hair"—is ever really on display, and then only in a gently satiric fashion. The male characters, by contrast, include Cowboy Curtis, a conventionally good-looking guy in the unconventional role of a black cowboy, and, most conspicuously, Tito, a body-building lifeguard who rarely wears more than a bathing suit.[2] The one time Tito is compelled to dress up, he wears a purple tuxedo jacket without shirt, tie, or pants. It is Tito, rather than any of the women, who ranks as the most eligible and desirable libidinal attachment in the topsy-turvy world of the playhouse.

A fleeting moment between Pee-wee and Tito will begin to illustrate how Pee-wee's show works almost systematically to skew gender stereotypes and to disturb what can only with difficulty be called the viewer's "identification" with the characters on the screen. One time when Miss Yvonne and Tito are dancing at a playhouse party, Pee-wee sidles up to the couple and asks to be allowed to cut in. Miss Yvonne graciously nods her approval, only to find that Pee-wee turns to Tito and starts dancing with him. No more than two or three seconds pass before Pee-wee chuckles his all-purpose laugh and begins dancing with Miss Yvonne as he was supposed to in the first place. Sexual order is restored, but the disruptive effect of the moment lingers on well after the plot has passed it by. The most elaborate and spectacular of these disruptive moments occurs when, in one episode, Cowboy Curtis has to be coached for his upcoming date with Miss Yvonne. Curtis complains of having never been out on a fancy date with a woman—one wonders if he's been on any kind of date with a woman— and the Cowntess (a cow who occasionally wears a muumuu) ropes Pee-wee into pretending to be Miss Yvonne for Curtis's benefit. Pee-wee protests at first that he doesn't "want to be a girl." But the Cowntess urges him to "Have some fun with it." Pee-wee then cheerfully adopts a falsetto voice and revels in his role as a woman for a long while, an interlude (or maybe just a lude) of some thirty seconds, a veritable eternity in Pee-wee time. Pee-wee muses about lipstick, hairspray and the dress he'll wear, while flirting with Cowboy Curtis, and decorum is only restored at the moment when Pee-wee balks at Curtis's attempt to kiss him goodnight. The explicit moral of this episode of *Pee-wee*—and there is hardly an episode that does not claim some high moral ground—is "Be Yourself," a motto that can be construed in more than one way. One imagines the reading the network and sponsors could offer with a sigh of relief: "Be Yourself," that is to say, boys will be boys, girls will be girls. For in the end the traditional shakedown of masculine boys and feminine girls is duly restored. But again the narrative resolution hardly obviates all that has gone before it. A principal effect of Pee-wee's histrionics, whatever the outcome of the episode, is to unsettle culturally codified notions of masculine and feminine, indeed to twist them around. When Captain Carl points out to Pee-wee that there's "a really twisted side" to him, Pee-wee's only response is "Thanks, Captain Carl." And his response is the same when Reba tells him that his is the most twisted address on her route. The exhortation "Be Yourself" includes the possibility of being your twisted self, which is to say a self less twisted according to prefabricated structures of desire.

The motif of a kiss that was not meant to be occurs in another crucial episode where gender roles are again staged. It's a rainy day and Miss Yvonne proposes that the members of the playhouse "play house." Miss Yvonne takes the role of Mommy and persuades a reluctant Pee-wee to be the Daddy. Daddy has to go off to work and as it happens Pee-wee wants to be an astronaut. When he returns home from out of this world with the gift of a moon rock, the gift isn't enough for Miss Yvonne and she asks if she can't have a little kiss? Pee-wee balks at the suggestion and declares that the game is over. Miss Yvonne, however, insists on continuing to play and it is only the arrival of the mail-lady that successfully interrupts and ends the game. Is Pee-wee here the little macho boy grossed out by the prospect of consorting with girls, or is he rather another sort of boy, one who simply isn't interested in girls? The film *Pee-wee's Big Adventure* features a scene in which Pee-wee resists the advances of Dotty and explains to her that there are some things about Pee-wee that she "couldn't understand, shouldn't understand." The visual and verbal signs of *Pee-wee's Playhouse* help us understand just what it was that Dotty shouldn't.

If the role of the mail-lady is somewhat enigmatic in the episode where she interrupts Pee-wee and Miss Yvonne, her message becomes louder and clearer in this last of the "gender" episodes I want to consider. This episode features a more explicit insistence on the letter and letters delivered by the mail-lady. One day when Reba arrives to deliver the mail, she has letters for everyone in the playhouse except Pee-wee, which prompts him to ask "Where's my mail?" Reba doesn't turn up any mail for Pee-wee who exclaims "That can't be! There must be some mistake! Everybody got mail except me!" The question "Where's my mail?"—not unlike Reagan's "Where's the rest of me?—is, among other things, a question about manhood. In an oblique response to Pee-wee's question, a number of "signifiers" are quickly summoned up, as if to dispel any doubts in the viewer's mind. Reba explains, commonsensically, that you have to write letters to get letters, whereupon Pee-wee takes up an elongated and swelled pencil (more or less a foot long) to begin a letter to Captain Carl, one of his many pen pals. The mail-lady asks Pee-wee whether he thinks he's got a big

enough pencil there and since "there" is the secret word of the day, the playhouse can erupt—has to erupt—in a communal scream. I scream, you scream, we all scream. Pee-wee's writing produces instantaneous results: Captain Carl shows up immediately, as if summoned by the letter addressed but not delivered to him. He hands Pee-wee another in a series of what used to be called phallic symbols: a telescope. (Pee-wee, one might say, suffers from telescopophilia.) Through this telescope Pee-wee sees a film clip of Errol Flynn gazing right back through a telescope at him. Pee-wee's "manhood" is confirmed momentarily by this specular, reflective chain of events, but even so the upshot of the scene is not quite enough to make the question "Where's my mail?" magically disappear.[3]

The harmless little phrase "the mail-lady." then, epitomizes a complex visual/verbal play linked to what is most disruptive and progressive in Pee-wee's show. We might well ask whether these tricks are for kids? The answer I think has to be: yes and no. The possibility of double or multiple reading marks Pee-wee's whole program from the beginning: and these readings do not always neatly divide between children's and adult's, though *Pee-wee's Playhouse* seems like the show to have most successfully walked this allegorical line. Much of the verbal banter relies on allusions, puns, and clichés that can hardly have any resonance for an audience of young children. But by the same token or rather by a different token (the token of difference), the "adult" sexual play in the playhouse can hardly be directed only to adults. Neither the subject constructed on the screen nor the viewer-subject constructed in the television audience is a homogenous one: indeed, there is no "subject" to speak of.

When Freud divided the neuroses of hysteria and obsession roughly along gender lines, hysteria aligned with the female and obsession with the male, he left room, as so often, for a certain or uncertain crossover. In a paper on "Hysterical Phantasies and Their Relation to Bisexuality," Freud proposed nine theses, the last and most tentative of which reads: "An hysterical symptom is the expression of both a masculine and a feminine unconscious sexual phantasy."[4] Freud goes on to qualify this claim, wondering about the universality of its validity, but he nonetheless feels able to express it first of all as a thesis. Hysterical symptoms, for Freud, tend to occur more often at some ages than others: it is primarily in the daydreams of adolescents that Freud locates the origins of hysteria.[5] (And Pee-wee is arguably television's adolescent daydreamer par excellence.) Thus Freud allows for the pronounced bisexual character of hysterical symptoms and for the possibility of a specifiably male hysteria. If we combine Freud's hypothesis on the bisexual character of hysteria with the haunting formulation from

Freud and Breuer that "hysterics suffer principally from reminiscences," then we have the formula for much of the action in *Pee-wee's Playhouse*. What is remarkable in this second formulation of Freud and Breuer is the general, the unqualified character of "reminiscences" which are not specified here as being traumatic ones.[6] It is perhaps too much to say that Pee-wee "suffers" from reminiscences, but certainly he is constituted by them: the show would be nowhere without its immense web of echoes, allusions and citations from television history and popular culture generally. (The network of citations, as it were, is usually quite medium-specific in Pee-wee's work: that is to say, the TV show is replete with TV references, whereas the film *Pee-wee's Big Adventure* is a parody and pastiche of a dozen film genres.) Pee-wee, at least the Pee-wee of the televised playhouse, can surely say, in David Byrne's words, "Television made me what I am," even if that "I" is suspended in a kind of permanent oscillation.

II. The Monster

The rhetoric of sexual difference that permeates *Pee-wee's Playhouse* is inscribed in a more encompassing text of cultural difference, whose messages are also conveyed largely via the letter. The actual letters delivered by Reba the mail-lady come from pen pals all over the world. Their contents are somewhat predictable, even cliched: a Japanese writes to Pee-wee-San telling of living in a house with paper walls, watching Godzilla and eating raw fish; an English child writes about Big Ben and explains that it's not a person but a clock, and so on. The "world" of *Pee-wee's Playhouse* is large enough to include even the People's Republic of China, where Pee-wee also has a pen pal. The character of Globy is always on hand to point out where the letters originate and to offer geography lessons emphasizing that there is something more to the world than the United States: in its most utopian moments, the world emerges as something of a Globy Village. Attention to geographical difference is complemented by an attention to linguistic difference unparalleled on Saturday morning television. Foreign phrases riddle especially the episodes featuring pen pals and, in the second season (which originates no longer from New York but L.A.), the character of Ricardo often speaks at length in Spanish, sometimes translating and sometimes not. In addition to this worldly difference, the other-worldly often impinges on the territory of the playhouse in the form of aliens. A number of the "Penny" cartoons feature reveries about aliens and the not so clear boundaries between them and us. A whole episode of the second season is structured around a character named Zyzzybalubah who is literally out of this world: virtually every segment addresses translation and transportation, from the whole bag of mail Pee-wee receives from the mail-lady to a Penny cartoon about Christopher Columbus, from a magic screen documentary on the solar system to a French cartoon with a song by Edith Piaf. The humanist's motto has always been "nothing human is alien to me"; the unwritten motto in Pee-wee's playhouse reads "nothing alien is alien to me."

The most extreme instance of cultural difference occurs in one episode where a gigantic green one-eyed monster stalks the playhouse. The monster succeeds in scaring everyone, including the family of dinosaurs that live in the mouse-hole.[7] He terrorizes the playhouse screaming real loud until Pee-wee invokes his weekly wish and asks Jambi to translate from the original monsterese. The green giant turns out to be a jolly kid named Roger who explains that he and his friends—regular viewers of *Pee-wee's Playhouse*—were frightened at first by the show but that they felt a lot better now that they understood it. The magical translation permits the playhouse to get back to normal, or almost. There remains one absolutely frightening thing, frightening even to Roger the monster. A certain grotesque saleman arrives every episode at the playhouse claiming to make an incredible offer, whereupon the door is promptly slammed in his immense face. (I return later to speculate on why this salesman is so scary.) As far as it goes, this monstrous fable of cultural difference may be delivering the merely liberal message that everyone is tolerable in their own way. We can call it liberal though it is certainly radical by Saturday morning TV standards. Far more radical is the Penny cartoon which follows the monster sequence, for it contains a virtual manifesto on kids' rights— it takes up the questions of why kids don't have the right to live where they want to live, to go to school only when they please, and so forth. Penny posits that parents might be "totally different" from the kids or again that parents might "never be at all like the kid." So relentless is *Pee-wee's Playhouse* in its pursuit of difference that it threatens to dissolve even the bonds of filiation and family resemblance, making of them mere legal fictions.

What then about Pee-wee's own parents? We never get a glimpse of them or even hear of them second-hand. For all we know, Pee-wee may have generated spontaneously into the adolescent age he is stuck in. Pee-wee often dons a helmet that features a single eye, giving him three in all, which identifies tangentially with Oedipus, at least in one reading of the Oedipus myth. "Oedipus had one eye too many," Hölderlin could write. Is Pee-wee really an Oedipus figure who has successfully done away with his father? Not exactly, because if it is television that has made Pee-wee what he is, then his real relations are his TV ancestors: Captain Kangaroo, Howdy-Doody, Soupy Sales,

Mr. Rogers, and, in a somewhat different vein, Jerry Lewis. At the thematic level, the many differences between Pee-wee and his precursors hardly need to be rehearsed: no kid's show has staged sexual difference, for example, quite in the manner of Pee-wee. The principal formal quality that divides Pee-wee's program from that of his TV parents is speed. Indeed, the show looks something like *Mister Rogers* on speed. In a half-hour show three or four visitors might saunter by Mr. Rogers's house, at a pace that befits the cardigan and slippers lifestyle. The first episode of Pee-wee introduces a bewildering array of two dozen characters, of all shapes and sizes: live people, talking animals, and objects personified. The viewer of *Sesame Street* may learn arithmetic but the viewer of Pee-wee experiences what Kant called the mathematical sublime, in which the imagination is so overloaded that comprehension cannot keep up with apprehension.[8] The manic pace of the show might be ascribed to television's gradual erosion of the attention span, which has created the necessity of providing the viewer with something new and different every few moments. But this same speed celebrates as much as it taxes the imagination. "Think fast," Pee-wee once says to Mr. Window as he throws something in his direction, and it's this advice to think fast that is the principle, the motto, and the threat of Pee-wee's program.

III. The Salesman

On Saturday morning network television, Pee-wee's is the only show with live people. Totally surrounded by cartoons, Pee-wee's program is defined in relation to them. No Pee-wee episode passes without the screening of part of an old cartoon—usually its tail end—and the segment often has an oblique or allegorical relation to the enveloping action of the show. So for example, in the "sexual difference" episode— the one where Pee-wee pretends to be Miss Yvonne on a date—the cartoon features a young boy prancing around on stage and crooning in a falsetto voice, echoing, as it were, Pee-wee's own role in the show. But aside from any thematic connections, the main interest of the old cartoons lies in their formal function, for Pee-wee's show surrounds the cartoon, not unlike the way cartoons surround Pee-wee. The rhythm of the show is such that the old cartoon clip from the 30s or 40s usually precedes by several minutes the Penny cartoon, the spectacular clay animation sequence that is one of the signatures of the show. The Penny cartoon, so thoroughly postmodern in its uncanny primitiveness, displaces and transfigures the older cartoon format even as it cites its predecessor.

The very first Pee-wee episode was marked by an almost rigorous system of citations from popular culture of every period since the 20s: cartoons from the 30s, beatnik jazz musician puppets from the 50s, Go-Go dancers from the 60s, and so on. The three kids on the shows of the first season are named Opal, Elvis, and Cher. Pee-wee's program, then, becomes something of an epitome of pop cultural television history, its brief allegory. This is not a claim one can prove exactly but I can report to you an anecdote—and this marks the empirical moment of this study—that the two-year-old of a friend of mine was so taken with the first few Pee-wee episodes she saw that she began to call the television set "Pee-wee." It may be too much simply to identify Pee-wee and TV, but few programs have quite the pervasively citational, recombinant texture of Pee-wee's program.

Fredric Jameson has taught us to think of the products of mass culture in terms of reification and utopia, the two poles of a dialectic at work in every text simultaneously.[9] Much as Walter Benjamin argued that there is no document of culture that is not at the same time a document of barbarism, so Jameson suggests, in polemical opposition to aestheticist defenders of high art, that a utopian element lurks in even the most transparently reified object of late consumer capitalism. In the first volume of *Capital*, Marx had contended that a certain movement of reification was built into the commodity and its world, as one moment of a double movement that takes the rhetorical form of a chiasmus, in which things are personified and people are reified. Marx speaks of "an antithesis, immanent in the commodity, between use-value and value, between private labour which must simultaneously manifest itself as directly social labour, and a particular concrete labour, between the conversion of things into persons, and persons into things; the antithetical phases of the metamorphosis of the commodity are the developed forms of motion of this immanent contradiction.[10] No network television show can resist the gravitational pull of the commodity, but the Pee-wee show does its unlevel best to resist or reroute that force. The strategy seems to be that in order to counter the reification of people, one should personify everything in sight. Personification, for Marx, is the master trope of commodity fetishism, and Pee-wee counteracts a certain commodity fetishism precisely through an excessive, hyperbolic reveling in personification. We always knew chairs had arms and legs but in Pee-wee's world the chair, named Chairy, also has a face and a voice, like you and me. Conky, the beatbox robot, Globey the globe, Mr. Window: these are all characters among others. It's difficult to tell the people from the things and vice versa. This relentless personification works in two registers, low tech and high tech—or perhaps as we should now say "mecka-lecka high tech." The latter is the medium for the astonishing visual effects of the clay animation sequences, effects that make the surrounding Saturday morning cartoons pale in comparison. The achievement of these effects are ascribable in no small measure to the resources of capital in the first place. Yet this force is countered thematically by the celebration of a whole range of low tech activities: making a puppet out of an old sock, a space helmet out of a paper bag, a little monster out of a potato and four pencils.

Somewhat in the same vein—and here we return to the scary figure of the salesman—*Pee-wee's Playhouse* does its best to keep the cash nexus and the commodity world at bay, figured each week in the

shutting out of the salesman and his incredible offer. The primary form of exchange in the playhouse is barter, and its medium—at least for the first season—is tin foil, material for the primitive accumulation of Pee-wee's foil ball. Literal money almost never appears on the show except as it forms the eyes of Penny, which are soon transmuted in a kind of Blakean fantasy into the medium of imagination and desire. The one time the salesman actually gets in the door of the playhouse, it turns out that he really does have an incredible offer: free foil. But the salesman only enters the playhouse during a party, a saturnalian or carnivalesque moment in which the world is momentarily turned upside down. This entry of the salesman with his offer of free foil clearly marks it as the most patently utopian moment of the show because as everyone knows, there is no such thing as free foil.

IV. The Sphinx

All of the characters in the playhouse take their place under the presiding deity of a sphinx, whom we see in the opening sequence of every show, perched on top of the playhouse, shifting his or her head and smiling knowingly. It's as much an American as an Egyptian or Greek sphinx, because its head resembles the immense bust of George Washington on Hitchcock's Mount Rushmore. The sphinx of Greek antiquity, the reader will recall, has the head and breasts of a woman, the body of a dog, the tail of a serpent, the wings of a bird, the paws of a lion, and a human voice: in other words, a Pee-wee character *avant la lettre*. The classical sphinx proposed a riddle, a question whose answer, as only Oedipus knew, was "man." And the consequence of a wrong answer to the riddle was death. In *Pee-wee's Playhouse*, "man" is the question not the answer, but a question whose consequences are only somewhat less grave.

NOTES

1. One incident goes against the grain of this movement, namely, when in a carnivalesque party atmosphere, Pee-wee returns his regular gift of a wish to Jambi. Against all expectation, Jambi chooses to have a female genie head as his companion. But this is the sort of exceptional moment that proves the contrary rule (which is the rule of the contrary).

2. The Tito figure is replaced in the second season by Ricardo, though the two do not entirely overlap in their functions.

3. For all the unsettling of gender stereotypes, however, *Pee- wee's Playhouse* remains largely phallocentric. When this paper was first given as part of a conference "On Television" at Johns Hopkins University, Neil Hertz remarked that a viewing of several episodes suggested that the show was "about a little boy's penis," as something of an autonomous signifier. That is to say, the show is not even about a little boy's relation to his penis but simply about the "thing" itself.

4. Sigmund Freud, *Collected Papers,* trans. Joan Rivière (Basic Books: New York, 1959), Vol. 2: 57.

5. Sigmund Freud, *Collected Papers* 51.

6. In the first of Freud's theses, there is no absolute specification that the reminiscence be a traumatic one. Freud writes: "The hysterical symptom is the memory-symbol of the operation of certain (traumatic) impressions and experiences." *Collected Papers* 55. Here trauma appears in parenthesis, which is a good way to describe the status of hysteria in cultural representation and production.

7. When this paper was given at the University of Toronto, one member of the audience rightly pointed out that the dinosaur family is the only family unit given any prominence in the show, which implies perhaps that, from the point of view(s) of the playhouse, the nuclear family has gone the way of the dinosaur.

8. The Kantian motif of the infinite as it pertains to the analytic of the sublime surfaces at the verbal level in *Pee-wee's Playhouse* and *Pee Wee's Big Adventure* when in order to put an end, paradoxically, to an exchange of lines like "Did not"—"Did so"—"Did not"—"Did so," Pee-wee will simply blurt out: "Infinity."

9. See Fredric Jameson's important essay, "Reification and Utopia in Mass Culture," *Social Text* vol.1, no.1: 130–148.

10. Karl Marx, *Capital*, Volume 1, trans. Ben Fowkes (Harmondsworth: Penguin, 1976): 209.

"Going Bonkers!": Children, Play and Pee-wee
Henry Jenkins III

We've watched them gaping at the screen.
They loll and slop and lounge about,
and stare until their eyes pop out. . . .
They sit and stare and stare and sit
until they're hypnotized by it,
until they're absolutely drunk
with all that shocking ghastly junk.

Roald Dahl, 1964 (145–146)

Roald Dahl's *Charlie and the Chocolate Factory*, a Dantesque vision of the faults and foibles of contemporary children, reserves special ire for the young television addict, Mike Teavee. When we first encounter Mike, he is so preoccupied with a television gunfight, "his eyes glued to the screen," eighteen cap guns assembled at his side, that he refuses to be distracted even by the news that he is the recipient of one of the much coveted Golden Tickets: "Didn't I tell you not to interrupt! This show's an absolute Whiz-banger! It's terrific! I watch it every day! I watch all of them every day, even the crummy ones, where there's no shooting!" (39). Once inside the mysterious chocolate factory, where the punishment always fits the crime, the sensation-crazed youngster receives his just deserts; he is "televised." A giant camera "split[s him] up into millions of tiny little pieces which are so small that you can't see them, and these little pieces are shot out into the sky by electricity" (134). In order to be projected through the medium which he loves, Mike must be transformed, atomized and shrunk to fit within the cramped confines of the television world. Meanwhile, the moralistic Oompa-Loompas sing of the dire consequences of excessive viewing:

It rots the senses in the head!
It kills the imagination dead!
It clogs and clutters up the mind!
It makes the child so dull and blind
he can no longer understand
a fantasy, a fairyland!
His brain becomes as soft as cheese!
His powers of thinking rust and freeze!
He cannot think—he only sees! (146)

157

Dahl's nightmarish parable about a youngster physically confined within the television set that has already totally captured his imagination merely exaggerates the hyperbolic claims activists and empirical researchers make about the negative "effects" of television viewing on children. Such accounts reject, from the outset, any notion that children might exercise selective viewing strategies or that they may bring their own agenda to bear on television rather than remaining passive consumers of its preset curriculum. Befitting their roles as academic apologists for the media reformers, their research questions already presume that what is to be investigated is the impact which television has on children and not the impact that children's viewing strategies might have on program-preferred meanings. Children are preconceived as victims, not users, of television and their viewing habits are stripped of any social context, allowing the researchers, and the activists who feed upon their work, to rationalize their own efforts to exert greater control over the children's playtime.

More recently, however, several scholars, working within the Anglo-American Cultural Studies tradition, have sounded a welcome note of discord to the monotonous chorus of professional Oompa-Loompas. Robert Hodge and David Tripp (1986) insist that we should begin from the assumption that youngsters find the shows they watch somehow meaningful and that we should pay closer attention to the process by which these television meanings are negotiated between young viewers, texts and contexts. Hodge and Tripp effectively reverse the logic of existing media research; no longer is Mike Teavee perceived as transformed by his encounters with television, rather, Mike fragments television content and reshapes it to respond to his own cultural, social, cognitive and emotional needs:

> Television sends out messages, which are interpreted and acted on by social agents responsible for their actions. . . . We need to know how television carries meanings; how different minds will interpret and use these meanings, particularly children's growing and developing minds; and how such meanings are likely to be enacted in the real world of the child viewer. (2–3)

This article represents my own provisional response, as a concerned father as well as a media scholar, to those central questions: an examination of the ways in which a particular group of five Madison Kindergartners made sense of and found pleasure in a specific Saturday morning show, *Pee-wee's Playhouse*. The nature of the meanings produced, and even to some degree, the strategies for meaning production are particular to the reception context, the broadcast material, and the specific socio-cultural experience of the individual child. But a Geertzian "thick description" (Geertz 1973) of how a limited group responds to a favored show can illustrate how social factors shape the kinds of meanings produced and how children's characteristic viewing strategies reflect the process of making sense of program materials.

As a parent, I felt I might bring special insight to the discussion. While "Kidspeak" proves highly resistent to adult interpretation and, as we will see, works to create an autonomous space for children, my prior exposure to the rituals, slang, and norms of kindergarten society and my familiarity with most of the children's common cultural references helped me to recognize at least some of the complex connections underlying their fragmentary and often poorly articulated comments about the program content. My own enthusiasm for *Pee-wee's Playhouse* granted me freer interaction with the children than traditional media effects researchers for whom all "kidvid" is treated as the "same stuff" without much regard to the particulars of program content.

In researching this paper, I sought to create a more natural environment than the traditional laboratory setting, one in which the children could interact with each other and the television program in a more spontaneous fashion. Four of my son's classmates were invited to our apartment to participate in a "Pee-wee Party."[1] While some activities (drawing, storytelling, etc.) were designed to provoke specific feedback about the program content, plenty of time was available for children to simply play with each other in an unstructured, often unnervingly chaotic fashion. The party setting provided a catalyst that intensified children's normal responses to program content, creating a situation where they would be more open to examination. It also allowed me to examine not simply how individual children reacted to program content but how those responses were used in their interaction with their social peers, how they provided content for play, jokes, and conversations, and how television meanings were integrated back into lived experience.

Watching Children Watch TV: Play as a Viewing Strategy

> Q: What did you think of the way they watched the show? Did they, er, seem to be having a good time?
> A: (long pause) well, ah, most of the time. But, some of the time, they were going wild—bonkers!. . . . They were hopping on the hoppity-hop and not watching the show! They were paying no attention to the show!—Henry, 5 1/2

Henry's distress over his playmates' conduct at our "Pee-wee Party" echoes concerns many parents feel when they witness the frankly irreverent attitude young viewers display toward a particularly favored text. Although television viewing is obviously a source of pleasure for children, they rarely watch the screen with rapt attention and frequently dash from one activity to another with only occasional glances towards the screen (Palmer 1986). At our "party," children dragged several of Henry's toys into the living room. A large stuffed He-Man doll was used alternately as a "seat belt," lying across the lap of several children, or as an imaginary playmate, addressed as a "naughty" child and even spanked, to the objection of some participants who felt he was not being "bad." One girl watched part of the episode through the eyes of a Man-at-Arms mask. One boy pushed a firetruck around on the floor. A Silverhawks doll, with a telescopic eye, was passed around the circle so that all could get a chance to look at the "tiny tiny tiny TV set" through its distorting lens. Kids grabbed for grapes or raced to the bathroom. To adult eyes, this mode of reception may appear haphazard or lackadaisical. If, however, a parent attempts to recapture the set or worse, turn it off, they are apt to receive resounding protests. For the children involved, the interaction is of immense importance and the challenge facing the researcher is to account for the kinds of pleasures and meanings that could be produced in this context.

We might begin with a deceptively simple assertion: for children, watching television is a type of play. Those attempting to describe the cognitive activity of spectators frequently resort to the metaphor of a game played between viewer and text. David Bordwell (1986) writes, for instance, "The perceiver in effect bets on what he or she takes to be the most likely perceptual hypothesis" (31). Bordwell's game is goal-centered and rule-governed. Participants seek to reconstruct the event chain and the textual world, to make predictions about likely outcomes of story actions and to learn whether or not they have guessed correctly, to achieve a sense of "unity" and "coherence" from the fragments of the text. In doing so, their projections are constrained, at least in part, by textual properties, by reading "rules" imposed upon them intrinsically by the work itself and extrinsically by their interpretive community. "Grown-ups" like to play games of this type; preschoolers rarely do. Bruno Bettelheim (1987) draws sharp distinctions between children's play and adult games:

> Generally speaking, play refers to the young child's activities characterized by freedom from all but personally imposed rules (which are changed at will), by free-wheeling fantasy involvement, and by the absence of any goals outside of the activity itself. Games, however, are usually competitive and are characterized by agreed-upon, often externally imposed, rules, by a requirement to use the implements of the activity in the manner for which they were intended and not as fancy suggests, and frequently by a goal or

purpose outside the activity, such as winning the game. Children recognize early on that play is an opportunity for pure enjoyment, whereas games may involve considerable stress. (37)

For young children, watching television lacks the textual imperatives that confront adults. Their viewing is unstructured and exploratory. It is responsive to self-imposed rules only, and those are often temporary and provisional. Left to their own devices, children frequently display little interest in "following the plot" or locating the moral behind a particular episode, "games" that require skills which they have imperfectly mastered and that assume goals which they do not yet share. Rather, they watch to have "fun," a pleasure that is found more often in "sensation," and even incoherence, rather than in causality and unity. Spectacle displaces narrative as the dominant appeal of the text. A youngster who has a favorite film or program on videotape often fastforwards past the slow expository passages on a second viewing to get to the "good parts," to find the place where Large Marge's eyes pop from her head or where Slimer smears the Ghostbusters with noxious green goo, displaying increasingly less interest in character motivation or causal logic.

This difference is readily apparent in the kinds of stories that children choose to create about their favorite television characters. Consider an excerpt from a bedtime storytelling session with my son:

> Once upon, er, next, he goes back to his place and then he goes to sleep and then at the crack of dawn, he wakes up and then plays with his toys and right when it's. . . . Then when it's 6:30 he rushed to the TV set to watch He-Man and She-Ra. He likes to do the same things I do on Saturday morning. . . . And, then, after he watches the show, he goes out and wakes his dog, Speck, and he asks him, "Should we have breakfast right now today?" and he goes, "Not right now," and then Pee-wee says "Okay" and then he goes play with his toys some more and then after that, he takes a piece of paper and puts it in front of his paper ball and then he crumbles it up with that and then he says, he asks to his dog, "should we have breakfast now?" and then his dog says, "Yes, let's" and then the breakfast song again from the movie . . . And then he takes his fortune and it says, "Leave the house today, Urgent." . . . [Whispers] He has some books and he has to take them back to the library and the library will be boiling up mad at him because he bringed the book back a hundred days later from the day he is supposed to.

I view this story as a transitional work between child-like emphasis on "sensation" and adult-like emphasis on linearity and causality. Henry has partially accepted more adult story structures but still chooses to pursue childish pleasures that draw him from narrative logic. While there is a kind of rough sequential patterning here ("and then"), borrowed from his own Saturday morning routine and from the opening of *Pee-wee's Big Adventure*, there is only limited causal logic linking the various story events. We are well into it before Pee-wee's narrative goal is firmly established: he needs to return some books to the library. But, even then, he is consistently sidetracked along the way to water the neighbor's lawn, to play with mechanical gadgets, to fight with the boy next-door, etc:

> And then he can't get past Francis's house. Francis is out, outdoors and he is right where Pee-wee is about to step and he says [mimics], "Good morning, Pee-wee Herman," and he says, "It's my birthday and my father says I can have anything that I want and guess what I want?" and he says, "A new bank teller?" and he says, "No! Your bike!" and then Pee-wee says, then Pee-wee rolls down on the ground and goes HAHAHAHA! and then Francis says, "What's so funny, Pee-wee?" and then Pee-wee says, "It's not for sale" and then the people start arguing and it sounds like this: "I know you are but what am I?" "You're an idiot!" "I know you are but what am I? I know you are but what am I?" . . . . and then after that, he says he wouldn't sell his bike for all the money in the world and he says, "Well, I will just drive through galaxies and get money from two worlds" and then he says, "not even for that price." Pee-wee says that and then he goes to the library. And he drops the books off in the inside of the thing and the library-man walks around and says [shouts], "Pee-wee Herman! You stop that! You got this book here a hundred days late and you have to give us the money from two galaxies!" and Pee-wee says, "I can't give you that price!" and then the librarian says, "you have to!" and Pee-wee says, "It's not a deal, okay!" and the librarian says, "Okay, we'll get out this gun and kill you!" . . . .

An adult telling this same story might have drawn the obvious connection between Francis's offer of money for the bike and the library's absurd demand that Pee-wee pay them "all the money in two galaxies," thereby creating unity and closure within the work. Henry does not. Problems are not so much resolved as forgotten. Yet, what may sound to adult ears like digressions are really the heart of the tale, an important source of pleasure.

Although, as Hodge and Tripp note, children have generally absorbed adult viewing strategies by age 12, these skills develop slowly and often under some duress: these skills depend upon social knowledge that must be learned over time; the very notion of rule-governed or goal-centered games requires a certain degree of cognitive and social development; the rules represent adult-imposed restraints upon the interpretive process that may repress or redirect the joy found in "pure" play with media content. Learning to play (or read) by the sanctioned rules may allow for their admission into adult society, but at the high cost of repressed spontaneity. All too often, such socialization is accompanied by feelings of inadequacy and anxiety.

Children's play is not ideologically innocent; it is the primary means by which children absorb the values of their society and master both their own bodies and other culturally-significant materials (Vygotsky 1976). It is by experimenting with various social roles, by toying with a variety of different rules for structuring experience, that the child comes to explore the preferred meanings of his or her cultural community and to develop self-mastery. Such play may and often does reinforce parental values, but it also contains a countersocial potential; it may be used to express the child's feelings of outrage over the expectations imposed upon him or her by the social formation, over the pressure to conform to rules that constrain instinctual life and frustrate personal desire.

Over time, as the reality principle comes to restrain the pleasure principle, the "pure" enjoyment of childhood play becomes a kind of "guilty pleasure" that must be rationalized through the guise of some more purposeful or goal-centered activity. Consequently, parents often defend their children's television viewing through appeals to educational benefits or "pro-social" values. Asked to describe the qualities they regard as "desirable in a program aimed at kindergarten age children," all of my adult respondents emphasized education over entertainment:

"The show must have a point to it. It must educate her either with a situation she could encounter or something she would face at school."

"Programs that teach the child something as well as entertain."

"Any show where there is a moral at the end. Even the action/ adventure cartoons (He-Man, She-Ra, etc.) have a lesson to teach."

"We have normal concerns about sex and violence and nonsensical shows."

Some openly acknowledged the contradiction between their goals and those of their children:

"I would like her to watch more educational type shows, but I also want her to enjoy it."

Others expressed discomfort over their child's indiscriminate pursuit of pleasure:

"He would overindulge in cartoons if I let him . . . but I limit what he can watch. He could watch cartoons for hours."

When parents watch television with their children, they frequently spend much of their time instructing them in the "rules," the "normal" interpretive strategies, they use in making sense of narratives, encouraging the children to make predictions about the plot or to locate character motivations, directing wandering attention back toward the screen at moments that seem of especial importance in the unfolding story. But children watching television without adult interference make very different kinds of comments and adopt very different kinds of reading strategies. Their "fun" comes precisely from their unbounded play with program material. They may cluster together events across a limited time span and seem to respond quite emotionally to these two- or three-minute segments. But little attempt is made to integrate narrative material across the full span of the episode. Rather, the kids watch the show in short spurts, allowing their attention to wander to other things, until it is again drawn back toward full concentration during moments of intense spectacle or heightened sensation. In a social viewing situation such as I observed, their sudden and insistent outbursts cue each other to watch a particularly promising passage:

Bill: Dinosaurs! Dinosaurs!
. . . .
Cassandra: The ants!
Henry!:   Yeah. That's the ant family
. . . .
Bill: A vacuum cleaner?!!
Henry: This is a silly family. I mean, see what the vacuum cleaner does. It just sucks up their carpet and it just gets everything sucked.
Bill: They really know how to clean up! They sucked the ball up! Maybe they'll suck themselves up!
. . . .
Jackie: Hey, these cartoons look funny!

Regular viewers of *Pee-wee's Playhouse* develop a strong sense of its formulaic structure that they rely on to determine which moments offer the greatest potential reward and which can be missed in good conscience:

Several: Watch the crazy fridge!
Henry: Yeah, Look at his refridge. Something crazy is going to happen. It's a crazy refridge. I mean, see—why!!!

The remainder of this paper will offer a description of children at play with the materials of their cultural environment and with the roles they are invited to assume as socialized members of the kindergarten community. Such a viewing strategy is far more experiential than interpretive, far more interested in finding pleasure than in making meanings. But it does produce meanings, however atomistically, that are of vital importance to the children involved. These meanings are localized and transitory, reflecting an immediate response both to specific program content and to particular concerns of pre-school life. But the meaning-production process described here—the resistance to adult dominance over their cultural space, the process of textual fragmentation and the accruing of associated meanings around the bits of program material, the translation of narrative content into images for drawings and jokes, the forging of intertextual linkages between seemingly disparate texts, the manipulation of modal relations to create proximity or distance from represented material, etc.—reflect children's characteristic ways of making sense of television texts.

TV "Ket": Childhood as (Candy) Counter-culture

"You'll love it! It's really gross!"—Cassandra, 5 1/2

"The most fun we had writing the show was when we could come up with stuff we knew was going to kill the five-year-olds."—Paul Reubens (a.k.a. Pee-wee Herman) (Gertler, 1987, 102)

These youngsters, undergoing an awkward transition from the relative freedom of their pre-school lives into the institutional demands of kindergarten, generally found great pleasure in the unstructured activity of watching children's television: "Saturdays are really neat. I get up and I don't have school and then I watch what I want to watch" (Bill). But parental opposition to the kinds of sensation-centered programming preferred by children can transform gratification into an act of open defiance. Although it has attracted a cult following among some college students, many adults find *Pee-wee's Playhouse* highly abrasive, and experience discomfort over its flashing colors and screeching noises, over the androgyny and spasticity of its central figure, over the playhouse that *Rolling Stone* (1987) described as "the collision of *The Cabinet of Dr. Caligari* with a raspberry-and-lime Jell-O mold constructed by Disney technicians recovering from Taiwan flu" (38). It is precisely the kind of "pointless" or "nonsensical" show that parents hate. Bill reported that his father "won't let me watch that crazy show." Kate, acknowledging that "it's kinda funny-talking," said that her father does not like her to watch it either, though she frequently views it anyway. My son responded that "finally, at last," they would be able to watch *Pee-wee* at our party: "And your parents won't be able to do anything about it!" Several of the children giggled appreciatively. For these children, part of the appeal of watching *Pee-wee* at a friend's house was the opportunity to circumvent parental authority, to push toward greater control over their recreational life and thereby to assert a degree of autonomy from the adult-dominated world. These playful children are discovering the pleasures of resistance.

Alison James (1979) offers a similar vision of a children's culture cast in opposition to adult norms and satisfying the growing youngster's need for greater personal autonomy. Her examination of children's consumption of cheap confections (called "kets" in certain British children's slang, a term also used by adults to refer to "rubbish") suggests that youngster's favorite sweets may provide entry into an "alternative" cultural system, constructed from the "rubbish" and remnants of adult society, satisfying drives and desires basic to prepubescent sexuality while opposing parental efforts to bring those drives under control: "The eating of dirty, decaying 'kets' is condemned by adults and it is this very condemnation which allows the child to assume control over at least one of his orifices" (306). This confectionery economy operates, consciously or unconsciously, to confuse adult categories and to resist parental intrusion, placing the greatest value on precisely those things that "grown-ups" find worthless and undesirable:

> By confusing the adult order children create for themselves considerable room for movement within the limits imposed upon them by the adult society. This deflection of adult perception is crucial for both the maintenance and continuation of the child's culture and for the growth of the concept of the self of the individual child. (295)

Children's candies adopt names of things "grown-ups" find distasteful or of things that would not normally be consumed (candy cigarettes, bubble gum cigars, jelly worms, gummy mummies, etc.), assume unusual textures (rubbery, slimy, etc.) or synthetic flavors, provoke strong and sometimes unpleasant sensations (Pop Rocks that literally explode on the tongue), demand to be eaten in unsanitary ways (sucking, slurping, fingering, blowing), and come in flamboyant patterns or clashing color combinations that disturb our normal aestheticsensibility. Such sugary delights seduce children into playing with their food, even though they recognize parental prohibitions against doing so. Semi-digested chewing gum is removed and stretched into saliva-coated sculptures. Slobbery suckers are passed from mouth to mouth as a kind of kiddie communion. Children take pleasure in confections that sizzle and crackle in their mouths and turn their tongues lurid purple: "Kets are not distanced from the body . . . .Hands become covered in 'ket' and the normal eating conventions, instilled by parents during early childhood, are flagrantly disregarded" (304).

Such logic pervades the cultural world of contemporary children. TOYS Я US has been transformed into junior galleries of the grotesque.

Its shelves are crammed with Mad Balls with protruding eyeballs, cans of mucus-like green slime, dolls with bad breath or which make "disgusting noises, Garbage Pail Kids bubble gum cards which crudely parody popular consumer goods and playfully represent various bodily functions, monster labs where would-be "mad scientists" can watch acid decay the flesh from the body of hideous toy monsters. Playground slang abounds with frank references to "fungus," "snot" and "poop." The cable children's channel, Nickelodeon, features scatological comedy programs like *Turkey Television* and *You Can't Do That on Television*, offering *Monty Python*-style humor for the youngsters. Their most successful program, *Double Dare*, invites kids to swim through vats of assorted goops and to fling food at each other. *Finders Keepers*, another popular children's game show, has the young contestants trash a model house, with rooms like Granny's Kitchen and Dad's Den, in search of prizes.

James's analysis would suggest that children find these "gross" things appealing precisely because their parents find them so unappealing. Their meaning comes through opposition, through allowing youngsters to carve for themselves a cultural space "just for kids," to construct a society that is responsive to their whims and that allows them a momentary release from adult control.

Pee-wee's Playhouse seems ideally constructed for these preschoolers' needs: a garishly-colored, sensation-saturated, slickly-packaged televisual "ket," something like "Pop Rocks" for the mind. Its fragmentary structure encourages a playful response from its fans while its abrasive edge keeps (at least some) parents from intruding into their play space and claiming it as their own or imposing strictures upon its use. If Pee-wee actively offends some parents, so much the better, since it is through resistance to parental pressures that the kids are able to make the program truly their own. Like all good "kets," it lacks obvious nutritional value and resists transformation into an "educational" experience. "It's just fun, that's all!"

"A Place Where Anything Can Happen": Domesticity, Disorder and Desire

> There will be no more nappin', we're going to a place where anything can happen. We've given fair warnin', it's gonna be that kind of mornin' for getting wacky, for being snotty, for going cuckoo at Pee-wee's Playhouse.
> —theme song, *Pee-wee's Playhouse*

Like "ket" or its American counterpart, "junk," such words as "fun," "neat," "bonkers," "crazy," "cuckoo," "silly," etc., which occur so frequently in children's conversation, are open to a broad range of significations. Their polyvocality makes them particularly obscure to adult ears. They describe a wide variety of cultural experiences and qualities, but what many of these share is their displacement of adult-imposed rules, their disruption of the tidy realm of the school room and the family dinner table, their transgressions of the cultural categories and social norms that order "grown-up" society. Having "fun" or acting "crazy" frequently represents a momentary release from the intense pressures of the socialization process, a brief resurrection of the infantile pleasures that are being sublimated in the name of maturity.

Figure one

What makes *Pee-wee's Playhouse* "fun" for these preschoolers, then, is the way that it operates as a kind of anti-kindergarten where playful "misbehavior" takes precedence over "good conduct," children are urged to "scream real loud" at the slightest provocation, making a mess is an acknowledged source of pleasure, "grown-ups" act like children and parental strictures no longer apply. Many of *Pee-wee's Playhouse*'s most appealing segments deal with the disruption of domestic space, the undermining of adult authority or the violation of basic cultural categories: the "crazy fridge" scenes where fruits and vegetables dance and perform acrobatics while making a shambles of Pee-wee's icebox, the dinosaur family whose patriarch is constantly being humiliated by the pranks and misconduct of his offspring, the robot who keeps bumping into the furniture, Penny whose satirical comments often ridicule adult values and the enormous foil ball that threatens to overwhelm everything in its path. Pee-wee invites us to enter an anarchic realm where desire and disorder are indistinguishable and where infantile urges are given free rein.

The children seem fascinated with the playhouse and its oddly-shaped doors, off-kilter roof, impenetrable clutter, and anthropomorphized furnishings: "Pee-wee's playhouse is a funhouse. You never know what's going to happen" (Jackie). The playhouse figures prominently in children's drawings of the program, sometimes even displacing the show's star altogether: "He's inside the house where you

Figure two

can't see him" (Jackie) [figure one]. The playhouse represents for these children an unruly, disorderly, and cluttered domestic space, where normal categories do not seem to apply, where nothing is in its proper place either literally or figuratively. One girl drew a picture of the playhouse with an anthropomorphized television that looked remarkably like a young girl [figure two]: "Pee-wee's house is a funny place. He has a TV with long hair and eyes and a nose and a mouth and . . . hahaha freckles." Later, seeing a friend's portrait of Pee-wee as a punk rocker, which appears to have been modeled after a Strawberry Shortcake doll [figure three], she decides her own picture really depicted the show's star too, suggesting just how malleable the program materials (and children's drawings) can be. Another girl included a talking door, an image consistent with program content though no such character exists on the show [figure one]. Several children speculated, with great amusement, about what such a door might say:

Q: What do you think a talking door would say?
Bill: (deep voice) Hello, Mister. I'm a talking door.
(All laugh.)
Cassandra: Stop knocking on me. I've got a splitting headache!
(All laugh.)
Bill: Knock, knock.
Q: Who's there?
Bill: Ding Dong!
Jackie: Ding dong who?
Bill: Awk! Awk! It's a Silverhawk! Awk!
Kate: You're pretty crazy.
(All laugh.)[4]

Figure three

Henry drew a picture of Pee-wee's "crazy closet" full of an assortment of "crazy toys" that did "crazy things all the time."

Young children, whose own comprehension of the world around them is far from perfect, and who feel highly dependent upon adult authorities for guidance, sometimes take great pleasure in phenomena that call into question the more rigid cultural categories by which "grown-ups" order their social environment and that openly acknowledge the inconsistencies of adult conduct. Martha Wolfenstein (1954) attributes the persistent images of disorderly worlds, of the destruction of property and the breakdown of social order found in children's jokes, to their confusion and anxiety over the apparently contradictory behavior of their parents. These ambiguities are vividly expressed in Kate's attempt to recount the plot of a particular episode:

Q: Can you tell me what happened during the episode today? What do you remember about it?

Kate: I remember that Pee-wee said stop all that racket and stuff because the people, they were doing all this stuff that was wrong to do.

Q: Oh, what sort of stuff?

A: Jumping on the coach, spinning the round head too fast, and that's all I remember. You see, sometimes, people do all that racket. And see, when it does that, some people next door says something to them, that they can't do it anymore. And then sometimes I have a neighbor at my house and sometimes my mom and dad fight and Lucy hears it and gripes at them about it.

Kate's description suggests a compelling need to comprehend the paradoxes of the adult world: how could her parents maintain authority over her if, at the same time, they face rebuke from other adults because of their own childish conduct? How can they be both parent and child? To resolve these contradictions, she must overlook Pee-wee's own infantile behavior, casting the program's star as an idealized father who, through analogy, may discipline her own parents when they act in childish ways. For Wolfenstein, children's jokes, through their representation of worlds where the Law of the Father no longer applies, are the playful manifestation of Oedipal tensions and allow for a harmless outlet for the youngsters' fundamental need to create some distance from parental authority in order to come to terms with its inconsistencies. Not atypically, Kate's account suggests that she finds the prospect of a world that makes as little sense to adults as it does to children, where the certainties of the adult order break down, a source of real fascination, capable of producing both great pleasure and great anxiety.

Similarly, the children were drawn toward the grotesque figures of some of the program characters: the oversized head and minuscule body of the door-to-door salesman, the disembodied head of the genie, the mismatched heads and bodies of Pee-wee's toy collection, the talking fist with the lipstick mouth and eyes, and Pee-wee's mask-like face which must be shrunk in one episode so that he may extract it from a mousehole. For children just gaining mastery over their bodily functions, still a bit confused about how the various parts work together and intrigued by the range of different physiques they encounter as they move more and more outside of the relatively homogenous space of the home, these mutant misshapen bodies are an object of intense interest, and perhaps, a little anxiety. Such figures appear frequently in their drawings, though the more normal-looking characters (Dixie, Captain Karl, etc.) rarely do. Pee-wee's all-too-obvious lack of bodily control and his equally apparent joy in manipulating his face strikes a familiar chord for these youngsters.

References to the body run through their conversations, both in direct reference to the program content ("She looks like a pig!," "How did he get such a big head?!!") and more generally. A girl, drawing a portrait of herself and a friend watching television [figure four], obsessively enumerates the various body parts as she draws them: "Here's my head and nose, ears, eyes, arm, okay, and here's another arm. Then leg, leg, then Jackie's head, heh heh, fat head! heh heh. And here's your arms and here's your legs and your other arm and an eye and a

Figure four

nose. There. All done." Another remarks seemingly at random and to no one in particular, "Have you ever seen a boy with orange hair?"

Although such questions do not originate from watching the show, Pee-wee provides the children with one way in which they can explore their feelings toward their own bodies and their fascination with physical difference, topics which frequently make adults feel uncomfortable. Befitting their roles as socializing agents, parents discuss the body with children in a prohibitory fashion ("Don't pick your nose!"). Pee-wee, subversive spokesman for spontaneity and childishness, addresses such concerns in an open and exploratory fashion ("See what I can do with my nose!"), justifying the pleasures kids find in playing with their bodies. Here, again, we find that *Pee-wee's Playhouse* becomes a perfect program for children to explore their feelings about themselves and their world precisely because it transgresses adult standards of taste and decorum and upholds child meanings over those of their parents.

The Importance of Being Bonkers: Pee-wee and the Preschool
Experience

> Q: Do you think, er, do you think most kids think Pee-wee is a grown-
> up or a kid?
> A: A kid.
> Q: A kid. How can you tell?
> A: Because they see that he goes bonkers all of the time and no grown-
> up acts like Pee-wee. Pee-wee acts like a one-year-old.
> Q: He does, doesn't he?
> A: Yeah. Except he doesn't cry and whine and stuff.
>
> —Henry, 5 1/2

Figure five

For these preschoolers, the fascination of *Pee-wee's Playhouse* predominantly rests on the ambiguity surrounding its central character—
Pee-wee's "otherness," which one boy described as "the greatest mystery of them all," and his uncontrollable and frequently disruptive
conduct. Children often represent Pee-wee as a blur of scribbled activity; Henry reproduced the character's face as a great spiral which
he drew with such intensity that his pencil shredded the page [figure
five]. While adults often attribute the uneasiness which Pee-wee provokes to a sense of sexual ambiguity, of androgyny, or perhaps, homosexuality, these children perceive it as a question of immaturity.
For some, Pee-wee represents an adult who lacks the social skills

necessary to function in the "grown-up" world: "No grown-up acts like Pee-wee" (Henry). For others, Pee-wee represents an over-size child who has somehow stumbled into a world of his own, outside of adult control, where he is free to indulge in his most infantile pleasures.

The question of social maturity is a central concern in these preschoolers' lives. Their entry into kindergarten marks the end of an era of relative freedom. (Only one of the children had daycare experience prior to kindergarten; the others had remained at home under their parents' care and supervision). Now, they must respond to institutional demands for conformity and decorum. Impulsiveness must give way to regimentation as they learn new rules of conduct and new ways of organizing their lives.

Children absorb these institutional norms to a surprising degree, often criticizing each other for their failure to behave appropriately. The threat of discovering that they are "still too little," not really mature enough yet to move on to first grade, is never far from the surface, and as a result, the children feel compelled to distance themselves from any signs of infantile behavior. Those with younger siblings obnoxiously remind people that they are old enough to go to school while the others are not. The worst insult is to be accused of "acting like a baby." Henry explicitly rejected several classmates from his guest list because he felt uncomfortable with their classroom conduct. One boy was characterized as a "clown" who "always acts crazy." Another was described as "always going bonkers" and "knocking things over." Such inappropriate conduct is ill-received by children struggling to suppress all signs of their own childishness. But at the same time, these children experience feelings of nostalgia for their earlier years when they did not face such pressures, frequently dragging out family albums with a disbelief that they could ever have been "that little," reverting to earlier types of conduct when they are tired or hungry. The pleasures of infantilism compete with their pride over their newly discovered maturity.

The duality of the man/child, Pee-wee, makes him a useful vehicle for exploring children's conflicting desires. Frequently, these children employ the same words to denigrate their own misconduct and to praise Pee-wee's antics that they find particularly amusing. One girl drew a picture of Pee-wee with very long hair and characterized him as a "punk rocker" [figure three]. Her discussion of that drawing suggests that she has created a vague mental category that includes a range of social figures who violate institutional norms or cause disruptions through their inappropriate behavior:

Cassandra: Here's Pee-wee acting crazy as ever. Wee wee wee.

Jackie:	Pee-wee's got long hair as ever. Aw gawd! Now he's a punk rocker!!! and now mine has hair sticking out on top of him!
Cassandra:	Now, my Pee-wee is a punk rocker too!
Jackie:	. . . Pee-wee has as long as hair as ever so don't laugh at Pee-wee no matter what anybody calls him!
Bill:	You're as funny as a bug!
(All laugh.)	
Jackie:	It would be worser if he went to school, don't you think?
Q:	What's a punk rocker do?
Jackie:	He acts crazy, just like Pee-wee does.

Her references to Pee-wee going to school and to the names other children might call him suggests just how close a link exists in her mind between Pee-wee and her own impulsive behavior. Similarly, Henry's anxiety about conforming to institutional norms and confronting adult authorities finds direct expression in his story about Pee-wee's late library book. The absurd overstatement—the library's demand for "all the money in two galaxies" as a penalty for a book that is only "one hundred days late," the disruption caused by his refusal to pay that price, and the librarian's grotesque response—gives comic release to very real tensions about his own powerlessness before the kinds of seemingly unreasonable demands that adult authorities place upon him. For Henry, as for Jackie, Pee-wee becomes a focal point for his confusion about the gap between the need to act maturely and his own infantile desires and impulses. The very personification of the return of the repressed, Pee-wee embodies their unfulfilled desires and sublimated urges, allowing them to experience the triumph of the pleasure principle over rational control. But he can act in this role only by becoming an *other*, both adult and infant, belonging fully to neither camp.

Pee-wee's grey suit and red bow tie, which persistently appear in children's representations of him [figure six], allow children to deny the obvious parallels between this eccentric figure and their own social position and thereby to contain some of the tensions that he might otherwise produce. No matter how childlike he may act, he dresses and looks like a "grown-up." Wolfenstein (1954) and Erikson (1950) consider it essential for comic figures, like circus clowns and moron jokes, to mask their essentially infantile nature in order to allow children a way to break from too intense an identification with them.

In fact, Pee-wee may be doubly displaced from the realm of their lived experience since children also describe him as "acting like he was just born" or "acting like a two-year-old," phrases that mean something fundamentally different to a five-year-old than they do to an adult. Pee-wee is perceived as the younger sibling, not yet mature enough to handle the responsibilities of kindergarten, allowing the children to feel a strong sense of superiority over him. He does things that they would never do.

Several of the children felt a compelling need to place Pee-wee in a world well beyond their reach, a space greatly distanced from the realm of their lived experience. Hodge and Tripp employ the term "modality" to describe the relationship that young viewers ascribe to the difference between a given media representation and social reality, a choice that helps to determine their emotional response to the depicted events. Through their manipulation of modality, viewers may pull a represented event toward them so that it may be experienced

Figure six

more immediately and more intensely, or shove it away to create necessary emotional and psychological distance from it.

Bill constructs a land of make-believe to contain his brief Pee-wee story:

> Once upon a time there was a little boy, er, man named Pee-wee. He lived far far away in Pee-wee Land where all the people (who) looked like Pee-wee come to play with Pee-wee and live with him happily ever after. The end.

Bill's ambiguity about Pee-wee's age, his dependence upon traditional fairy tale structures, and his need to create a world ("Pee-wee Land") where the star's usually anomalous appearance and behavior is normal and rational ("all the people looked like Pee-wee") suggest the degree to which he is relying upon modality to deny any obvious connection between himself and the show's comic hero and to contain the disturbing questions that his otherness provokes.

Kate makes a subtler, though no less significant, attempt to define the program events as occupying a space quite distinct from the world of her own experience. Asked to write a story about Pee-wee, she instead imagined what it might be like to own her own construction company. Attempting to direct discussion back onto the program, my wife asked her how she might respond if Pee-wee came to her with a commission:

> Q: What would you do if you got an order from Pee-wee to build a new playhouse?
> A: Um. No! I don't watch TV because I work all day.
> Q: Ah. Well, what if he hired you to build his house for his new TV show?
> A: I would, er. One day, I would go home and I would watch TV and then, I would be done and I would go back to work . . . and then, you know, I would tell them that I saw that show that they wanted but I have a lot of work to do and I can't do it . . . .And I don't like, when I go home, you see, my boss, he likes me to work and not go home to watch TV all the time.

While Kate's story concerns a real world of adult concerns, Pee-wee can exist in such a world only on television; no direct interaction with him is possible.

Not all children create such sharp distinctions between *Pee-wee's Playhouse* and their own lives. In my son's stories, Pee-wee awakens early on Saturday mornings to watch some of Henry's favorite television shows and even comes to visit his apartment and play with some of his toys: "He likes the same things I do." Although we must be cautious about making psychological claims about the individual children, such differences in the assignment of modality may be indicative of very real differences in the ways that these kids resolve the kinds of tensions which the figure of Pee-wee provokes. Those who feel the greatest anxiety about the socialization process or about disorderly conditions within their surroundings may find it relatively difficult to allow Pee-wee to remain in close proximity to the realm of their lived experience because his spontaneity might call into question the kinds of painful compromises they are forced to make in their adjustments to the demands of school life. Yet, even these children, frightened though they may be of the things he represents, feel a need to play with the potent meanings that the Pee-wee man/child suggests to them. The dilemmas that he poses are too central to the socialization process to be long ignored.

The Uses of Immaturity: Television Play and Socialization

For children of the television age, the most readily available play materials are those that the media bring into their homes. Children draw upon the prefabricated characters and situations of popular culture to make sense of their own social experience, reworking them to satisfy their own needs and desires. The children's manipulation of these televisual materials rarely stops when the broadcast does. Rather, program content is fragmented and dissected and the most meaningful bits, the "good parts," are integrated into the child's other play activities, into dreams and into waking thoughts. The parents in my study reported that their children often drew upon their favorite shows to give content to their drawings and pretend games. All of the children owned dolls or other toys directly tied to television programs. In such play, children feel little compulsion to remain faithful to the original series concepts, to "stay within the lines." In fact, children seem almost compulsively intertextual, blurring the normal boundaries between texts, mixing and matching the contents of multiple shows at their whim, creating stories where, say, Batman and Dr. Who join forces to combat Count Dracula and the Stay-Puft Marshmallow Man,or parodying, albeit crudely, the codes and conventions of favored programs. Henry wrote a story "making fun" of Mr. Rogers by showing how differently Pee-wee would act in the same situations. Just as the children at the party treated a He-Man stuffed toy as, interchangeably, a seat belt and a naughty boy, a child may take a "pro-social" program and endow it with countercultural meanings, or with equal dexterity, may find rational logic behind the most nonsensical elements of their favorite shows.

These skills are not totally lost as the child is molded into a young adult. Indeed, many of the activities enjoyed by adult media fans reflect these same kinds of play with program content (Jenkins 1988). Rather, newer interpretive skills are layered over them as he or she learns to read television in more socially sanctioned ways. Fragmentation and association may come to coexist with integration and interpretation as alternative (and perhaps complementary) ways of responding to popular texts. Yet, the reality principle dictates that pleasure will be more frequently subordinated to some "higher purpose" as our impulsiveness is constrained by our inclusion within a larger cultural community. Maturation should be perceived as a process whereby basic emotional needs are embedded within new mental structures necessary for future survival and yet potentially antagonistic to human impulsiveness. As Hodge and Tripp write, "Earlier stages survive because they are functional. They are the site of pleasure and the play of emotional energy. If later stages are essential for power, earlier stages are essential for desire" (85). Nobody wants a world in which children never reach maturity, a kind of "never-never land" where one can act infantile forever. The socialization process is essential for human accomplishment and fulfillment. But we must be cautious that in furthering the development of our children, we do not push too hard towards the rationalization of all experience, destroying within them those qualities which make them most human: their capacity to play, to find pleasure, to be creative. If, as adults, we feel compelled to find something educational and pro-social in all of children's television, perhaps this is the lesson we can learn from a visit to *Pee-wee's Playhouse*: the importance of "going bonkers."

NOTES

I am indebted to John Fiske, David Bordwell, Richard Lachman, Murray Smith, and Kristine Karnick, for their helpful suggestions in preparing this manuscript for publication. I am especially grateful to the active participation, inspiration and support of Cindy Benson Jenkins and Henry Jenkins IV, without whom this project would not have been possible.

1. While the parents were informed that the party constituted a type of scholarly research and completed open-ended survey forms about their children and their viewing habits, they were asked to treat the gathering as any other that their son or daughter might attend. As far as the children were concerned, it was simply another opportunity to share a good time with some friends. My son, Henry, was active at all stages of the planning process, selecting which children to invite, designing and making the invitations, determining the menu, and deciding what program episodes we would show. Such a child-centered research design helped to eliminate, though not entirely, the youngster's tendencies to conform to the expectations of authorities, tendencies that unmistakably color more traditional approaches to children and the media.

2. For examples of how adults might confront a similar problem—that of recounting their experience of a text—see David Bleich (1986).

3. Although more research is needed here, my own experience with Henry's viewing of a variety of different types of texts suggests that the more fragmented structure of *Pee-wee's Playhouse* is not a major determinant of this sensation-centered reading strategy. Even programs with more linear constructions, such as *Masters of the Universe,* are often read atomistically with little or no interest in the larger narrative context within which a particularly compelling scene might be embedded.

4. Note how Bill's Knock-Knock joke follows adult rules only long enough to sucker his playmates into participation and then gleefully abandons them for a punchline which seems totally beside the point. His reference

to *Silverhawks* here reflects Bill's general strategy throughout the party to deflect attention away from *Pee-wee's Playhouse*, a show which he was forbidden to watch by his father, onto the more comfortable terrain of his own favorite television program, and suggests rather vividly the degree to which the ability to make in-references to popular programs may be a real source of social power within kindergarten society.

WORKS CITED

Bettelheim, B. 1987. "The Importance of Play." Atlantic. March: 35–46.

Bleich, D. 1985. "Gender Interests in Reading and Language." E. A. Flynn and P. P. Schweickart, eds. *Gender and Reading: Essays on Readers, Texts and Contexts*. Baltimore: Johns Hopkins University Press.

Bordwell, D. 1985. *Narration in the Fiction Film*. Madison: University of Wisconsin Press.

Dahl, R. 1964. *Charlie and the Chocolate Factory*. New York: Alfred A. Knopf.

Elias, N. 1978. *The History of Manners*. New York: Pantheon.

Erikson, E. 1950. *Childhood and Society*. New York: W. W. Norton.

Geertz, C. 1973. *The Interpretation of Cultures*. New York: Basic.

Gertler, T. 1987. "The Pee-wee Perplex." *Rolling Stone*. 12 Feb. 1987: 37–41.

Hearn, F. 1976. "Towards a Critical Theory of Play." *Telos* 30: 145–160.

Hodge, R. and D. Tripp. 1986. *Children and Television: A Semiotic Approach*. Cambridge: Polity Press.

James, A. 1982. "Confections, Concoctions and Conceptions." B. Waites, T. Bennett and G. Martins, eds. *Popular Culture: Past and Present*. London: Croom Helm/Open University Press.

Jenkins, H. 1988. "Star Trek Rerun, Reread, Rewritten: Fan Writing as Textual Poaching," *Critical Studies in Mass Communication 5*, 2: 85–107.

Lévi-Strauss, C. 1962. *The Savage Mind*. Chicago: University of Chicago Press.

Miller, S. 1973. "Ends, Means and Galumphing: Some Leitmotifs of Play." *American Anthropologist* 1: 87-98.

Palmer, P. 1986. *The Lively Audience*. Sidney: Allen and Unwin.

Vygotsky, L. S. 1933. "Play and Its Role in the Mental Development of the Child." J. S. Bruner, A. Jolly and K. Sylva, eds. *Play: Its Role in Development and Evolution*. New York: Penguin, 1976.

Wolfenstein, M. 1954. *Children's Humor: A Psychological Analysis*. Bloomington: Indiana University Press.

The Sissy Boy, The Fat Ladies, and The Dykes: Queerness and/as Gender in Pee-wee's World
Alexander Doty

In all the things I've read or heard about Pee-wee Herman, his shows, and his films, only two commentators even begin to consider the specifically queer gender dynamics centered around Pee-wee/Paul Reubens.[1] Bryan Bruce, in "Pee Wee Herman: The Homosexual Subtext," is right on the money when he says "The most exciting aspect of Pee Wee Herman, so far, remains his role as vindicator of the sissies," adding elsewhere that Pee-wee tends to "undercut masculinity . . . by feminizing it."[2] "The Mail-Lady," the first section of Ian Balfour's "The Playhouse of the Signifier: Reading Pee-wee Herman" toys with, but never directly engages, the idea that Pee-wee's gay sexuality (and the queerness of other characters) might be spoken through gender. Consider this pair of quotations, which follow each other early in the article:

> For Pee-wee's mail man is a "mail-lady," a phrase that—given the over-determined encoded by the sexual hijinks on the show—takes on an added resonance: the *male*-lady. And, indeed, the phrase the "mail-lady" can be switched into its converse, the lady-male, faster than one can change channels by remote.
>
> It doesn't take very long to recognize the gay subtext, intertext, or just plain text of the Pee-wee episodes, most clearly legible in the figure of Jambi, the drag queen genie adorned with a turban, flaming red lipstick, and a single earring.[3]

Here and elsewhere, Balfour is on the verge of linking the show's gender destabilization with queerness (or is that linking the show's queerness to gender destabilization?), but he can't seem to bring himself to do it explicitly. To be fair, Balfour's reluctance probably arises from an attempt to avoid stereotypically aligning gayness with the feminine/effeminate and lesbianism with the masculine/butch. In any case, after the first page, the word "gay" is dropped, and the "Mail-Lady" section opts for the suggestive, innuendo-like approach to speaking homosexuality through heterocentric notions of cross-gender identification which Balfour seems to wish to avoid:

> He [Pee-wee] then perks up to advise the boys and girls that next time he will tell the story of the "part-time boy." The part-time boy is, of course,

183

Pee-wee: and this phrase too has to be understood in more than one sense. Part-time *boy*, because Pee-wee is part-time boy and part-time girl, if only in his most hysterical and histrionic moments. But also *part-time* boy because the other part of the time Pee-wee is something like a man.[4]

Without a specifically queer cultural-historical context to clarify things here, Balfour's parallel between Pee-wee as a "hysterical and histrionic" girl and Pee-wee as "*something like* a man" can only be read as a reiteration of two heterosexist standards about gay men: (1) they are screaming queens/woman wannabes, and (2) they are less than/something other than "real" (read: heterosexual) men. Given this, it's no surprise that the only appearance of the word "gay" in the essay is connected to Jambi ("the drag queen genie") and men wearing lipstick ("Jambi . . . is one of the few male characters on television to wear lipstick, and Pee-wee may be the only other one").[5]

Having said this, I still think Balfour's initially suggestive juxtaposition of gender (mail-lady/lady-male) and (homo)sexuality (implicitly lesbian/more explictly gay) is an important one to work with in discussing Pee-wee and his texts. I will carry out this discussion within a particular queer context: that of the feminine gay man.[6] Even more specifically, this reading of Pee-wee and his texts will be influenced by the positions of, and discourses surrounding, feminine gay men and boys growing up in white, heterosexual America in the 1950s and 1960s—a cultural and historical heritage Paul Reubens and thousands of gay men share.

In this light, Pee-wee's queerness needs to be analyzed in relation to the then-popular understanding of homosexuality as always a case of gender inversion, where gender is patriarchally heterosexualized and the gay or lesbian is put in the cultural position of a substitute for (and an inferior imitation of) the opposite gender. Connected to this position is the cultural reinforcement of rigid gender roles that subordinated everything considered "womanly" and "feminine." But it is also important to recall that the articulation of Pee-wee's gender position as a sissy gay within 1950s and 1960s discourse is mediated by, and negotiated within, homosexualized gender discourses of the 1980s and 1990s. That is, in Pee-wee's world gender is often reconceptualized through queerness as much as queerness is expressed through traditional heterosexualized cross-gender positions.

In "The Cabinet of Dr. Pee-wee: Consumerism and Sexual Terror," Constance Penley points out that "the periods, styles and objects [of *Pee-wee's Playhouse*] are, of course, not arbitrarily chosen: they have been selected for parodic recycling because they have their origins in what must have been the childhood and adolescence of the 'real' Pee-wee Herman, the thirty-five [now thirty-seven] year old Paul Reubens."[7] I would add to this that the attitudes toward gender and sexuality (and the relationship between the two) that Pee-wee and his texts express also "have their origins in what must have been the childhood and adolescence" of Reubens. The popular press has often called Pee-wee "thirty-five (or thirty-six) going on ten," and it is within this complex and often contradictory attempt to work alternately or simultaneously with(in) the past (childhood; the 50s and 60s; pre-Stonewall) and and the present (adulthood; the 80s and 90s; post-Stonewall) that Reubens, through Pee-wee, expresses his "sissy boy" and woman-identified gay worldview. Given this postmodern time-warp, it is often difficult to form clear-cut political readings for Reubens's queer deployment of gender in the Pee-wee universe. Frequently the most conventional codes of queerness as heterosexualized cross-gender identification will be juxtaposed or co-exist with more progressive queer reworkings of the masculine and the feminine.[8]

Of course, the possibility of reading the Pee-wee texts' presentation of queerness and/as gender in a camp register makes coming to an ideological bottom line even more tricky. Penley finds that Reubens is relatively even-handed in his uses of camp in order to have "subversive fun" with gender and sexuality: if Miss Yvonne becomes "the Burlesque Queen of camp theater, her femininity exaggerated into a parody of itself," then Pee-wee's feminine gay persona is campily coded through his "mincing step, affected gestures, exaggerated speech, obvious makeup and extreme fastidiousness."[9] If this is the case, then camp's impulse to "satirize and celebrate," which Penley points out, might give us more pause to wonder just what about gender and sexuality is being satirized and/or celebrated in Pee-wee's world—and why. If Miss Yvonne's character is a parody of a caricature, is Pee-wee's "mincing" fag the same? Or are they both celebrations of these (stereo)types? Perhaps the answer to these questions depends on the gender and sexuality agendas of the camp reader, as well as the particular example of camp she/he is faced with. For example, I find it difficult to read Miss Yvonne's camp parody of conventional 1950s–1960s femininity in exactly the same way that I interpret Pee-wee's campy comment on the codes of feminine gayness. While both satirize popular notions of gender and sexuality, Pee-wee's character also seems to function for many queer viewers as an affirmation of the look, behavior, and attitude of the feminine gay.

In "The Incredible Shrinking He[r]man: Male Regression, the Male Body, and Film," Tania Modleski places Pee-wee's camp within the context of postmodernism—and then condemns both camp and post-modernism for their attempts "to escape accountability by relying on

the alibi of the figurative—indeed on the alibi of the alibi: nothing is
what it seems or where it seems; nothing is taken seriously."[10] Relating
all this to our culture's tradition of regressive male "escapist fantasy—
even if its function is to serve as a cover story for a hidden gay text,"
Modleski finds that "insofar as Pee-wee can 'become woman' and at
the same time revile through comic exaggeration the very traits that
constitute 'womanliness,' he reveals how the desire to appropriate and
the need to denigrate can easily coexist in male attitudes towards
femininity."[11] In first separating, then conflating, straight men and gay
men in this section of her essay, Modleski does her otherwise provocative argument, as well as gay men, a disservice. Men may have
misogyny in common, but gay men's misogyny, particularly that of
feminine gay men, needs to be discussed with more attention to its
specific queer psychological and cultural foundations and patterns.
Besides, as a queer character, Pee-wee less "becomes woman," than
represents an expression of gay femininity, less "reviles . . . womanliness" as some sort of essential category, than reviles its various cultural constructions and surfaces. In saying this, I don't want to suggest
that all the instances of gender representation and gender play in Pee-
wee's world are free of misogyny. What I do want to suggest is that
one might want to consider more carefully the particular gay context
in which this postmodern camp is produced, as well as the possibility
of variant audience readings of these particular texts' uses of camp in
relation to gender and sexuality.[12]

But, aside from Bryan Bruce's article, most academic and popular
writing about Pee-wee Herman has forgrounded gender concerns in a
heterocentrist manner. That is, these articles implicitly set up straight
men and straight women as the ultimate reference points for their
analysis of gender because their authors don't seriously consider the
possibility that the gayness, lesbianism, and bisexuality in Pee-wee's
image and texts might be crucial to that destabilization of gender roles
they're all so excited about. If anything, it is the queer tone and context
of Pee-wee and his world that allows for, and encourages, most of the
gender confusion and reconceptualization. When homosexuality does
enter the discussion in these articles, it is usually in the form of questioning, or being suggestively vague about, Pee-wee's *exact* sexual
orientation (anything to keep from acknowledging he is fundamentally
a gay boy-man), or of acknowledging the character's and the text's
gayness at one point, only to render explicit gayness invisible again at
another (the Balfour article), or to downplay its importance (the Penley
article: "Perhaps too much has been made of the homosexual subtext
in *Pee-wee's Playhouse*.")[13] Investigating how differences in sexualities
are culturally gendered from childhood, and how, therefore, the gender

play in Pee-wee's world is inextricably bound up in the play of queerness across its characters and texts seems not to be on most commentators' critical agendas.[14]

To return to an earlier point for the moment, while the Playhouse, its inhabitants, and its visitors attempt to recreate a 1950s–1960s sissy boy's perceptions and fantasies, we can't forget that Pee-wee is the 1980s creation of an adult gay man, Paul Reubens. This being the case, Pee-wee and other Reubens creations must also be considered against the backdrop of queer attitudes, politics, and styles that developed between the 1950s and the 1980s. As a feminine gay, Reubens might decide to have lots of athletic, traditionally masculine-looking men as Pee-wee's "friends"[15]: Tito, the lifeguard; Cowboy Curtis; Ricardo, the soccer player; Mickey, the weightlifting escaped convict; Captain Carl, the ship's skipper; a Marine Corps chorus. But if these men are coded as (stereo)typically butch in an "old-fashioned" gay way, they are simultaneously presented as soft and pretty (as gay "boy toys," and/or boyfriends).[16] And while many of these men are erotically displayed as ethnic exotics, and therefore, as regressively racist examples of "forbidden" (homo)sexual desires, when they speak and interact with Pee-wee they seem as friendly and familiar as the multiracial cast of men on *Sesame Street.*

Pee-wee's 1950s sissy boy can't, however, take direct erotic notice of these butch-looking men, so, as many feminine gay viewers have done (or have felt culturally compelled to do), he usually expresses his desire for them by using women as his erotic representatives. To this end, Reubens creates women characters — Miss Yvonne, especially, but also Mrs. René, Mrs. Steve, and Winnie the schoolteacher in *Big Top Pee-Wee*—who can verbalize and/or act out Pee-wee's desires. Yet these women are (stereo)typed by certain excesses, which might be explained as part of an overdetermined coding of Pee-Wee's/Reubens's hidden and projected gay desires. These marks of excess could also be the result of a sissy boy's/feminine gay man's love-hate relationship with the gender that he recognizes his affinities are with even while he feels restricted by conventional heterosexualized definitions of that gender. Reubens/Pee-wee is the sissy boy/feminine gay man who both enjoys and resents his connection with women. This position is even more intensely held for having been developed in a period like the 1950s and the 1960s in the United States, when gender was rigidly heterosexualized and publicly defined in a manner that attempted to keep women second-class citizens. The sissy boy/effeminate gay man knows he's not like men, not "masculine," in the way it is defined by straight patriarchal culture. But to be told by that same culture that he is, therefore, like a woman, is heterosexually "feminine," and that he functions as a woman substitute or as an imitation woman, isn't usually a welcomed or enviable alternative—although it often seems the only one, given the absence of homosexuality as a male/masculine choice. Given these circumstances, the resentment and dislike of women that has been (stereo)typically part of the way in which straight culture, and even much of queer culture, has characterized gay men—particularly feminine gay men—is often less about gay men's problems with actual women than it is about their problems with the heterocentrist and patriarchal cultural definitions and depictions of women forced upon them. For this reason alone, the "one-size-fits-all" approach to male misogyny Modleski and others employ when criticizing Paul Reubens's work with women characters is not very sensitive to how the particular position of gay men within patriarchy has been constructed in relation to concepts of "woman" and the "feminine." Many things Reubens does with women characters might be misogynistic, but, as mentioned earlier, we need to consider more carefully how these instances may express misogyny of a distinctly queer variety, with complicated psychological and cultural foundations of its own—perhaps more comparable to straight women's misogyny than to straight men's.

So, in Pee-wee's world, Miss Yvonne has the "biggest [bouffant] hair" and is a vain hyper-1950s feminine type. Mrs. Steve and Mrs. René are food-obsessed and fat. The schoolteacher progresses from being an extra-nice and prim 1960s blonde girl-next-door to becoming the lover of an entire troupe of Eastern European acrobats who are brothers. But while these excessive women may express Pee-wee/Reubens's gay desires (Miss Yvonne, Winnie, sometimes Mrs. René as man-eaters) or his sexual frustrations (Mrs. René, Mrs. Steve as over-eaters), these women are not passive tokens of homosocial or homoerotic exchange between men. Their energy and aggressiveness parallel Pee-wee's hyperactivity, and they all stand in contrast to the rather bland pleasantness of the male sex objects on the show. These women are as much counterparts to, and examples for, the closeted Pee-wee as they are unwitting beards for him. For every moment when Pee-wee does something like cut in on Miss Yvonne in order to dance with Tito, there is another like the one in which he watches Miss Yvonne intently as she seduces the Conky repairman (or some other hunk) with lines such as "Is that a wrench in your pocket?," and then provides the camera/audience with a sly, knowing, and approving look after Miss Yvonne has made a successful pick-up.

At least some of these "excessive" women can also be read in specifically adult gay culture terms as one half of a classic team: feminine gay man and "fag hag," or, to use a more recent term, "fag moll." In its stereotypical form this pair consists of a thin, witty-bitchy, stylish young man and a fat and/or flashily-dressed and made-up woman, who often appears to be emulating the look of drag queens rather than that of conventional straight feminine glamour. Indeed, fag moll Mrs. Steve can be read as a drag queen—at least one commentator dubbed her "the Divine stand-in."[17] As fag molls, Mrs. Steve, Mrs. René, Miss Yvonne, and even the Cowntess often receive the cruel and bitchy end of Pee-wee's schtick, with fat jokes, vanity jokes, and sexual double-entendres aplenty at their expense.[18] Even seeing Pee-wee as "one of the girls," doesn't help matters in these cases—it only makes certain moments on the television shows and specials seem like remakes of *The Women*, with a different feminine gay man (Paul Reubens rather than George Cukor or R.W. Fassbinder) directing, as well as partici-pating in, the action.[19]

For balance and counterpoint, however, there are many examples of Pee-wee's comraderie with women characters, including suggestions that Mrs. René and Miss Yvonne on the televison series, and Simone the waitress in *Pee-wee's Big Adventure* serve as Pee-wee's female "doubles," representing parallels to his gay femininity in all its prob-lemmatic construction—as when Pee-wee gives his wish to Miss Yvonne (on *The Pee-wee Herman Show*) by asking Jambi to make Captain Carl "really like her," or when Pee-wee leaves Mrs. René in charge of the Playhouse when he goes "camping" with Cowboy Curtis, or when Pee-wee and Simone sit in the head of a large model dinosaur, share their dreams, and realize they are soulmates. These, and other, examples of Pee-wee and women characters bonding and doubling are generally worked out as moments of gay femininity connecting with straight femininity rather than as moments in which heterocentrist notions of gayness as a masquerade of straight femaleness are being evoked. The much-cited episode in which Pee-wee plays Miss Yvonne on a practice date with Cowboy Curtis stands as an excellent illus-tration of the kind of heterosexualized gay gender positioning Pee-wee usually refuses to accept. Initially reluctant to substitute for Miss Yvonne in a date rehearsal staged by the Cowntess, Pee-wee reluctantly gives in, but remains uncomfortable until he begins a camp parody of the traditional straight female position. When the Cowntess urges Curtis to kiss Pee-wee for the grand finale, Pee-wee stops the pro-ceedings. While it is possible to read this scene as an (unsuccessful) attempt to establish Pee-wee's heterosexual credentials, seen queerly, this moment reveals that gay Pee-wee doesn't want to be seen or used as a substitute for a straight woman—he may be *like* Miss Yvonne in many ways (being attracted to Cowboy Curtis is only one of them), but he isn't Miss Yvonne.

While Modleski is concerned about how other essays on Pee-wee implicitly treat his lack of interest in girls as examples of the old idea that "homosexuality is a result of arrested development and involv[es] man's turning away from the 'mature' object choice, woman," she proceeds to argue her points in a heterocentrist manner.[20] Modleski's ultimate criticism seems not that the statements about Pee-wee being uninterested in, or "grossed out" by, girls-women might be homophobic, but that Pee-wee's rejection of girls-women is let off the hook with only "lighthearted" commentary. Finally, Modleski condemns Pee-wee along with all other little boy-men: "this dismissive attitude . . . is congruent with the misogyny of patriarchal ideology and reveals a contempt for females Freud saw as characteristic of 'normal' masculinity."[21] From this position, it might not occur to Modleski to question and more carefully examine the heterocentrist assumptions behind assertions in the essays she criticizes that Pee-wee "is . . . another sort of boy, one who simply isn't interested in girls."[22] It is one thing to say Pee-wee isn't romantically or sexually interested in girls-women (or that he rejects them on these counts); it is quite another to have this represent a general rejection and dismissal of women.

But this is just what is done in Modleski's critical discussion of Pee-wee, as much as in the work of others she cites (Balfour, Penley). As a sissy boy/feminine gay man, Pee-wee might not be sexually interested in girls-women, but he is certainly very interested in them in many other ways that cannot be called "dismissive" or "misogynistic" — he's interested in them as friends. To briefly bring in the example of a similar heterocentrist take on another Playhouse character, Balfour argues that there is one "exceptional moment" on the series in which Jambi seems to become "the stereotypical masculinist male." This is when "[a]gainst all expectations, Jambi chooses to have a female genie head as his companion."[23] Given Jambi's character as feminine gay, this moment is hardly atypical: Jambi wishes to have a girl friend, not a girlfriend. With its fixation on sex as the primary bond between men and women, heterocentrist positions and readings constantly attempt to recast the relationships (real and representational) between women and gay men in terms of sexual antagonism. By these terms, gay men hate and dismiss women because they don't want to have sex with them, or jealously want to be women, or covet their men.

Besides his straight women friends, another group of women important to defining Pee-wee's sissy boy/feminine gay position as queer, as well as central to establishing the general queerness of Pee-wee's world, are the tomboys/dykes. Not surprisingly, this group has gone almost totally unacknowledged in discussions of Pee-wee Herman texts. Aside from John Goss's short film *"Out"takes* (1990, which "outs" Dixie as a dyke), and the occasional informal conversation, lesbians seem to be invisible to most people looking at Pee-wee's television shows and the films. Taken together, these dykes represent further illustration of the mediation between 1950s–1960s and 1980s–1990s styles and attitudes typical of Reuben's work: the codes of butch-as-heterosexualied-male and femme-as-heterosexualized-female meet, and often mingle with, more homosexualized gendered lesbian looks, attitudes, and behaviors, including butch and femme. Often, dyke characters coded as butch are used as counterparts to Pee-wee's/Reubens's feminine gay personality: Reba the mail-male lady, Dixie the cab driver, Herman Hattie (*The Pee-wee Herman Show*), Large Marge (*Pee-wee's Big Adventure*), and k.d. lang (*Pee-wee's Christmas Special*). Whether you read these butches as heterosexually masculinized or queerly masculine often depends upon the episode, the scene, the moment, and the spectator.

Most often, however, the heterosexually masculine codes of dress and behavior surrounding these butch dykes are combined with just enough androgynous or feminine coding to suggest that they operate in the space of some lesbian reconceptualizing of masculinity rather than as imitations of straight men. That is, they seem to be butches who are both woman-identified and masculine. In any case, it makes queer sense that Reba is in the Playhouse with Pee-wee when it becomes lost in space and enters an alternative universe in which Miss Yvonne's double appears as a bald alien. Or that when Reba and Dixie appear in dresses at one Playhouse party they elicit the same type of surprised comment as when Pee-wee gets out of his prissy plaid suit and red bow tie and into more butch attire (a baseball uniform, a cowboy outfit). Or that Herman Hattie (note the first name) echos Pee-wee's dialogue to Miss Yvonne and will trust only Pee-wee to guard her jeep's tools and paraphernalia ("with your life"). Or that k.d. lang is the only guest star on the Christmas special who interacts with the entire Playhouse crew during a spirited rendition of "Jingle Bell Rock."

But there is another side to these suggestions of complementariness between sissy Pee-wee and the butch dykes. For if these dykes are depicted as Pee-wee's "opposite" homosexualized gender comrades, they are also often presented as uncomprehending of the world of the feminine gay man, as well as incomprehensible within this world. Reba is constantly befuddled by what happens in the Playhouse (one time calling the Playhouse and its inhabitants "twisted"), Dixie is abrupt and uncommunicative, k.d. lang tries too hard to fit in and appears awkwardly hyperkinetic, Herman Hattie is a laughable hillbilly with a skunk stuck to her "butt," and Large Marge metamorphoses into a monster. But this ambivalent presentation of butches in Pee-wee's world accurately reflects queer cultural history, past and present, as it suggests the longstanding suspicion and distrust between lesbians and gays (particularly between butches and sissies) that has only recently begun to change in any significant way with the revival of queer coalition politics, particularly around AIDS and women's health issues.

If the femmes in Pee-wee's world are treated more benignly, it is perhaps because they seem less like "others" to the sissy boy—he has the expression of queerly reconfigured femininity in common with them. The only femme Pee-wee seems uncomfortable with is Sandra Bernhard, appearing in one episode as a telephone operator who aggressively vamps Pee-wee over the picture phone. Bernhard's charade of heterosexualized femininity here (which parallels her off-screen "I'm not a lesbian" pronouncements at the time) causes Pee-wee great irritation, and he quickly cuts off her parodic seduction scene. But Pee-wee can enthusiastically greet each cartoon featuring Penny, a femme tomboy who has interesting relationships with a mermaid, an imaginary twin sister, a real sister, and Dorothy Lamour, among other females; and he can have fun singing "Hey Good Lookin'" with Dolly Parton in her visit to Pee-wee's Playhouse on an episode of her own variety series (that is, until he suspects her of getting romantic with him).

And then there's Miss Yvonne, the character who has been with Pee-wee since his nightclub beginnings—at once the hyperfeminine straight woman who expresses Pee-wee's gay desires, the fag moll, and the femme dyke. Miss Yvonne's position as (unaware?) femme lesbian is most clearly articulated in *The Pee-wee Herman Show* when Herman Hattie, the hillbilly butch in coonskin cap and buckskin, romances "Miss Y" by presenting her with a bottle of "Rocky Mountain Valley Violet Perfume." Later, in the beauty makeover episode of *Pee-wee's Playhouse*, Dixie asks Miss Yvonne if she could "do her" after she finishes with Mrs. Steve. But Miss Yvonne's queer textual status as femme isn't consistent. Rather, it seems a case of Reubens-as-Pee-wee working out his own feminine gay character through Miss Yvonne in a way that will implicitly homosexualize his own cross-gender identification by connecting its feminized erotic expression to queerness. Miss Yvonne is thus the ultra-fem(inine) figure who lusts after the Playhouse hunks while occasionally being sexually paired through double entendres with butch dyke figures like Dixie, Herman Hattie, and Reba.

If the queer readings offered thus far seem either tentative or tenuous, it is probably because the queerness of Pee-wee's world is usually signaled by connotation, like the queerness in most mainstream cultural texts. To quote D.A. Miller in a discussion of Alfred Hitchcock's *Rope*:

> Now, defined in contrast to the immediate self-evidence (however on re-flection deconstructible) of denotation, connotation will always manifest a certain semiotic insufficiency. . . . [C]onnotation enjoys, or suffers from, an abiding deniability. . . . *Rope* exploits the particular aptitude of con-notation for allowing homosexual meaning to be elided even as it is also being elaborated. . . . In this sense, the cultural work performed by *Rope*, toiling alongside other films . . . and other cultural productions . . . consists in helping construct a homosexuality held definitionally in suspense on no less than a question of its own existence—and in helping to produce in the process homosexual subjects doubtful of the validity and even the reality of their desire, which *may only be, does not necessarily mean*, and all the rest.[24]

Substitute *Pee-wee's Playhouse, Pee-wee's Big Adventure, Big Top Pee-wee*, and the other Pee-wee texts for *Rope* in the quotation above, and Miller's observations about homosexuality and/as connotation will indicate both the pleasures and the painful limitations of Pee-wee's world for queer audiences. The air of insider, "wink wink," double entendre queer cultural connotative referentiality, linked to instances of more "obvious" queer cross-gender codes (but are they denotative only to queerly-positioned readers?), have opened the space for my analysis above. However the queer-deniability factor Miller refers to is powerfully at work in Pee-wee's world, allowing for readings that downplay queerness, separate it from other topics (most notably from gender concerns), or render it invisible. Not surprisingly, this last category of reading Pee-wee is the one favored in articles written for mass market newspapers and journals, which typically cast Pee-wee as a wacky and disconcerting asexual or presexual man-boy who encourages outrageous and "naughty" behavior in similarly asexual or presexual child viewers. It is a reading of his character and his work that the closeted Reubens has encouraged in interviews conducted as Pee-wee, while also coyly hinting at "offscreen" women admirers for his character.[25] But at least one child viewer cited in Henry Jenkins's essay unwittingly provided the best metaphor for the Pee-wee universe, as embodied in his (in)famous Playhouse, when he called it a "crazy closet."[26] The television Playhouse as "crazy" queer closet has its parallels in Pee-wee's film house and farm, which offer similar self-contained, queer-connotative environments set apart from the "nor-mal" world (it makes sense that in *Big Top Pee-wee* a stranded circus is quickly and easily integrated into Pee-wee's farm).

Perhaps it is to be expected that Pee-wee and his friends are stuck in a closet of queer representation-as-connotation, as most of Pee-wee's world is constructed to fit into the conventions of children's television and mainstream filmmaking, while it is also placed within that time warp between the 1950s–1960s and the 1980s–1990s.[27] To make matters more difficult for Reubens to directly express queerness in his work, the 1980s–1990s seem to be shaping up as a period in which America is reworking the conservative ideologies of the 1950s and 1960s. So Pee-wee's world is one in which safe sex is referred to, but only by way of the sight of Miss Yvonne quickly changing into a plastic raincoat and "a transparent plastic cap to protect her large, dome-shaped bouffant hairdo."[28] It is also a world where muscular men can be erotically displayed, but where Pee-wee can't even touch them. And where Dixie's demand that Miss Yvonne "do" her after doing Mrs. Steve can only result in a femme-inizing beauty makeover.

But there are closets within the closet of the Playhouse. In *Pee-wee's Big Adventure* there is the hidden and excessively guarded garage that houses Pee-wee's prized bicycle. *Pee-wee's Playhouse* contains a secret room that stores this same bike (and a bizarre monster helmet). While the series and *The Pee-wee Herman Show* both feature the box containing Jambi, the queeny genie, a.k.a. "The Wish Man." Only *Big Top Pee-wee*, with its (albeit often parodic) heterosexual romance narrative lacks a clear closet-within-the-closet. For if Pee-wee's (Play)house becomes, in many ways, a closet of and for queer connotative expression (with "secret words," campy bric-a-brac, and everything), and, as such, the prisonhouse of open queer expression, the closets-within-closets represent a desire to "come out"—the desire of the closeted sissy boy to directly express himself in the outside world.

At the end of each episode of *Pee-wee's Playhouse*, Pee-wee pulls down the arm of a reproduction of the famous Greek discus thrower statue, releasing his bike and "one-eyed monster" (slang for penis) helmet. Once helmeted and on the bike, he bids his Playhouse pals and the audience goodbye before magically zooming out of a previously unseen boarded-up and padlocked door; taking this route rather than going out by the front door, which is presided over by a reproduction of the Venus de Milo. So Pee-wee's "outing" of himself is provocatively presented here as a move from the "Venus de Milo" (the incomplete figure of desire) Playhouse door which leads into and out of the space of indirectly expressing queerness (or expressing it strictly in cross-gender terms), to the revelation of hidden "Greek discus thrower" doors/spaces—spaces of potentially open, and even culturally-sanctioned, gay identities and desires.

But the desire to be "out" and therefore to "be" is still expressed symbolically through the play of connotation, and even within these terms, coming out is cast as a dream, a fantasy, a wish. In *Pee-wee's Big Adventure*, Pee-wee wins the Tour de France and public acclaim with his unconventional (read: unathletic, unmasculine) biking style, but wakes up to find it was only a dream. Later in the film, his forays into the outside world on his bike end in humiliation (he falls off his bike in front of a group of boys) or disaster (his bike is stolen by another sissy boy who must sense its sexually symbolic importance).[29] Pee-wee's public reunion with his (homo)sexualized bike in this film is initially set to take place in the *basement* of the Alamo, which proves to be nonexistent in any case, as Pee-wee discovers to his mortification while his tour group laughs derisively. When he finally locates the bike, it is on a movie set, where he must cross-dress as a movie nun to get it back. And while Pee-wee may blast out of his fantastic Playhouse on his bike at the end of each episode, he always lands in an equally fantastic "outside" environment in the form of obvious back projections of the open road. The episode of *Pee-wee's Playhouse* where the secret word is "out," metaphorically translates the process of coming out into Pee-wee developing an illness that makes his "emotions lie very close to the surface," as he tells Ricardo. But having come "very close" to blurting out these "emotions" to one of his love objects, Pee-wee retreats to his bed and soon becomes better. His bout of coming out jitters passed, he is once again ready to take charge of his *implicitly* queer Playhouse-as-closet.

More and more, it seems to me that Jambi, the queeny genie, might be the key to the closeted, yet richly queer-connotative, time-warp Zeitgeist of Pee-wee's world. As the deep-voiced drag diva hidden in a bejeweled box, and the model for the coyly winking sphinx high atop the Playhouse, Jambi flamboyantly expresses a queer femininity that is both the "embarrassing" secret and the cause for celebration— in Pee-wee's world, and often in the queer world outside. He is the fairy godmother who grants Pee-wee wishes (like making him visible again after he has made himself vanish during a magic show), as well as the (older queer generation?) voice of Pee-wee's conscience, often encouraging him to examine his motives and emotions before making a wish. Connected as he is with effeminacy, queer femininity, drag culture, and magic/witchcraft, Jambi is a compelling and disturbing figure whose power and threat is contained because usually he can appear only at Pee-wee's behest (and only in the form of a disembodied head, at that). As the most overtly queer character, Jambi and his magic powers must be carefully guarded and monitored by the regime of the closet of connotation that is Pee-wee's world. But, to quote D.A. Miller again, "if connotation . . . has the advantage of constructing an essentially insubstantial homosexuality, it has the corresponding inconvenience of tending to raise this ghost all over the place."[30] Locked away in his box most of the time, Jambi's queeny spirit still presides on the Playhouse roof as a campy sphinx — at once guarding the secret of Mondo Pee-wee's queerness while announcing it to the world at the beginning of each episode.[31]

NOTES

This article has benefited from the encouragement and critical insights of Jean Rosales, Colin Bailey, Michael Chesonis, and Constance Penley.

1. As a flexible, and activism-charged, term that can refer to gays, lesbians, bisexuals, and those of other non-heterosexual, non-straight sexual desires, identities, and politics, I prefer to use "queer" in this essay as a unifying label, rather than "homosexual" or "gay" (the latter seems to have lost some of its currency as a label under which to unite men and women). This essay will move between "queer" and more specific terms like "lesbian," "gay," "feminine gay," "butch dyke," etc. as the context of discussions dictates. When related to cultural studies, and used in phrases like "queer readings," "queer positions," and "queer pleasures," the word queer is meant to suggest a range of non-heterosexual, non-straight responses to culture that can be experienced by anyone, regardless of their "real life" sexual identity. See my article "There's Something Queer Here," *Screen* (forthcoming), for a more detailed account of these ideas.

2. Bryan Bruce, "Pee Wee Herman: The Homosexual Subtext," *CineAction!* no. 9 (Summer 1987): 6.

3. Ian Balfour, "The Playhouse of the Signifier: Reading Pee-wee Herman," *Camera Obscura* no. 17 (1988): 155–156.

4. Balfour 156.

5. Balfour 156.

6. I use "feminine" and "masculine" in the context of discussing queerness and gender in this essay because these terms evoke a sense of the cultural construction of gender positions and, therefore, they can be used to suggest meanings which range from traditional patriarchal notions that naturalize the masculine and the feminine by conflating them with essentializing biology-based concepts of "man" and "woman," to expressions of radical queer gender identities which deny or ignore this type of straight gender ideology. Some gay men will prefer the terms "effeminate" or "woman-identified" where I use "feminine." I find the former term still too closely connected to straight uses which simultaneously trash gay men and women, while the latter term might appear to place gay men in the position of essentializing theoretical transsexuals. Where I use "effeminate" in this

essay, it should be understood as describing culturally dictated heterosexist ideas about gays and gender (which queers might also employ). My use of "sissy" and "sissy boy" to describe pre-adult feminine gay men is an attempt to capture the position of many homosexual men, like Paul Reubens, who as children in the 1950s and 1960s were defined and labeled as "sissies" (or "girly") by the straight world. The challenge for these gay men (who I count myself among) in later years is to work with, through, or around the pejorative heterosexualized gender connotations that come with being labeled "sissy" or "effeminate."

7. Constance Penley, "The Cabinet of Dr. Pee-wee: Consumerism and Sexual Terror," *Camera Obscura* no. 17 (1988): 147.

8. The following sources provide invaluable queer cultural and historical background for working through visual and aural codings of queerness and gender—in life and in representation: Derek Cohen and Richard Dyer, "The Politics of Gay Culture," *Homosexualities Power and Politics*, ed. Gay Left Collective (London and New York: Allison and Busby, 1980) 172–186; Christine Riddiough, "Culture and Politics," *Pink Triangles*, ed. Pam Mitchell (Boston: Alyson Publishers, 1980) 14–33; Jackie Goldsby, "What It Means To Be Colored Me," *Outlook* vol. 3, no. 1 (Summer 1990): 8–17; Marlon Riggs, "Black Macho Revisited: Reflections of a Snap! Queen," *The Independent* (April 1991): 32–34; Marlon Riggs, "Ruminations of a Snap Queen: What Time Is It?," *Outlook* vol. 12 (1991): 12–19; Kobena Mercer and Isaac Julien, "Race, Sexual Politics and Black Masculinity: A Dossier," *Male Order: Unwrapping Masculinity*, ed. Rowena Chapman and Jonathan Rutherford (London: Lawrence and Wishart, 1988) 97–164; Amber Hollinbaugh and Cherrie Moraga, "What We're Rollin Around in Bed With: Sexual Silences in Feminism," *Powers of Desire: The Politics of Sexuality*, ed. Ann Snitow, Christine Stansell, and Sharon Thompson (New York: Monthly Review Press, 1983) 394–405; Joan Nestle, "The Fem Question," *Pleasure and Danger: Exploring Female Sexuality*, ed. Carole Vance (London: Pandora Press, 1989) 232–241; Joan Nestle, "Butch-Femme Relationships: Sexual Courage in the 1950s," *A Restricted Country* (Ithaca, NY: Firebrand Books, 1987) 100–109; "Sensibility and Survival," New Gay Arts, A Special Issue, *Village Voice* 28 June 1988: 21–39; Esther Newton, "Of Yams, Grinders, & Gays," *Outlook* vol. 1, no. 1 (Spring 1988): 28–37; Madeline Davis and Elizabeth Lapovsky, "Oral History and the Study of Sexuality in the Lesbian Community: Buffalo, New York, 1940–1960," *Hidden From History*, ed. Martin Duberman, Martha Vicinus, and George Chauncy (New York: New American Library, 1989) 426–440; Sue-Ellen Case, "Toward a Butch-Femme Aesthetic," *Discourse* vol. 11, no. 1 (Fall-Winter 1988–1989): 55–71; Lisa Duggan, "The Anguished Cry of an 80s Fem: I Want to Be a Drag Queen," *Outlook* vol. 1, no. 1 (Spring 1988): 62–65; Jan Brown, "Sex, Lies, & Penetration: A Butch Finally 'Fesses Up,'" *Outlook* no. 7 (Winter 1990): 30–34; Arlene Stein, "All Dressed Up, But No Place to Go?: Style Wars and the New Lesbianism," *Outlook*

vol. 1, no. 4 (Winter 1989): 34–44; Mark Leger, "The Boy Look," *Outlook* vol. 1, no. 4 (Winter 1989): 45; Julia Creet, "Lesbian Sex/Gay Sex: What's the Difference?," *Outlook* no. 11 (Winter 1991): 29–34; Jan Zita Grover, "The Demise of the Zippered Sweatshirt: Hal Fischer's *Gay Semiotics*," *Outlook* no. 11 (Winter 1991): 44–47; Michaelangelo Signorelli, "Clone Wars," *Outweek* 28 November 1990: 39–45; Martin Humphries, "Gay Machismo," *The Sexuality of Men*, ed. Andy Metcalf and Martin Humphries (London: Pluto Press, 1985) 70–85; Seymour Kleinberg, "Where Have All The Sissies Gone?," *Alienated Affections* (New York: St. Martin's Press, 1980) 143–156. Besides these specific pieces, many issues of *Outlook*, *Outweek*, *The Advocate*, *On Our Backs*, and *Bad Attitude* (as well as local and more "underground" lesbian, gay and bisexual papers and magazines) have articles, columns, photographs, and drawings that touch upon issues of queer style, gender and sexuality attitudes, and media/art representation.

9. Penley 147.

10. Tania Modleski, "The Incredible Shrinking He[r]man: Male Regression, the Male Body, and Film," *differences* vol. 2, no. 2 (Summer 1990): 64.

11. Modleski 66.

12. Of particular interest to the ongoing discussions of camp in general and in relation to Pee-wee Herman in particular, is the "Where Have All The Sissies Gone?" chapter of Seymour Kleinberg's *Alienated Affections: Being Gay in America* (New York: St. Martin's Press, 1980) 143–156. In part a defense of camp by a feminine gay man (a "sissy"), Kleinberg's comments are are compelling reminders that camp critiques referring to queer texts like *Pee-wee's Playhouse* need to be careful and rigorous about considering queer cultures and queer spectators in their working through the ideological meanings of camp's uses: "Camping did express self-denigration, but it was a complex criticism. . . . [C]amping also released for gay men some of their anger at their closeted lives. . . . Between the values of virility that they did not question and their rage at having no apparent alternatives, gay men would camp out their frustrations." (149–150)

13. Penley 145.

14. This queer blindness takes its most extreme form in an article like Rob Winning's "Pee Wee Herman Un-Mascs Our Cultural Myths About Masculinity" (*Journal of American Culture* vol. 11, no. 2 [Summer 1988]: 57–63), which discusses Pee-wee's reconceptualization of masculinity in heterocentrist terms. Aside from noting that Pee-wee's "movements vacillate between those of a frenetic child and an effeminate male" (and thus suggesting that homosexuality is an immature form of behavior), Winning's article fully recuperates the character and his texts as examples of a kinder, gentler straight masculinity. (57)

15. Along these lines, one might place various aspects of Pee-wee's world

sharply within the range of feminine gay experiences as described by a man quoted in Kleinberg: "We fell for masculinity when we were twelve; there must be something to it because it made us gay. Most of us didn't become gay because we fell in love with sissies; we became sissies because we fell in love with men, usually jocks." (154) With critical irony, Kleinberg follows this quote by saying, "It sounds familiar. And so what if one chooses to make one's life pornographic?" (154) See note 16 for a discussion of Pee-wee's jocks as "pornographic."

16. Cited in Penley's article, but worth repeating here, is Bryan Bruce's observation that each "attractive man" on *Pee-wee's Playhouse* "represents a specific gay male icon, prominent fantasy figures in homosexual pornography . . . including the sailor (Captain Carl), the black cowboy (Cowboy Curtis), and the muscular, scantily-clad lifeguard (Tito), not to mention the escaped con (Mickey) in *Pee Wee's Big Adventure*." (5)

17. Penley 147.

18. Other specific cultural and psychological contexts would complicate straight(forward) readings of Pee-wee and the fat women characters in his texts that foreground misogyny. Some of these contexts are suggested in Michael Moon and Eve Kosofsky Sedgwick's dialogue essay "Divinity: A Dossier, A Performance Piece, A Little-Understood Emotion," *Discourse* vol. 13, no. 1 (Fall-Winter 1990–1991).

Michael Moon: It was a deep fear of mine as a twelve-year-old boy putting on pubescent weight that after having been a slender child, I was at puberty freakish and unaccountably developing feminine hips and breasts. . . . One happy aspect of the story of my own and other gay men's formation of our adolescent and adult body-images is that the fat, beaming figure of the diva has never been entirely absent from our *imaginaire* . . . as an alternative body-identity fantasy. (13)

Eve Kosofsky Sedgwick: John Waters and Divine were a celebrated gay-man-and-diva couple. (15)

Michael Moon: Divine seems to offer a powerful condensation of some emotional and identity linkages—historically dense ones—between fat women and gay men. Specifically, a certain interface between abjection and defiance . . . [which] seems to be related to the interlocking histories of stigma, self-constitution, and epistemological complication proper to fat women and gay men in this century. (15)

Eve Kosofsky Sedgwick: It follows from all this, however, that there *is* such a process as *coming out as a fat woman*. Like the other, more materially dangerous kind of coming out, it involves a risk—here, a certainty—of uttering bathetically as a brave declaration that truth which can scarcely in this instance ever have been less than self-evident. Also, like the other kind of coming out, however, denomination of oneself as a fat woman is a way in the first place of making clear to others that their cultural meanings will be, and will be heard as, assaultive and diminishing to the degree that they are not fat-affirmative. In the second place and far more importantly, it is a way of staking one's claim to insist on, and participate actively in, a renegotiation of the *representational contract* between one's body and one's world. (27)

Throughout this dialogue, Moon and Sedgwick's comments about the often symbiotic relationships of (feminine) gay men and fat women—which are pitched somewhere between "abjection and defiance"—suggest a number of provocative approaches to queerly reading Reubens's construction of, and Pee-wee's interactions with, Mrs. Steve, Mrs. René, the Cowntess, and even the voluptuous Miss Yvonne as something other than examples of misogyny.

19. The works referred to here are *The Women* (1939, MGM, George Cukor); and *Frauen in New York* (1977, Ndr Television, R.W. Fassbinder).

20. Modleski 63.

21. Modleski 63–64.

22. Balfour 158.

23. Balfour 156, 166 (note 1).

24. D. A. Miller, "Anal Rope," *Representations* vol. 32 (Fall 1990): 118–119.

25. Among these sorts of articles and interviews published at the height of the Pee-wee craze were Ian Penman, "America's Sweetheart," *The Face* no. 87 (July 1987): 14–19, 75; Barry Walters, "Triumph of the Twerp," *The Village Voice* 23 Sept. 1986: 43–44; Jack Barth, "Pee Wee TV," *Film Comment* vol. 22, no. 6 (Nov.-Dec. 1986): 79; T. Gertler, "The Pee-Wee Perplex," *Rolling Stone* 12 Feb. 1987: 37–40, 100, 102–103; Margy Rochlin, "Pee-wee Herman," *Interview* vol. 17, no. 7 (July 1987): 45–50.

26. Henry Jenkins III, " 'Going Bonkers!': Children, Play and Pee-wee," *Camera Obscura* no. 17 (1988): 182.

27. The Penley article does an excellent job of critically analyzing the production history of *Pee-wee's Playhouse*, making a good case for the conscious "risks" the network took in "transforming a sexually risqué work of performance art [*The Pee-wee Herman Show*] into a children's television program." Penley goes on to say that "[w]hat is surprising is that CBS never questioned or censored the show's presentation of sexuality, including its clear allusions to homosexuality." (144–145)

28. Penley 136.

29. My queer reading of the sexual connotations surrounding Pee-wee's bicycle is, in part, a response to Winning's interpretation of the bike in conventional pop Freud dream-fantasy terms as "a potent phallic symbol," because it is "something which is fast, red, has a head, and most importantly, fits between his [Pee-wee's] legs." (58) In the context of Winning's

straight reading of Pee-wee's character, this makes sense, as does seeing the loss of the bike as representing castration anxiety. But I'd like to offer a queer—specifically a gay male—reading of this same bicycle and its symbolic sexual functions in Pee-wee's world. As much as something that "fits between his legs," the bike is something Pee-wee sits on. In his Tour de France dream, Pee-wee "is riding erect," as Winning notes, as he excitedly peddles his bike over the finish line. Rather than Pee-wee's own lost penis or phallus, the bike could represent that of another man. Rather than autoeroticism and castration, the sexual pleasure and loss here could be connected to anal sex or dildo play and the loss of a sex partner or a sex toy.

30. Miller 119.

31. At the end of his article, Balfour reminds readers that "the classical sphinx proposed a riddle, a question whose answer, as only Oedipus knew, was 'man.' " (166) While Balfour suggests that "man" is the question, not the answer, in *Pee-wee's Playhouse*, I would queerly propose that "man" is indeed the answer (as in "I want/need a man"), considering queeny Jambi is the sphinx and gay Pee-wee is our Oedipus. Perhaps a gay version of the Oedipus myth is being suggested here?

I assume in this essay that Paul Reubens is queer, as I do also for Dolly Parton. Although having my assumptions validated by public statements might be important to some of my points, such public disclosures would not significantly alter most of my discussions about Pee-wee and queerness. In any case, Reubens (like a number of celebrities) is *considered to be* queer/gay by some portion of the queer and straight publics because this is how they read his Pee-wee Herman persona. By rarely appearing out of character, Reubens encouraged the near erasure of his private life, and the substitution of the public figure of Pee-wee in its place. Therefore, gayness (or a less specific queerness) is part of the range of readings audiences have given Reubens and/as Pee-wee. For an interesting examination of Dolly Parton's place in lesbian culture, see Jean Carlomusto's *L Is For the Way You Look* (1991). As for Sandra Bernhard and k. d. lang, whom I also mention, both have more or less come out/come forward about their queer sexuality: Bernhard through remarks about a lover she refers to as "she" in *Madonna: Truth or Dare* (1991, Miramax, Alex Keshishian), and lang in an interview with Brendan Lemon for *The Advocate*, issue 605 (16 June 1992): 34–46.

COLUMBIA PICTURES
IS PROUD TO PRESENT
THE PULITZER PRIZE PLAY
ON THE SCREEN

WILLIAM HOLDEN

in his most sensational role. as the stranger
in

picnic

with

KIM NOVAK

as the pretty sister

BETTY FIELD
as the mother

SUSAN STRASBERG
as the teen-age sister

CLIFF ROBERTSON
as the rich man's son

AND
CO-STARRING

ROSALIND RUSSELL

AS ROSEMARY

CINEMASCOPE
COLOR BY
TECHNICOLOR

Screen play by   Based upon the play "Picnic"   Produced on the stage by
DANIEL TARADASH • by WILLIAM INGE • THEATRE GUILD, Inc. and JOSHUA LOGAN
(prize-winning screen writer
of "From Here to Eternity")
Directed by JOSHUA LOGAN • Produced by FRED KOHLMAR

Masquerading As the American Male in the Fifties: *Picnic,* William Holden and the Spectacle of Masculinity in Hollywood Film
Steven Cohan

"Whatever does she see in *him?*" is a common female crack about another girl's beau or husband. Or about her movie hero. Marilyn Monroe appeals to almost all men, but there is no male movie star who universally sends the girls. Some like them tough, some like them tender. Some like them wistful and in need of a mother while some others like them as protective as a father. Rippling muscles and a bare chest give some women shivers of delight while still others feel that Hathaway has done more for men than nature. A dimple in the chin is deliciously sexy to dimple doters while other women want to fill it up with putty. Feats of strength and prowess make certain women feel all weak and swoony though some want to say, "Come off it, you big baboon!" ("Stronger" 93)

This opening paragraph of *Life* magazine's pictorial survey of popular male movie stars in 1954 is significant for a number of reasons. In stating that "almost all men" see the same thing in Monroe, the article assumes that masculine desire is universal and uncomplicated; but in going on to comment that, in contrast, "there is no male star who universally sends the girls," *Life* openly acknowledges that women go to films to look at men too and, what's more, that the male image, no less a marketable commodity than the female image, is marked to be looked at in multiple and contradictory ways. As the article reads them, some stars like Burt Lancaster are tough, with an "unshaved brute force" (93), while others like Robert Francis are tender, with "an innocent clean-shaven face" (94).[1] More significantly, the commentary accompanying the photographs goes so far as to suggest that a star's power as an actor in a narrative is deeply implicated in his sexual value on screen. The article's description of Rock Hudson in this respect is quite telling: "In pictures he rides horses and fights off attacking armies and has the physique for this work, being 6 feet 4 inches tall." After offering this very conventional picture of heroic masculinity in action, the text then goes on to point out a much more spectacular dimension of Hudson's star image: "Students of fan appeal are undecided whether Hudson's lies primarily in his 'basic honesty' or his bare chest" (96). Clearly, this "Hollywood album of male appeal" (as the magazine cover called it), appreciates that it is the *sight* of these men on screen which provides the source of their tremendous appeal to female viewers.[2]

In taking the attraction of male stars at face value, quite literally so in the descriptions of Lancaster and Francis, the *Life* article poses something of a problem for the central assumption of much contemporary film criticism, which concentrates on the female and not the male body as the given stake of cinematic representation and spectatorial pleasure. "In their traditional exhibitionist role," Laura Mulvey states in her well known and much reprinted essay, "women are simultaneously looked at and displayed, with their appearance coded for strong visual and erotic impact so that they can be said to connote *to-be-looked-at-ness*" (19). As an explicit contrast to the female star's spectacularity, Mulvey continues, "a male movie star's glamorous characteristics are thus not those of the erotic object of the gaze, but those of the more perfect, more complete, more powerful ideal ego" (20). Anyone interested in Hollywood film as both a representational system and an institutionalized regime of scopic pleasure is indebted to Mulvey's analysis, and this debt cannot be underestimated.[3] However, it is a mistake to conclude from the important critique her essay has inspired that "traditionally male stars did not necessarily (or even primarily) derive their 'glamor' from their looks or their sexuality but from the power they were able to wield within the filmic world in which they functioned" (Kaplan 28). Whether promoting Douglas Fairbanks Sr. and Rudolph Valentino or Robert Redford and Mel Gibson, the Hollywood studios have made it their business to sell the imagery of male stars as part of the film product, holding out to the spectator, female or male, an opportunity to take pleasure in looking at men.[4]

Picnic (1956, Joshua Logan), a popular film from the midfifties, is an especially revealing (in all senses of the word) example of Hollywood cinema's investment in the spectacle of the male body. This film is quite blatantly organized, in both its cinematic address and its narrative, around questions of looking at the body of its male star, William Holden—whose face, not too coincidentally, was on the cover of that *Life* issue promoting its "Hollywood Album of Male Appeal." Ultimately I want to situate this film's visual attention to Holden's body in its historical context, but what interests me about this film to start with is the highly contradictory marking of its star. On one hand, the narrative of *Picnic* conforms to the familiar practice of classic Hollywood cinema, jeopardizing the masculinity of the Holden character only to restore it at the end. On the other hand, the film repeatedly makes a point of visually foregrounding Holden's seminude body as the object of a number of female and male gazes in the diegesis as well as the cinema auditorium, and such unabashed erotic attention to the body of a major male movie star prevents the film's closure from easily serving as an affirmation of traditional masculinity. In response to this problematic marking of Holden as active hero/passive pinup, the film tends to deny its own terms of visual representation. To borrow the significant phrasing of *Life*'s description of Rock Hudson's ambiguous appeal, *Picnic* exploits the sight of Holden's "bare chest" as a primary site of his virility; but then, as a Hollywood product, it also tries to minimize that disturbing male spectacle through an extratextual institutional reliance upon Holden's star image, which exemplifies the "basic honesty" of the American male, though again not without a high degree of contradiction.

1

William Holden may not be remembered as an icon of fifties male sexuality but one should not underestimate his importance to the studio system at that time. He ranked near the top of exhibition polls during the decade, and was number one at the time *Picnic* was released. Nor should one discount his erotic value as a movie star. Scenes displaying him barechested seemed to be a veritable convention of his 1950s films, and his muscular body was prominently used in advertising his most famous and successful ones, *Love is a Many Splendored Thing* (1955) and *Bridge on the River Kwai* (1957), as well as *Picnic*. Given his popularity in the midfifties, it made perfect sense for *Life* to promote its story about sexy male movie stars with his face on the cover. After all, he was the very first movie star that Lucy Ricardo saw upon arriving in Hollywood, when she stared at his "dreamy" face from her booth at the Brown Derby (in a famous episode of *I Love Lucy* which first aired on CBS in February, 1955).

Prominently featuring its two leads as sexual bodies—Kim Novak costars with Holden, and their most famous moment together is choreographed in an erotically charged dance to "Moonglow"—*Picnic* was not an exploitation film by any means but a prestige production of Columbia Pictures. It opened in Beverly Hills to qualify for Academy Award consideration in late December 1955 (it was nominated for six, including Picture and Direction, and it won two) and then premiered officially at Radio City Music Hall the following February. Adapted from William Inge's Pulitzer Prize-winning play and directed by Joshua Logan, who had also done the play, the film begins with the arrival of Hal (Holden) in a small Kansas town on Labor day, and then shows how he disrupts the quiet desperation of a group of unattached women: Flo Owens (Betty Field), her older daughter Madge (Kim Novak), her younger daughter Milly (Susan Strasberg), her boarder Rosemary Sidney, a self-described old-maid schoolteacher (Rosalind Russell), and her neighbor Mrs. Potts (Verna Felton). As in the play, the narrative of the film works to replace the attraction of class and status—represented both by Flo's eagerness to have Madge marry the wealthy Alan Benson (Cliff Robertson) and Hal's need, as he says, to "get someplace in this world"—with the "liberating" sexual desire signified in the lead characters' reciprocal looks and in the camera's gaze at the stars portraying them.

While *Picnic* was the breakthrough film for Kim Novak, even more provocative is its visual as well as narrative and institutional reliance on the spectacle of Holden's body. Indeed, the impression persists that Logan uses any excuse to get Holden to take off his shirt: the star appears barechested during the opening credits, when he is washing in a stream; during the first extended scene in the yard, when he is burning trash for Mrs. Potts and meets the other women; during the afternoon, when he goes swimming with his friend Alan and the two Owens daughters; during the last part of the picnic, when, after he dances with Madge to "Moonglow," Rosemary verbally and physically attacks him, ripping open his shirt; and finally during his love scene with Madge. All of this amounts to quite a lot of bare skin for an actor who wasn't working for DeMille or playing Tarzan.

Holden's shirtlessness, furthermore, does not go without comment in the film itself. The female characters refer to Hal's body in their dialogue; what's more, they look at him quite openly. Mrs. Potts initially encourages Hal to take off his shirt so that she can wash it for him. "You think anyone would mind?" he asks, to which she replies, matter-of-factly, "You're a man. What's the difference?" Her question is rhetorical insofar as she assumes that no one pays attention to a man working out of doors without his shirt; once barechested, however, he proves otherwise.

The scene in the yard, which begins with Hal taking off his shirt to work, is structured around a series of looks which Hal does not initiate and which focus on his body. To begin with, Milly stares at him from the next yard as he burns the trash: after she looks to see who is working there, he looks back at her in a reverse shot. Likewise, after

Hal strips off his shirt to work, Rosemary initiates a secreted look of interest, turning away defensively when Hal returns it. "Working over there, naked as an Indian," she mutters scornfully after she looks, "who does he think is interested?" Rosemary's sarcastic comment leads Milly to take more notice of Hal's body ("*Who*'s naked as an Indian?"), so much so that the newspaper boy Bomber (Nick Adams) has to physically interrupt her voyeurism in order to get her attention. Madge then appears outside on the front porch, and when Hal walks over to rescue her from Bomber's pestering, he restores the familiar dominant position of masculine viewing, which this visual attention to Hal/ Holden's body has been threatening. With Hal's entrance from Mrs. Potts's yard off-screen, the camera retroactively links its viewing position of this scene to his, just as the imposing physical difference between Holden's body and Nick Adams's—marked by the camera's framing as well as commented on by the dialogue ("I'm biggern' you," Hal warns Bomber)—justifies Hal's possession of this feminine space in the name of the phallic male. But despite the attempt to establish a dominant male gaze, this is, significantly, also the point at which Hal first sees Madge and she looks right back, their reciprocal gaze indicating mutual sexual attraction. Furthermore, when Flo, Madge's mother, interrupts that exchange, she makes Hal embarrassed by his nakedness, which connotes his social inferiority as well as his immodesty: in acknowledgment of *her* visual positioning of *his* body, he looks down and covers his bare chest with his arms. And while Madge is still watching Hal as he leaves and shows off his virility on the basketball court, so is her mother, who has driven him out of the yard with her determined stare. After Mrs. Potts calls her over to the more neutral territory of her yard, Madge and Hal gaze at each other again, and her point of view from within the house then closes this sequence as she looks back at Hal through the screen door.

Jackie Byars argues that this scene in the yard exemplifies how the narrative address of the film establishes a gaze "consistently under female control" (123), and to the extent that she is talking about the viewing going on in the diegesis, I agree. The looking that occurs in this scene collapses the kind of binary scopic regime defined by Mulvey, since it places Hal in the same position of "to-be-looked-at-ness" occupied by Madge, who later complains that she is "tired of being pretty" and "tired of only being looked at." But it does not follow, as Byars goes on to claim, that "*Picnic* maintains Madge as its central focus and as its primary discursive agent" (124). First of all, the film allows Hal to be looked at from *multiple* viewing positions: Mrs. Potts's admiration, Milly's curiosity, Rosemary's hostility, Bomber's rivalry, Madge's attraction, Flo's suspicion, and, later in the film, Alan's identification and then jealousy. Secondly, all of this visual attention to Hal keeps turning the film's narrative around the problem of his masculinity, which gets played out at the site of his body, and not Madge's sexuality, as in the play. Madge therefore does not dominate the film's focalization or discourse as Byars assumes.

The film's shift of emphasis from Madge to Hal seems to have been a commercial decision on Columbia's part to turn the play into a star vehicle for Holden, who was still under contract to the studio at the time. Holden was the only star with above-the-title billing, and the film establishes the importance of his character with the first title card superimposed over an image of his body. The action occurring under the credits, moreover, opens up the play to show Hal arriving by box car in the Kansas town. This opening establishes a narrative frame that directs the viewer's attention to watch him serving as the catalyst of the film's action, first disrupting the stasis of the female community to expose its sexual desperation, and then unequivocally motivating the revised ending Joshua Logan insisted upon when directing the play on Broadway, with Madge leaving home to follow Hal to Tulsa rather than remaining in the town with her reputation as a "good girl" forever tarnished, as Inge originally intended.[5] The closure of the film thus occurs for audiences at the moment of Hal's decision to accept the proper breadwinner role (he proposes to Madge the morning after they make love, and then leaves for Oklahoma in search of gainful employment to support her), instead of her decision to break with her mother's hypocritical middle-class values (when she leaves to follow him). The adaptation, in short, gives the story to Hal and the film to Holden, which is how the review in *Photoplay* read *Picnic*: "Holden plays a light-hearted drifter who hits a Kansas town one summer day, lifting the spirits of many of its people (especially the women). . . . At the annual picnic . . . matters come to a climax. . . . And the picnic's last hours also bring Holden to a moment of decision" (Graves).

This reorientation of the play's storyline around Hal meant that Madge's desire for independence had to be subordinated to his growth as a "man." In effect, what the studio did was to redirect the play's emphases more along the lines of a conventional family melodrama, one of the favorite fifties genres for displaying American masculinity in crisis and then resolving it through the successful formation of a heterosexual couple. Much more so than in the play, Brandon French points out, "the film's subliminal message is that it takes *two* people to make a 'real man,' the man himself and the woman who sacrifices herself to his welfare" (119). To secure the conditions for turning Hal into such a "real man," *Picnic* "eliminates or changes most of the basis of the women's internal conflict," concentrating instead on Hal's longings and insecurities (116). Most notably, Daniel Taradash's screenplay discredits Flo's dreams for Madge by making them tantamount to pandering, it motivates Rosemary's resentment of Hal and Madge solely out of jealousy, and it uses the nonconforming, tomboyish Milly to validate Madge's choice to follow Hal. "In this way," French concludes, "the film makes room for Hal's considerable deficiency—his desperate lies and foolish dreams of grandeur and superficial bravado—without endangering his position as the romantic hero. In fact, it makes enough room to accommodate a hero whose vulnerability, beneath all those rippling muscles, is the basis of his appeal" (117).

But the film's considerable visual interest in Hal's body ends up subverting the kind of recuperation of conventional masculinity which French attributes to the narrative's closure. Thus, while the film may appear to be telling Hal's story, and valorizing him as "another [fifties] natural man" (Biskind 325) in a nostalgic yearning for an obsolete form of masculinity—that is, one made antiquated by the suburban American ranch house and back yard—it is still the spectacle of his bare chest, particularly as reinforced by the sight of Holden's oiled muscular body in CinemaScope, that sparks the action from scene to scene, continually attracting the camera's gaze and establishing the male body as the film's primary image of sexual difference.

2

From the very moment that Hal/Holden first takes off his shirt behind the opening credits, *Picnic* challenges the fifties orthodoxy of a "real man": the white, middle-class, married business man, whose stereotypical profession (Madison Avenue advertising executive) and bland uniform (the ubiquitous grey flannel suit) well represented his power over the image. To start with, the spectacle of Hal's body immediately disturbs the social and sexual binaries which uphold that conventional representation of masculinity. If, as Richard Dyer comments about the male pinup, "a man's athletic body may be much admired, but only on condition that it has been acquired through sports not labour" (*Stars* 43), then the sight of Hal working in Mrs. Potts's yard obscures the significant class difference between a male body praised for its athleticism (one of Hollywood's primary excuses for showing off a star's body, going back to Douglas Fairbanks), and a male body marked with the effects of hard physical labor. Originally a college sports hero with a physique appropriate for display, Hal now uses his body to work. Physical labor is the reason for his present fitness, as well as the occasion for the spectacle of his body in the yard scene, which positions him as an erotic object for the various female viewers.

Hal's "rippling muscles" may therefore signify phallic superiority in comparison to the other more diminutive male bodies on screen, but it also reminds the women characters of his social inferiority as an itinerant laborer, which is, in turn, linked to his very unmanly capacity to be turned into a sexual object for them, into what one British reviewer called, significantly enough, "a male Marilyn Monroe, halfway between a threat and a promise" (Brien). Or as *Time* put it, drawing a comparison that also suggests Hal's similarity to a female movie star, he "is a sex bomb" ("Conquest" 63). Since Hal's very appealing virility has its undeniable basis in the spectacle of his muscular body, the film encodes him with the value of "to-be-looked-at-ness"; this marking then turns him, figuratively speaking, into a male version of the desirable female, the bombshell epitomized in the fifties by Monroe, as the only way the dominant culture could comprehend male spectacle. After all, in the fifties a "real man" simply didn't take off his shirt and strut in solicitation of another's gaze without calling into question his virility and, with that, his sexual identity.

The problem which the spectacle of Hal poses for fifties masculinity is made immediately apparent after the yard scene establishes the powerful erotic appeal of his body. Leaving Mrs. Potts's house, Hal goes to find his rich college friend Alan Benson, and entertains him with a bawdy account of his life since leaving college. The importance of this next scene lies in certain particulars of the story Hal tells Alan as they engage in frat-boy banter and physical play. Their exchange probably resonates more forcefully in the film than on stage because Hal's account of his past begins by calling attention to the spectacle of men in the movies. After working in a gas station and a stint in the army, Hal says he went to Hollywood to become a "big movie hero." Renamed "Brush Carter," he expected a big career but failed his screen test because of his teeth: "Out there you gotta have a certain kind of teeth or they can't use you," he tells Alan. "Don't ask me why. Anyway, this babe told me they'd have to pull all my teeth and give me new ones, so naturally . . ." Naturally, Hal refused (though both actors playing this scene on film probably had their teeth capped). Even more striking is what happened to Hal next. Hitchhiking in Texas, he confides, "two babes pull up in this big yellow convertible. And one of 'em slams on the brakes and hollers, 'get in, Beefcake!' So I got in." The two babes get him drunk on martinis. Indeed, though he boasts, "they musta thought I was Superman," when he tires out before they do, "one of 'em sticks a gun in my back. She says, 'This party's goin' on till we say it's over, Buck!' You'da thought she was Humphrey Bogart!" Exhausted, Hal passes out and, while asleep, gets rolled of his life savings by the two women. To add insult to his injury, when he goes to the police they don't believe him but call his story "wishful thinking." "I'm telling you, Benson," he warns, "women are getting desperate."

Hal is using his autobiographical narrative to show off his virility to Alan, and not surprisingly his friend responds with admiration and envy, wondering why such sexual adventures never happen to him. But at the same time it is important to notice that Hal gains Alan's attention by telling a story of male sexual *failure*, which he then turns into an allegory of the female desperation that jeopardizes virility. In doing this Hal helps brings the film into line with the new discourses of sexuality that emerged from the bestselling Kinsey reports on sexual behavior in men (1948) and women (1953). The conclusions of the first volume were highly publicized, quickly entering the public idiom, and the findings of the second report were even more widely circulated through the mainstream press, which stressed this unexpected difference between men and women according to Kinsey: the sexuality of men peaks in their late teens, *Time* reported, "the height of their physical power for sexual activity," and then "the man's curve keeps on dropping, *i.e.*, his need for sexual activity generally declines while the woman's stays fairly high" ("5,940" 54). *Newsweek* went so far as to italicize the point so that no one would miss the troubling implications of this "bomb" dropped by Kinsey:[6] "*Females are most sexually responsive in their late 20s and early 30s, and their capacity remains more or less constant into their 50s and 60s*" ("All" 70).

Viewed in this context, Hal's autobiographical narrative gives him a rather obvious ideological function: he translates the social and economic implications of the female characters' desperation into sexual and thus more personalized terms. His presence exposes the unhealthy repression of female sexuality so that the hostility of the deserted wife Flo and spinster schoolteacher Rosemary appears as a symptom of what they "really" desire as women in the age of Kinsey; and he then cures female repression by liberating Madge's sexuality and, to a lesser extent, Milly's from that cloistered and oppressive feminine environment. In short, Hal reconfirms the power of the phallus to bring out the sexuality of the women in this matriarchal community, thereby implicitly regenerating exhausted male sexuality for American men past the age of nineteen. However, as Hal serves this symbolic function, he ends up performing the role which Mulvey attributes to the female in Hollywood film: "Ultimately, the meaning of woman is sexual difference" (21). As Mrs. Potts declares to Flo after Hal's departure: "He clomped through the place like he was still outdoors. There was a man in the house, and it seemed good."[7]

Mrs. Potts's admiration for Hal's masculinity is essentially un-changed from the play, which used Hal to define sexual difference around the phallus so blatantly that *New Republic* reviewer Eric Bent-ley accused Inge of waving, as a symbolic banner, "the torn shirt of Stanley Kowalski," which "stands for the new phallus worship. . . . so much is made of the hero's body and . . . he has so little else" (71–72). This response was a common one. By now it is an unfortunate cliche that "the figure of the stud [in *Picnic* as well as in Tennessee Williams' plays and films] . . . is, like the sex-starved woman, largely a figment of male homosexual fantasy" (Haskell 250). So it is important to remember what Kinsey's research called attention to regarding sex-ual behavior and dysfunction in American men. Heterosexual mas-culinity, it turned out, was not quite the monolithic identity the culture supposed; and the figure of the stud — along with the movie stars who personified him — spoke compellingly of a fantasized masculinity to heterosexual men too, especially when they were told by science that female sexual desire exceeded male performance.

Brought to public attention by Kinsey, male sexual inadequacy be-came increasingly visible throughout the decade, referred to in both scholarly journals and the popular press as the primary problem of the contemporary American male's psychology; a related symptom that American masculinity was in deep trouble was the mounting evidence that middle-class men were susceptible to employment stress and heart disease, since this fact further underscored the fragility and vulnerability of the male body in comparison to the female (Ehrenreich 73–81). As *Look* magazine reported in a 1955 article, men may have larger and stronger bodies "but despite these superiorities, men are actually weaker than women — in health, longevity and other ways" (Frank 52). The resulting crisis in masculinity — the failure to experi-ence male identity happily let alone define it with any degree of con-sistency — led sociologist Helen Mayer Hacker to comment in 1957: "Virility used to be conceived as a unilateral expression of male sex-uality, but is regarded today in terms of the ability to evoke a full sexual response on the part of the female" (231). In response to this inflated and yet narrow ideal of masculinity, Hacker proposed, "ho-mosexuality may be viewed as one index of the burdens of masculin-ity" — a "flight from masculinity" that indicates both a confusing mul-tiplication of the qualities comprising a "real man" (who should be able effortlessly to negotiate the conflicting demands of the board room, the bedroom, and the family room), and an excessive raising of the sexual stakes of manhood by fifties American culture, which taught that "sexual performance is more inextricably linked to feelings of masculine self-worth than even motherhood is to women" (231).

That American men failed the test of manliness because of American women was a complaint repeated in the popular press again and again. *Look,* for instance, picked up Hacker's criticism of the excessive cultural burdens imposed on masculine identity and male sexuality but missed the point of her critique. "Scientists who study human behavior fear that the American male is now dominated by the American female," *Look* warned, ". . . he is no longer the masculine, strong-minded man who pioneered the continent and built America's greatness" (Moskin 77). The contemporary American male, the article continued, "has even lost much of his sexual initiative and control; some authorities believe that his capacity is being lowered" (78). Taking to task "women's new aggressiveness and demand for sexual satisfaction" (78) as the reason for "the decline in male sexual potency" (80), the article then turned around the implications of Kinsey's findings by arguing that the male's "withdrawing from sex relations" (80) is not due to a biological clock but is another symptomatic defense—like bachelorhood and homosexuality—against the female-dominated society that fifties America had become following the Second World War. With woman regulating sexual contact, repressing "the male's recognized biological nature, which impels him to seek the company of a variety of females" (77), and then demanding that he defer his own pleasure for her total satisfaction—"she cannot accept compromises" (78)—it is small wonder that men were said to be suffering from "fatigue," "passivity," "anxiety," and "impotency" (78–79) or that, as the article quotes one sexologist, "our younger generation [already] shows signs of being fagged out . . ." (78).

If I have seemed to digress, it is only to underscore the discursive field of Hal's sexuality; for whatever sexual connotations fifties audiences read in him were loaded, to say the least. He is by no means characterized as a homosexual in his sexual behavior (although his physical horseplay with Alan and their competition for Madge suggests such an undercurrent); and his muscular body seems to belie the effeminacy which the culture equated with homosexuality. Yet the film not only puts his body on display as an object of desire, turning him into "a male Marilyn Monroe," it also shows his attractiveness to all the characters, the other men (Alan, Howard Bevans, Mr. Benson) as well as the women. Hal, furthermore, is that most reviled and "unmanly" of fifties male figures, the bum, as exemplified by his many itinerant occupations: football hero, soldier, Hollywood "starlet," cowboy, and artist's model, he tells Milly, posing "almost in the raw." That these jobs are also all gender stereotypes is significant. Immature, insecure, and most of all an imposter, Hal's appealing virility turns out to depend upon his *posing* as a stud, lying and bragging to cover up his inability to make good on his muscles.

From the perspective of the dominant culture of breadwinning males, Hal encodes the failure of orthodox masculinity, which is the specific meaning fifties America read into homosexuality, treating it as a question of gender inversion and social irresponsibility rather than as a difference of sexuality. With the breadwinning ethic the unquestioned norm of heterosexual masculinity in the domestic distribution of gender in the home (men earned and women spent), "homosexuality" was the pejorative term encoding sexual immaturity, domestic irresponsibility, and professional failure, all covered up by the homosexual's pretense of being a "real man" (the able lover, wise father, successful provider). "Since a man couldn't actually become a woman (Christine Jorgenson was the only publicized exception throughout the fifties), heterosexual failures and overt homosexuals could only be understood as living in a state of constant deception. And this was perhaps the most despicable thing about them: They *looked like* men, but they weren't really men" (Ehrenreich 26). Once read as a form of social *deception,* the very category of "homosexuality" called into question the culture's assumption of a stable and automatic relation between male sexuality and masculine identity, implying instead that gender is an effect of social *reception.* Consequently, when Hal's adventure with the two women in Texas seems to encode a homosexual stud fantasy for audiences, it does so in large part because what he tries to conceal through the sexual bravado of that narrative ("they musta thought I was Superman") is the objectification of his body in the eyes of a desiring other, which results in the exposure of his sexual inadequacy. Rather than proving his virility, then, his body does just the opposite, letting slip its concealment of his failed manhood. Not only do the women exhaust *him,* but one of them figuratively turns into a man, sticking a gun in his back to "motivate" his sexual services: "You'da thought she was Humphrey Bogart!" (So what does that make him? Lauren Bacall?)

This troubling suspicion that Hal's virile brand of masculinity is bogus—nothing more than a series of poses, what with his frequent posturing and bragging and muscle-flexing—comes to the film from its source material in the play; and so does the ambivalence with which Hal is at once valued for his idealized manliness, particularly his ability to satisfy every kind of sexual fantasy, and yet rejected for turning the desperations of masculinity into a public spectacle. From the very beginning of its tryout run outside New York, just how to pitch Hal caused difficulties for the production. Logan attributed the mixed reactions of the audience to discomfort on the part of men even more than women with the excessive posturing of Hal's character. To solve this problem, Logan inserted, with Inge's permission, a speech for Alan

Benson—"the most reliable character"—establishing explicit disapproval of his friend's exhibitionism (Logan *Josh* 354–55). Alan tells Flo that, like the other boys in their fraternity, he too didn't like Hal until they shared a room and he got to know him better, that is, could see what genuine manliness was underneath the bragging and posing. In the film this dialogue occurs as Flo and Alan drive to the picnic. This criticism of Hal, though, seems only halfhearted at best since in both play and film Alan still responds favorably (and vicariously) to Hal's sexual bragging about those two "babes."

On film *Picnic* makes a greater effort to redeem Hal's masculinity through Rosemary's drunken attack on him at the picnic. Visibly shaming him with her lascivious attentions when she pulls him away from Madge and rips open his shirt, Rosemary causes a scandal which he does not deserve, for all his bragging and posturing. With the curious crowd gathering on the bridge to witness his embarrassment and a searchlight illuminating his humiliating nakedness, Hal is made a public spectacle as the result of her drunken outburst, which shows her up, in turn, as a hysterical, repressed, vindictive and, most of all, sexually desperate woman castrating the natural phallic man. Madge must consequently step in "to restore and sustain Hal's crumbling manhood; and making him 'something' makes her 'something' in turn. That is the symbiotic nature of 'real manhood' and 'real womanhood' which the film doggedly celebrates" (French 118). Yes, but . . . it is not easy to forget Hal's anecdote about those two "babes." That little allegory of castrating female desperation recounts how *he*, reduced to a sexual object by those two women, was unable to keep (it) up with them. He lacked the potency to begin with, so Rosemary's outburst cannot be dismissed simply as a spiteful and undeserved belittling of his genuine masculinity, even though that is the inflection of Rosalind Russell's shrill performance in this scene.

When she cuts in on his dance with Madge, Rosemary treats Hal in the same way that the two "babes" and the camera have done, as an object of erotic scopic interest. "You know what?" she whispers, holding him so tightly that her earrings dig into his neck, "You remind me of one of those old statues. One of those Roman gladiators. All they had on was a shield!" Then, after he tries to get away, she tears his shirt in her effort to cling to him, and he tries to cover up his exposed chest. "You been stompin' around here in those boots like you owned the place," she yells, "thinking every woman you saw was gonna fall madly in love." Rosemary's beau Howard Bevans (Arthur O'Connell) tries to defend Hal against her accusation that he got Milly drunk, saying, "The boy didn't do anything," but Rosemary goes on: "You think just 'cause you act young you can walk in here and make off with whatever you like. But let me tell you something—you're a fake! You're no jive kid—you're just scared to act your age!" Rosemary's accusation literally brings Hal to his knees. "She looked right though me like an X-ray machine," he tells Madge afterwards, and what Rosemary exposes is the castration motivating a male form of masquerade that constitutes virility out of fakery and spectacle. Based in spectacle from the start and then exposed as a fake, Hal's impersonation of masculinity crosses gender lines insofar as both the spectacle and the fakery link him to what Hollywood has routinely and historically defined as the feminine position in representation.[8] Hal's masquerade of masculinity is undeniably attractive to both women and men in the film because of those two significant characteristics, and for that reason, it is also deeply disturbing, as first Rosemary's attack indicates and then Alan's repudiation of Hal before Flo immediately afterwards confirms.

Rosemary's stinging accusation that Hal is "no jive kid" is made even more problematic in the film because of the casting of the 37-year old Holden in the part. The final draft of the script (May 2, 1955) repeats the text of Inge's script by describing Hal as "an exceedingly handsome, husky youth," and then adds: "sure of his attraction, but down deep, unsure of himself." To uphold this characterization, the film equates the sexual attraction and liberating value of Hal's masculinity with his youth and boyishness: he is called "a boy" several times by both Flo and Howard, and he is Oedipalized through his inheritance of his father's boots and criminal past. After Rosemary's attack, Madge attempts to reassure Hal of his youthfulness: "Don't pay any attention to her—you *are* young. . . . Not so young that you're not a man, too." With this kind of double-talk Madge hits the proverbial problem right on the button: for in its visual register the film keeps representing Hal's masculinity in terms of his highly developed body, which does not look boyish at all. As a result, Rosemary's sarcastic admonition that he look into a mirror and see his real age rings truer than the lines may have ever intended, suggesting an additional dimension of Hal's masquerade in the film. The Hal we see performed by William Holden is no jive kid at all but another kind of fake, a husky man masquerading as a youth strutting before the interested gaze of the camera.

Picnic makes no pretense of disguising Holden's age since a great deal of the visual impact of his performance depends upon the sight of his physically mature body. The muscular definition of his build—with its clean lines, smooth surface, thick chest, lean stomach—differentiates Holden from younger stars like James Dean on the one hand, and older stars like James Stewart on the other. In the photograph and poster art used to publicize the film, which produced what is arguably the most famous image of *Picnic* (though it is not actually from the film), Holden stands with his shirt ripped open and hanging off his arms, his pectorals bared, biceps flexed, stomach held in tightly; while Novak, positioned to his side somewhat at knee-level, pulls at the sleeve of his torn shirt (see figures 1 and 2). In addition, the studio produced a series of stills based on the same visual theme (see figure 3 for the one from the set now being used to sell the video). Holden's body dominates Novak's in every spatial variation of this scene; so while her breasts are not ignored by any means, his body functions just as much if not more than hers to draw the viewer's gaze toward the photograph. Indeed, as one chronicler of Holden's career notes about *Picnic*: "The two [Holden and Novak] made a lusty pair, though it's a toss up for the more photogenic chest" (Holtzman 115). One could never make that claim of James Stewart in either of his two films with Novak (not after seeing him take off his shirt in *Rear Window*), nor of James Dean with Natalie Wood in *Rebel Without a Cause*.

The film text itself emphasizes the erotic value of the male body as spectacle by stylizing the visual treatment of Hal/Holden in a manner more befitting a biblical epic than a melodrama. It is therefore highly appropriate that Hal reminds Rosemary of a Roman gladiator and a statue. Like the epic genre, *Picnic* draws on conventions of the bodybuilding exhibition for its representational codes: celebrating the muscularity of a hard, tensed, oiled and hairless body in an ostensible if sometimes kitschy reference to antique statuary. To be sure, lacking the overall muscular density of a bodybuilder, Holden's build is actually more characteristic of a prize fighter's, which should not be all that surprising since he made his screen debut in *Golden Boy* (1939) as a boxer. The boxer, perhaps because his sport shows off his torso so easily, has always been the movies' prototype of a well-developed, well-proportioned body. Whether displaying this body type in a sports arena or ancient Rome or a Kansas backyard, fifties Hollywood in particular pretty much followed conventions of male spectacle which the biblical epic exemplified and which found their source in body building and so-called "art" or "athletic" male photography. Filling up the wide screen "with straining muscular flesh" (Foster 12), these spectacles reinscribed a very orthodox understanding of masculinity, one which assumes "that it is precisely *straining* that is held to be the great good, what makes a man a man" (Dyer "Don't" 72).

One feels compelled to ask, however: straining for whose benefit? Antony Easthope's comments about photographs of sports figures, who routinely make a public show of straining their muscles, applies

Figure one

to the imagery of Holden's body in *Picnic* and to the movies' display of athletic physiques in general: "these images of the hard, trained, disciplined body under rational control are not just there to be identified with—they are there to be looked at" (53). Once spectacularized in this fashion, the movie or sports hero may be straining his muscular body as vainly (or, I would say, as effectively) as Hal does at the picnic to prove his manliness: for while the image may invite viewers to

Figure two

COLUMBIA PICTURES
IS PROUD TO PRESENT
THE PULITZER PRIZE PLAY
ON THE SCREEN

WILLIAM HOLDEN
in his most sensational role, as the stranger
in

picnic

with

KIM NOVAK
as the pretty sister

BETTY FIELD
as the mother

SUSAN STRASBERG
as the teen-age sister

CLIFF ROBERTSON
as the rich man's son

AND
CO-STARRING

ROSALIND RUSSELL
AS ROSEMARY

CinemaScope
COLOR BY
TECHNICOLOR

Screen play by
DANIEL TARADASH • by WILLIAM INGE • THEATRE GUILD, Inc. and JOSHUA LOGAN
(prize-winning screen writer
of "From Here to Eternity")   Directed by JOSHUA LOGAN • Produced by FRED KOHLMAR

Based upon the play "Picnic"
Produced on the stage by

Figure three

identify with the man's powerful muscular body as a phallocratic ideal ego, his presence *in* the image also confuses the difference between who is visible as spectacle (usually the female) and who does the looking (usually the male). Hal's claim to sexual power as an actor in the diegesis, no less than Holden's erotic appeal as an actor on the screen, depends upon his being seen, in direct violation of the expected sexual differentiation of looking/being looked at.

As *Picnic* fashions Holden's body into a recurring visual reference to the epic's conventionalized style of male exhibitionism, furthermore, the imagery cannot help reminding viewers of the fact that a highly-defined and developed body like his is not natural at all. Bulging, well articulated muscles may be phallic but they are also the result of repeated labor and discipline and, in a lot of cases, a careful regimen of diet and steroids. As Margaret Walters comments: "paradoxically, body-building is the most purely narcissistic and, in that sense, most feminine, of pastimes. The body-builder's goal is appearance not action. He is less like the sportsman trying to improve on his time or performance, than he is like the woman, who sees her body as raw material to be pummeled, pounded, starved and even cut into better shape" (294–95). Consequently, rather than inflating Hal's importance as a physical symbol of patriarchal domination of women, as one might expect from all the attention lavished on his muscles, the visual comparison implied between Holden's body and the biblical epic hero/bodybuilder keeps foregrounding what in the Hollywood star system is perhaps most fundamental to the representation of masculinity on screen, and most disturbing to the symbolic phallic support of male power: the extent to which an actor's appearance, no less than his female counterpart's, has to be artificially fashioned into an *image* of physical virility for the eye of the camera—with a little bit of help from toupees, shoe lifts, and Max Factor, that goes without saying.

The cosmetic aspect of screen performance is crucial to the particular look of movie stars of both genders, although for men it runs against the grain of the cultural assumption that masculinity is the essential and spontaneous expression of maleness. As illustrated by Hitchcock's use of Kim Novak in *Vertigo*, which plays the artifice of her lavender blonde star image against her own Midwest (and brunette) origins, the appeal of a female actress usually gives her star image a cultural materiality inflected—through the tropes of clothes, voice, makeup, and hair—with specific references (even if faked) to class, age, and ethnic identity as the measure of her feminine authenticity. And as James Stewart illustrates in the same film, it is the comparative absence of those social references that inscribes the apparent invisibility and, hence, naturalness of his masculinity. That naturalness, however, is just another type of mask, since the actor is costumed, lit, madeup— just like the actress. For this reason, as Michael Malone observes, "acting itself is seen as tinged with unmanliness" (6); it is not a manly art like one of the professional or amateur sports precisely because "a real man" should not have to depend upon art for his virility. Screen acting in particular blows the cover of a "natural" man in its technical acknowledgment that gendered sexualities are constituted out of fakery and spectacle—out of what I have been calling "masquerade" and what Judith Butler terms "performance."[9] Given the fifties' anxiety about masculinity becoming feminized, there was every reason for

Photoplay to ask "Are Actors Sissies?" at the thought of "big handsome he-men of the wide open spaces primping and prancing in make-up before they go into a scene" (Armstrong 53).[10]

Sissies or no, for a film like *Picnic* to follow the example of the biblical epic in observing the "unwritten rule" of art photography that "male nudes should be smooth" as a way of suggesting "associations with marble" (Foster 43) which help to aestheticize the male body—and also, I assume, help to make it appear younger and less differentiated as a *sexed* body—the makeup department has to make-over the star with more attention to his body than usual, in the process violating another one of the most time-honored assumptions about sexual difference: the law of Samson's razor. "If a man manicures his nails or shaves his legs," Rosalind Coward remarks, "he's likely to be mocked; a woman shaving her legs, though, is seen as expressing her natural femininity" (230). In Hollywood, however, baring the chest to represent the classical ideal of smooth muscularity required an actor like Holden (and Brando, and Clift, and so on down the line) to shave his hirsute body. Susan Strasberg recalls that Holden "complained when he had to shave his chest" but, as she adds, "No hair was allowed in 1955" (Strasberg 46), so he had to submit to the razor, no doubt more than once given the amount of screen time Logan devoted to his chest.

The particular physical features connoting Holden's "virility," as inscribed by the makeup department on his body, are thus no different than those connoting the "sexiness" of a female star like Monroe or Novak; and they are just as historically inflected to conform the star's appearance to popular tastes of the period, although the male's star's body is cosmetically marked to produce the opposite effect, representing his maleness as a universal condition of nature. Nonetheless, no matter how hard Hollywood tries to naturalize maleness, the apparatus of the star system proves otherwise, because male sexual identity on screen is the effect of an actor performing a historically specific version of masculinity. *Picnic* makes this dimension of male star performance quite clear in the way it foregrounds the spectacle of Holden's body.

3

Even more so than Hal's account of his brief brush with Hollywood stardom, I have been arguing, the continual spectacle of Holden's body in *Picnic* challenges the film's ostensible project of recuperating Hal for conventional masculinity. This is not to suggest, though, that the casting of Holden as Hal was a careless decision on the studio's part which worked against the impact of the film. On the contrary, I believe that "William Holden" was fundamental to the film's economic *and* ideological success in refuting what it simultaneously exploits in making (and marketing) the image of the male body as the primary stake of Hal's (and Holden's) masculinity. Holden's secure star image of being "solid citizen on screen and off" ("Stronger" 93) could help overcome the role's disturbing implication that masculinity is constituted in a performance of virility, so it is a considerable extratextual dimension of the film's complex attitude toward Hal and, more importantly, toward the male body as an object of cinematic fascination.

In the fifties Holden's star image actually went to the opposite extreme of Hal in openly disclaiming performance. Although he was not the only male star in Hollywood to disavow his craft because of its "unmanly" associations with fakery and spectacle, the acclaim for the naturalness of Holden's performance style stands out in a period dominated by the discourse of self-conscious Method acting (particularly given the ties which the play *Picnic* had to the New York background circulating that discourse). Unlike Brando, Clift, or Dean, say, in the words of Billy Wilder, his director in three major pictures, Holden "is beyond acting" (quoted in "Conquest" 64). "Only actors who are ashamed to act are worth their salt," Wilder is supposed to have said as well, and "that's why I'm fond of Holden. He dies every time he has to act" (quoted in Malone 6). With this kind of press from his best director, it followed that a large part of the "authenticity" of Holden's star image was based on his supposed transcendence of screen performance so that there could be no question about *his* masculinity even when the character's was in doubt. Consequently, the age and personality differences between "William Holden" and the character he played in *Picnic* could accentuate the actor's own safe distance from his impersonation of the bragging, swaggering Hal.

The naturalness of Holden's performance style, which serves to ground the potentially explosive implications of the role of Hal, is a dominant characteristic of the Hollywood movie star generally. "Naturalness" supplies one of the key performance codes through which the star system helps to structure the meaning of a film. As Richard Dyer explains:

> There is a whole litany in the fan literature surrounding stars in which certain adjectives endlessly recur—sincere, immediate, spontaneous, real, direct, genuine and so on. All of these words can be seen as relating to a general notion of "authenticity." It is these qualities that we demand of a star if we accept her or him in the spirit in which she or he is offered. Outside of a camp appreciation, it is the star's really seeming to be what s/he is supposed to be that secures his/her star status, "star quality" or charisma. Authenticity is both a quality necessary to the star phenomenon

to make it work, and also the quality that guarantees the authenticity of the other particular values a star embodies (such as girl-next-door-ness, etc.) It is this effect of authenticating authenticity that gives the star charisma . . . (Dyer "Star" 14)

A male movie star's supposed authenticity as a nonperformer is what usually supports Hollywood's equation of "seeming natural" with "being male." However, since the apparatus promotes, as Dyer puts it, only an "effect of authenticating authenticity" — that is, for an actor like Holden, the simulation of virility, deeply convincing perhaps but artificial just the same — then the screen actor's quite literal performance of masculinity on film always implicates male sexual identity and desire in a masquerade no less artificial (or no more natural) than the female star's — or Hal's, for that matter.

In the specific case of Holden, his discomfort with the artifice of screen performance is made evident in accounts of his temper, his drinking, and his daredevil stunts, and these are stressed in opposition to — and as a means of recuperating — the way his semi-nude body is positioned as an erotic spectacle on screen in *Picnic*. Is it simply coincidence that every anecdotal account of the film's production not only mentions Holden's discomfort with the role of Hal because of age and temperament but goes on to stress the actor's own display of youthfulness and virility on the set? Susan Strasberg, for one, remembers Holden being "very unhappy about his role. 'Christ, Josh, I can't swing around like a monkey. I'm too old for that crap. I'm going to look like an idiot' " (46). Yet at the same time it appears that Holden *did* more than his share of swinging around on the set. One repeated story has him hanging off the ledge of a tenth (or seventh, or fourteenth — the number varies in each account of the episode) floor hotel window in order (and, again, the point of the story varies with the source) to get Logan to apologize for something he said (in Strasberg 47); or to prove his athletic ability with a daredevil stunt (in Logan *Movie* 16–17); or to show it off in a fit of drunkenness (in Russell 186); or to relax because, "for some reason, Holden, a trained gymnast, likes to lower himself from outside a window-sill, hang there, and look around" (as reported by *Time* in "Conquest" 63). In short, as Logan puts it, "he was simply a red-blooded American boy who wanted to have a good time, and believe me, he did" (*Movie* 11).

Time's cover story on Holden, "The Conquest of Smiling Jim," timed to the national release of *Picnic* in February 1956, is an important document in this regard because it promotes his star image as "a red-blooded American boy" by using criticism of his performance as evidence of the authenticity of his masculinity, which, like Logan, the magazine also understands in national rather than erotic terms, thus going against the very grain of *Picnic*'s visual text. Unlike Hal, Holden's "driving sincerity," "his almost complete lack of pretentiousness" ("Conquest" 67), shine forth in the *Time* article as proof of his genuine virility on screen and off. "Holden's talent as an actor is not large, as he readily admits, but he uses it with an almost ferocious sincerity, and with an intelligence much keener than some men with greater gifts enjoy" (63). Miscast in *Picnic,* the article continues,

> Bill was asked not only to portray a man far younger than himself, but to animate a type, completely opposite to his own—a feat especially difficult on the screen. For a good cinemactor, there is only one way to act: don't. The camera comes so close that the slightest insincerity can be seen. Bill's whole experience has taught him not to play a part, but to play himself in the part. . . . In the *Picnic* part, however, the old way would not work, and Bill was made most mightily to stretch his soul. It would not always stretch. . . . Even so, in the balance, the lapses in Bill's acting weigh the most, and the greatest of these failures is emotional. In playing the part of a man who is little more than an animal, Bill seems unable to free the animal forces in himself. (63–64)

As *Time* accounts for it, the miscasting of Holden as Hal shows up most in the highly "emotional" acting required of him—which is to say that the *failure* of this star performance appears to guarantee the transparency with which Holden openly fakes Hal's brand of bogus masculinity in order to establish the authenticity of his own.

The "William Holden" which *Time* magazine reproduces as the man that Hal could not coopt is an unlikely romantic movie hero: an ordinary American Joe with no pretensions toward high art, a long lasting marriage, and a face resembling, in an often-repeated quotation, "a map of the United States. . . . All those meaningless straight lines" (62). The adjectives that immediately stand out in the article's description of Holden are "likable," "forthright" and "suburban" (62), words coming straight out of the fan magazines' homages to the ordinariness of Holden's middle-class life, from P.T.A. and scout meetings to the Sunday barbecues with the family in the patio of their valley home.[11] These qualities were important to Holden's star image because they linked the sincerity of his screen presence to his middle-class family life as a means of conforming his masculinity to an homogeneous national identity: that all-American boy next door, who grew up, went to war and came back to put on a grey flannel suit and live in the suburbs. Holden was by no means the only star whose persona was defined in such nationalistic terms; but it is extremely significant that *Time* goes so far as to equate his screen appeal with his face, pictured as a kind of monument to postwar America, with its highways and waterways inscribed there as metaphors for the greater authority which age had brought to his indistinct pretty-boy looks, and not with his "athletic type [of body], with a graceful flow of well-conditioned muscle" (62), which is what sold *Picnic* in its advertisements.

In *Time*'s reading of Holden, the opposition between mature face and youthful body signifies a contradiction, etched into the very surface of the actor's star image, which catches his "tensions and complexities" (67) to suggest a depth of personality off-screen. With this turn to Holden's "hidden" side, the magazine simply repeats the star's screen persona, indirectly documenting how the actor had indeed learned "to play himself in the part" as the reason for his great success as a "cinemactor" in the fifties. In the three starmaking films Holden made for Billy Wilder—*Sunset Boulevard* (1950), *Stalag 17* (1953), and *Sabrina* (1954)—his parts somewhat darkened his brash and earnest *Golden Boy* (1939) and *Dear Ruth* (1947) screen image by exposing a cynicism and egoism lurking underneath his boyish charm, only to temper that nasty edge in the story's end with a heavy streak of sentimentality posing as honor. As *Time* goes on to characterize Holden, revealing that "the grey flannel suit has a scarlet lining," it shows a man similarly divided: at home, the "solid citizen," but at work, the boozing bad boy who needs to "warm up the ice cubes" before *and* after performing a scene ("Conquest" 63).

The cover story in *Time* reportedly "incensed" Holden because of what it revealed about his temper, recklessness and heavy drinking (Thomas 111). As in his film roles, though, these two different sides to Holden's persona are not all that incompatible, because together they produce the particular masculine inflection of his star image. With his "mature" side written all over his all-American face to inscribe his male identity quite clearly, his "boyish" side can then safely give expression to his body, as manifested in "his need for danger" ("Conquest" 63). Thus, even if motivated by heavy drinking, when cited as evidence of his athletic prowess, a grandstanding stunt such as hanging from a window ledge functions in several ways to define Holden's star image in contrast to a character like Hal. It serves as proof not only of the expert physical control Holden has over his body, but also of his being in remarkably fit condition for a thirty-seven-year-old man; at the same time, in its impulsiveness as a prank, the stunt offers evidence that the American boy next door is still father to that thirty-seven-year-old man. Most of all, this type of reckless physical activity authenticates Holden's screen image as an action hero, since it is simply another version of what Holden does professionally when he performs his own stunts for his films. Emphasizing male action over spectacle, Holden's off-screen behavior on the set serves to reproduce his manliness all the way down the line, denying his cinematic value as an object of desire in *Picnic* and insisting instead upon his attraction as an ego-ideal more consistent with the culture's understanding of masculinity. The various reports of this type of grandstanding performance of virility, in short, ensure that Hal remains "a type, completely opposite to his own," even though both of them *do* swing around like monkeys.

4

The attempt to contain the film by the extratextual representation of masculinity supplied by Holden's star image is a direct response to the way *Picnic* puts that representation under pressure because of the recurring spectacle of his body, which collapses the difference between star and part: both are, after all, produced in the same image. The spectacle of Holden's body on film, this is to say, epitomizes the problems which the apparatus potentially causes for the masculinity of the Hollywood movie hero in general, even when he does not take off his shirt, by making him an object of vision on the screen. Since the camera always subjects him to its gaze, placing him in the position of exhibitionist and focussing on his body with the kind of look supposedly reserved only for the female star, his masculinity can all too easily turn out to be the effect of a masquerade just like Hal's.

The masquerade of masculinity in *Picnic* thus has far-reaching theoretical implications for an understanding of Hollywood's representation of sexual difference on screen because it acknowledges—textually, in the diegetic characterization of Hal and the erotic spectacle of Holden, and extratextually, when Holden's star image is brought to bear upon the film in an effort to differentiate him from the role—that gender is an ongoing performance which requires an audience for the recognition of sexual identities and so positions men as well as women as the object of an other's look. As the *Life* article with which I began suggests, the apparatus of the star system does not simply link the male to the controlling look of the camera, as most critics have assumed. Rather, Hollywood's treatment of the male star implies a doubly engendered viewer: the visual address invites erotic interest from an ostensible female spectator as well as narcissistic identification from an ostensible male one, and it then goes even further to raise the additional possibility that the appeal of the male screen star like Holden—oscillating between the ego ideal of his basic honesty and the erotic objectification of his bare chest—actually breaks down a strictly gendered alignment of narcissistic and libidinal investments in Hollywood's representation of the male body.

More specifically, I have also been arguing, the spectacle of Holden's body in *Picnic* makes the film complicit in the crisis of masculinity which characterizes the representation of sexual identities on screen and off during the fifties. A full elaboration of the representation of masculinity in Hollywood film during this historical conjuncture will have to await another occasion. What I have been able to show here in this essay is how *Picnic* uses male spectacle to foreground the basis of masculinity in masquerade, in a performance of virility, and how the film attempts to recuperate a more traditional version of masculinity, textually and extratextually, for its star. The film's particular treatment of Holden repeats the ambivalence with which Hollywood cinema as an institution has depended upon the spectacle of a male star's body, but just as significantly, it is also symptomatic of the breakdown of consensus in the fifties about the constitution of masculinity. In *Picnic* the pressures which the spectacle of the male body brings to bear upon Hollywood's traditional understanding of a homogenized American masculinity are what inscribe the real "tensions and complexities" in both Holden's star image and the part he plays in the film.

NOTES

1. Robert Francis, the male ingenue in *The Caine Mutiny* in 1954, died in an air crash the year later, which is why his name is unfamiliar.

2. In citing the significance of the *Life* article's representation of the male star I do not mean to imply that it is somehow free of a phallic bias, because it is not. Even while calling attention to the erotic status of male stars in Hollywood cinema, *Life*'s coverage of their fan appeal still retains a presumption of male dominance throughout—in the active poses of the stars in the photographs, as well as through the accompanying text's engendering of who is looking at these exemplars of the "stronger sex": either teenage girls infatuated with star idols or "their older sisters" seeking husbands modeled on a star's masculine image (94). Nor does the article comment on the possible attractiveness of these stars as ego-ideals or libidinal objects for *male* viewers, who surely contributed to these stars' box-office "muscle." (Regarding the latter point, this silence in 1954 is not all that surprising, though, because of what the spectacle of male stars implies for men about the objectification, homoeroticism, and narcissism underlying the solicitation of their look by the apparatus.) Nevertheless, the article's attention to men as spectacle—as having faces that, shaved or not, are meant to be looked at—shows the extent to which the star system breaks with the accepted differentiation of the look according to gender, which assumes that men exclusively do the looking and women exclusively are looked at.

3. The wideranging influence of Laura Mulvey's essay, "Visual Pleasure and Narrative Cinema," reprinted in her volume *Visual and Other Pleasures*, is impossible to document in a short note. As an indication of both the impact of that essay and the focussed attention on the female spectator which followed as a consequence of it, see the special issue of *Camera Obscura* on "The Spectatrix" (ed., Bergstrom and Doane), which features various national surveys of scholarship on the topic (including one by Mulvey), individual responses by feminist film critics, and a comprehensive bibliography.

4. Although there is little scholarship on the subject of male stars as spectacle in classic Hollywood cinema, the topic has not been completely ignored. In addition to the work cited in my essay, two articles in particular have helped me, if only indirectly, to establish the ground of my study of *Picnic*. In "Masculinity as Spectacle," Steve Neale expands upon Mulvey to discuss the relation between sadistic narrative elements and the spectacle of male bodies in the western and gangster film; in both genres, Neale argues, the sadism disavows the homoerotic implications of looking at men on screen. And in "Pleasure, Ambivalence, Identification," Miriam Hansen examines the spectacle of Valentino, paying close attention to the theatricality with which his films mark his body as an erotic object, to consider its implications for female spectatorship and the "powerful challenge [his films pose] to myths of masculinity in American culture between the wars" (23).

5. Inge published the original ending in *Summer Brave*, his alternative version of *Picnic*.

6. A week later the magazine actually equated the Kinsey report on female sexuality with the successful testing of an H-bomb by the Soviets ("Bombs").

7. In the final revised script, as in the play, Mrs. Potts continues, making the point even clearer: "And that reminded me—I'm a woman. And that seemed good, too."

8. In describing Hal's virility as the effect of a masquerade (his muscle-flexing, his showing-off, his lying), I am not using this term casually but do intend to evoke the history with which femininity has been analyzed as a masquerade in implied contrast to the "naturalness" of masculinity. Thus when I say that Hal's masculinity is similarly based in a masquerade, I do not mean to erase the problematic status of femininity, nor do I want to empty gender of the difference between masculinity and femininity; but I do want to use the term to underscore the problematic dimension of Hal's masculinity precisely because the feminine has always been equated with the masquerade as a means of normalizing masculinity and authenticating it. See the account of the feminine masquerade in Joan Riviere's case study, which originated the discussion, and then the essays by Stephen Heath, Mary Ann Doane, and John Fletcher, who extend it to the problem of sexual representation in film.

9. For her discussion of gender as performance see Butler, especially 24–25 and 134–41. In brief, she argues that gender signs—"acts, gestures, and desires"—"are *performative* in the sense that the essence or identity that they otherwise purport to express [on the surface of the body] are *fabrications* manufactured and sustained through corporeal signs and other discursive means. That the gendered body is performative suggests that it has no ontological status apart from the various acts which constitute its reality" (136).

10. Not surprisingly, the magazine's answer was a resounding, "no, they are not!" As far as *Photoplay* was concerned, the job may require men to dress up, thus acting like sissies, but it cannot subvert the essential manliness covered up by the pancake base. All those he-men, the article stressed, "try to compensate for the frills and furbelows of their film careers by leaning over backwards in private life to be very, very masculine. . . . the boys, embarrassed by the powder puff routine, spend a lot of time off stage proving they're as rugged as the parts they play. And that's very rugged indeed" (Armstrong 97). *Photoplay*'s question may have been rhetorical but it nonetheless indicates a disturbing suspicion about Hollywood masculinity that results from the problematic status of the male body in the apparatus. For the "proof" of virility turns out to be the star's reliance on phallic props and display; and to pull the rug out from under Hollywood ruggedness with an even more abrupt if unintended yank, at the same time that the article stresses the off-camera manliness of Hollywood's he-men, it prominently features photographs of Tony Curtis and Ricardo Montalban with captions emphasizing their physical activity but pictures displaying their semi-nude torsos.

11. See Dee Philips's profile of Holden for an example of this type of domestic discourse about the actor, published at around the time of his first award from *Photoplay* for male star of the year.

WORKS CITED

_____. "All About Eve: Kinsey Reports on American Women." *Newsweek* 24 Aug. 1953: 68–71.

Armstrong, George. "Are Actors Sissies?" *Photoplay* Feb. 1953: 52–53, 97.

Bentley, Eric. "Pathetic Phalluses." *What is Theatre? Incorporating The Dramatic Event and Other Reviews, 1944–1967.* New York: Atheneum, 1968.

Bergstrom, Janet and Doane, Mary Ann, eds. Special Issue: "The Spectatrix." *Camera Obscura* 20–21 (1989).

Biskind, Peter. *Seeing is Believing: How Hollywood Taught Us to Stop Worrying and Love the Fifties.* New York: Pantheon, 1983.

Brien, Alan. "Mr. Holden is the Magnet." London *Evening Standard* 9 Feb. 1956: 7.

_____. "Bombs, H and K." *Newsweek* 31 Aug. 1953: 57.

Butler, Judith. *Gender Trouble: Feminism and the Subversion of Identity.* New York: Routledge, 1990.

Byars, Jackie. "Gazes/Voices/Power: Expanding Psychoanalysis for Feminist Film and Television Theory." *Female Spectators: Looking at Film and Television.* Ed. E. Deidre Pribram. London: Verso, 1988. 110–131.

_____. "The Conquest of Smiling Jim." *Time* 27 Feb. 1956: 62–67.

Coward, Rosalind. *Female Desires: How they are Sought, Bought and Packaged.* New York: Grove Press, 1985.

Doane, Mary Ann. "Film and the Masquerade: Theorizing the Female Spectator." *Screen* 23.3–4 (Sept.–Oct. 1982): 74–88.

Dyer, Richard. "Don't Look Now." *Screen* 23.3-4 (Sept.-Oct. 1982): 61–73.

_____. "*A Star is Born* and the Construction of Authenticity." *Star Signs: Papers from a Weekend Workshop.* London: BFI Education, 1982. 13–22.

_____. *Stars.* London: British Film Institute, 1979.

Easthope, Antony. *What a Man's Gotta Do: The Masculine Myth in Popular Culture.* London: Paladin, 1986.

Ehrenreich, Barbara. *The Hearts of Men: American Dreams and the Flight from Commitment.* New York: Anchor Press, 1983.

_____. "5,940 Women." *Time* 24 Aug. 1953: 51–58.

Fletcher, John. "Versions of Masquerade." *Screen* 29.3 (Summer 1988): 43–69.

Foster, Alasdair. *Behold the Man: The Male Nude in Photography.* Edinburgh: Sills Gallery, 1988.

Frank, Lawrence K. "How Much Do We Know About Men?" *Look* 17 May 1955: 52–56.

French, Brandon. *On the Verge of Revolt: Women in American Films of the Fifties.* New York: Frederick Ungar, 1978.

Graves, Janet. Rev. of *Picnic. Photoplay* March 1956: 10.

Hacker, Helen Mayer. "The New Burdens of Masculinity." *Marriage and Family Living* 19.3 (Aug. 1957): 227–33.

Hansen, Miriam. "Pleasure, Ambivalence, Identification: Valentino and Female Spectatorship." *Cinema Journal* 25.4 (Summer 1986): 6–32.

Haskell, Molly. *From Reverence to Rape: The Treatment of Women in the Movies.* New York: Penguin, 1974.

Heath, Stephen. "Joan Riviere and the Masquerade." *Formations of Fantasy.* Eds. Victor Burgin, James Donald, and Cora Kaplan. New York: Methuen, 1986. 45–61.

Holtzman, Will. *William Holden.* New York: Pyramid, 1976.

Inge, William. *Picnic.* New York: Bantam, 1956.

_____. *Summer Brave and Eleven Short Plays.* New York: Random House, 1955.

Kaplan, E. Ann. *Women and Film: Both Sides of the Camera.* New York: Methuen, 1983.

Logan, Joshua. *Josh: My Up and Down, In and Out Life.* New York: Delacorte Press, 1976.

_____. *Movie Stars, Real People, and Me.* New York: Delacorte Press, 1978.

Malone, Michael. *Heroes of Eroes: Male Sexuality in the Movies.* New York: Dutton, 1979.

Moskin, J. Robert. "The American Male: Why do WOMEN Dominate Him?" *Look* 4 Feb.1958: 77–80.

Mulvey, Laura. *Visual and Other Pleasures*. Bloomington: Indiana University Press, 1989.

Neale, Steve. "Masculinity as Spectacle." *Screen* 24.6 (Nov.-Dec. 1983): 2–16.

Phillips, Dee. "Average Score: Terrific!" *Photoplay* April 1955: 36–37, 109–112.

Riviere, Joan. "Womanliness as a Masquerade." *Formations of Fantasy*. Eds. Victor Burgin, James Donald, and Cora Kaplan. New York: Methuen, 1986.

Russell, Rosalind and Chris Chase. *Life is a Banquet*. New York: Random House, 1977.

Strasberg, Susan. *Bittersweet*. New York: G.P. Putnam's Sons, 1980.

Taradash, Daniel. *Picnic*. Revised Final Draft: May 2, 1955.

Thomas, Bob. *Golden Boy: The Untold Story of William Holden*. New York: St. Martin's Press, 1983.

———. "The Stronger Sex Makes Strong Box Office." *Life* 31 May 1954: 93–96.

Walters, Margaret. *The Nude Male: A New Perspective*. London: Penguin, 1978.

"Crisscross": Paranoia and Projection in *Strangers on a Train*

Sabrina Barton

> Isn't it a fascinating design? You could study it forever.
>
> Hitchcock on *Strangers on a Train*

Like the hero, the camera, and the spectator, feminist film theory has fixed its gaze on Hitchcock's blonde: we can't take our eyes off her. And with good reason. Hollywood's dream machine thrives on her fetishized surfaces. It is precisely because she is the object of the "male" gaze that she must also be taken as an object of feminist study. Singled out for theoretical scrutiny by Laura Mulvey and Raymond Bellour in the mid-seventies, the Hitchcock blonde has since come to stand for the "to-be-looked-at-ness" of cinematic femininity in general.[1] Investigations of cinematic subjectivity and spectatorship regularly return to what are now, as a consequence, the canonical Hitchcock texts, all linked by the spectacle of the blonde: Grace Kelly in *Rear Window,* Kim Novak in *Vertigo,* Janet Leigh in *Psycho,* Tippi Hedren in *The Birds* and *Marnie,* and Eva Marie Saint in *North By Northwest.*[2] To understand the function of Hitchcock's blonde is thus to understand something fundamental about the imperatives of desire and representation in classical Hollywood cinema.

In an effort to depart from the rigid gender alignments of our by now all too familiar male gaze/female object model of classical Hollywood cinema, and in order to reconsider the constitution of the female subject, feminist criticism has recently taken a surprising turn: the interrogation of the male subject. For example, during a feminist film conference at Cornell University in the fall of 1988 called "Feminist Film Theory and Cultural Critique," many of the papers chose to take another look at representations of male subjectivity, especially gay male subjectivity, under the aegis of directors as different as Friedkin, Fassbinder, and Jarman, in order to consider various formations of "masculinity."[3] Though drawing sharp comments from some members of the audience disturbed by the predominance of "man talk" at a feminist conference, this shift of focus has rapidly become a favored feminist strategy for a more complicated understanding of the role of sexual difference in theories of the cinema.

235

Feminist film criticism's interest in male subjectivity parallels feminist literary criticism's explorations of the fissures in patriarchy, in homosociality, and in the phallus.[4] By refuting the conventional gender ideology promoted by most texts, and by examining ways in which male subjects are as constructed and, potentially, as fragmented and attenuated as female subjects, recent readings make available important forms of female empowerment. I would like to take up the question of representations of male subjectivity in film as a strategy for rethinking the singularly unempowered role assigned to the female subject in certain areas of film theory. In so doing, I hope to reopen the case of the director around whose preponderate *oeuvre* the debate over cinematic constitutions of female subjectivity has taken place, Alfred Hitchcock.

My focus will be on *Strangers on a Train*, a film obviously, even narrowly, focused on male subjectivity.[5] Just as *Vertigo* self-consciously explores blonde specularization—that is, the reducing of a female subject (Judy) to a mirroring blonde object (Madeleine)—*Strangers on a Train* explores the structuration of a male subject, an exploration from which what I will call the "blonde-function" is notably absent in any recognizable form. As a result, the film demarcates the position and function of "Woman" within patriarchy's plots in a way that rapt attention to a spectacular blonde object can (and perhaps is intended to) obscure. Unlike the narrative design of canonical Hitchcock films, *Strangers on a Train* offers no men in pursuit of blondes, nor blondes in pursuit of men. The first few minutes of the film, with its self-announcing singleminded interest in the movements between two men, at once explains this film's previous absence from feminist attention and indicates its relevance to the current feminist debate about representations of masculinity.

After the credit sequence, the camera lowers its angle, hovering around knee-level, and crosscuts (in time to Dmitri Tiomkin's score) between two pairs of men's legs departing from taxis and walking briskly through Washington D.C.'s Union Station toward a train. While this camera angle remains a familiar cinematic device for the male scrutiny of female legs, Hitchcock's witty, stylized opening instead directs the audience to track the promenading of men. There are no diegetic glances, male or female, within the sequence to provide an alibi for the camera's fixation. Hitchcock's formal technique, crosscutting, proleptically indicates the film's narrative interest in the crisscrossing and doubling of desire between men that will be developed and played out in *Strangers on a Train*.

The narrative trajectory is propelled by the efforts of the two male protagonists to deny or acknowledge their "chance" crossing of paths on the train, a crisscrossing that will shortly result in the murder of

Guy's wife, Miriam. When Bruno, voicing Guy's desire to be free from Miriam, proposes over lambchops that they "swap murders . . . crisscross" (the deal would be that Bruno murder Guy's lower-class, blackmailing wife in exchange for Guy murdering Bruno's domineering father), Bruno's proposition narrativizes the symmetrical relation between the two men textually inscribed by the opening crosscutting ("crisscross"). The homosexual valence of this symmetry is emphasized by Bruno's quick exclamation at their first meeting, "I like you—I'd do anything for you!" A profusion of doubling motifs crops up during their encounter—including Guy's tennis doubles, Guy's "bigamy" joke, Bruno's drink order ("scotch and plain water—a *pair—doubles*"), the pair of crisscrossed tennis rackets on Guy's lighter—all reinforcing the linkage of the two men by inviting us to read Bruno Anthony as Guy Haines's double.

The film's concern with the slippage of male identity is further underlined by Guy's lighter, which he "forgets" in Bruno's train compartment: the initials "A to G" may refer to Ann or An/thony. The eroticization of Bruno's threat, and the paranoia it triggers in Guy, completes this film's hyperbolically Freudian and homophobic account of how the paranoid subject, suffering from the repression and distortion of homosexual desire, projects a persecuting double.[6] With the loss of the lighter to Bruno, Guy loses crucial evidence of his heterosexual identity and of his innocence: he may now be blackmailed by the threatening other who commits his murder ("It's *your* murder," Bruno will later remind Guy).[7] The murder of Miriam makes possible Guy's social advancement but at the same time equates Guy with his partner in crime, an equation that anticipates the film's central concern: the destabilization and restabilization of Guy's subjectivity.

While *Strangers on a Train* does not seem to critique the privilege of the bourgeois male subject, it takes a more than perverse pleasure in exposing the mechanisms of, and Guy's guilty complicity in, the displaced violence required to ensure that privilege. On the one hand, the film's two deaths (Miriam and Bruno) are represented as necessary, even deserved by the two scapegoated stereotypes (and stereotypical scapegoats)—the voracious tramp and the deranged homosexual—who threaten Guy's stable identity. But on the other hand, the film makes visible the secret of Guy's success, the mechanisms of paranoia and projection through which the other is cast out and punished. To describe the film as simply being about Guy's "dark underside,"[8] is to miss *Strangers on a Train*'s special interest to the feminist film critic for its suggestion that a masterful male subject position is at once produced and continually threatened by its own paranoid homophobic and misogynist plots, the plots familiar from so much classical Hollywood cinema.

Crisscrossing/Coupling

Those familiar Hollywood plots obsessively center around a male Oedipal resolution and the formation of the heterosexual couple. Raymond Bellour argues that a process of "alternation" distributes similarities and dissimilarities across every register of the text to produce and naturalize the couple. For example, in *The Big Sleep* the lighting, shot/reverse shot editing, and dialogue duration of a twelve-shot sequence generate the aura of "inevitability" around the Bacall/Bogart coupling and clearly define Bogart's "masculinity" and Bacall's "femininity." The primary goal of coded repetitions and differences is "to ensure the natural continuity of the narrative—that is, to sustain its artifice, but without ever making it too obvious."[9] The not-too-obvious obviousness of a narrative flow into heterosexual coupledom anchors mainstream American cinema.

What, then, do we make of the fact that the first twelve shots of *Strangers on a Train* work to produce the obviousness and inevitability of a same-sex male couple? This question is especially interesting in light of Thierry Kuntzel's claim that a film's opening serves as a microcosm or "matrix" for the film as a whole, the manifest "dream" from which the rest of the film unfolds, repeats, and resolves itself.[10] Before exploring Guy and Bruno's relationship as a couple, I will look first at how crisscrossing codes generate this coupling-effect. Although conventional exposition is deferred until *Strangers*' second segment, the layering of crisscrossing codes already "narrates" an inevitable meeting/clash between these two anonymous strangers. In this way, narrative desire resonates within the elaborate enunciation—the "fascinating design"—of Hitchcock's *Strangers on a Train*.

Overall, the chart reveals a strikingly balanced alternation of camera angles, framing, movement, and shot duration between the Bruno and

Guy "sides" of the opening sequence. The crisscrossing symmetries of the first twelve shots produce the two male protagonists as mirroring
doubles (a doubling echoed by the pairs of porter
legs that share the frame with Guy and Bruno).
Freud explains scenarios of uncanny doubling
in terms of a rift within the subject. *Strangers
on a Train* divides the hero's "normal" (Guy)
self from the murderous, sexual (Bruno) self that
the ego represses and projects outward as
"other." Doubling motifs divide the "two"
selves, while crosscutting motifs reveal that they
are destined for one another.

At the same time, however, the heavily codified symmetries of the opening matrix work to
render the dissymmetries all the more telling,
dissymmetries that reassuringly invite us to distinguish between the doubles. Most obvious is
the detail of mise-en-scène that immediately asserts the basic difference between the two men:
their shoes. This figure condenses the thematics
of sexuality and class about to unfold. One of
the men (who turns out to be the hero, Guy
Haines) wears inconspicuous brown lace-ups
suitable to his status as the mild-mannered, up-
wardly mobile tennis celebrity whose political
aspirations include marriage to a Senator's
daughter (Ann Morton). The other (his antagonistic Other, Bruno Anthony) sports decadent
two-toned, wing-tipped shoes whose semiotics
in this film signal his eccentricity and effeminacy,
traits associated with his membership in the decaying upper classes. Taste in shoes is determining in this film: Guy wouldn't be caught dead
in Bruno's shoes; Bruno will be both caught and
dead. And when Miriam warns Guy, "You can't
throw me away like an old shoe," she is mistaken. As her analogy predicts, old wives *are*
like old shoes—easily discarded.

A more subtle dissymmetry lies in the inscrip-
tion of Bruno's priority in this segment, the im-
balance of power that the rest of the film will

CHART:

Shot:	Punctuation	Angle	Framing	S/M	Characters	Speech	Duration
1	[estab. shot]	l to /	(L to) MC	(S to)M	B		+ +
2	cut	\	MC	MC	G		+
3	cut	\	MC	S	B		-
4	cut	/	MC	S*	G		-
5	cut	\	M	S*	B		—
6	cut	/	M	S*	G		—
7	cut	l	MC to L	M	B		+ +
8	dissolve	l to /	M to L	M	X		+
9	dissolve	l to \	MC	M	B		+
10	cut	l to /	MC	M	G		+
11	cut	/	C	M	G & B		-
12	cut	l	ML	S	G & B	B: "Excuse me"	-

KEY TO CHART:[11]

Angle = / (low camera angle from upper right); \ (low angle from upper left); l (straight-on)

Framing = L (long shot); ML (medium long); M (medium); MC (medium close); C (close-up)

Static or Moving Camera = S (static); S* (camera adjusts to keep character centered but "feels" static); M (moving)

Characters = presence or absence of G (Guy) or B (Bruno) in frame

Speech = presence or absence of dialogue

Time = + + (longer), + (long), - (short), -- (shorter) relative duration of shot

Punctuation = the join between shots

struggle to correct. The exterior space of the film's establishing shot of Union Station, over which the credits roll, is appropriated by Bruno when he steps from his cab, compelling the camera to assume its low-angle position. In shot 8, Bruno will again have priority in entering the interior space of the train. (Bruno uncannily is always already in the place Guy intends to be: train stations, tennis courts, the museum, the Senator's party, the amusement park.) As a result, when Guy steps into the exterior space from his cab (shot 2) and enters the interior space of the train (shot 10), his movement has a secondary status. At one point, Guy even loses "his" shot (shot 8), which the strict alternation of shots 1/2, 3/4, 5/6 has led us to expect. Instead of a cut, the camera watches Guy enter Bruno's (shot 7) "dissolving" him into an insert of crisscrossing train tracks from the moving train's "point of view." This literalized "tracking" shot alludes to Guy not only in its serial placement but also in its movement from left to right (just as the camera has been "tracking" Guy from left to right): the splitting tracks metaphorize the hero's splitting self. A second dissolve returns us to Bruno walking from right to left along the aisle of the train, confirming that the previous figure of splitting was an adequate substitute for Guy. Alternation has been sustained. The double dissolves that frame shot 7 function as a hinge at which the segment divides itself, a division marked by the absence of the hero.

Guy (in another reverse-image of his other) walks along the train aisle from left to right and sits directly across from Bruno, kicking Bruno's flamboyantly-shod foot as he does so: Guy, not Bruno, makes the first move, a move we view voyeuristically from our low-angle vantage point. This point of contact not only anthropomorphizes the earlier figure of the train tracks—that is, a figure of splitting and crisscrossing—it also rhymes with a prior crisscrossing between Guy and Bruno traced solely by the reversal of camera angles in the first four shots. A chart of the camera angles' movement reveals an inaugural chiasmus or "X," a figure for the subsequent series of textual and thematic crisscrossing exchanges between Guy and Bruno:

Segment 1. (shot 2)G.————————————————————————————B.(shot 1)
         (3)B.————————————————————————————G.(4)
      (5)B.   G.(6)
        (7)B.   X.(8)
              B.(9). G.(10)
              B.& G.(11)
              B.& G.(12)

Guy's transgressive "kick" sets the plot in motion by triggering the quick splicing together of both pairs of feet in shot 11, which culminates in the tableaux of Guy and Bruno, face to face, finally sharing a single frame in shot 12. The sequence of filmic crisscrossing that opens the film thus resolves itself in a bit of physical crisscrossing (in fact, a bit of footsie), sustaining the film's fetishistic fascination with shoes. However, Guy's desire is coded as "accident," while Bruno's apology for Guy's accident indicates the instantaneous transfer of guilt to the other. The carousel scene at the end of the film will complete the rewriting of Guy's "accident" as Bruno's perversion: there the scapegoated homosexual villain intentionally kicks at Guy until the carousel collapses and the pair are explosively hurled apart.

The threat implicit in the initial crisscrossing sequence culminates in a question concerning identity: "Is your name Guy Haines?". The audience, like Bruno, lacks an iconic James Stewart or Cary Grant to secure instant identification. The opening matrix of *Strangers on a Train* generates an uneasy confusion over who these two guys are, a confusion central to the film's thematics of destabilized male identity. The second narrative sequence answers Bruno's question by identifying the two main characters and introducing the murder-swapping plot. Once again, Bruno dominates shot and dialogue duration, further occluding Guy's own desire and agency. However, editing codes function to sustain a crisscrossing symmetry between the two men: out of the sixty-seven shots in this segment on the train, fifty-eight (roughly 86%) are paired into twenty-nine sets of reverse-angles. When Bruno proposes that they "swap murders—crisscross," shot/reverse shot editing becomes especially pronounced with the camera flipping back to Guy each time he tries to interrupt, as if itself destabilized, as if itself caught between two points of view. Perhaps because it encodes Hollywood heterosexuality ("Classic Hollywood cinema abounds in shot/reverse shot formations in which men look at women"),[12] *Strangers'* use of shot/reverse shot becomes frenetic as it places Guy in the "feminine" position. The segment concludes with Bruno alone in his train compartment, once again naming with hushed pleasure the formation that binds him to Guy: "crisscross," he murmurs. Later, when Bruno reminds Guy of his role in Miriam's murder—"we planned it together on the train: crisscross"—the camera will resume its intensive shot/reverse shot structuration. Guy's complicity, denied at the level of narrative, infiltrates the textual codes.

The crisscrossing game of Guy's tennis playing, which emblematizes the textual codes of this film and of Hollywood cinema generally, is only the most explicit instance of the crisscrossing games that Guy must win: the illicit crisscrossing of desire (or coupling) between himself and Bruno; the crisscrossing murder-swapping plan; and the homosocial crisscrossing between Guy and the Senator (that is, the swapping of the father's daughter for the surrogate son's advancement).[13] Guy's identity as an acceptable Hollywood hero turns on winning these games. The film as a whole suggests that winning requires the playing out of the very misogynist and homophobic impulses that render male normality a contest (contested) in the first place.

Destabilization

While much of Hollywood's misogynist and homophobic plotting is so conventionalized as to manage to pass itself off as "natural," *Strangers on a Train* is striking for how explicitly it links plots against the female and homosexual other to the paranoid projections of a contested male subject. Guy's initial encounters with Miriam and Bruno produce increasingly intense forms of paranoia: our hero, who supposedly hasn't *done* anything, rapidly becomes a nervous wreck before our eyes. (Unlike Cary Grant's easy mastery in *North By Northwest* over the stranger he meets on a train, Eva Marie Saint, Guy lacks a blonde-function and therefore lacks mastery.) To underline the degree to which Guy's dilemma is essentially psychic and self-induced, the film lets us overhear a police detective reveal that they "don't have a thing on him." In contrast to the standard doubles plots of, say, Clint Eastwood's *Tightrope* or TV evil-twin movies, Hitchcock never represents Guy's dilemma as the problem of what act of violence his evil double will commit next. Rather, the film's suspense turns on Guy's ability to act "normal." Should Guy report to the office? Should he keep practicing for Forest Hills?—these are the urgent questions Guy discusses with the Mortons after they learn of Miriam's death. *Strangers on a Train* explores not the mystery of Miriam's murder but the mystery behind Guy's "normal" subjectivity.[14]

The role of paranoia and projection in eliminating the "abnormal" is clarified by Laplanche and Pontalis in their exploration of Freud's dual structure of paranoia as either a "not wishing to know" or a "not wishing to be": the first is understood as a *"refusal to recognize (méconnaissance)* which has as its counterpart the subject's ability to recognize in others what he refuses to acknowledge in himself"; the second is understood as "a quasi-real process of expulsion: the subject ejects something he does not want and later rediscovers it in the outside reality."[15] The narrative trajectory of *Strangers on a Train* may be mapped according to these two senses of paranoia: first Guy, refusing to recognize his own murderous desire, recognizes that desire in Bruno; the film then charts Guy's disavowal, rediscovery, and expulsion of (himself as) Bruno. Paranoid projection grounds the masculine subject and at the same time reveals the violence and precariousness of that grounding. On the train, Bruno reads our repressed, paranoid hero like an open book (Guy warns him that maybe he "read[s] too much"). Next, when Guy visits the music store where Miriam works, she, like Bruno, is uncannily able to read or penetrate Guy's secrets. After listening to her mocking refusal to grant him a divorce and her insinuating remarks about his new friends, his new money, and his new liaison with Ann Morton, Guy becomes enraged and abusive: he calls her a "doublecrosser," implicitly threatening her with the crisscross scheme. The music store's glass listening booth serves as a figure for Guy's vulnerability to Miriam's knowing look. Although Guy retreats there for privacy, the booth puts him on display, just as he has found

his interiority suddenly on display before Bruno's "close reading" and Miriam's penetrating glasses. Together, the glasses and the glass booth trigger Guy's panicked sensation of lost mastery. Like the space of the listening booth, the supposedly sealed-off space of Guy's subjectivity has become utterly transparent and vulnerable to the gaze from the outside. (A young couple, always visible in the adjoining booth, serves as our spectator-surrogates, watching with curiosity the pantomime of the unfolding narrative.)

The destabilization of Guy continues when he leaves the music store for another glass booth, this time a phone booth from which he calls Ann—a booth that again makes his inner voice "transparent." In what the startled Ann describes as a "savage" voice, he shouts over the noise of a train that he'd like to break Miriam's "foul useless little neck . . . . I said I could strangle her!" Hitchcock's next cut, from Guy in the phone booth to Bruno at home, filmically dramatizes a psychic projection from self (Guy) to other (Bruno), a projection of the desire to strangle.

Instantly, Guy's murderous desire gets transmitted, as if through an accidental crisscrossing of wires, to Bruno. In this extraordinary cut from the phone booth to a close-up shot of a pair of hands held in a strangling position, the word "strangle" is literally projected—the murderous signifier cast out by Guy and metonymically transferred into the hands of the double, Bruno, who commits the crime. A subsequent motif of close-ups on Bruno's hands (while he waits outside Guy's house, stalks Miriam at the amusement park, struggles to regain Guy's lighter) reinforces a reading of Bruno's hands as the auxiliary device of Guy's agency. The editing of this shot—the jarring suddenness of the cut from Guy's voice to Bruno's hands, heightened by the musical score's dissonant orchestral accompaniment—enacts Guy's psychic disavowal of the cast-out image. This moment also alludes to the spectator's complicity in the process of cinematic projection. The glass booth and the telephone stand in for film's image and sound apparatus, whose projections enable the audience's own disavowal of projected desires: we do not seek or speak our desires, but passively sit back and let them speak us. Like Guy, we never need to dial direct.[16]

However, in *Strangers on a Train* the male spectator harbors an excessively paranoid relation to his projected images. The scene depicting Guy's anticipatory dread of Miriam's murder is aptly characterized by Laplanche and Pontalis's formulation of paranoia as "comparable to the cinematographic"; that is, Guy "sends out into the external world an image of something that exists in him in an unconscious way" (354). Arriving home late from a tennis match, Guy steps from his cab into a disorientingly canted camera frame and dark, shadowy lighting; he then hears the weird echoing sound of Bruno's voice invisibly calling, as if ventriloquized and projected outward: "Guy . . . Guy. . . ." But when Guy turns from his doorway back toward the darkened courtyard, instead of innocent bewilderment we see the haunted expression that insists on his guilt. Although he hasn't yet been told, the film suggests that unconsciously Guy already "knows" his wife has been strangled to death. Guy is a man who knows too much, and his repressed knowledge quite literally emanates from him.

Guy's attempts to stabilize himself through conversations with his fiancée, Ann, are repeatedly interrupted by his association with Bruno. For example, at the museum just before Bruno appears, Guy confesses to Ann that he feels like he's living in a "glass bowl": his words performatively summon his double and refer back to the earlier figures of his own transparency. Ann's failure to mediate the threat this "other man" poses to Guy's masculinity (her failure as a blonde-function) complicates Bellour's account of cinema's preoccupation with Woman as "the mirror-effect of the narcissistic doubling that makes possible the constitution of the male subject through the woman's body." Ann fails to mirror Guy because the site of "the woman's body"[17] is already occupied by Bruno.[18] The priority of the other man suggests that the heterosexual version of "narcissistic doubling" by way of a blonde-function may founder before same-sex narcissistic identifications.

Freud's work on paranoia repeatedly betrays the tenuousness of his own opposition between homosexual desire and "normal" heterosexual functioning:

> So long as the individual is functioning normally and it is consequently impossible to see into the depths of his mental life, we may doubt whether his emotional relations to his neighbors in society have anything to do with sexuality. . . . But delusions never fail to uncover these relations. . . .[19]

"Uncover[ing]" relations with one's neighbors will disclose a sexual, often homosexual, content. Unable to conceal "the depths of his mental life," Guy no longer "function[s] normally" as a heterosexual male. Hitchcock's film dramatizes Freud's insight into the imposture of "functioning normally," even as it subscribes to Freud's own investment in that imposture. Freud also pointed out that it is through the "attempt to master" so-called abnormal unconscious desires that we "come to grief" (60). *Strangers on a Train* seems fascinated by the inevitability of coming to grief, by the inevitability of paranoia in a society that requires the repression of all "abnormal" desires.

The mise-en-scène of *Strangers* charts the abnormal within the normal as we follow Bruno following Guy, repeatedly erupting into the well-lit Washington D.C. public spaces Guy eagerly inhabits in an effort to distance himself from his double. Bruno materializes as a dark, spectral silhouette at a museum, at the steps of the Jefferson Memorial, the tennis courts, even the Senator's house, contaminating these clean havens of patriarchal order. Shadows repeatedly cut across—cut and divide—Guy's body. As Bruno remarks, "You're not yourself, Guy." Hitchcock's films persistently uncover the "non-self" within the "self," the gothic deviancy lodged within realist normalcy.

The gothicism associated with Bruno can be elucidated by considering Eve Sedgwick's work on the "eroticized, paranoid double." In her reading of James Hogg's gothic classic, *Confessions of a Justified Sinner,* Sedgwick discusses the threat that "slipperiness of identity" poses for the male subject in the homosocial order.[20] The character of Bruno, with his decaying aristocratic legacy, his effeminacy, his insanity, his incestuous relationship with his mother, and his positioning as the persecuting double of Guy, is right out of the gothic tradition. In fact, Hogg's account of an ambitious tennis player pursued by a persecuting double may even be a source for the film's revision of Guy's profession from architect (in Highsmith's novel) to tennis player. Hogg's emphasis on his protagonist's paranoid horror of his double's "hideous glances"—identifying the problem of male subjectivity with a problem of visual mastery—makes the following passage a strikingly cinematic anticipation of Guy's subjection to Bruno's "hideous glances":

> To whatever place of amusement he [George] betook himself, and however well he concealed his intentions of going there from all flesh living, there was his brother . . . also, and always within a few yards of him, generally about the same distance, and ever and anon darting looks at him that chilled his very soul. . . . all whose eyes caught a glimpse of these hideous glances followed them to the object toward which they darted. . . .[21]

This passage vividly captures the coercive effect of "hideous glances" on object and spectator alike.

Those soul-chilling "darting looks" that violate the boundaries of the self neatly characterize the threat that Jacqueline Rose argues is inherent in cinema's scopic system. In her critique of Bellour's account of the masterful male gaze, Rose claims, like Freud, that "normal" self/other relations are destabilized by the narcissistic projections that may so easily flip into fears of persecution:

> Paranoia is latent to the reversibility of the ego's self-alienation. Furthermore, since the projective alienation of the subject's own image is the precondition for the identification of an object world, all systems of objectification can be related to the structure of paranoia. Aggressivity is latent to the system, but it will also be discharged where the stability of the system is threatened.[22]

If a "projective alienation of the subject's own image" underwrites the differentiation of ego and object world—the organization of self and other—then the systematic expelling of otherness can backfire; polarization is always susceptible of reversal; the subject may suddenly become an object of her or his own outcast images; and any destabilization will unleash the paranoia and aggressivity "latent to the system." Narcissism, difference, and the look, are not so easily managed.

In *Strangers on a Train* the threat of reversibility inherent in the cinematic system is played out, so to speak, in a tennis court sequence where the back-and-forth shots (shot/reverse shots) emblematize the subject's attempts at mastery. The sequence begins with a shot of Guy watching (what else) a doubles match while awaiting his turn to practice for Forest Hills. The camera then reverses to show us, directly across the courts, the bleachers full of spectators who, like Guy, are watching the game. A reverse angle back to Guy shows his expression suddenly become anxious and paranoid. Still another reverse angle of the spectators' heads rhythmically following the back-and-forth movement of the ball invites the film audience to laugh at their coerced looking, superior in our privileged alignment with the gaze of the camera.

All this occurs within seconds until, with a shock, we see what Guy sees: Bruno's single head fixed and staring right at us. The spectator/camera/Guy are all caught in an act of imaginary mastery—visible and vulnerable after all. Like Guy's crisscrossed relation to Bruno, we are placed in a mirroring relation to the automaton-like tennis spectators across the court whose "freely" shifting look, like ours, is an illusion, an illusion punctured for us by the reversal of the look from Bruno. As Rose argues, when "the subject is looked at from the point of its own projections" it causes "the look . . . itself [to] be externalized" (Rose 147). This moment of reversal and externalization invariably elicits gasps and surprised laughter from the *Strangers* audience: we enjoy being startled by a vertiginous glimpse of ourselves constituted as objects rather than subjects of the gaze. But only for a moment. As the camera zooms in toward Bruno, we instantly register that his look is slightly to the side of the camera—he sees Guy but not us—an obliquity that recuperates our sense of visual mastery, safely outside that mise-en-abîme of interspecularity. The predicament of violent reversal inherent in crisscrossing glances later resurfaces in another unusual shot/reverse shot during the Morton party sequence. In an upstairs bedroom, after Bruno has caused a scene, Guy calls him a "mad, crazy maniac." When Bruno pleads, "But Guy, I like you," Guy punches him.[23] Bruno's plea triggers a cut to his point of view, just in time to record Guy's oncoming fist as a blow to the camera's/spectator's/Bruno's "face," a collision registered by a brief fade to black, obliterating our view altogether. An instantaneous reverse angle has Bruno's chin snapping back from the camera's/spectator's/ Guy's point of view. Guy's aggressivity—his fist—works to suture his point of view to that of the apparatus.

A reversal of power between men is thus accompanied by the surfacing of the means of enunciation. ("Aggressivity . . . will also be discharged where the stability of the system is threatened," Rose.) At stake in violent struggles against the double is the goal of securely realigning the hero with the discursive apparatus. However, *Strangers on a Train*'s crisscrossing motifs make visible the always reversible hinge of psychic and cinematic mastery. And the opacity of the blackened screen lingers as a figure for the failures of point of view.

The Dangerous Game of Restabilization— "You're not yourself, Guy"

The problem of not being oneself, of failing to master a stable subject position with a unitary point of view, is a problem that Lacanian theory views as endemic to a fissured ego structure ceaselessly projecting the self onto external objects or screens. *Strangers on a Train* shows how seamlessly Guy's "normal" irritation with Miriam slides into murderous projection, and it is this very continuity from "normal" to violent projection that discloses the mechanism by which unstable male subjectivity gets re-narrativized as a paranoid fear of the female or homosexual other.

The paranoid male subject, as represented in *Strangers on a Train*, thus counters the conventional evocation of a male subject who (in theory, at least) enjoys a safely distanced fetishistic or voyeuristic relation to the image. That invincible figure is usually opposed to women who "lacking castration anxiety [are] also deprived of the possibility of fetishism"—woman can only *be* the fetishized object or image.[24] But woman holds no monopoly on an unstable proximity to signification; sexual differentiation marks only the most dramatic of an endless series of efforts on the part of all subjects to position a self within our culture's signifying systems. Nonetheless, an ideological form like film is likely to reflect not a shared psychic predicament but our gendered positions under patriarchy—woman's exclusion, powerlessness, difference. Feminist film theory ought therefore to remain suspicious of claiming "loss and difference" for femininity. After all, the feminist strategy of valorizing the disruptive potential of woman's proximity to the image repeats an association that has already been happily offered up by the film itself.

Without losing sight of the profound asymmetries in Hollywood's representations of gender, we can explore the fissures in "masculinity" revealed by these representations in order to help free femininity from bearing the entire burden of split subjectivity. Disruption is not a glamorous thing that a woman "does" through her own agency. But perhaps disruption—or the ruptured representation—of subjectivity is something a marginalized female or male subject may recognize and read.[25] After all, the two marginalized subjects in *Strangers*, Miriam and Bruno, are the insightful and playful readers who question Guy's unitary point of view, reminding us that the "normal" male subject also harbors a dangerously reversible (or crisscrossed) relation of ego to image.

Not surprisingly, Guy's climactic Forest Hills match near the end of the film seems calculated to produce him as a clear winner. Earlier crosscutting and tennis sequences are repeated for this resolution, but with a difference. Guy is now a player, not a spectator, and (the sports announcer tells us) he has changed his style and become fast, aggressive, hardhitting. Watching him from the stands is not Bruno but Ann, her head not fixed but obediently following Guy's shots. Bruno is excluded, in spite of the resurgence of the crosscutting technique that first established the link between the two men. For, in contrast to the opening sequence, this latter alternation between Bruno (trying to plant Guy's incriminating lighter at the scene of the crime) and Guy (who must win his match and get on a train to stop Bruno) works mainly as scaffolding for an elaborate narrative suspense that all but absorbs the "fascinating design" of formal crisscrossing codes. Furthermore, instead of the visual and aural matching in the opening segment, these codes reinforce narrative difference: shots of Guy are associated with open space, rapid cutting, vigorous narrative action, bright lighting and lively music; Bruno's shots are associated with claustrophobic space, longer takes, thwarted action, dark lighting, and sonorous music: Guy will go free, Bruno will not.

And yet, in a perfectly Hitchcockian twist, the entire sequence is played under the sign of "sameness." Entering the stadium, the camera glides over an awning inscribed with a line from Kipling: "And treat those two imposters just the same."[26] The line ironizes the tidy polarization of Hollywood closure to come. At the very moment that every textual register in the film encourages us to root for Guy's victory over the match, over Bruno, and over the Senator's daughter, a literary citation reminds us that these so-called opposites (named in the poem

"Triumph" and "Disaster") are "the same." The hero is called an "imposter": his mastery—his "triumphant" phallus—an imposture.

Learning how to assume the props and posturing of masculinity is, in fact, the subject of Kipling's poem, "If—," whose rhetorical structure is an address from a father to his son. The poem offers a lesson in negotiating the tricky balance—the "if"—of "normal" patriarchal subjectivity. *If* the boy can succeed: "Yours is the Earth and everything that's in it, / And—which is more—you'll be a Man, my son!" (ll.31–32). To possess everything, including the "more" of Manhood, depends in this poem on a logic of paranoia, on a rigid guarding of self from other, on holding everything in and treating all others alike (with the same degree of suspicious distance) so that "neither foes nor loving friends can hurt you." The moral of the poem becomes the moral of the epilogue of *Strangers on a Train*: when a minister on a train repeats Bruno's destabilizing question—"Aren't you Guy Haines?"—Guy and Ann silently leave the compartment. Guy has learned not to talk to strangers.

However, the silence of conjugal closure echoes with the screams of the carousel sequence that precedes and produces it. Guy's restabilized identity only barely emerges from the disordering confusion of "those two imposters." "That's him," says the ticket-taker at the carousel, identifying the criminal, Bruno; "Yes, we know," respond the policemen, meaning Guy. As if in response to this failure of reference (who is "him"?) a policeman's wild gunshot misses its indistinct double-target and instead kills the operator hidden within the apparatus of the carousel. The troubling question of male identity ("Aren't you Guy Haines?") once again bespeaks the instability of the subject constituted in language.

The question also bespeaks the instability of the spectator's own processes of identification within the language of cinema. It is curious, then, that apparatus theory has tended to promote the concept of a spectator who achieves a sublime imaginary unity before the flickering screen. Joan Copjec diagnoses that critical claim as itself a paranoid masculine fantasy of a "phallic machine" that can reproduce stable male subject positions. She cites Freud's observation that "It is highly probable that all complicated machinery and apparatus occurring in dreams stand for the genitals—and as a rule the male ones." Copjec also argues that the disruptive complications of sexual difference have been evaded, in part by collapsing Jean-Louis Baudry's two distinct terms—*appareil* and *dispositif*—into the single and phallic concept of "apparatus," which elides the more mobile, multiform concept of "arrangement" that *dispositif* offers.[27] It seems to me that the "fascinating design" of Hitchcock's apparatus (the film text, the carousel) similarly strains against, yet also reveals, multiform sexual arrangements.

The carousel-apparatus initially seems an innocent enough pleasure, evoking an early form of the cinema: the amusement park setting, the purchasing of tickets, the revolving images, the spritely music on the soundtrack, the painted props, the interested spectators. Then the hidden agent of amusement (the director?) is eliminated by a random gunshot. With his death, our spectator-surrogates lose their illusion of control and begin to scream in terror: the game is a dangerous one. The visual and aural confusion that follows breaks up orderly spectatorial positioning and produces the film's highest pitch of excitement: pleasure-in-order gives way to a (pleasurable) panic-in-disorder.

The film has already hinted at the allure of disordered cinematic subjectivity by revealing the instability inherent in shot/reverse shot. The carousel scene pursues the logic of an inherent instability to its extreme. The vertiginous 360 degree whirling circularity of the merry-go-round "describes" the breaking of the 180 degree rule that governs both shot/reverse shot and orderly continuity editing.[28] The film's figure for an "unrealistic" spinning camera—for out-of-control apparatus and 360 degrees of taboo space—represents the collapse of the linear, 180-degree editing logic that divided Guy from Bruno; that collapse discloses the "other scene" of crisscrossing: intercourse. The camera moves in for a tight framing of Guy and Bruno writhing around on the floor of the merry-go-round, lying on top of one another, clenched together, with phallic poles and a horse's hoof pumping up and down, in and out of the frame (the foot fetish returning as a sign of homoerotic desire). Hitchcock fragments the space surrounding the grappling men through disorientingly blurred and spliced together rear-projection footage. Subject/object relations are disjoined; distorting close-ups animate the inanimate machine-horses; screams mingle in a cacophony of diegetic and nondiegetic music; textual codes explode into confusion.

The erotic charge of this sensational confusion lies in the fusing of images of "disordering" homosexuality with disordered cinematic representation. The carousel scene betrays "the temptation" that normative textual codes are "intended to overcome: the temptation to refuse cultural re-integration, to skid off-course, out-of-control, to prefer castration to false plenitude."[29] In the carousel scene, transgressive desire disorders the film's symbolic law and allows two men to spin out of control. Desire unbinds a figural and sexual energy that is at once celebratory and apocalyptic.

Ultimately, the film's horror of destabilization ensures the scene's restabilizing resolution. The film allows dangerous unbinding in order to motivate rebinding; it allows disordered desire in order to motivate the reordering of desire.[30] *Strangers on a Train* associates the ruptured cinematic codes with Bruno, and then proceeds to eliminate both at once. Bruno is literally buried in the confusion-effects he "caused," in the cracked, dismantled machinery of the carousel-apparatus. Although all subjects are at once located and dislocated within signification, *Strangers* reinstates an opposition: Guy is back on track, while Bruno is literally "dislocated" ("I think his neck is broken.")

In terms of the film's closure, then, the apparatus does function with some success as a machine for restabilizing masculinity. As if to emphasize this, the carousel sequence alludes to Hollywood's most popular genre for the cinematic construction of masculinity: the western. The scene includes good guys and bad guys, guns, horses, a chase, a fistfight, screaming women, the law, a mother and her son. The film's attention to the son on the merry-go-round, a young boy who advances from spectator to player when he begins to hit Bruno in imitation of Guy, establishes a rhetorical situation analogous to that of the Kipling poem: the boy-spectator must learn how to "be a Man," only in this case through the witnessing of violent male spectacle.[31] Cultural representations supply the tropes through which male identity gets constituted.

This moment repeats and reverses a prior scene between Bruno and a young boy. While trailing Miriam about the amusement park, Bruno encounters a young boy wearing a cowboy suit and hat who points a toy gun at him and says "Bang! Bang!" In response, Bruno bursts the boy's balloon with his cigar, transforming pretend violence into real violence with a bang. Bruno mimes the little boy's violent gesture just as the boy himself is miming the gestures and costume of masculinity produced by the western. The film erodes the distinction between innocent and intentional violence, between playacting and aggressive acts. Bruno's "pretend" strangulation at the Morton's party quickly turns murderous; Guy's "innocent" idiom—"I could strangle her"—assumes performative efficacy. The boy's toy gun alludes to Bruno's "perfect murder" game at the Morton party ("Bang, bang, bang, blood all over the place"); the toy gun also refers to Guy's playacting of his "perfect murder" of Mr. Anthony—he creeps up the stairs holding Bruno's gun like a prop or toy that will later turn lethal in the hands of his double. Once again, the game is dangerous. But out of dangerous games emerge heroes and villains.

Narrative codes complete the work of reestablishing difference between Guy and Bruno (narrative once again proving itself able to recuperate textual perturbance.) Most importantly, Guy saves the little boy-spectator whom Bruno almost pushes off the ride, thus securing an instant polarity of family-protector versus child-murderer. Responding to the mother's terrified appeal, "My little boy!", Guy's heroics sever his relation to Bruno as he inserts himself into the paternal slot of an Oedipal triangle. Bruno's deviance is reasserted in a final trope as he, snarling, grasps the eroticized horse's hoof and kicks Guy's hands. The weird metonymic relation scripts Bruno as the sole bestial aggressor, no longer in the pedo-symmetry with Guy established by the film's opening sequence.

The spectacle of the exploding carousel marks the dismantling of the apparatus by an eruption of homosexual panic. I want to argue that the carousel scene also refers back to a fissure within the apparently smoothly-functioning apparatus of the murdered-woman plot. I am thinking of the moment when a woman, Miriam, sees herself trapped within a murderous male projection, Guy's/Bruno's, just before his strangling hands cause her eyeglasses to fall to the ground and crack. Bruno's casual post-murder joke to Guy—"Nobody saw—only Miriam"—will later redound with a vengeance. Miriam's look, signified by her cracked glasses, returns in the trope of the broken carousel.

Broken Spectacles

As the murdered-woman sequence begins, however, Miriam's looks seem far from disruptive; she blindly mistakes Bruno's murderous stalking for innocent flirtation. Hitchcock plays the sequence for comedy. By displacing the film's horror of doubleness onto a feminine object, he invites the audience to feel that Miriam is asking for it. Miriam herself is "double," or pregnant; sexually, she is doubly guilty, out with two young men; and she has just doublecrossed Guy. Miriam's voraciousness—she hungrily eats and lasciviously looks throughout this sequence—seems implicitly to cause her own murder. Women who eat too much, like women who see too much, deserve to die.

In his role as murderer, Bruno functions as a projected figure for the male director, actor, and spectator: he enacts the revenge of the threatened and paranoid male subject on both sides of the camera. Before following Miriam and her doubled dates into the Tunnel of Love, Bruno pauses to buy popcorn, like the paradigmatic moviegoer, from an old-fashioned machine whose spinning wheel and flickering lights allude to the film projector itself.[32] When the camera films the shadows hugely projected by Miriam grappling with her dates inside the Tunnel, it is as if sexual gropings in the darkness of the theater were themselves indistinguishable from the projected screen images.

The camera then cuts outside in time for Miriam's off-screen scream, cuing the audience to project—to imagine and desire—her murder; we repeat Guy's own projection of Miriam's murder. By linking Guy's paranoia and projection to tropes for cinematic projection, this scene hints at a causal link between male paranoia and movies' murdered-women plots.

The murder sequence concludes on the island when Bruno as director holds Guy's lighter under the female object's chin, creating his desired effect of underlighting; he then as spectator asks "Is your name Miriam?"; and, finally, as actor—the actor who enacts Guy's desire—he begins to strangle her. Guy's desire—"I could strangle her"—writes the script that is played out or projected through Bruno.[33] Hitchcock films even the murder as another shadow show, another staging of projected images. The strangulation is filmed from the mirroring lens of a huge replica of Miriam's glasses that Hitchcock designed to achieve this effect.

Instead of using a spectacular blonde object, Hitchcock has literalized the function of woman as a specular screen for male projections. In contrast to *Vertigo* where the blonde's body becomes the fetish, in *Strangers on a Train* the fetish is not Miriam-as-spectacle but Miriam's spectacles. What becomes visible as a result is the disjunctive space between Miriam as a screen for projected images (that is, the "blonde-function"), and Miriam as a subject and viewer in her own right. Again unlike *Vertigo*'s victimized female object of male desire, Miriam has fun with her playacting ("I can be very pathetic as the deserted little mother in the courtroom" she threatens Guy) and has fun with her flirtations (her seductive gazing at Guy and Bruno). As a woman with spectacles, rather than a blonde spectacle, Miriam continues, even after her death, to make visible male paranoia and projection. For example, Barbara's Miriam-like eyeglasses will later betray Guy's complicity to his fiancée, Ann.

Strangers on a Train is punctuated with examples of female spectators who enjoy an alarming facility around and pleasure in representation: Mrs. Anthony's irreverently surreal painting of St. Francis onto which Bruno projects a monstrous portrait of his father; Miriam's "pretty story" as she mockingly threatens to perform the role of "deserted little mother" in the courtroom; Barbara's eager launching into the discourse of detective fiction, referring to Guy as a "suspect" who might be "thrown in the can and left all night" (she openly voices her pleasure in narratives in which "a man loves you so much he'd kill for you" until sharply reprimanded by her father, the Senator); Mrs. Cunningham and Mrs. Anderson at the Morton party gleefully spinning out conventional plots for husband-murdering; Miriam's scream of laughter in the Tunnel of Love, indicating her irreverent distance from the games of love and murder in which she is supposed to be the helpless object; Ann's sharp glances as she recognizes the congruences between Guy and Bruno, and between Barbara and Miriam, and pieces the puzzle together; and even the old woman in the back of the car the police appropriate to chase Guy to the train station: "Excuse us ma'am, we're chasing a man" to which she responds with delight "Oh really? How exciting!" What links these different examples together is a refusal of the high seriousness and masochistic identification often associated with woman's reading of patriarchal narrative.

But, as Guy's rage at Miriam indicates (rather like Scottie's rage at Midge when she parodically paints herself as a blonde-function sporting spectacles, in *Vertigo*), in *Strangers on a Train* active female spectating is no joke. Interestingly enough, Hitchcock's own appearance in the film seems to imply a less paranoid solution to the problem of the threatening other. He climbs onto the train, carrying the figure for his own double—a double bass. Like the tennis-celebrity Guy, Hitchcock is a public figure; he is precisely *not* a stranger on a train. His paranoid sense of being seen, recognized, and pursued is borne out by the critical tradition that has followed on his death. Yet his appearance contradicts the solution that the film's ideology promotes for Guy (and a link is established when Guy crosses the director's path on the steps of the train). While Guy, like the addressed son of "If—," is to cultivate a suspicious silence and a quest for invisibility as a guarantee, as Kipling put it, of being a "Man," Hitchcock's appearance parodically deconstructs masculine identity. Unlike Guy's disavowed, gendered, sexualized other, the director's "other," the bass fiddle, is simply a shape or figure that he carries with him—a shape resembling his own, a figure indeterminately masculine or feminine.

I am, certainly, overreading a joke. But the image of Hitchcock with his humorous double not only condenses the film's thematics of male paranoia and projection, but also works to associate the director with his own female other. The musical instrument, like the pair of spectacles, is linked with Miriam in the music store. Thus, the film's two primary figures for vision and voice both allude to the woman who saw too much, who said too much, who ate too much. Hitchcock's repressed double may be this projected "overweight" woman, whose hungers he finds intolerable. We do not, of course, see the director wearing glasses; his "spectacles" are the camera itself that, when it chooses to film the director, makes visible the mechanisms of projection whose invisibility is conventionally so important to the "complicated machinery" of classical Hollywood cinema. Where, by the way, are

Miriam's broken spectacles at the film's end? Those missing spectacles function as a loose end, an unrecuperated figure for female insight, for the possibility of reasserting distance from the image and for reading the paranoid projections of male subjectivity.

NOTES

1. Laura Mulvey, "Visual Pleasure and Narrative Cinema," *Screen* 16, 3 (Autumn 1975); Raymond Bellour, *"The Birds," Cahiers du Cinéma* 216 (Oct. 1969), English translation from the BFI Educational Advisory Service; "Hitchcock the Enunciator," *Camera Obscura* 2 (Fall 1977); "Psychosis, Neurosis, Perversion," *Camera Obscura* 3–4 (Summer 1979).

2. Some examples: Jacqueline Rose, "Paranoia and the Film System," *Screen* 17, 4 (Winter 1976–77); Robert Stam and Roberta Pearson. "Hitchcock's *Rear Window*: Reflexivity and the Critique of Voyeurism," *Enclitic* 7, 1 (1983); Tania Modleski, *The Women Who Knew Too Much: Hitchcock and Feminist Theory* (New York and London: Methuen, Inc., 1988).

3. Papers interested in male subjectivity were Timothy Murray's "Dirty Stills: Retrospection, Hieroglyphs, and Filmic Phantoms," Kaja Silverman's "Male Subjectivity at the Margins," and Sharon Willis's "Disputed Territories: Masculinity and Social Space." Article versions of the latter two pieces appear in *Camera Obscura* 19 (Jan. 1989), Silverman's under the title "Fassbinder and Lacan: A Reconsideration of Gaze, Look, and Image." Murray's "Le cliché tâché: rétrospection et décomposition cinématographique" was published in *L'annuaire théâtrale* (Fall 1988/Spring 1989), with a longer version forthcoming in his *Subliminal Libraries: Writing the Death Drive of Vision* (New York: Routledge).

4. See for example, Eve Kosofsky Sedgwick's work on male homosociality (*Between Men: English Literature and Male Homosocial Desire* [New York: Columbia University Press, 1985]), and recent feminist accounts of the novel, including Mary Poovey's work on the contradictions of patriarchal ideology (*Uneven Developments: The Ideological Work of Gender in Mid-Victorian England* [Chicago: University of Chicago Press, 1988]) and Nancy Armstrong's analysis of how eighteenth-century "female" subjectivity becomes nineteenth-century "male" subjectivity (*Desire and Domestic Fiction: A Political History of the Novel* [New York: Oxford University Press, 1987]); also see critiques of phallocentrism in psychoanalysis such as Jane Gallop's *Reading Lacan* (Ithaca, NY: Cornell University Press, 1985), and Luce Irigaray's *This Sex Which Is Not One*, trans. Catherine Porter (Ithaca, NY: Cornell University Press, 1985).

5. My thinking about this film owes much to discussions with Phil Barrish, as well as with Amanda Anderson, Debra Fried, and the Writing About

Film staff led by Lynda Bogel (Fall 1988). I also want to thank Tim Murray and Sasha Torres for their advice about revisions, and Constance Penley for her interest in my project.

6. Sigmund Freud, "Psycho-Analytic Notes on an Autobiographical Account of a Case of Paranoia," *The Standard Edition of the Complete Psychological Works of Sigmund Freud* vol. 12, trans. James Strachey (London: Hogarth Press, 1911; rpt. 1953) 59–79.

7. On the link between homosociality and blackmail in narratives concerned with male doubles, see Eve Kosofsky Sedgwick's "Toward the Gothic: Terrorism and Homosexual Panic" in *Between Men: English Literature and Male Homosocial Desire* (New York: Columbia University Press, 1985) 97–117.

8. Donald Spoto, *The Art of Alfred Hitchcock: Fifty Years of His Motion Pictures* (New York: Hopkinson and Blake, Pub., 1976) 209–210.

9. Raymond Bellour, "The Obvious and the Code," *Narrative, Apparatus, Ideology: A Film Theory Reader*, ed. Philip Rosen (New York: Columbia University Press, 1986) 100.

10. Thierry Kuntzel, "The Film-Work, 2," *Camera Obscura* 5 (Spring, 1980): 7–68.

11. I am using Bellour's chart of specific and nonspecific cinematic codes from "The Obvious and the Code," with the exception of his "elements of narration" category, which does not strictly apply to this opening segment.

12. Kaja Silverman, *The Subject of Semiotics* (New York: Oxford University Press, 1983) 225. By contrast, the scene between Guy and Miriam in the music store is filmed primarily in two-shot framing, both figures contained in a single camera frame, with far fewer cuts. A "pop" explanation of shot/reverse shot suture is found in Roger Ebert's account of the "Seeing Eye Man"—"Function performed by most men in Hollywood feature films. Involves a series of shots in which (1) the man sees something, (2) he points it out to the woman, (3) she then sees it too, often nodding in agreement, gratitude, amusement, or relief."

13. In contrast to Hitchcock's use of a "fascinating design" to channel the crisscrossing of desire between men (thus satisfying personal and professional censors), Patricia Highsmith's novel *Strangers on a Train* (New York: Harper and Brothers, 1950), from which the film derives, makes the attraction and aggression between Guy and Bruno much more explicit.

14. A recent Hitchcockian treatment of doubles is David Cronenberg's *Dead Ringers* (1988) in which destabilized male subjectivity, paranoid projection, and murderous rage are all triggered by the intrusion of a female (Geneviève Bujold's) sexually aggressive look. Unlike *Strangers*, however, *Dead Ringers* retains its focus on the logic of a self-destructive male pathology: instead of murdering the woman, the identical twins—a literalized split self—destroy each other.

15. J. Laplanche and J.B. Pontalis, *The Language of Psychoanalysis* (New York: W.W. Norton and Co., 1973) 354. I am indebted to Mary Ann Doane's *The Desire to Desire: The Woman's Film of the 1940s* (Bloomington: Indiana University Press, 1987) for stimulating my interest in paranoia and gender, and for calling my attention to the Laplanche and Pontalis definition.

16. See Debra Fried's "The Men in *The Women*," *Women and Film*, ed. Janet Todd (Holmes and Meier Pub., Inc., 1988) 43–69, for an account of phones as markers of the apparatus.

17. Raymond Bellour, "Psychosis, Neurosis, Perversion": 118–19.

18. Although Ann will ultimately replace Bruno and become Guy's conjugal "double," I think it is important to notice (to denaturalize or "de-obvious-ize") the difficulty of the process along the way.

19. *Standard Edition of the Complete Psychological Works of Sigmund Freud* 60.

20. Sedgwick, *Between Men* 105.

21. James Hogg, *The Private Memoirs and Confessions of a Justified Sinner*, ed. John Carey (London: Oxford University Press, 1969; first pub. in 1824) 35–6.

22. Jacqueline Rose, "Paranoia and the Film System," *Feminism and Film Theory*, ed. Constance Penley (New York: Routledge, 1988) 144.

23. Interestingly, following his angry assault on Bruno, Guy tenderly reties Bruno's tie ("Here, let me" he says) as if the tie between them, between the self and the other, were a possible one, briefly opening up a space for a different articulation of masculinity. But the drive to resecure Guy's heterosexual "manhood" ultimately produces the expulsion of the homosexual other.

24. Doane, *The Desire to Desire* 169.

25. Patricia Highsmith, who wrote lesbian fiction under the pseudonym "Claire Morgan," might be considered such a reader.

26. "If—", *Rudyard Kipling's Verse: The Definitive Edition* (London: Hodder and Stoughton, 1940) 576–7.

27. As Copjec notes, Baudry actually used the term *dispositif* (a disposition or arrangement) rather than *appareil* (apparatus) in his second essay on the workings of cinema, but both were translated as "apparatus" (Copjec 58); Baudry himself retains an investment in the cinematic machine as capable of completing the subject. See Jean-Louis Baudry, "The Apparatus: Metapsychological Approaches to the Impression of Reality in the Cinema," *Narrative, Apparatus, Ideology: A Film Theory Reader* (New York: Columbia University Press, 1986) 299–318. The subject of the "dispositif" is less positioned than dispositioned, less singular than mul-

tiple: "Patriarchy can only be an effect of a particular arrangement of competing discourses" and these competing discourses include "the multiformity of the construction of sexual differences" (Copjec 58–9). It is crucial for feminist film theory to recover this distinction since a cinematic *dispositif* or "arrangement," as Constance Penley explains, implies not the "singular subject of the optical apparatus" but the subject (and here she quotes Derrida) of a "system of relations between strata . . . of the psyche, of society, of the world" (Penley, "Feminism, Film Theory, and the Bachelor Machines," *The Future of an Illusion: Film, Feminism, and Psychoanalysis* [Minneapolis: University of Minnesota Press, 1989] 70).

28. As Kaja Silverman explains, the 180 degree rule is "predicated on the assumption that a complete camera revolution would be 'unrealistic,' defining a space larger than the 'naked eye' would normally cover," *The Subject of Semiotics* 201.

29. Silverman, *Subject* 232.

30. Kuntzel's insights into textual disorder in *The Most Dangerous Game* inform my reading of this scene: "Let's not be mistaken: narrative-representational film only allows discharge of energy, excess, disorder, confusion, on condition that all of these ruptures of code take on meaning— and *value*—with respect to the global economy of narration and representation" (Kuntzel, *Camera Obscura*: 48).

31. This is the familiar form of address in films preoccupied with the formation of male subjectivity. See, for example, the role of the boy-spectator and his mimetic imitation of a TV superhero (whom his father also therefore imitates) in *Robocop* (1987), a self-conscious reworking of the father/son thematic in *Shane*—most obviously in Shane's signature "gun-twirling" gesture so admired by Joey.

32. Debra Fried's helpful observation.

33. To complete the fantasy, her death enables a displaced version of a male couple, Miriam's doubled boyfriends, to go off together into the night.

Courtesy of the Museum of Modern Art/Film Stills Archive.

To Live and Die in L.A. (William Friedkin, 1985)

Disputed Territories: Masculinity and Social Space
Sharon Willis

A cop stealthily enters the tract house bedroom of his occasional lover, a young blond woman whose parole he oversees. Her observance of parole consists in passing him information and sleeping with him upon demand. This familiar pornographic formula (where seduction is tinged with sadism in the imposed authority of the police, and linked to the forced prostitution of an innocent looking wide-eyed victim) is enacted in a scene that renders the male body as spectacle. While the woman remains in the bed where she has just awakened, the cop, backlit by dawn light through the window which frames him, performs a rapid striptease that ends in a pose, arms folded, legs apart—an aggressive full frontal display reminiscent of male nude magazines. This almost parodic rehearsal of a stylized porn scenario is one of the two moments of heterosexual sex that punctuate William Freidkin's *To Live and Die in LA* (1985).

The second of these moments centers on Rick Masters, the adversary of Richie Chance, the cop of the first scene. Masters is shown making love with his girlfriend, while they watch videotapes of themselves making love. Our gaze is directed by Masters away from the current sexual scene to the image, just as he is immobilized by fascination with it. It is as if this scene figured the concentration of all erotic energy in the gaze, a gaze captivated by a pornographic home movie; that is, as if the image of sex were more seductive and engaging than the fictional "real" sex.

At the same time, this scene participates in the film's general tendency to frame the male body as spectacle, constructing masculinity as image, as body-to-be-displayed, an inversion of traditional cinematic codings of sexual difference. But the context of this construction of masculinity is crucial. The film is charged with a homoerotic subtext, just as it is haunted by sexual ambivalence, and by the threat of castration or feminization. *To Live and Die*'s principal antagonists are locked in a

---

A longer version of this essay appears in *Seduction and Theory*, edited by Dianne Hunter, University of Illinois Press, 1989.

cycle of homosocial aggression. Further, the narrative scenes of seduction are peripheral to the most powerful seductive circuits of this film, which is intensely fascinated with seduction and simulation. This fascination focuses on displacements and dissolutions of boundaries, between the "real" and its simulacra, between the art object and the object of consumption, between the "authentic" and the counterfeit.

Sexual difference here becomes one of several problems, arrayed in a network of insufficiently established differences, which the film sets out to order. Questions of differentiation are organized in spaces coded to represent "culture," "high art," and good taste, which are established in contrast to the menace of the common, the vulgar, the popular and the "lower class." These ambivalent cinematic constructions of sexual difference thus coincide with aesthetic ambivalence, with instability of value in the circulation of objects and the mapping of space. The construction of the male body as spectacle here seems to depend on its articulation as part of a captivating consumer space.

In its construction of space, *To Live and Die* reproduces the spaces and fascinations of the postmodern urban scene. It's not incidental, it seems to me, that the film was shot in Los Angeles, a city that has been constructed as the "capital of postmodernism," in part because its version of urban landscape seems to embody the theoretical features of postmodernism. Its heterogeneous ethnicity is dispersed in a fragmented topography, where spaces seem not to communicate, much less interlock, because one can only circulate through them by driving. The city, then, appears as centerless, depthless, a vast extension of scenery, framed by a windshield, viewed at a distance, and at high speed. Further, as a major production site for cinema and television, Los Angeles is ideally suited to figure effects of endless reproducibility; the city is pure image endlessly reproducing itself.[1]

Since *To Live and Die*'s narrative stages a confrontation between the artist and the law (in the figures of Masters, the Neo-Expressionist painter and counterfeiter, and Chance, the maniacally macho Treasury agent), in which the character who has the most style and taste is the most seductive, the film rehearses certain preoccupations of postmodernist theories of representational strategy. By presenting the artist as a transgressive figure with a strong resemblance to the media mythologized Neo-Expressionists of the contemporary art scene, and casting him within a mass cultural vehicle—a fairly formulaic detective thriller scenario—it forces the emergence of a confrontation between high culture and consumer culture, a displacement of boundaries that is articulated around the figures of counterfeit and simulation. Part of the seductiveness of such a mass cultural object may be that it shares current theoretical preoccupations, that it theorizes on the same ground as so-called "high culture" and its criticism. Seductiveness of this sort, however, must be polyvalent, operating in different registers with respect to varying spectator positions, positions which must be at least in part conditioned by their social and cultural situations. A significant question here is how such seductive effects may displace spectators's social and cultural locations, how social boundaries and the way they are imagined may shift, and what pleasures such shifts might involve.

Seduction always entails pleasure, a term whose analysis is complicated by its ambiguity, by the difficulty of elaborating the relation of subjective experience to the social. Colin Mercer argues that pleasure is ambiguous "probably because it also implies the unspoken figure to which it applies—the individual pleasure is about individual taste and preferences. More than any other notion (except perhaps those of taste or choice), it entails individual sovereignty. This is the 'unsaid' of pleasure, its presupposition when mobilized in any discourse (collective pleasures are always a bit tacky)."[2] Pleasure, like aggression, is especially complicated because it emerges with greatest clarity within the framework of individual subjectivity, however abstractly conceived. Even on the individual level, pleasure is unstable, elusive, subject to loss in analysis. To try to "socialize" pleasure seems to risk dispersing it completely. But if we want to understand intrapsychic processes to be socially inflected, and to have social effects, it is particularly important to avoid reducing social operations to simple analogs of an individual psychic model.

However, the operations of the cinematic apparatus are social, and the subject they construct and seduce is a social one. Cinema does not work, then, only upon the subjective imaginary. Rather, we must consider it as a "ceaseless working up of social imaginaries," in Jean-Louis Comolli's phrase.[3] Consequently, we must focus on the framing mechanisms that condition representational practices (including distribution and circulation, the institutions governing consumption), and on the forms of address that locate a spectator *for* these representations. Framing mechanisms are the threshold of complex exchanges that continually dissolve and reconstitute these imaginary zones ("public" and "private") and that rework boundaries between high and popular culture.

Because, even while offering the pleasures and the lure of an illusory highly privatized space, cinematic experience is, in many ways, the most eminently social form of consumption, we must work on the contradictions common to the subject constructed through cinematic forms of address and to the apparatus itself; upon the crucial ideological formation that splits "public" from "private." Cinematic production and consumption, reciprocally conditioning as they are, are embedded in social power formations. Produced within cultural exchange and circulation, images also construct the conditions of their reception, the positions the spectator occupies or invests. The spectator's act of filmic consumption involves accepting its forms of address, but it also entails producing its legibility, and negotiating its disjunctions, the elaborate exchanges among its semiotic registers.

However, as a discourse generated in a social field, the film itself incorporates, or *consumes* messages, collective representations. Consumer as well as producer of discourses and images, popular commercial cinema works the way mass culture in general does, according to Laura Kipnis, "by *transforming* elements at large in the culture — not through inventing or imposing arbitrary materials on a stunned and passive populace."[4] To stress the work of transformation this way is to argue for considering mass culture and cinema as processes that operate in a circuit of exchanges, and to leave room for the possibility of ambivalence, resistances and contradictions within them. This is the space of oppositional discourses and culture which may be available, to be activated or repressed, within the fabric of apparently dominant order film.

Once we decide to consider popular culture and its cinema not as imposed from without on a passive public, but as responsive to certain collective demands or desires, however vaguely articulated, we are in a better position to study both social fantasies and the strategies designed to activate and regulate them. This is why Simon Frith argues for replacing the terms "popular" or "mass" culture with the term "capitalist" culture: "culture defined, that is, not in terms of production and consumption of commodities (though this is involved), but as the way in which people deal with/symbolise/articulate/share/resist the *experience* of capitalism (including, but not exclusively, the ideological experience of capitalism)."[5] He seeks to eliminate the hierarchical and static suggestions of "mass culture" (stressing the consumers subjection to producers), and to render historically specific the *form* of mass culture; in capitalism it is a culture in a state of permanent crisis.

We need to analyze a cinema that responds to, reads, and maps collective fantasies, utopian and anxious, a cinema that is always reading us — reading our social configurations of power and desire, pleasure and violence. This is part of film's allure: as we read it, it also reads us. But if cinema mobilizes and channels pleasure, violence and resistances, it often does so only to capture or manage them. Popular cinema's machine of pleasure announces itself as gratuitous, as socially and politically irresponsible, luxuriously abundant in simulacra, asserting the comforting reproducibility of reality — at a distance, and in consumable form. This is a cinema that claims legibility without work, code without pertinent message, that claims to produce nothing, but rather, to reproduce the entirely consumable, already-read.[6]

To analyze cinema as a social machine entails understanding seduction in general, not as a privatized exchange, but as part of social libidinal channeling and mapping. Seduction here cannot be confined to sexual exchange that is thematized in images of sexual activity, or of the body, or in narrated thematics of desire. Seduction does not just lead *towards*; it always leads *away* from something as well. I am interested in those moments and details that we may be seduced into *not* seeing.

In the postmodern moment, mass culture increasingly operates through strategies it shares with experimental art. Dana Polan argues that it tends to work with "montage that produces collisions of messages that continually destabilize and negate each other."[7] Confronted with this kind of practice, we can only posit a spectator who goes to cinema precisely for a loss of reality, to continually reactivate that loss in simulation effects. This is a spectator who uses the apparatus, with all its reality effects, to give him/herself away to a lure, but one which is already understood as such, understood as spectacle, in a kind of self-seduction.

I want to argue that To Live and Die invites us to abandon ourselves to just such a fascination, an absorption in simulation effects. But these effects interrupt and re-route narrative and gaze all at once, and activate seduction quite self-consciously through editing and shot composition. Indeed, their exhilaration within effects of simulation are their critical edge, precisely because these effects are both thematized and performed. Simulation and fakery are central narrative issues, which are also quite explicitly and self-consciously staged in the work of the camera—in its production of space and spectator positions for that space.

The first three sequences of To Live and Die embed the totality of its plot and mark out the multilayered space in which it will unfold. An aerial shot of the LA skyline resolves into a sharper image with the digital time reading printed across it: December 20, 1410 hours (in a standard cue of police timekeeping that will punctuate the film throughout). Under Wang Chung's sound track, a presidential motorcade leads into the action sequence which will introduce one of the film's two antagonists. Before they appear, the first voice of the film sets its terms. Ronald Reagan is heard in voice-over, speaking about death and taxes, terms which emerge in the film's central nexus, where not only money, but also the Treasury Department, is connected to murder. The next sequence literally and figuratively mobilizes Richie

Chance, the Treasury agent, and his older partner/mentor, whose subsequent murder will launch Chance's relentless pursuit of Rick Masters, the counterfeiter. The punning similarity of first names insists that the contest we will witness pits chance against mastery.

In this sequence, however, the adversary is, in a completely unaccountable turn, an Arab terrorist, wrapped in sticks of dynamite, who plunges to his death from the hotel roof, shouting a parody of terrorist discourse: "Death to Israel and America and all enemies of Islam." In a gratuitous, glancing gesture towards the "topical," we are given a construction of an enemy Other whose behavior is motivated only by insanity, while the really unaccountable violence is that which is played out through the rest of the film. This moment has become a common one in recent popular film, (think of the narratively incomprehensible appearance of the fantasmatic hybrids, Palestinian-Libyan terrorists, in *Back to the Future*, for instance). In *To Live and Die*, this embedded figure of American foreign policy anxiety also allows the film the occasion to blow the Third World off the screen, so to speak, leaving only its resonances with the "domestic" Third World, the Black characters.

The cut to the next sequence fixes on the LA skyline again, obscured and transformed through dusky light. This sequence involves rapid cross cutting between images of paintings in the contemporary Neo-Expressionist style of Schnabel and Salle, and sections of LA—mostly industrial sites, like oil tanks, and a movie set—a sort of map of LA's "production sites." At the same time, this is the credit sequence. The kind of montage effects commonly seen under television credits now appear to interrupt the film, but also to establish a space beyond the narrative instance we've just seen, and to indicate, across the disjunctions of its tense, jumpy editing, a "context." But narrative context is precisely the film's most unstable area, one that it constantly renegotiates and obscures or dissolves. The most prominent series of images here is that of transactions—money changing hands, moving from one anonymous hand to another. Interestingly, what emerges from this anonymity is, first, a kind of racial mapping: Black men exchange money, Black and Hispanic men exchange money, then a Black man and a white man, a Black woman and a white man, a white woman and Black men, a Black man and a white man. If this film is to be about money circulating, we must assume that it will circulate across race and gender; money will structure racial and sexual exchanges. This circuit of exchanges, however, closes with a photograph of Masters, the artist-counterfeiter, set up as "master" and source of these circulating effects. Not surprisingly, but amusingly enough, the name which crosses the screen at this point is Friedkin's own.

This last image is matched on a shot of Masters in his studio, surrounded by his paintings. The next shot shows a canvas unrolled against a wall. After a cut to a close-up of Masters's gaze at his own work, we see him light a corner of it with his cigarette lighter and watch it go up in flames. If these two sequences begin to articulate money and art across Masters's image, they also anticipate his end— when he is immolated in his studio. That is, in the end, Masters becomes his image, in two ways: he burns up like this first painting, and he persists as an image on the videotapes that his girlfriend takes away with her at the end of the film.

Masters is also figured as the gaze of mastery—frequently shown in medium close-up, facing off, aggressively or sexually, with another character, or regarding his own images (and here the ambiguity of the possessive is apt: this figure conflates production and reproduction bound together in his own narcissism), and finally appearing in the mirror, surveying his girlfriend, or his adversaries. Often, we can't locate him spatially; he is most present as image projected or reflected.

But Masters's mastery also figures several kinds of power which are staged as intersecting, and which produce a certain spatial trajectory. His power is located on the axis of art and culture, accompanied by connoisseurship, as well as on that of economics, and finally on that of sexualized violence and aggression. His economic power, reflected in his glimmering museum-home, with its network of electronic apparatuses, is supported by his engagement with the technology of reproduction. For the artist here is a counterfeiter; we watch, with the fascinated camera, as the process of mechanical reproduction of twenty dollar bills unfolds. This is a long sequence which presents the "hand of the artist" in immense detail, as it produces a plate and prints and colors the bills, with particularly captivating close-ups of the mixing of luxurious gobs of paint—red, black, green, and white together. Here the postmodern in-joking of the film's discourse operates on several levels: Masters is an enfant terrible Neo-Expressionist whose artistic talent translates directly into cash. Of course, the cash is fake, just as he is. This sequence also plays on a fascination with surface detail, and upon the infinite extension of serial reproduction.

Counterfeit money, the reproduced image of a mass produced image, is only valuable if exchanged. It must circulate, and keep on circulating, if it is to remain undetected, if it is to continue to convert directly into "real" money. Now, on the first level of legibility, the film is about the collapse of the simulacrum and the "real," a proposition which it repeatedly asserts. Chance and his new partner want to pose as potential customers in order to entrap Masters, so they have to become outlaws in order to get enough real money for the deposit that will both permit delivery of the counterfeit, and "prove" the authenticity of their pose. They will authenticate themselves with real money. On the other hand, the film here carries its almost parodically excessive libertarian discourse to the limit; since the government won't put up the money for their venture, Chance has to steal it. As his partner points out, they've had to steal thirty thousand dollars of real money, taxpayer's money at that, to buy counterfeit. So it is the simulacrum that turns the law into an outlaw. There is no difference between the pose and the reality: to impersonate outlaws, they must become outlaws. Further, given both Chance's ardent pursuit of Masters, and Chance's replacement, at the end of the film, by his partner, who "takes over his life," continuing his work, adopting his traits, and becoming the lover of his parolee charge, it seems that the law somehow both desires the simulacrum, and is itself a simulacrum.

But if counterfeit must circulate endlessly in order to maintain its value, Masters too is constantly circulating. His passage from one social space to another, one milieu to another, defines the spacing of the film. At once classless and classy, Masters moves from the underworld gym where he is surrounded by thugs, to his girlfriend's trendy nightclub dance performances, to the offices of lawyers like Grimes and Waxman, glassed in exhibition spaces—the one showcasing the LA skyline, the other presenting an art collection.

It is money or its simulacrum (counterfeit, style, or connoisseurship) that negotiates among spaces, weaves them together, cuts a path through them, and finally, equalizes them. Similarly, in a narrative universe where everyone is corrupt, where no character sustains a positive affective charge for the spectator, it is the one with the best taste and the most style who wins. That is, even though Chance's partner survives him and Masters, basically by becoming a replica of Chance, Masters outlasts Chance, who gets his head blown off first. In a stunning moment of competing "tastes," Masters confronts Max Waxman, a yuppie lawyer who has tried to cheat him. When Masters is ordering Waxman to open his safe, and is temporarily distracted, Waxman hits him with a statue. After retaliating by shooting the lawyer in the crotch, Masters evaluates the statue: "18th century Cameroon? Your taste is in your ass," before firing the lethal shot, to the face this time. Leaving aside for the moment the sadistic cast to this homoerotic imagery, and the camera's adoption of the look of the victim, which is a recurrent motif, for now, I want to focus on the issue of taste. Waxman is an unequal contender in this masculine cycle of aggression because his taste is bad. However, the question of bad taste (and indeed, of poor taste, given the relentless relay of anal erotic innuendos in *To Live and Die*), is encoded, played out, in a montage and mise en scène that foreground style, and indeed, a collision of styles. Just as the credit sequence recalls rock video editing and relation to sound, a later sequence contains shots which resemble contemporary beer commercials. When Chance enters a bar, the camera is angled as if from the point of view of one seated at the bar, and the joking exchange of camaraderie takes place in a scene where the frame's horizon-line is dominated by an array of Miller beer bottles and glasses. It is those objects which are the focus of the scene. A later scene of tense exchange between Chance and his partner is also compositionally structured by beer bottles, again with the camera at bar level. (Whatever Miller paid for this kind of representation, surely the film's explicit reproduction of beer commercial motifs is in excess of advertising). But it is precisely this kind of juxtaposition of codes, the commercial with the artistic, that may constitute the film's critical edge.

Otherwise, why use a cameraman like Robby Muller (formerly best known for his work with Wim Wenders), whose camera specializes in a density of texture, and a startling and highly contrasted shot composition, a lingering attention to detail that seems here to mark "European art film style"? However much the distinct photographic style may be read as yet another of the excesses with which this film is fascinated, the still life compositions here seem to have another function as well. It lays out a superabundance of objects, a luxury in detail that implies a kind of fetishization, where object and sign reduce to one another. The object's production, use and context are effaced in its appropriation as sign, its encoding of a particular aesthetic and consumer space.[8]

Using a cinematographer who displays a highly individualized, signature style, the film rather aggressively mixes modes to suggest an equivalency, in this case, given the narrative frame, an equivalency established on the commercial level. This film operates most critically through its display of the shared ground of art and advertising. Indeed, it seems bound to demonstrate Laura Kipnis's assertion that, "in postmodernism, the artistic subject produced in high art, in mass culture, in advertising and consumption *is* the bourgeois subject" (27).

The questions that are central to this analysis, then, involve constructions of space, where space is saturated with value, and embedded in power relations. Within these cinematic spaces, seductive effects emerge out of our "implication" as both producers and consumers of space, since the film's "real effects" are focused by a simulation of postmodern lived spaces—both urban and domestic landscapes, in which the home is a museum-like cloister sealed off from the menace of the under- or over-territorialized urban landscape. Such a combination of codes of consumption seems to be increasingly a feature of cinematic pleasure. One remarkable example is the recent *Year of the Dragon* (Cimino, 1985), in which a loft apartment becomes one primary site of intrigue. The film's particularly detailed examination of its space is ratified and reasserted in the final credits, where the name of the loft designer is noted. Our seduction occurs through our relation to those spaces. Figuratively, space presents itself as a screen for our projections, or a surface reflecting our desire. At the same time, our gaze circulates through it, unimpeded by its boundaries and divisions. Finally, because the space is a display space, offering itself to our visual exploration, we may feel that it acquires depth through our look, that our look produces it.

To *Live and Die* seems to embrace/reproduce the postmodern breakdown of spatial boundaries in its sacrifice of the "scene" to extended, endlessly unfolding spaces of simulation and spectacle in a kind of "hyperspace,"[9] where the terms public and private no longer make sense. According to Jean Baudrillard, such a breakdown depends on the loss of spectacle in the public domain, and the loss of secrecy in the private one. Our contemporary architecture, he argues, is "not a public scene, or a true public space, but gigantic spaces of circulation, ventilation and ephemeral connections."[10] Concomitantly, private space must collapse in the loss of distinction between interior and exterior, and with it, what Baudrillard calls, "the sovereignty of a symbolic space which was also that of the subject" (130).

Yet, however much *To Live and Die* both reproduces and celebrates this exhilarating or vertiginous circulation in and of spaces, its fantasmatic cartography of the city reconstructs a set of spatial divisions which map the power relations of our culture. Museum-like home and business spaces may be indistinguishable from each other, but they are radically different from the homes on the industrial side of Los Angeles, in the shadow of oil tanks, like that inhabited by Chance's sexual slave, and from the Black neighborhood of Masters's associate, Jeff. Space remains implicitly social, and class and race relations are spatialized in a particularly intense fashion. The seductiveness of certain spaces depends upon and is haunted by another space which they hold off or evacuate—this is the space that remains firmly grounded in social power relations.

The spaces of fetishization, of glistening surface, of display and collection (lawyers's offices, Masters's studio)—the consumer space par excellence—taken in the frame of the film's overall development, seem to participate in a rhetoric of spatialization, where history and social formation become matters of space. It is as if spatial division, and the accumulation of objects it permits, entailed an accumulation and containment of history as well, space calculated to function as a museum does.

Such composed spaces tend to negate the gaze, to produce mortifying immobilization of the gaze, along with a negation of traces of use or production.[11] Our gaze, then, is fascinated by a sealed space which excludes us, and which reduces all objects—including human ones—to the same status. This fetishization parallels a technical fetishization in camerawork on the compositional level, and in certain other "excesses." One of To Live and Die's most stunning excesses is the exceptionally long and virtuoso chase scene for which the film is noted. Grounded in gratuitous intensification of anxiety, as are most chase scenes, this sequence presents a chase through a dry river bed, through a truck loading yard, with the camera racing head-on towards enormous tractor-trailers, to culminate in a race against the flow of dense freeway traffic. We see it from a point of view within the car, and later shot from above, pulling away in relief, as we gleefully watch the havoc on the freeway. An explicit excess, based on commuter traffic anxiety, this sequence rehearses the pleasure of seeing traffic entirely disrupted, while one is not involved. Such a sequence participates in a certain rhetoric of expenditure which structures the film; here it is articulated in terms of cost, tricks, affect and anxiety. However, this move is also mean-spirited in its focus of affect on simple, everyday commuter anxiety and stress. Ultimately, the sequence stresses virtuoso performance, the staged quality of the spectacle, and serves to re-encode other instances of excessive violence and aggression as equally random and nonpertinent, playful or incidental occasions for affective discharge.

If To Live and Die's vertiginous circulation is emblematized in a credit sequence of financial transactions and their social map, its later chase sequence is designed to stage an excessive expenditure. The chase produces a rhythmic anxiety/unpleasure and release/pleasure mechanism built around the figure of circulation—the car appears capable of going anywhere, to circulate even against the flow of traffic. Two kinds of flow collide. But this excess, mapped as expenditure (financial and affective), is picked up on another relay, channeled through a circuit of violent masculine homophobic exchanges, which operate both visually and verbally. Verbal violence operates in reciprocal challenge and insult, in phrases organized by an aggressive anal erotic subtext. Indeed, this form of aggressivity is the zone of most intense narrative affectivity—the only zone of consistent affect, where the term "to fuck" is continually employed as a term of threat and aggression, to the point that its connection with sexual intercourse evaporates: "to fuck" becomes "to fuck over."

In its aggressive rhetoric and its thematization of horrific violence between men (Chance has his brains blown out; he is shot in the face like Waxman, who is also shot in the groin; Masters intimidates the Black character, Jeff, by sitting on him and putting a revolver in his mouth; Carl, the prisoner Chance wants to use as an informer, escapes by kicking him first in the groin and then in the face), the film represents an almost parodically hyper-masculinized genre. In Mary Ann Doane's assessment, "feminine" genres, like the love story, and "masculine" genres, like Westerns and detective films, are constructed upon an opposition between emotionalism and violence. She writes, "theories of scopophilia, the imaginary relation of spectator to film, and the mirror phase all suggest that aggressivity is an inevitable component of the imaginary relation in the cinema. In the Western and detective film aggressivity or violence is internalized as narrative content."[12] In so-called "women's films," she argues, "the violence is displaced onto affect." By its very excessive violence, To Live and Die manages to maintain both levels of intensity; it thematizes violence and it produces bursts of affect channeled as spectator horror. It is as if the film sadistically exposes the aggressive component in cinematic fascination, just as it cleverly plays on castration anxiety: male characters accuse each other of "having no balls," fights involve an attack, a kick, jab, or shot, to the groin.

Homoerotic suggestions repeatedly emerge in an endless relay of "jokes" about asses, anality, and even in the early gift exchange between Chance and his mentor—giving the older man his retirement gift, a fishing rod, before the official retirement party, Chance allows as how "it's been burning a hole in my truck." In the epithets shouted during the chase scene, or between Chance and his series of adversaries, the film emits a barrage of anal sadistic slang.

But why? This film sets up an endless circulation effect, a circulation of affect among figures who are all enemies. The one exception to this rule is Chance's first partner, the only one to whom he is not antagonistic, and whose murder launches the central pursuit of the film. But this character, a father-mentor on the point of his retirement, is figured as somewhat "out of style," archaic, unprepared for the new rules of the game, for the new kind of criminality Masters embodies. After his death, all characters are equally "bad," or "perverse" and menacing; there is no stable point of identification in a continual escalation of reciprocal aggression. The film's construction of masculinity as male hysteria is designed to ward off feminization, but in the process it exposes the homoerotics of mimetic rivalry which so frequently structures classic Hollywood narratives of equal adversaries. Sexual difference is re-mapped in this film—erotic heterosexual attractions are doubled by homoerotic ones (in various triangulations: Chance and Bukovitch and the parolee, Masters, his girlfriend and Waxman, and in the peculiar parallel between Masters's physical position and framing in relation to his girlfriend at the moment of a kiss, and his aggressive confrontations with Chance). Further, the film's logic suggests that the winner is the one who gets to say "fuck you" last.[13] I don't mean this lightly, because it is the case that all the male characters systematically say this to each other in moments of rage. On this reading, the final triumph belongs to Masters's girlfriend and her lesbian lover, since they ride off together in the end, in Masters's car, with his money. Indeed, part of the vicious thrust of the film is displaced onto the lesbian couple, which is cast as the most corrupt and most affectless.

In a central moment, Masters meets his girlfriend just after a dance performance. The dancers, all masked and short-haired, are entirely androgynous. The next shot shows the dressing room and Masters looking into the camera as he is approached by a tall broad-shouldered figure, shot from the back in medium close-up. As they kiss, the camera turns slowly to the side of the heads and we discover that the partner is a woman. This seems to be the moment of the film's most aggressive assertion of its seductive powers: a "Fuck you" to the audience. This is the moment of our awareness that the film can dupe us, mislead us. It is as if the film asserted: "This is not what you expected to see, but what you really wanted to see." It is also the scene where the girlfriend's relation to her woman lover is first established, in a relay of gazes over Master's shoulder and through dressing room mirrors — as if they have already mastered him. Notably, the homosexual charge in the kiss is immediately displaced and reconfigured upon the women.

But why all this violence in connection with homoerotics? It seems that one could argue, as Tania Modleski does concerning the pleasures of horror films, that horrific violence may be pleasurable if certain anxieties and fantasies are managed and contained at some other level of the film's operation. She wonders what sort of pleasure or stable position of mastery spectators obtain from films that seem only to rehearse a random "lust for destruction," within a narrative that presents interchangeable and unsympathetic "villains and victims," without offering the satisfaction of a logically coherent narrative closure. She concludes that, "the mastery these popular texts no longer permit through effecting closure or eliciting narcissistic identification is often reasserted through projecting the experience of submission and defenselessness onto the female body."[14]

This reading is particularly useful for *To Live and Die*, where the homoerotic violence seems to repress and reveal a subterranean homophobia, an anxiety about displacement or reconfigurations of power and sexual difference. Male homosocial bonding, to use Eve Sedgwick's term, depends on keeping its distance, through repression and violence, from male homosexuality; hence it depends, in its historical construction, upon homophobia. The thrust of the dancers's dressing room scene is to reinsert the reassuring woman, to rehearse homophobia and hold off homosexual panic.

As Sedgwick argues: "To draw the 'homosocial' back into the orbit of 'desire' of the potentially erotic, then, is to hypothesize the potential unbrokenness of a continuum between the homosocial and the homosexual—a continuum whose visibility, for men in our society, is radically disrupted."[15] The intense aggressive energy of this film, then, is, as it were, powered or fueled by homosexual panic, which can be read in the repeated connection of homoerotics to insult.

But this particular configuration of male homosocial agonistics and the violent affect it is designed to rehearse, places the spectator in a masochistic position, as the gaze of the victim caught up in a paranoiac universe—in the titillating fear of being taken unawares. Some recent studies, notably, the work of Kaja Silverman and Tania Modleski, have pushed beyond the limitations of cinematic analyses that focus exclusively on voyeurism and sadistic scopophilia, where sexual difference is organized by the figures of a feminine object of aggression and a masculine subject of aggressive pleasure. These studies suggest that a spectator's pleasure in the image of someone submitting to violent domination is not a simple, unified, "pure" sadistic pleasure, but rather, that it involves a split: a sadistic identification with the aggressor and a masochistic one with the victim.[16] This argument not only provides a means of interrogating more than one type of spectator pleasure, but it accounts for a more complex reading of the play of identification and desire in spectator seduction, such that a spectator could both desire to control and desire to submit, just as it allows for a "masculine" spectator position based in both desire for and identification with the woman as image. But it also allows us to analyze the pleasure and seductive effects of a film like To Live and Die, where the spectator is agitated by violence, and where there is no stable point of identification, but rather a steady rhythm of reciprocal aggression.

Aggression, here, however, also works out a distribution of power along racial lines. In one of the most brutal scenes of the film, a scene that partakes of the same excess as the chase scene, an excessive implausibility, a racial anxiety seems to be at work. Masters enters the Black neighborhood (shown in ample detail as a neighborhood) for the second time, since the contract he has purchased from Jeff, which guarantees that Black prisoners will kill his captured associate before he passes any information, has not been fulfilled. Accompanied by only one other white man, he defeats five Black men in Jeff's home, that is, "on their own turf," even though these men are armed with knives and all display martial arts training, which Masters doesn't seem to possess. Thus, the narrative rehearses particular white fantasies, of dark nights in Black neighborhoods, and manages them with Masters's brutal conquest of Jeff. This is a fantasy of rape, articulated when Masters places a pistol in Jeff's mouth, while saying "you'll have to suck on this until you shit that money," where the anal reference effects a fantasmatic displacement. Now this is coded as a minor scene, one of the narrative peripeteia, a pretext for more violent excesses in the filmic economy of expenditure. Yet in the context of the film's fantasmatic relays, the circulation through spaces, it constructs a territory off limits, a space to be partitioned off, a threat put to rest. This, then, is the social side which is made to appear and disappear, the space where simulacra can't circulate. Masters wants his money back, so he can burn it, because, as he says, "it's no good to me after they've handled it." It has circulated in the wrong space, mis-circulated in that other space, a space of labor, industry and poverty which must be held off. It would seem that what Modleski describes as the pleasure of reasserted mastery appears here as an identification with space, or spatial boundaries. Spectator desire and identification come to be focused upon spaces, constructed scenes, which separate Masters's zone from that of the Black men, upon whose bodies the film inscribes submission and defeat.

Beneath and beyond the narrative movements they offer, this film concerns the conquest of space by money, an operation reproduced in the filmic spectacle, where simulation wards off social referentiality. Yet if we refuse to disavow the referential level, we see another picture altogether. And we must refuse this disavowal, for the film's fictional production of nonpertinent differences, its reduction of social power differences to equivalent effects in spectacle, *depends* fundamentally upon maintaining at least a trace, a residue of referential charge. That is, part of the narrative titillation resides in the display of real social differences, the lived power distributions and antagonisms which structure contemporary social life. But these social differences are presented as elements in an array of diverse details, proliferating differences in texture and intensity that structure the spectacle, or that motivate narrative disjunctions, obstacles and shifts. The point is that these are not just any details; manifestly, they are particular social pressure points that this film regulates and manages.

Such work upon social difference within representations is characterized by Judith Williamson as fundamental to cultural domination and ideological reproduction: "These differences represented within, which our culture so liberally offers, are to a great extent reconstructions of captured external differences. Our culture, deeply rooted in imperialism, needs to destroy genuine difference, to capture what is beyond its reach; at the same time, it needs constructs of difference in order to signify itself at all."[17] That is, our cultural objects tend to occlude the specificity and significance of differences, making them appear as arbitrary and nonsignifying, by presenting them as part of a totality of random differences.

In *To Live and Die*, the spectacle achieves its regulation of social contradictions not by direct confrontation, but rather, by distraction. If we can ignore the social referentiality here, it is because we are seduced: we look aside, look elsewhere, give ourselves to spectacle produced on the ground of these differences. It is in this sense that the film participates in the cultural dominance that reduces differences in power distributed according to gender, race, class and sexuality to a play of equivalent differences. At the same time, these "differences," rendered as spectacle, do constitute a reconstruction of social antagonisms and the anxiety they generate for members of the dominant or privileged groups. The seductive effects of spatial circulation, of style and surface, as well as of narrative affect, relegate the film's rehearsal and management of white middle class heterosexual anxieties to a peripheral position. Almost out of frame, but everywhere glimpsed at its edge, as a kind of border (like the Black men who pass before us in the opening credit sequence), men of color and homosexuals emerge only as recipients of the violence which is continually routed towards them. It is because this aggression is not the primary filmic focus, but rather appears as a byproduct, a residue of the simulation machine, that it is so seductive, so effective. No spectator is obliged to take entirely seriously his or her pleasure or relief in these outbursts; they are only vaguely noticed, peripheral, incidental, immaterial and substitutable. But *To Live and Die* produces a series of confusing and conflicting messages around these sites as well. It manages to set up the homosexual and the Black man as sometimes competing, sometimes merging, sometimes conflicting figures. There is yet another turn of the screw, however: the "homoeroticization" of violence against Jeff switches the channels of violence and rage. The homoerotic subtext to this scene displaces responsibility for the violence onto homosexual desire; homophobic charges are worked out across a Black character as victim, with the residual effect of pitting the two groups against each other. These effects are possible because the film exhibits and circulate differences, among which there are no stable oppositions or positions; everyone is corrupt, confused, and "perverted," or "turned aside."

Because this film depends upon collisions of categories, of differences, and upon perpetual exchangeability, in which all figures are corrupt and perverse, seduced and seductive, then the seductive effects upon the spectator are related to circulation and collision. Such representations reduce social and cultural points of resistance to mere frictions, a stimulation of spectator affect with no referential charge. If *To Live and Die* mixes its messages as it mixes editing styles, it produces spectator pleasure in the reassurance that there are no positions to take, only postures, that there are no contradictions, only frictions and collisions. Our pleasure, then, and our seduction, may arise from submission to a lack of positioning. The global message of the spectacle may boil down to something quite simple: that there are no positions and no possibility of resistance. This is Dana Polan's contention about the way postmodern culture functions to induce an exhilarating sense of impotence: "More than ever, mass culture can come to encourage a powerlessness . . . powerlessness in post-modern mass culture now comes from a situation in which the montage of elements calls into question each and every position one might care to adopt" (183). In the particular context of this film, the dominant seductive effect here is an exhilarating dislocation, a loss of referentiality.

Doesn't it seduce us by its very denial of referentiality, its rendering of social contradictions as equivalent and nonmeaningful disjunctions in a fragmented play of heterogeneous elements? Such representation would seem to leave us captivated by analysis of our own auto-seductions, at the expense of examining our insertion as historical and cultural subjects in a social field. That finally narcissistic pleasure permits the film's incorporation of social antagonisms as mere props for spectacular scenes. Staging us as spectators, the film constructs us as consumers, consumers of social conflict as well as of stylish spaces. If we buy this, we accept the comfortable notion that social conflict can be reduced to a consumable and containable form, as an exciting spectacle. Once staged as spectacle, such political and social antagonisms can be evacuated, exhausted, just as the figures who represent them are made to disappear. Finally, then, the scene is an old and familiar one, for as aggressive as straight white men are towards each other in this film, it is always *some* straight white male who focuses the scene, who commands the space.

NOTES

1. For a good discussion of the particular features of Los Angeles's urban space and architecture, as well as an example of the privilege accorded to it by postmodern theoretical writing, see Fredric Jameson, "Postmodernism and The Cultural Logic of Late Capitalism," *New Left Review* 146 (1984): 80–84.

2. "A Poverty of Desire," *Formations* collective, *Formations of Pleasure* (London: Routledge and Kegan Paul, 1983) 95–6.

3. Jean-Louis Comolli, "Machines of the Visible," *The Cinematic Apparatus*, eds. Teresa de Lauretis and Stephen Heath (New York: St. Martin's Press, 1980) 121.

4. Laura Kipnis, " 'Re-functioning' reconsidered: Towards a left popular culture," *High Theory/Low Culture: Analysing Popular Television and Film*, ed. Colin MacCabe (New York: St. Martin's Press, 1986) 31.

5. Simon Frith, "Hearing Secret Harmonies," *High Theory/Low Culture* 55.

6. Jean Baudrillard examines the postmodern fetishism of the code in a passage that links it to consumption whereby we read for the "already-read," the message reduced to a function of the code. He writes: "The role of the message is no longer information, but testing and polling, and finally control ('contra-role,' in the sense that your answers are already inscribed in the 'role,' on the anticipated registers of the code). Montage and codification demand, in effect, that the receiver construe and decode by observing the same procedure whereby the work was assembled. The reading of the message is then only a perpetual examination of the code," *Simulations* (New York: *Semiotext(e)*, 1983) 119–120.

7. Dana Polan, "Brief Encounters: Mass Culture and the Evacuation of Sense," *Studies in Entertainment: Critical Approaches to Mass Culture*, ed. Tania Modleski (Bloomington: Indiana University Press, 1986) 182.

8. As Hal Foster describes aesthetic fetishism, it is linked to coding: "it is the purity and uniformity of our system of object-signs that fascinates. This clue, together with the fact that what we consume in the code is the difference of object-signs, suggests that fetishism is involved. . . . Like the narcissism of the child, the perfection of the code excludes us, seduces us — precisely because it seems to offer another side or beyond to castration and to labor," *Recodings: Art, Spectacle, Cultural Politics*, ed. Hal Foster (Port Townsend, Washington: Bay Press, 1985) 175.

9. See Jameson, "Post-modernism and the Cultural Logic of Late Capitalism" 80–81.

10. Jean Baudrillard, "The Ecstasy of Communication," *The Anti-Aesthetic* 130.

11. This effect participates in what Baudrillard designates as the "hyperreal"

produced by simulation: "the collapse of the real into hyperrealism, in the minute duplication of the real, preferably on the basis of another reproductive medium—advertising, photography, etc. . . . From medium to medium the real is volatilized . . . it becomes the real for the real, fetish of the lost object—no longer object of representation, but ecstasy of denegation and of its own ritual extermination," *Simulations* 141–2. If our relation to objects becomes entirely fetishistic through this process, at the same time, the fetishistic channeling of our gaze immobilizes it, freezes it in fascination, mortifies or annihilates it. If simulation destroys the object of representation, it simultaneously negates the subject of representation.

12. Mary Ann Doane, *The Desire to Desire: The Woman's Film of the 1940s* (Bloomington: Indiana University Press, 1987) 95.

13. I thank Jeffrey Nunokawa for this deft formulation of the problem; it very economically engages with the film's vicious logic.

14. Tania Modleski, "The Terror of Pleasure," *Studies in Entertainment* 163.

15. Eva Sedgwick, *Between Men: English Literature and Male Homosocial Desire* (New York: Columbia University Press, 1985) 1–2.

16. See Tania Modleski, *The Women Who Knew Too Much: Hitchcock and Feminist Theory*; Kaja Silverman, "Masochism and Male Subjectivity," *Camera Obscura* no. 17 (May 1988).

17. Judith Williamson, "Woman is an Island: Femininity and Colonization," *Studies in Entertainment* 100–101.

Melodrama, Masculinity and the Family: *thirtysomething* as Therapy
Sasha Torres

I. Genre and Gender

In an interview with *The New York Times*, Edward Zwick, one of the producers and creators of ABC's *thirtysomething*, contrasts the show's attention to a "mandate of smallness, worlds of incremental change" with the "galloping narrative" of traditional prime-time: "The idea is 'to try to look more closely to home for episodic drama rather than looking at the more melodramatic,' said Mr. Zwick. 'There's a lot to be mined.' "[1]

The explicit aim of Zwick's remark is to demonstrate *thirtysomething*'s difference from other prime-time programming, and in many respects *thirtysomething is* different. It is stylistically innovative, beautifully shot, and unusually and explicitly playful with the relation between television and film.[2] Given these ways in which the series differs from other contemporary prime-time dramas, it is curious that Zwick seizes upon an aspect of the show which is not very unusual or innovative—attention to the domestic—in an attempt to claim its difference from them. His remark is even more odd, though, considering just how obviously "melodramatic" *thirtysomething* is. The series is crucially concerned with precisely the issues that have preoccupied recent melodrama: the constitution and consolidation of family, the maintenance of the suburban home, the regulation of sexuality, the display and displacement of emotion. That Zwick's offhand remark is so counterintuitive suggests that it is worth unpacking: read as an attempt to situate *thirtysomething* generically, his comment offers a crucial clue to the show's representational practices and sexual politics.

Zwick's statement relies on the commonsense pejorative definition of "melodramatic"—overwrought, excessive, *déclassé*. And in this sense of the term, the series is to be contrasted with the melodramatic: nothing could be more tasteful and measured in its display of bourgeois affect than *thirtysomething*. The series represents ABC's first contribution to the trend begun by NBC's *L.A. Law*, and continued by series

283

like *The Wonder Years*, *Baby Boom* and *Almost Grown*: television's attempt to reach the demographic group most desirable to advertisers — 18-49 year old baby boomers — by mirroring them back to themselves.[3] Thus *thirtysomething* addresses an audience comprised predominantly of those who are, like the characters, white, urban, upper-middle class, and well endowed with cultural capital — conversant, for example, with allusions to David Hockney and Bergman's *oeuvre*. The result, in ABC head Brandon Stoddard's words, is that *thirtysomething*'s demographics are "fabulous, absolutely wonderful."[4]

Attempts like *thirtysomething* to win baby boomers' attention come at a moment of crisis for all three networks, which is no doubt felt particularly keenly by third-ranked ABC. Competition from cable, home video, and independent stations, which means lower ratings and declining advertising revenues, makes baby boomers an especially promising audience for several reasons. For one thing, there are a lot of them. More importantly though, they have grown up with television and are thus thought to be especially receptive to television advertising. And their supposed sophistication with high-tech button pushing leads some to speculate that it may be easier for "people meters," the new technology being used to measure ratings, to count them than to assess other demographic groups.[5]

But despite the fact that *thirtysomething* is unambiguously bourgeois, Zwick's attempt to distance the series from "the melodramatic" is complicated by melodrama's historically uneasy status as, at different moments, a bourgeois and a "popular" form.[6] And contrary to Zwick's assertion, *thirtysomething* is perfectly evoked by Geoffrey Nowell-Smith's description of melodrama: "the address is from one bourgeois to another bourgeois, and the subject matter is the life of the bourgeoisie."[7]

Another way to explain Zwick's statement might be to suggest that it opposes *thirtysomething* to melodrama by aligning the show with another mode of representing domestic life: realism.[8] Indeed, the phrase "mandate of smallness" recalls (for example) Jane Austen's description of her fictional project, perhaps transmuting it as follows: two yuppie couples and their single friends in Philadelphia are the perfect thing to work on.[9] Peter Horton, one of the actors on the series, has discussed the series' commitment to realism this way: "There's not much fiction in this ... All of this stuff seems to come from our lives." The endeavor of the show, he adds, is "finding a little bit of truth."[10] And, as the following quote from *Health* magazine's interview with actress Mel Harris indicates, Horton's assertion is echoed by much of the popular discourse about the show: "... *thirtysomething*," the interviewer notes, "is incontrovertibly really *real*."[11]

But *thirtysomething* often includes explicitly *anti*-realist moments, as well, which depict dreams or fantasies in ways that disrupt realist representational conventions. Further, Zwick's efforts to oppose *thirtysomething* to melodrama by aligning the show with realism are undermined not only by the series' intermittent anti-realism, but also by the fact that both realism and melodrama may be deployed to depict domestic detail. Thus Zwick's distinction gets blurry when he contrasts *thirtysomething*'s project of "looking more closely to home," with "looking at the more melodramatic," since melodrama has always been predominantly a genre that "looks to home." In Laura Mulvey's words, melodrama is "associated with the dramas of domesticity, women, love and sexuality. . . . [It] drew its source material from unease and contradiction within the very icon of American life, the home, and its sacred figure, the mother."[13] Mulvey's definition brings into focus what is at stake in Zwick's attempts to ward off melodrama: he is affirming the series' interest in the domestic sphere, while disavowing the associations of that interest with women and femininity.[14]

Although Mulvey is concerned, in these passages, with Hollywood family melodramas of the 1950's, Lynne Joyrich has recently argued that melodrama is the paradigmatic televisual form, harnessed to manage the crisis of postmodernity.[15] While soap operas are the most obvious examples of television melodrama, adopting such characteristics of filmic melodrama as the use of "concentrated visual metaphors" and music to convey emotional effects (131), Joyrich also cites the made-for-TV movie, television cop shows, network news programming, and even explicit investigations of postmodern culture like *Max Headroom* as linked to the melodrama (132–133). As these various forms become increasingly melodramatic, they come to share melodrama's interest in "emotional pressure, familial concerns, and gender or class position" (132), as well as the form's tendency to express "what are primarily ideological and social conflicts in emotional terms" (131).[16]

For Joyrich, the expansion of what we might generally call melodramatic tendencies, and, more specifically, of the crucially ideological work of television melodrama has a twofold effect. First, television melodrama both reproduces and contains two disquieting aspects of postmodernism: the contradictions that inhere in consumer culture in the age of multinational capital, and the collapse of representation brought about by simulation (136–7). TV melodrama effects this cultural work by "bring[ing] the strands of passivity and domesticity associated with both melodrama and TV together in a simulated plenitude, thereby positioning all viewers as susceptible consumers" (131). In addition, TV melodrama has emerged, Joyrich argues, as a "therapeutic" discourse, which attempts to produce the real in the form of authentic emotion and ethical imperative (138):

> Melodrama helps us place ourselves in a confusing world—its insistence on the validity of moral or experiential truths and its faith in the reality of the stakes creates a space from which to act. . . . Melodrama's promise of universally legible meaning seems to be particularly compelling in the postmodern era, experienced by many as desperately in need of some kind of grounding. (147)

But if television melodrama provides solace in "the postmodern era," Joyrich suggests that it also makes some of postmodernism's troubling features visible, in part because it tends to disperse "the 'feminine' connotations traditionally attached to melodrama—and to both consumerism and television viewing . . . onto a general audience" (131). That is, the tension produced by the possibility that femininity will be diffused onto men forces TV melodrama to reveal some of the ideological and representational stakes it tries to manage. *thirtysomething* wants to harness melodrama's therapeutic potential through its insistently insular concern with family, but chafes against the form's association with femininity.

thirtysomething focuses on an extended "family" of friends who live in or around Philadelphia: the happily married Michael and Hope, the emotional centers of the show; Elliot, Michael's best friend and business partner, and his wife Nancy; Michael's unmarried childhood friend, Gary, an English professor; Hope's unmarried childhood friend Ellen, a civil servant; and Melissa, Michael's cousin, a photographer who is also unmarried. As opposed to MTM series like *The Mary Tyler Moore Show*, which depict a "family" of co-workers,[17] *thirtysomething* represents work as always already familialized and domestic: Elliot and Michael's friendship predated their partnership in an advertising firm; Hope and Nancy have both deferred their careers (as magazine editor and artist) to stay home with their children; Melissa's darkroom is in her apartment; Ellen is having an affair with her boss; and the show is very unsure about what constitutes work for Gary, the academic.[18]

Further, *thirtysomething* is only about the imbrications of work and family. I say "only," because, unlike, say, *Cagney and Lacey*, *St. Elsewhere*, or *L.A. Law* (all have been cited as precursors to *thirtysomething*), which at least allude to a world beyond that of the characters, *thirtysomething* rarely makes such an attempt, a fact which has not eluded reviewers. Ella Taylor, for example, writes that the series has "become engrossed in its own claustrophobic detail," and that the characters' "connection to public life is severed altogether, or reduced to a trite shorthand of pop-cultural icons . . . that casually cue us into time, place and generation, and then shrink back into the politics of the personal."[19] The ahistorical tendencies Taylor laments are, according to Joyrich, central features of television melodrama: "Invoking history and memory even as they refuse historical grounding, TV melodramas deny the spectator any sense of coherent time, position, or identity, thereby allowing the manipulation of past TV history to instigate present viewing and consumption" (141).[20]

Ken Olin, the actor who plays Michael, responded implicitly to Taylor's and Joyrich's charges when he told the *Times*:

> Nobody on this show is presuming that the problems of these characters are as serious as the problems of the homeless and the mentally ill and the tragedy of war . . . [b]ut that is not to say that this generation doesn't face a set of issues that is valid too.[21]

Olin's remark, with its assertion that the issues faced by "this generation" are precisely *not* the problems of homelessness, mental illness or war, reflects the series' founding assumption that the most compelling problems baby boomers confront are interpersonal ones, and enacts *thirtysomething*'s melodramatic tendency to collapse a sociopolitical "outside" onto a familialized and domestic "inside." In other words, *thirtysomething* works ideologically by representing affect as unconnected to the social, economic, or political realms.

The series' attention to Michael and Elliot's advertising firm makes *thirtysomething* into a particularly self-referential melodramatic text, by incorporating into the narrative precisely those elements Joyrich suggests melodrama is deployed to manage. Advertising, as the exemplary mechanism of simulation and the ur-text of consumer culture, claims to refer to the real even as it endlessly reproduces differences that don't exist. The series often plays on the relation between advertising and the postmodern by making Elliot and Michael's office the site of anti-realist moments, suggesting that it is a postmodern locale. The office is linked to postmodernity not only by its metonymic connection to consumption, but also by strategies of representation which can only be called pastiche: *thirtysomething*'s anti-realism is generally marked by the appearance of elements from other genres such as science fiction (as when Elliot and Michael pick up toy rayguns from their desks and use them to make a troublesome secretary disappear), or the sitcom (for example, Michael's fantasy of the *thirtysomething* cast transported into the *Dick Van Dyke Show*).[22] But if the series calls attention to certain aspects of postmodern life, it also recapitulates their containment by giving us an extremely anachronistic picture of the advertising industry. Michael and Elliot's work seems to consist mostly of searching for inspired slogans, as opposed to studying market research, or learning how to use that new computer graphics program. That is, *thirtysomething* shows us a nostalgic representation of advertising in the age of *Bewitched* rather than in the late '80s. Of course, this extremely pre-postmodern depiction disassociates advertising from simulation, and thus reassures *thirtysomething*'s viewers of advertising's relation to the real.[23]

Given the ways in which *thirtysomething* is quintessentially melodramatic, Zwick may seem to be protesting too much. But there is an important way in which his effort to distance the show from melodrama rings true, and suggests that his protestations are not excessive, only misdirected. For while *thirtysomething* is certainly engaged with traditional notions of home and family, and insistently puts women at the center of its domestic spaces, the unanswered and persistent question for the show is masculinity, not femininity. *thirtysomething* knows, or at least thinks it knows, where women's "place," spatially and affectively, is; what it doesn't know is where men fit in. Its project is thus not the repudiation of family melodrama, but rather the renegotiation of domestic melodrama's boundaries to encompass male subjectivity, too.[25]

The necessity of this renegotiation is suggested by the final shot of the first season's credit sequence. As New Age guitar music twangs gently in the background, we see Hope holding Janey, her daughter, in the nursery. The camera backs out of the baby's room and pans to a view of Michael, looking at Hope and Janey through the banister rails. The camera's movement tells us that the initial view of Hope was from Michael's point of view, but disavows that knowledge by showing us Michael in the same shot, without an intervening cut. And, in addition to appropriating Michael's point of view, the camera also contrasts his expression, an unreadable mix of emotions, with the simplicity of Hope's maternal contentment. It is impossible to tell what Michael is thinking or feeling: he might be reveling in domestic plenitude or regretting his domestic entanglement. And his separation from Hope and Janey, effected by the banister rails, and accentuated by the shadows they cast against his face, emphasizes his spatial marginality with respect to them. The end of the credit sequence for the second season has a strikingly similar effect, using a shot of Michael against a reverse shot of Hope and Janey, suffused by candlelight, with Hope the perfect picture of maternal plenitude. Both sequences end by asking the same question: in a world dominated by domesticity, where do men belong?

I want to continue to track the implications of this question, and of its corollary—how do men and women fit together?—through a reading of one episode from the first season, in which Elliot and Nancy begin marriage counseling. Though the choice to focus on a single episode is methodologically problematic, it seems to me to be justified in light of what Joyrich says about melodrama as a therapeutic discourse: these scenes of therapy, which deploy affect in an attempt to divert attention from socio-political issues, may be read as exemplary melodramatic moments. That Marshall Herskovitz, Zwick's cocreator and producer, plays the therapist suggests how high the stakes are in the literalization of the show's therapeutic impulse. Indeed, his appearance may be read as thematizing the work the series has come to do in the culture: therapists on both coasts have taken to using taped episodes of *thirtysomething* in their practices, to help clients talk about their feelings.[26]

The episode is also interesting because of the kinds of questions it asks about the relation between feminine and masculine sexuality. These questions are important in thinking about the series as a whole, since the ideological and social conflicts *thirtysomething* most wants to represent in emotional terms have to do with gender and sexuality, and since it is against this unacknowledged field of conflict that the series tries to place masculinity in the '80s. But if this episode asks questions, it also tries to answer them in quite conventional ways, and thus recapitulates the ideological movement charted by the series generally, in which spaces for critique are persistently opened up and closed down. For while this episode explicitly investigates the disruptive effects of the traditional sexual division of labor on the nuclear family, its central project is the attempt to locate both normative heterosexuality and emotional contentment within that family. The "problem" of domesticating masculine sexuality remains, however, one which the episode cannot quite recuperate.

II. "So obscene and . . . so great": The Secret of Women's Sexuality

thirtysomething's most basic assumption about sexuality is that it is fundamentally different for men and women. The first scene of the marriage counseling episode takes up the construction of those differences. The opening shot dwells on Janey and Brittany (Nancy and Elliot's daughter), playing under a table in Michael and Elliot's office, while their parents discuss how they learned about sex. The shot establishes this sequence as a scene of instruction, and introduces the intertwining of sexuality and parenting that the rest of the episode will try to elaborate and untangle.[27] As the camera pans up to the adults, the assemblage, which includes Michael and Elliot's staff, sings

"Happy Birthday" to Elliot. The mix of families and co-workers underscores the familial quality of the workplace, even as the subsequent discussion between Michael, Hope, Elliot and Nancy emphasizes the role of the family in reproducing gendered sexuality: Elliot says that his father took him to *Goldfinger* to teach him about sex, Nancy that her mother brought her a book. The scene, then, underscores the textual construction of sexuality for both men and women, but insists on the differences among those texts, differences between the popular and the educational, between films and books, between one's father's discourse and one's mother's. Those differences, finally, boil down to levels of engagement: Elliot and Michael still remember the name of the female lead in *Goldfinger*, while Nancy asked her mother to take the book back "and bring me *National Velvet* instead."

The suggestion that women are basically—if not essentially—less interested in sex than men dovetails with the episode's common sense representation of women's sexuality as predictable, conservative and self-evident. This representation is worked out most clearly in the episode's subplot, about Ellen's "Mellow Yellow" tattoo, acquired after a Donovan concert on her sixteenth birthday. The obvious link between this and the main plot, about Nancy and Elliot's therapy and crumbling marriage, is the issue of individual privacy vs. collective gossip: Elliot asks Michael not to tell others about the marriage counseling, but Michael tells Melissa, who tells Gary, who calls Elliot; Ellen asks Michael not to divulge the secret of the tattoo, but he tells Gary and Elliot, and eventually the entire cast gathers at Michael and Hope's, where the by-now public nature of Ellen's "secret" is revealed. Less obviously, though, and more importantly, both plots deal with sexuality and its relation to the nuclear family.

The subplot's importance lies in the ways in which it establishes women's sexuality as the already known. The pleasure—and the scandal—of Ellen's tattoo for the men is that it is unpredictable, out of character and secret. After aggressively prying the story of the tattoo out of Ellen and Hope while playing Scrabble ("I hate secrets. Come on. Give."), Michael says "Oh Ellen, this is the most wonderful thing I've ever heard." Elliot tells Nancy, "The other day I heard this thing about Ellen. She has a tattoo on her tush. . . . Yeah, I thought that was so obscene and . . . so great." Gary's response, when Michael tells him, is to shriek with laughter and exclaim "Silk suit, briefcase-carrying Ellen?!"—here he and Michael exchange an exuberant high five—"Oh I love this. Think she'd let me touch it?"

Gary's remark emphasizes the difference between the dressed-for-success Ellen they all know, and the youthful, sexually aggressive Ellen who attended that Donovan concert. Indeed, the exchange between

Michael and Gary begins with Michael saying "I can tell you one person who's changed since she was sixteen." But if the men are surprised by the secret of the tattoo, the Scrabble scene establishes that, in contrast, Ellen is also shockingly staid (read repressed) these days: Michael is scandalized when he learns that Ellen leaves the lights out while making love with her boyfriend, in part to conceal the tattoo, because, she says, "he just doesn't think of me that way."

One effect of this insistence upon the drastic difference between Ellen at sixteen and Ellen at thirtysomething is to define women's sexual aggression (for this is clearly what the tattoo signifies for Michael, Elliot and Gary) as anachronistic. The tattoo is heavily coded as a product of its time, both by its allusive relation to Donovan, and by Ellen's comment that, on the night of the concert, she was wearing a "pink satin pantsuit with a Nehru collar."

The other consequence of this insistence is that Ellen comes to represent two extreme varieties of female sexuality, against which the show can define its ideal, Hope, who falls neatly between the two extremes. As Michael encourages Gary to guess who's got the tattoo, Gary says "Well it's not Hope," and Michael replies "Of course not." On the other hand, though, Hope clearly doesn't leave the lights out during sex, or Michael's incredulity would be directed at her, not at Ellen. In short, Hope represents the brand of female sexuality the show most wants to endorse—the feminine and fun-loving but basically conservative sexuality of the married mother. As an unmarried woman, in contrast, Ellen cannot command the kind of sexual and emotional authority Hope does, as demonstrated by the Scrabble scene, in which Ellen, ambivalent about her current relationship, asks Hope to reassure her:

> Hope: You really like him.
> Ellen: I think I like him. I do like him. Do you think I like him?

This scene, which depicts Ellen as emotionally inept, occurs in Michael and Hope's living room (the single characters rarely entertain), where elements of the mise-en-scène insist upon the hegemony of the heterosexual nuclear family, and on Ellen's status as outsider to that configuration. They sit on the floor playing Scrabble, surrounded by a sleeping dog and various toys, some belonging to the dog, some to Janey. In the background, to the left, there is a large poster of a painting of a mother and child by Mary Cassatt, in a pose suggestive of Hope and Janey in the final shot of the credit sequence described earlier. This poster becomes visible behind Ellen's head as she reluctantly tells Michael the story of the tattoo; it reminds us that Ellen's sexuality, in either its late '60s or its late '80s incarnation, cannot rival the complex emotional experience offered by Hope's, because it exists outside the family.

Ellen is also structurally excluded from the two other spaces in which we see the secret of the tattoo revealed: Nancy and Elliot's therapist's office, and the male domain of the urban playground where Elliot, Michael and Gary play basketball. The scene at the basketball court, though, enacts other exclusions as well. Some of the graffiti on the walls of the playground says "Overbrook Rules." Overbrook is the town that forms the boundary between the affluent, predominantly white suburbs known as the Main Line, and West Philadelphia, the middle and lower-middle class, predominantly Black neighborhood that was the site of the MOVE inferno; it is currently being gentrified. The representation of three white men on a basketball court in Overbrook is thus highly charged politically. The series' refusal to address issues of race even in order to recuperate them is typical of *thirtysomething*'s first season (such recuperation has become more common in the second season, when Gary began tutoring Black high school students); the show has consistently been much more self-aware about gender than about other modes of social stratification. Indeed, the scene itself, which alludes to contemporary advertising for basketball shoes, both calls attention to and elides its own sexism, by beginning and ending with discourse about the white male body (specifically Elliot's poor physical condition), while the middle of the scene is taken up with Michael and Gary's prurient conversation about the tattoo.

The inaccessibility of the playground and the therapist's office to Ellen emphasizes that the "secret" of her marginalized sexuality is intriguing only in relation to a normative, familial female sexuality—Hope's—which is understood by the series to be basically unsurprising. That is, the secret reveals that there is no secret. Rather, it is male sexuality, in its uneasy relation to the nuclear family, that *thirtysomething* isn't sure about.

III. What does Elliot want?: The Vicissitudes of Masculine Desire

Michael is *thirtysomething*'s representative of idealized male sexuality. While he is clearly established by this episode as being very interested in sex, he is also established as not being *too* interested, since this episode reminds us repeatedly of how troubled he is by the fact that Elliot has had an extra-marital affair. And in one of the closing scenes, outside of the Museum of (appropriately enough) Natural History, he becomes the episode's most eloquent spokesperson for marriage:

Elliot: Are you supposed to like being married?

Michael: I like it. I know I groan and I complain, but yeah, my life feels complete in a way it never did before.

Elliot: It's all awry with us now. It's like when I'm with her I just don't feel anything anymore. It's like we're on opposite sides of a window.

Michael: Did you ever talk about the affair?

Elliot: Believe me Michael, it would kill everything. . . . You're in love with Hope, right?

Michael: Yeah, I am.

Michael's sexuality is containable within the boundaries of the nuclear family; Elliot's is not. While the contrast between Ellen's sexuality and Hope's is mapped onto the difference between their marital statuses, the opposition between Elliot and Michael must be worked out in different terms. The episode represents the difference between Elliot's unruly libido and Michael's domesticated one as directly related to the success of their marriages (and of course, vice versa), and specifically to the success of the two couples in managing the traditional sexual division of labor: during *thirtysomething*'s first season, both Michael and Elliot go out to work, while both Hope and Nancy stay home with the kids.

During their first counseling session, sex emerges as a central problem in Elliot and Nancy's marriage. We see Elliot saying, in response to an unheard question from the therapist, "Sex, oh . . . I don't know. Sex is . . . I'm still trying to remember what sex is like. Sex is . . . sex is fine. You know, sex is sex." Nancy encourages Elliot to talk about it; when he refuses, she says: "He thinks I'm not interested in sex anymore. He thinks that I don't take care of his needs." The discussion evolves into one, not about sex, but about their attitudes toward each other: she finds him angry and insulting; he thinks she is controlling and unwilling to compromise.

It is these more general issues that resurface during the next counseling scene, which is crucially concerned with the allocation of power and work within the marriage. We hear Elliot's controlling narrative: "I feel like she's on me all the time. Like I can't do anything right." Here we have a flashback to Elliot's abortive attempt to make his son a peanut butter sandwich: "Don't you know by now he only likes *grape* jelly?" Nancy says, taking the bread out of his hand. "Or take the whole issue of money," Elliot says, continuing his enumeration. Another flashback to an argument over Elliot's unilateral decision to spend a substantial sum on a health club membership. These flashbacks, and the subsequent discussion of Elliot's decision to start his own company, establish that much of the friction between them is the result of Elliot's economic power and Nancy's relative helplessness ("I've been driving the same car for seven years. . . ." she says, "You get to have everything you want when you want it"), and of the fact that Nancy has primary responsibility for childcare and thus knows all too well what kind of jelly Ethan likes on his sandwiches.

The next counseling scene establishes that these factors are completely imbricated with their struggles over sex. Elliot says he wants "more excitement . . . more experimenting." Here he cites Ellen's tattoo as an example of such excitement and "last night" as an example of its absence. Nancy responds that she was exhausted by the demands of taking care of Brittany:

> And you were grabbing and insisting. I mean one night it's one thing and the next night . . . or you want me to wear something—fine, whatever, it doesn't matter, because it's never about what I want. It's always about what you want. What does Elliot want? . . . I mean, where is that supposed to stop?

The therapist asks her "What do you want?"

> Nancy: Just to be left alone sometimes . . . . I mean I am so exhausted at the end of the day that I don't usually even remember that I am a sexual person. . . . [to Elliot] We have two kids that I take care of. I spend my whole day talking about Rainbow Brite and Transformers and wondering if Britty has had enough milk. All I'm saying is that I need some help in changing gears. Is that asking too much? I mean I am sorry that I am not like the women in the porno films who don't need any help.
> Elliot: You wouldn't even watch them with me. . . .
> Nancy: It was a big turnoff to me. It just made my flesh crawl. Those women are not real women, they're robots.
> Elliot: Why, because they don't mind making men happy? Why?
> Nancy: If you had any sexual or emotional maturity you would understand the difference, that's all.

What most interests me about this scene is the way in which it simultaneously reveals and effaces two ideologically loaded aspects of bourgeois marriage: the effects of women's responsibility for childcare on heterosexual relations, and the incommensurability of masculine and feminine desire. Within the scene, the effacement of each of these problems is effected by the presence of the other. That is, the problem of the relation between Nancy's lack of interest in sex and her role as primary caretaker for two small children is displaced onto the problem of Elliot's unruly desires for sex accompanied by costume and pornography, and vice versa. Thus the episode is able both to represent and to contain these issues. And then, in melodrama's paradigmatic gesture, it diverts our attention from both this tangle of representation and displacement, and from the political problems of the construction of gender and sexuality, insisting, rather, that we attend to Elliot and Nancy's emotional problems. The scene ends wrenchingly: while the camera remains almost motionless for nearly a full minute, Elliot and Nancy display a degree of affective agony rare on television, and extremely painful to watch. But watch we must, for the stationary camera offers us no chance to avert our eyes.

The remaining half hour of the episode recapitulates the melodramatic gestures of containment enacted by this scene, collapsing the structural problems in Elliot and Nancy's marriage back into the realm of "feelings." Both Elliot and Nancy try to make concessions in response to the scene I have just described: Nancy tries to become more sexually aggressive, and Elliot takes the kids to the park for the afternoon. But the scenes at the Museum of Natural History suggest that such changes will not be sufficient, and, indeed, that the issues so threatening to the nuclear family raised in the therapist's office are not the problem after all. In the first of these scenes, Nancy, walking through an exhibit with Hope and the children, hints for the first time that Elliot's unhappiness may have little to do with her: "I get this feeling that I'm just supposed to sit around and wait until he gets all the crap out, all the bad feelings out, so he doesn't have to turn it against me anymore. . . . At least I don't feel so weird about it because I don't feel like it's all my fault." Outside with Michael, Elliot is confirming Nancy's suspicions: "I don't know if I love her anymore. And it's like no matter what she does, I can't seem to forgive her for that." These exchanges, naturalized by their setting, effectively displace and recuperate the issues which were raised so powerfully by the first half of the episode: the stresses placed on the nuclear family by the sexual division of labor and by the gendered construction of sexuality.

Of course, the recuperative process is also facilitated by the presence of Michael and Hope in these scenes, whose successful marriage reassures us again and again that the traditional division of labor in the traditional nuclear family *can* work. Since Michael and Hope's marriage is structurally no different from Elliot and Nancy's, Elliot and Nancy's problems, the series suggests, must stem from something other than that structure. And Elliot and Nancy's sexual dissatisfaction is likewise managed by Michael and Hope's comfortable, active sex life.

The displacement of "issues" by "feelings" that occurs in the museum scenes is definitively reinscribed by the final scenes of the episode, and by the final shot in particular. When Elliot returns from taking the kids out for the day to allow Nancy to "do something nice" for herself, they embrace. The final shot lets us know simultaneously that they've had sex and that all is still not well. The camera pans over Nancy's body as she lies in bed, on her stomach, with the covers tangled around her lower body and her back naked. She is sleeping. As the camera moves across the bed, Elliot comes into the frame, and at first he appears to be sleeping as well. But as the camera comes to rest on his face, he opens his eyes, sits up (displacing Nancy's arm, which was draped over his chest), and, with a discontented look, begins reading a book as the camera backs away from the bed. The camera's movement here carefully undoes the tableau of marital contentment it constructed at the beginning of the shot. Elliot's expression, and his inability to sleep, suggest that he and Nancy have reached only a temporary truce. Thus this shot insists that changes like the reallocation of domestic duties, which might satisfy Nancy, will not be enough to quiet Elliot's dissatisfaction.

But if the second half of this episode labors to recuperate the troubling possibilities raised by the first, it is, of course, only partially successful. The problem of male sexuality's potential resistance to bourgeois domestication remains unaddressed: Nancy's attempts to be sexy in Elliot's terms—and thus to domesticate his desires—fail miserably, and while Elliot's attempts at self-domestication (via child-care) make it possible for them to have sex, his restlessness afterwards is palpable. The openendedness of this episode thus allows masculine sexuality, and its relation to the nuclear family, to remain a question, both for the series and for potentially resistant viewers. For our part, we may celebrate the pressure Elliot's intractable (if clichéd) cravings put on the show's valorization of the nuclear family. For *thirtysomething*, these same cravings provide fodder for the continued investigation of men and their feelings: while the ending's refusal to provide neat closure shuts down investigations of power and work within marriage, it carefully leaves room for continued scrutiny of men's emotional lives, by making Elliot's feelings the most important problem in his marriage.

IV. "Hotel. Hotel. Hotel": Recuperation as Therapy

I'll conclude with some thoughts about *thirtysomething*'s second season premiere, which provides another example of the ways in which the series gives voice to, and then tries to recuperate, ideological critique. As this episode opens, Hope has just gone back to work part time and Michael wants to have another baby. Most of the plot is taken up with their struggle over that decision, since Hope is reluctant to get pregnant again. The following conversation between Michael

and Elliot (who is now separated from Nancy) takes place as they try
to think of an idea for a floor wax ad:

Elliot: How can I have an idea? I'm separated.
Michael: How is Nancy anyway?
Elliot: Shrew-like, vindictive. I miss her.
Michael: Women. Can't live with 'em, can't kill 'em.
Elliot: What'd she do now?
Michael: Nothing, nothing. It's just last night, we were in bed. . . . Anyway,
           there we are. Things are progressing at their normal rate. But
           she doesn't have her diaphragm. So she wants to go get it and I
           don't want her to.
Elliot: Whoops.
Michael: Is that a crime? Because one kid doesn't feel like a family to me?
           I mean, there were two kids in my family. You have two kids.
Elliot: Yeah, but it was part of our pre-nuptial agreement. She agreed
           to have two kids and serve my every whim, and I agreed to
           systematically destroy all her confidence and self-esteem.
Michael: Maybe you were smart.
Elliot: Yeah, maybe. Maybe that's why when I go to sleep at night
           there's a neon sign flashing outside my window that says "Hotel.
           Hotel. Hotel."

If masculinity in the '80s is being modified in the direction of allowing
men easier access to their parental yearnings, this scene lays bare the
ways in which Michael's "new" masculinity looks a lot like the old:
it poses a familiar threat to women's autonomy, and is based on a
violent contempt for women which lurks just below its veneer of
sensitivity. Elliot's role here is to voice a critique of this mode, which,
after all, destroyed his marriage. He offers a poignant reminder of how
destructive the usual allocation of responsibility within the nuclear
family, engendered by the new/old masculinity, can be. This reminder
is effaced, however, by the end of the episode, in which Hope, motivated by a bizarre and complex machinery of nostalgia (she has been
reading the diary of a former occupant of her house, written during
World War II), elects to have sex with Michael *sans* diaphragm.

Joyrich argues that melodrama attempts to manage the anxiety endemic to the postmodern age by giving affect priority over politics and
collapsing socio-political issues into the home. This therapeutic potential can be disrupted, though, by anxiety about the dispersion of
the feminine "onto a general audience" (131).[29] I have argued that
thirtysomething's abiding interest is in the elaboration of contemporary
masculinity's relation to women and the domestic. Perhaps the show's
concern with masculinity suggests why it is compelled to call attention
to its prioritization of affect. That is, its anxiety about the feminizing

effects of thinking masculinity and domesticity together may explain why *thirtysomething* insistently displays and banishes the ideological contradictions inherent in the gendered arrangement of the contemporary family, why it gives voice to, and then represses, critiques of that family. Perhaps such dissenting voices serve implicitly to problematize the feminizing potential of the family. And perhaps this structure explains why the show consistently valorizes traditional gender roles.

In other words, to serve as therapeutic, male domestic melodrama like *thirtysomething* seems to require several imbricated gestures: the representation of social, economic and political issues in affective terms, the incorporation of ideological contradiction into the melodramatic narrative, and a structure of disavowal, in which the acknowledgement of critiques of the family somehow renders them unimportant. It is this structure of disavowal which makes *thirtysomething* at once so compelling and so repellant. But as a thoroughly self-ironic postmodern text, *thirtysomething* has already thematized and recuperated such discomfort, thereby recapitulating its provocation: alluding to audiences' love-hate relationship to the series, Edward Zwick quipped, as he accepted *thirtysomething*'s Emmy for Best Dramatic Series, "If there were another category for the most annoying show on television, I think we'd win that too."[30]

NOTES

I am grateful to Amanda Anderson, Sabrina Barton, Lisa Moore, Andrew Parker, and Sharon Willis for their attentive readings of this essay, and to Lila Hanft for her comments on a shorter version. Judy Frank first piqued my interest in *thirtysomething*, and I continue to be indebted to her insightful and sensitive spectatorship.

1. " 'Thirtysomething': A Chronicle of Everyday Life," *New York Times* 24 Feb. 1988: C26.

2. Indeed, much of *thirtysomething*'s visual interest stems from its filmic feel and camera work, products of Zwick and cocreator Marshall Herskovitz's interest in making "little movies." Episodes often revise films explicitly: during the first season, one episode was the occasion for an extended riff on Hitchcock, another alluded to Kurosawa. Zwick and Herskovitz also cite Woody Allen as an influence. For their accounts of the relation between filmmaking and television production, see Phoebe Hoban, "All in the Family: TV's 'thirtysomething' Hits Home," *New York Magazine* 29 Feb. 1988: 48–52; and Jeffrey Lantos, "Talking 'Bout My Generation," *American Film* Nov. 1987: 49–51.

3. On *L.A. Law*, see Judith Mayne's "*L.A. Law* and Prime Time Feminism," *Discourse* X.2 (1988): 30–47. Television's growing tendency to target programming toward baby boomers has not gone unnoticed in the popular press. For examples, see Jeremy Gerard, "TV Mirrors a New Generation," *New York Times* 30 Oct. 1988, sec. 2: 1; and "Yup, Yup and Away," *Time* 5 Oct. 1987: 89–90.

4. Stoddard quoted by Hoban 50. Cf. ABC executive Chad Hoffman's comments on *thirtysomething*'s demographics, quoted by Lantos 50. For an extremely useful history of the notion of "quality demographics" in network television, see Jane Feuer, Paul Kerr, and Tise Vahimagi, eds., *MTM: "Quality Television"* (London: BFI, 1984); especially Feuer's "MTM Enterprises: An Overview," 1–31; and Kerr's "The Making of (The) MTM (Show)" 61–98.

5. On baby boomers and television advertising, see Michael Smythe, "Television is the Key to Baby Boomers' Buying," *Broadcasting* 4 July 1988: 23. On the networks' reaction to the people meters, see, for example, Mark Potts, "Nielsen Ratings May be Axed by Networks," *Washington Post* 18 Jan. 1987: H1.

6. For a useful discussion of melodrama's history, see Christine Gledhill's "The Melodramatic Field: An Investigation," *Home is Where the Heart Is*, ed. Gledhill (London: BFI, 1987) 14–28.

7. Geoffrey Nowell-Smith, "Minnelli and Melodrama," *Home is Where the Heart Is* 71.

8. As Gledhill has demonstrated, this is at best a problematic opposition, given the historical imbrications of realism with melodrama. See her discussion in "The Melodramatic Field."

9. Austen: "Three or four families in a country village is the perfect thing to work on." Quoted in Ronald Blythe's introduction to the Penguin edition of *Emma* (New York, 1983) 8. Cf. Austen's other famous description of her work: "The little bit (two inches wide) of ivory on which I work with so fine a brush, as to produce little effect, after much labor" 8.

10. " 'Thirtysomething': A Chronicle of Everyday Life" C26.

11. Hank Herman, "*thirtysomething*'s Mel Harris: 'Prince Charming Lives,' " *Health* March 1988: 46, emphasis in original. Discussions of *thirtysomething*'s "realism" have come to completely pervade the popular discourse about the show. I don't think I've come across a single review that doesn't address its alleged verisimilitude. The most extensive discussion, which is usefully concerned with elements of mise-en-scène, is Hoban's 50–51.

12. For an account of *thirtysomething* which makes these moments into further evidence of the show's "realism," see Alice Hoffman, "Move Over Ozzie and Harriet," *New York Times* 14 Feb. 1988, sec. 2: 1.

13. Laura Mulvey, "Melodrama in and out of the Home," *High Theory/Low Culture*, ed. Colin MacCabe (New York: St. Martin's Press, 1986) 81.

14. *thirtysomething*'s remarkable engagement with film and film history seems to me to render it unlikely that the generic resonances of the term "melodramatic" would be inaccessible to Zwick.

15. Lynne Joyrich, "All That Television Allows: TV Melodrama, Postmodernism and Consumer Culture," *Camera Obscura* 16 (1988): 129–154. Subsequent references will be provided parenthetically. Like Joyrich, I read postmodernism and its effects through Jameson and Baudrillard. Another way of saying this is that postmodernism for my purposes here is what E. Ann Kaplan has called "commercial or co-opted postmodernism," rather than "utopian postmodernism." See her introduction to *Postmodernism and Its Discontents* (London: Verso, 1988) 4.

16. In suggesting that melodrama crosses television's generic boundaries, Joyrich is departing from Jane Feuer's earlier formulation, which locates the televisual melodramatic specifically within serial forms (daytime and prime time soaps, and such programs as *Hill Street Blues* and *St. Elsewhere*). See Feuer's "Melodrama, Serial Form and Television Today," *Screen* 25.1 (1984): 4–16. In this respect, Joyrich returns to David Thorburn's account of the pervasiveness of television melodrama. See his "Television Melodrama," in *Television: The Critical View*, ed. Horace Newcomb (New York: Oxford University Press, 1987) 628–644, especially 631.

17. Feuer, "Narrative Form in American Network Television," *High Theory/Low Culture* 107.

18. The first season episode which focused on Gary's tenure review in the English Department at Haverford College was so poorly researched that it betrayed almost no knowledge of how the tenure process—or even, for that matter, the pedagogical process—works in the contemporary academy. The writers cannot even begin to imagine what Gary's work life is like, even when that endeavor is their explicit subject.

19. Ella Taylor, "Forget Murder and Car Chases: Now It's 'Slice of Life' Shows," *New York Times* 17 April 1988: H39.

20. In particular, the TV history *thirtysomething* manipulates is television's representation of the '60s (with frequent references to *Leave it to Beaver* and *The Dick Van Dyke Show*); it also alludes, though, to other kinds of mass cultural productions of that era, especially music. A CBS series new this season, *Almost Grown*, which owes a lot, stylistically and thematically, to *thirtysomething*, takes this allusiveness as its narrative premise, chronicling the lives of a couple who met in the '60s, married in the '70s and divorced in the '80s. The plots are contemporary, but proceed largely through flashbacks, often motivated by pop music.

21. " 'Thirtysomething': A Chronicle of Everyday Life" C26. Cf. Zwick's statement that "It's not that we don't endorse the larger, sociopolitical

concerns of hunger, the homeless, and toxic waste; it's just that we think it's worth addressing the everyday concerns of a person's life" (Hoban 51).

22. On postmodernism and pastiche, see Fredric Jameson, "Postmodernism and Consumer Society," *Postmodernism and Its Discontents* 13–29; "Postmodernism, or The Cultural Logic of Late Capitalism," *New Left Review* 146 (1984): 53–92; and Anders Stephanson, "Regarding Postmodernism—A Conversation with Fredric Jameson," *Universal Abandon?: The Politics of Postmodernism,* ed. Andrew Ross (Minneapolis: University of Minnesota Press, 1988) 3–30.

23. My discussion here of the anachronistic aspects of the series's representation of advertising is indebted to a conversation with Judy Frank, Dec. 7, 1988.

24. Several of the commercials aired during the episode I'll analyze here suggest that sponsors believe that *thirtysomething*'s viewers are interested in the possibility of redefining masculinity's relation to the family. For instance, a promotional spot for *Good Morning, America,* opens with a man, holding a baby, waking up his wife. In the next shot he is shaving, holding a slightly older child. Finally, we see him, dressed in a shirt and tie, bringing a plateful of the fresh pancakes he has just made to the breakfast table, where his dressed-for-success wife entertains the two children. "Good morning America," a male voice sings in the background, "Family to family." *Good Morning, America*'s attempt to constitute its audience as comprised of conflict-free households, where domestic tasks do not have to be orchestrated by women, is a fascinating fantasy indeed (especially considering that it is women who do the domestic work on *thirtysomething*). Another ad, for a men's cologne called "Iron," depicts a series of men, one more brawny than the next, engaged in stereotypical masculine activities: a rock climber, an air traffic controller, a construction worker. But the commercial also shows us men's sensitive sides: closeups of the rock climber and the air traffic controller, a shot of a man lifting a woman up and swinging her through the air, a shot of an amply muscled naked male torso holding a baby. In the rapid editing of this spot, it is the latter shots that stand out, but this alternative (and anti-essentialist) depiction of masculinity is wholly recuperated by the lyrics of the song: a woman's voice sings "Here's to the men who are building our world," while shots of the construction worker literalize and naturalize the fact that it is still men who "build our world."

25. *thirtysomething* is certainly not unique in interrogating masculinity's relation to melodrama; such questions have a long history. The series is unusual, though, as a *domestic* melodrama (as opposed to more conventionally "male" melodramatic forms such as the western or the cop show) which resolutely focuses on masculinity within the format of an hour-long drama. On the gendered forms of melodrama, see Mulvey, "Notes on Sirk and Melodrama," *Home is Where the Heart Is* 75–79.

26. See Patricia Hersch, "thirtysomethingtherapy," *Psychology Today* Oct. 1988: 62–64; See also Hoban 52.

27. See Nowell-Smith: "In addition to the problems of adults, particularly women, in relation to their sexuality, the Hollywood melodrama is also fundamentally concerned with the child's problems of growing into a sexual identity within the family. . . ." 73.

28. In an episode which aired after the one I analyze here, Michael's college girlfriend comes to visit. Michael comes close to sleeping with her, but decides to stick with marital fidelity.

29. It is no accident that the *Psychology Today* article on "thirtysomething-therapy" begins with an anecdote about an irate husband who had been asked to watch the show by his therapist. His complaint: "I'll never watch that show again. Michael is such a wimp!" The article continues: "His reaction irritated his wife, who said she really enjoyed seeing Michael come home and spend time with Hope and the baby" 62.

30. Lee Margulies, "Baby Boom Programs win Major Emmys," *Los Angeles Times* 29 August 1988: 7.

Contributors

Parveen Adams teaches in the Department of Human Sciences of Brunel University, England. She was cofounder and coeditor of *m/f*, 1978–86. Her recent publications include "Of Female Bondage," in Teresa Brennan (ed.), *Between Feminism and Psychoanalysis* (1989); *The Woman in Question*, jointly edited with Elizabeth Cowie (1990); a special issue of *October*, "Rendering the Real," *October* 58 (1991); and "Waiving the Phallus," *Differences* (May 1992). She is currently working on a book on psychoanalysis and perverse sexualities.

Ian Balfour teaches in the Department of English and in the graduate program in social and political thought at York University. He is the author of *Northrop Frye* and is completing *The Rhetoric of Romantic Prophecy*. He has published on literary theory, Romanticism, television, and music in *MLN*, *Camera Obscura*, and elsewhere. He also serves on the editorial board of *Alphabet City*.

Ray Barrie is a native of England but now lives and works in New York City. He studied at St. Martin's School of Art in London and taught at the London Institute and more recently at the California Institute for the Arts in Los Angeles and the CSU Summer School for the Arts. His work has been exhibited in "Europa 79," Max Hetzler, Stuttgart, the Sydney Biennale, and "Difference: On Representation and Sexuality" at the New Museum of Contemporary Art, New York. He has held workshops on representations of masculinity for the Vancouver Art Gallery and the School for Contemporary Art, Simon Fraser University.

Sabrina Barton is an assistant professor in the Department of English at the University of Texas, Austin. For the 1992–93 academic year, she is a visiting professor in English at the University of California, Davis. Barton is currently working on a feminist rereading of mainstream fifties films entitled *Rearranging the Furniture: The Apparatus of Subjectivity in 1950s Cinema.*

Rey Chow is an associate professor of comparative literature at the University of Minnesota. She is the author of *Woman and Chinese Modernity: The Politics of Reading between West and East* (Minnesota, 1991) and *Writing Diaspora: Tactics of Intervention* (forthcoming).

Steven Cohan teaches narrative theory, the novel, and film at Syracuse University. He is coauthor of *Telling Stories: A Theoretical Analysis of Narrative Fiction* (1988) and coeditor of *Screening the Male: Exploring Masculinities in Hollywood Cinema* (forthcoming), for which his own contribution is an essay on the spectacle of Fred Astaire. At present he is writing a book on American masculinity and the movies during the fifties.

Mark Cousins teaches sociology at Thames Polytechnic in London. He is the author, with Athar Hussain, of *Michael Foucault.*

Alexander Doty teaches film and mass culture at Lehigh University. He has written articles on Lucille Ball, authorship and lesbian/gay cultures, and queer mass culture theory. His book *Making Things Perfectly Queer: Interpreting Mass Culture* is forthcoming from the University of Minnesota Press.

Henry Jenkins III, an assistant professor of literature at MIT, is a frequent contributor to *Camera Obscura*. He is the author of two books, *Textual Poachers: Television Fans and Participatory Culture* (1992) and *"What Made Pistachio Nuts?": Early Sound Comedy and the Vaudeville Aesthetic* (1992). His son, Henry, is now in sixth grade and likes Nintendo and WWF Wrestling.

Lynne Kirby holds a Ph.D. in critical studies in film and television from the University of California, Los Angeles. She works for the Independent Television Service in St. Paul, Minnesota.

Constance Penley teaches film studies and women's studies at the University of California, Santa Barbara. She is the author of *The Future of an Illusion: Film, Feminism, and Psychoanalysis* (Minnesota, 1989), editor of *Feminism and Film Theory*, and coeditor of *Technoculture* (Minnesota, 1991) and *Close Encounters: Film, Feminism, and Science Fiction* (Minnesota, 1991).

Kaja Silverman is professor of rhetoric at the University of California at Berkeley. She is the author of *Male Subjectivity at the Margins* (1992), *The Acoustic Mirror: The Female Voice in Psychoanalysis and Cinema* (1988), and *The Subject of Semiotics* (1983).

Sasha Torres teaches film and television at Dartmouth College. She is currently writing a book-length study of the representational relations between television and film, tentatively called *The Resistance to Television*, and editing an anthology of essays in television theory designed for undergraduate classroom use.

Sharon Willis is an associate professor in the Department of Foreign Languages, Literatures, and Linguistics at the University of Rochester, where she teaches French, comparative literature, film, and women's studies. Author of *Marguerite Duras: Writing on the Body* (1987), she is currently completing a book entitled *Public Fantasies: Gender and Race in Contemporary Film*.

Index

Compiled by Robin Jackson